THE JEWS OF ANCIENT ROME

Professor Morris Loeb, of New York, the distinguished chemist, scholar and public worker, who died on October 8, 1912, by his last Will and Testament, created a Fund under the following terms: "I give and bequeath to the Jewish Publication Society of America the sum of Ten Thousand Dollars as a permanent fund, the income of which alone shall, from time to time, be utilized for and applied to the preparation and publication of a scholarly work devoted to the interests of Judaism."

The present work is the fifth issued under this Fund. The first, SAADIA GAON—*His Life and Works*, by Henry Malter, was published in 1921. The second, THE PHARISEES—*The Sociological Background of Their Faith*, by Louis Finkelstein, was published in 1938. The third, THE JEWS IN SPAIN—*Their Social, Political and Cultural Life During the Middle Ages*, by Abraham Neuman, and the fourth, THE JEWISH COMMUNITY—*Its History and Structure to the American Revolution*, by Salo W. Baron, were published in 1942.

The

JEWS

of

ANCIENT
ROME

Updated Edition

HARRY J. LEON

with a new introduction by CAROLYN A. OSIEK

HENDRICKSON
PUBLISHERS

Copyright © 1960 by Hendrickson Publishers, Inc.
P. O. Box 3473
Peabody, Massachusetts 01961–3473

ISBN 1–56563–076–9

This edition of *The Jews of Ancient Rome,* originally published
by The Jewish Publication Society of America, is reprinted by
arrangement with the family of Harry J. Leon.

Printed in the United States of America

First Printing Updated Edition, April 1995

Library of Congress Cataloging-in-Publication Data

Leon, Harry J. (Harry Joshua)
    The Jews of ancient Rome   /   by Harry J. Leon
[introduction and appendix to the revised edition prepared
by Carolyn Osiek].—Rev. ed.
        p. cm.
    Originally published: Philadelphia: Jewish Publication
Society of America, 1960. (The Morris Loeb series). With
new introd. and appendix.
    Includes bibliographical references and index.
    ISBN 1–56563–076–9 (pbk.)
    1. Jews—Italy—Rome—History. 2. Jews—Italy—Rome—
Antiquities. 3. Rome (Italy)—Antiquities. 4. Catacombs—
Italy—Rome. 5. Inscriptions, Jewish—Italy—Rome.
I. Osiek, Carolyn. II. Title
DS135.I85R64 1995
937'.004924—dc20   95–6049
                                                        CIP

CONTENTS

PREFACE

The Jewish community of Rome has had a longer continuous existence than any other Jewish community of Europe —since Jews have lived in that city for more than two thousand years—yet no complete study of its ancient period has yet been made. Those who, like Berliner and Vogelstein, made extensive use of the literary sources had but small acquaintance with the archaeological materials. Besides, since their histories appeared, a large amount of new material has been yielded by the Jewish catacombs.

It is my purpose in this monograph to present all the available data on the Jews of ancient Rome. I have made a fresh study of the historical evidence, as culled from the ancient writers, comprising the period from the end of the second century B.C.E. to the fourth century C.E., and have offered new interpretations which, I hope, will meet with approval. The abundant archaeological and epigraphic material which the Jewish catacombs of Rome have made available is now for the first time completely and systematically presented. The numerous inscriptions are examined for information on the language, names, congregations, communal organization, and, to the limited extent possible, the customs and religious concepts of the Roman Jews of antiquity. Some attention is given to their art and their use of symbols both on their tomb inscriptions and in the decorations of their tombs and tomb chambers. An appendix offers carefully verified texts with translations of all the inscriptions from the Jewish catacombs of Rome, except those too fragmentary to be of any value.

I wish to acknowledge gratefully the courtesy of the Pontificia Commissione di Archeologia Sacra, which, through Father Antonio Ferrua, made it possible for me to explore and take photographs in the Jewish catacombs of the Via Appia and Via Nomentana. To this Commissione I am indebted also for a number of my illustrations. The following photographs are the property of the Pontificia Commissione di Archeologia Sacra and are used in this book with its permission: Figures 26, 27, 30, 32-39, 46-50, 52-67.

Most of all I wish to express my debt to my wife, Ernestine, a Fellow of the American Academy in Rome, who accompanied me on all my catacomb explorations, assisted me in transcribing the inscriptions, and offered numerous suggestions at every phase of this work.

Harry J. Leon

Austin, Texas
August, 1960

PREFACE TO THE REVISED EDITION

The original edition of Leon's book has long been out of print, and it remains the standard reference work for the Jewish inscriptions of Rome. New excavations and discoveries by Father Umberto Fasola in 1976, unfortunately too late to be incorporated in Baruch Lifshitz's revised edition of Frey's *CII* volume I, provided a second reason for bringing *The Jews of Ancient Rome* back into print, with the new material added.

While I was in Rome in 1973, doing research on the Christian and Jewish antiquities, I was privileged to have known Father Fasola of the Pontifical Institute of Christian Archaeology, which then had the care of the Jewish catacombs. He most graciously gave me access to many sites not open to the public, and in fact, the day before my departure from Rome, invited me to observe the excavation he was then conducting at Villa Torlonia. His untimely death a few years later was an inestimable loss.

My special thanks go to two persons without whom I could not have done this project. Dr. J. Albert Harrill, then adjunct assistant professor at the Catholic Theological Union, provided invaluable research assistance. William Burton, OFM, now a doctoral student at the Pontifical Biblical Institute in Rome, during his Masters study at Catholic Theological Union some years earlier, knowing how much I wanted a copy of the original edition, secretly combed the used bookstores of the country and surprised me with a gift of it in a most original fashion.

Carolyn Osiek
Catholic Theological Union
Chicago, Illinois
June 1994

ABBREVIATIONS

AJ	Antiquitates Iudaicae of Josephus
AJA	*American Journal of Archaeology*
AJP	*American Journal of Philology*
BAC	*Bullettino di Archeologia Cristiana*
BCACR	*Bullettino della Commissione Archeologica Communale di Roma*
BICA	*Bullettino dell' Instituto di Correspondenza Archeologica*
BJ	Bellum Iudaicum of Josephus
BL	H. W. Beyer and H. Lietzmann, Die jüdische Katakombe der Villa Torlonia in Rom.
Civ. Catt.	*Civiltà Cattolica*
CIG	Corpus Inscriptionum Graecarum
CII	Corpus Inscriptionum Iudaicarum
CIL	Corpus Inscriptionum Latinarum
CP	*Classical Philology*
DACL	Dictionnaire d'Archéologie Chrétienne et de Liturgie, by F. Cabrol and H. Leclercq
HTR	*Harvard Theological Review*
HUCA	*Hebrew Union College Annual*
JAOS	*Journal of the American Oriental Society*
JE	The Jewish Encyclopedia
JQR	*Jewish Quarterly Review*
JRS	*Journal of Roman Studies*
MB	N. Müller and N. A. Bees, Die Inschriften der jüdischen Katakombe am Monteverde zu Rom
NBAC	*Nuovo Bullettino di Archeologia Cristiana*
N. Sc.	*Notizie degli Scavi di Antichità*
RA	*Revue Archéologique*
RAC	*Rivista di Archeologia Cristiana*
RE	Pauly-Wissowa, Real-Encyclopädie der classischen Altertumswissenschaft
REJ	*Revue des Études Juives*
TAPA	*Transactions of the American Philological Association*
VR	H. Vogelstein and Paul Rieger, Geschichte der Juden in Rom, Vol. I

INTRODUCTION TO THE REVISED EDITION

The aim of this revised edition is to make Leon's work once more accessible in its original form, and to make more readily available the new materials discovered and published since its appearance. It would have been impossible to incorporate so much new data into the statistics and discussion of *The Jews of Ancient Rome* without rewriting the entire book. Thus, all new information is given here in this introduction and in the listing of the new inscriptions in the appendix of new inscriptions, while the original edition, except for the correction of a few typographical errors, is reprinted intact. It is not the purpose of this revised edition to provide extensive discussion of the new material, but simply to make it more widely available.

RECEPTION OF THE FIRST EDITION

Reception of the first edition of *The Jews of Ancient Rome* in 1960 and years following was overwhelmingly positive. While reviewers did not hesitate to call attention to its shortcomings, they received it as "un travail solide et tout à fait estimable,"[1] a "welcome addition,"[2] "a standard by which other scholars will have to guide themselves,"[3] an "authoritative treatise, . . . the culmination of a lifetime of study and publication,"[4] done "with a precisely observant eye and . . . sober common sense, most deserving of a welcome."[5] The most lengthy and detailed review, while liberal with disagreements and alternative suggestions, still concluded that the book

---

[1] J. Schwartz, *Revue de philologie* ser. 3, 36 (1963) 162–64.
[2] E. Mary Smallwood, *JRS* 51 (1961) 243–44.
[3] John E. Rexine, *Judaism* 11 (1962) 380–82.
[4] James E. Seaver, *Classical Journal* 57 (1961–62) 373–74.
[5] J. M. Reynolds, *Classical Review* n.s. 13 (1963) 332–33.

"could profitably be in every library since it places the reader in immediate contact with one of the great formative influences on the culture of the West."[6]

Critics were able to disagree only with minor points of interpretation and a few instances of drawing too much from too little evidence, such as attempts to draw conclusions about the differences of population of the various catacombs. J. M. Reynolds pointed to "a number of unsatisfactory historical judgments," e.g., the definition of *populares* as the "liberal democratic or people's party" (p. 8), when in fact the two rival parties of the late republic, the *optimates* and the *populares* were both aristocratic parties, the former in control of the Senate, thus forcing the latter to seek support in the tribal assembly.[7] Exception was also taken by both Reynolds and Smallwood to Leon's use of the *fiscus iudaicus* (pp. 31, 33, 36) as the tax paid by Jews, rather than the treasury and imperial administration set up to receive the tax.[8] Moreover, its existence after the middle of the second century is disputed.[9]

THE NEW INSCRIPTIONS

Since the appearance of the first edition, over forty new inscriptions were published by the late Umberto Fasola following the extensive re-excavation and exploration of the Villa Torlonia complex from November 1973 to June 1974.[10] Fasola's careful excavation enabled him to formulate some kind of picture of the stratigraphy and dating. He confirmed earlier theories of two originally independent Jewish cemeteries that eventually met, but saw the lower level as older than the higher. On the basis of brick stamps *in situ*, he dated the oldest part, section E, not before Septimius Severus

---

[6] M. Joseph Costelloe, S.J., *AJP* 83 (1962) 308–13.

[7] See H. H. Scullard, *From the Gracchi to Nero* (5th ed.; London: Methuen, 1982) 6–7.

[8] Cf. Smallwood, *The Jews under Roman Rule*, 371–78; *PW* 12 (1909) 2403–5.

[9] Cf. Tcherikover, *CPJ* 1.80–81.

[10] "Le due catacombe ebraiche di Villa Torlonia," *Rivista Archeologia Cristiana* 52 (1976) 7–62.

(d. 211 C.E.), whereas parts of section A in the upper catacomb, by the same criterion, were begun after Diocletian (d. 316 C.E.).[11]

Only those inscriptions that contain some kind of useful information are included in the new appendix. Those with only a few letters not distinguishable into a name or word other than part of a formula are omitted. Besides these fragmentary inscriptions mentioned by Fasola, he also notes many other painted inscriptions that were completely illegible.[12] Since the inscriptions in Fasola's article are not assigned numbers, and since only a few of them are published in *Année épigraphique* (1976), they are here assigned new numbers followed by # to distinguish them from the other series given by Leon.

In addition to the new inscriptions from Villa Torlonia, one other Jewish inscription not included by Leon (no. 40#), part of a private collection of Christian inscriptions, was published by Antonio Ferrua in 1983,[13] and new arguments have been put forth for the Jewish provenance of two previously known inscriptions (nos. 16#, 41#), which are included here.[14]

The names and other information in the new inscriptions are listed below.

GREEK NAMES

Amachios 13#	Gero[. . . .] 30#
An[as]tasios 15#	Hermias 41#
Ap[elles?] 28#	Hermione 41#
Athe[naios?] 31#	[L]eontis 32#
Cerdo 12#	Philippos 1#
Epa[. . . .] 37#	Spoudeos 10#
Eumenis 6#	Zosimos 2#
Euprepios 24#	[. . . .]theia 37#
Gaianos 4#	[. . . .]metos 18#
Gerontis 29#	[Philod]oxo[s?] 26#

---

[11] Discussion of chronology in Fasola, "Le due catacombe," 61–62; cf. further discussion in T. Rajak, "Reading the Jewish Catacombs of Rome," 229.

[12] "Le due catacombe," 14.

[13] "Iscrizioni paleocristiane in una raccolta privata," *Rivista Archeologia Cristiana* 59 (1983) 321–33.

[14] For no. 16#, see Horsley, *NewDocs* 1.76 (1981) 118–19; for no. 41#, Luigi Moretti, "Iscrizioni greco-giudaiche di Roma," *Rivista Archeologia Cristiana* 50 (1974) 215–18.

Latin Names

Anastasius 15#
Avia 33#
Cuspia 16#
Cuspius 16#
Julia 21#, 27#
Julius 21#, 22#
Justus 13#
Maximus 9#

Oc[la]tia Pia 25#
Rufinus 3#, 19#
Severu[s] 17#
Simpl[i]cius 8#
Verinus 7#
[Pom]ponia? 11#
[Ro]mana? 39#

Semitic Names

Joudas 23#
Maran 14#

Sarah 34#

Mixed Latin and Greek Names

[C]atilia Eutychi[a] 41#   Publius Catilius Hermias 41#

Uncertain

Abibo[s] 20#

If the name is Greek Ἀβîβος or Latin *Avivus*, it is rare or unattested. It may be Semitic, perhaps derived from Hebrew אבי, אביב, or even a poor transliteration of חביב, perhaps assumed by Fasola, who gives the rough breathing. But these can only be conjectures.

Provenance

Achaia 5#
Catania 13#

Lindos 20#
Thabraca 9#

Language of Inscription

Greek 35, Latin 5, bilingual 1

While Leon found a percentage of 76% Greek, 23% Latin, and 1% other (Semitic and bilingual in the original collection, the contrast between Greek and Latin percentages is even greater here: 87% Greek, 12% Latin, 1 bilingual inscription (no. 21#).

Sex of Persons

Men: 13 Greek, 10 Latin, 2 Semitic, 1 mixed (Latin and Greek)=26
Women: 2 Greek, 6 Latin, 1 Semitic, 1 mixed (Latin and Greek)=10
Sex uncertain: nos. 28#, 30#, 31#, 37#

The following spelling variants occur in the new inscriptions (many also occur in those previously published as well): ἰρήνη (4#, 5#, 10#, 12#, 13#, 21#, 40#), εἰρένη (8#), and ἐρήνη (37#) for εἰρήνη; ουκιν for ἐκείνου (41#); αεν for ἐν (8#); αἐτῶν (8#) and possibly οιτων (15#) for ἐτῶν; ἐπύησα for ἐποίησα (41#); γραμματέους for γραμματεύς (4#); κατανέου for κατανάιου (13#); κῖμαι for κεῖμαι (41#); κῖτε (4#, 5#, 6#, 10#, 15#, 29#) and κῖτε (13#) for κεῖται; νέπια for νήπια (33#); ὔκος for οἴκος (12#); and πεδίν for παιδίον (28#).

Titles of Office

ἄρχων 18#, 22#, and maybe 36#
ἀρχιγερουσιάρχης 15#
γραμματεύς 4#
ψαλμῳδός 4#

Ψαλμῳδός appears in the inscriptions here for the first time and is understood by Fasola[15] to correspond to the cantor of psalms in the synagogue service. One of the most sensational finds is the title of ἀρχιγερουσιάρχης in no. 15#. The consensus, as argued by Leon[16] and others, has been that the Roman Jews were organized in a loose association of synagogues, each governed by its own γερουσία rather than with any kind of centralized authority as at Alexandria. The presence of an ἀρχιγερουσιάρχης could indicate differently, but "this single occurence of the word ἀρχιγερουσιάρχης is too weak a basis to build such a hypothesis upon, the more so since there are other compounds as well in which the element ἀρχι– does not have the sense of 'leading.' "[17]

---

[15] "Le due catacombe," 20.
[16] Esp. pp. 167–70.
[17] P. W. van der Horst, *Ancient Jewish Epitaphs*, 91; cf. p. 85 n.1.

SERVILE STATUS

Contrary to the evidence of the literary sources, still there are no indicators in the Jewish inscriptions of Rome of servile or freed status. Various explanations have been offered: Jews avoided the designation for religious reasons that emphasized their allegiance to God alone;[18] the synagogues worked out ways of group patronage to avoid the patronal dependence of Jews on pagan patrons.[19] Probably the simplest explanation, however, lies in dating: the generations represented in the inscriptions are considerably later than their enslaved ancestors.[20]

---

[18] G. Fuks, "Where Have All the Freedmen Gone?"

[19] J. Albert Harrill, "The Social and Economic Position of Jewish Freedmen in Rome," unpublished paper, Social World of Formative Judaism and Christianity Group, Society of Biblical Literature Annual Meeting, 1992.

[20] Also the opinion of Dale Martin, "Slavery and the Ancient Jewish Family," in S. J. D. Cohen, ed., *The Jewish Family in Antiquity*, 120–21.

THE JEWS OF ANCIENT ROME

CHAPTER ONE

THE HISTORICAL RECORD

When King Agrippa addressed the Jews of Jerusalem as he sought to dissuade them from revolting against the power of Rome, he warned them that they would endanger the lives of their fellow Jews not only in Palestine but over the entire world, for, to quote his words as given by Josephus (*BJ* 2. 16.4.398),[1] "There is not a community in the entire world which does not have a portion of our people." This assertion, made during the reign of Nero, could have been uttered with equal truth a century and a half earlier, as we may gather from a statement of the celebrated geographer, Strabo, also quoted by Josephus (*AJ* 14. 7. 2. 114-115), to the effect that by the year 87 B.C.E. the world was full of Jews and that in Strabo's own time, the era of Augustus, this people had already spread to every city and that it would be difficult to find a place in the entire world which did not have a large and influential Jewish community.[2]

In fact, long before Titus destroyed Jerusalem and brought an end to the independent Jewish nation, numerous Jews had emigrated from Palestine and formed communities throughout the Mediterranean world. While not all of these Jewish groups could compare in size and importance with those of Alexandria or Cyrene or Antioch, Strabo's words, with due allowance for rhetorical exaggeration, would indicate, even if no other evidence were available, the extent and the significance of the spread of Jews over the civilized world.[3]

---

[1] The references to Josephus are given by book, chapter, section, and subsection, so that the passages can be readily located in either the older or the newer editions and translations. The text used here is that of B. Niese, 7 vols., Leipzig, 1885-1895.

[2] This testimony may be further amplified by a passage in the spurious Sibylline Oracles (*Orac. Sib.* 3.271) to the effect that the Jews fill every land and sea.

[3] On the extent of the Jews in the Diaspora, see especially E. Schürer, *Geschichte des jüdischen Volkes im Zeitalter Jesu Christi* (hereafter referred to as Schürer) III, 1-70; J. Juster, *Les juifs dans l'empire romain*, I, 179-212; S. Krauss, *Synagogale Altertümer*, 214-267.

It is, accordingly, not surprising that in the course of time an important Jewish community should have been formed at Rome. The surprising thing is that, despite the growing importance of Rome as a great cosmopolitan center, the Jews appear there relatively late. The reason may be that, even while Rome was expanding its territory and becoming a mighty imperial power, its people did not take to international trade until after they had become masters of the Mediterranean world. The Romans persistently regarded themselves as an agricultural people. Loving the soil and hating the sea, they retained for a long period their provincial outlook and remained suspicious of foreigners, especially of Greek and Oriental traders. The narrow nationalism of Cato the Censor was no unique phenomenon in the Rome of the second century B.C.E. [1] If, then, it is a fact (and this is far from certain, as we shall see) that the Jews were attracted to the larger commercial centers, prior to 100 B.C.E. there was comparatively little in Rome to draw them to that capital. Puteoli, for instance, was a more important Italian center for the Mediterranean trade and it may well be that it had a Jewish colony earlier than did Rome, although we have no tangible evidence to support any such conjecture. [2]

That the successive alliances between the mighty Roman republic and the tiny independent state set up in Palestine by Judas Maccabaeus brought permanent Jewish settlers to the city of Rome may well be doubted. The earliest indication that we have of the presence of Jews in Rome is to be found in a puzzling statement in Valerius Maximus, the author of a work on "Memorable Deeds and Sayings" (*Factorum ac Dictorum Memorabilium Libri IX*), published in the reign of the Emperor Tiberius about 170 years later than the incident to which he alludes. Under the heading "De Superstitionibus" (1. 3. 3) he observes that the praetor Gnaeus Cornelius Hispanus (the manuscripts of Valerius wrongly call him Hispalus), [3] who as *praetor peregrinus* was

---

[1] Cf. H. J. Leon, "One Hundred Per Cent Romanism," *South Atlantic Quarterly*, 26 (1927), 146-160.

[2] There was already a Jewish community in Puteoli (Dicaearchia) by the end of the pre-Christian era, but we do not know how long it had been there. See *AJ* 17.12.1.328; *BJ* 2.7.1.104.

[3] Since the name appears as Hispalus in the texts of Valerius, all

in charge of cases involving foreigners, expelled the Chaldaeans and astrologers from Rome in 139 B.C.E. because they were taking advantage of the credulity of the Romans, and that "he also compelled the Jews, who attempted to contaminate the morals of the Romans with the worship of Jupiter Sabazius, to go back to their own homes." Another version of the passage adds the detail that he cast their private altars out of the public places. [1]

Since the ambassadors of Simon Maccabaeus were probably in Rome at that time to renew the treaty between their state and Rome, it has been conjectured that this action by the praetor is in some way connected either with the ambassadors themselves or with members of their following who might have carried on religious propaganda while they were in the city. Especially puzzling is the reference to Jupiter Sabazius, who, far from being a Semitic deity, was a Phrygian god, whose rites had some connection with those of the Greek Bacchus and whose worship became popular in the eastern part of the Roman Empire. Some have seen here an allusion to the Lord of Hosts, Yahwe Sabaot, while others have found a confusion between the name of the Jewish Sabbath and the name of the god, a not improbable conjecture, since the observance of the Sabbath was one of the best known Jewish customs in the Roman world.

Whatever the actual fact may have been, it seems reasonably certain that the passage in Valerius refers not to a settled community but rather to a small group of temporary sojourners, whether they were merchants or in some way connected

---

modern historians have referred to him by that name. The praetor's name was actually Cn. Cornelius Scipio Hispanus, as is known from the inscription on his sarcophagus, which was found in the vault of the Scipio family on the Via Appia. His father, however, bore the second cognomen of Hispallus, and either Valerius or his source may have confused the two men. For the inscription, see *CIL* I (ed. 2) 15. For an account of Hispanus, see Pauly-Wissowa, RE, *s.v.* CORNELIUS, col. 1493. Cf. T. R. S. Broughton, *The Magistrates of the Roman Republic*, I (New York, 1951), 482.

[1]) The abridgement of Julius Paris states merely: *Idem (i.e.,* Hispallus) *Iudaeos, qui Sabazi Iovis cultu Romanos inficere mores conati erant repetere domos suas coegit.* The version of Nepotianus, which is generally considered less dependable, reads: *Iudaeos quoque, qui Romanis tradere sacra sua (i.e.* impart their religious rites) *conati erant, idem Hispalus urbe exterminavit arasque privatas e publicis locis abiecit.*

with the envoys from Palestine, who may have carried on an active religious propaganda which the Roman authorities found objectionable. These were requested to "go back home" (*repetere domos suas*), a phrase hardly applicable to permanent residents. There remains, of course, the possibility that these were not Jews at all, but that, because the name Sabazius was mistaken for the Jewish Sabbath, certain oriental propagandists were confused with Jews in Valerius' source.[1]

We are thus left without information as to when Rome received its first permanent Jewish settlers. During the first three or four decades of the first century B.C.E. the number of Jewish immigrants must have been considerable. The colony was substantially increased in the autumn of 61, when Gnaeus Pompey returned in triumph from his eastern conquests, bringing back numerous captives, among them many Jews taken at the capture of Jerusalem where the Roman general had intervened in behalf of Hyrcanus against Aristobulus, his younger brother and rival for the throne.

According to Philo (*Legatio* 23. 155) the nucleus of the Jewish community of Rome was made up chiefly of enslaved prisoners of war. Ransomed by fellow-Jews or freed by their owners, who must have found them intractable as slaves because of their insistence on observing the dietary laws, abstaining from work on the Sabbath, and practicing their exotic (to the Romans) religious rites, they acquired Roman citizenship and became a part of the city rabble. As most scholars have recognized, Philo's statement that the bulk of the Jewish group at Rome in the last generation of the Republic consisted of these ex-slaves can hardly be accepted,[2]

---

[1] Certainly the reference in the Nepotianus version to the private altars in public places would not be applicable to Jews. For a discussion of the entire matter, see Th. Reinach, *Textes d'auteurs grecs et romains relatifs au Judaisme*, 239,. note 3; Schürer, III, 58 f.; Vogelstein in Vogelstein and Rieger, *Geschichte der Juden in Rom,* I (hereafter referred to as *VR*), 3, and in his *Jews of Rome*, 10-14. In the last-mentioned work (p. 14), Vogelstein regards it as probable that the praetor actually abolished Jewish synagogues and prayer houses.

[2] C. Guignebert, *Le monde juif vers le temps de Jésus* (Paris, 1950), 235, suggests that these Jewish captives were brought to Rome as the result of Rome's successful war with Antiochus of Syria (192-188 B.C.E.), since he regards the Valerius Maximus passage as proof of a community in Rome by the year 139.

since we have clear contemporary evidence from a speech by Cicero that by the year 59, a mere two years after Pompey's triumphant return, the Jews of the city were already a formidable element in Roman politics, a definite indication that there must have been a solid nucleus of Jews in Rome for some years prior to 59. It was doubtless this group of well-established residents that saw to the freeing of their coreligionists and to assisting them in becoming an integrated part of the economic and social life of the Capital.

Cicero's speech, to which reference has been made, is the noted address which he delivered in October of 59 before a Roman jury in defense of Lucius Valerius Flaccus, a Roman aristocrat, who was charged with extortion and misappropriation of funds while serving as governor (propraetor) of the Roman province of Asia in the year 62. Among the charges against Flaccus was the accusation that he had confiscated the gold which the Jews of the province had collected for their annual contribution toward the maintenance of the Temple at Jerusalem. To this fund the Jews throughout the Diaspora contributed and, so far as we know, no difficulties had hitherto been raised about their sending the money to Jerusalem.

The trial of Flaccus aroused considerable attention, particularly among those who had interests in the province of Asia and most of all among the Jews, since, if Flaccus should be vindicated by acquittal, the Temple fund would be imperiled even to the point of being forbidden by the authorities. The case was tried before a jury at an open-air tribunal in the vicinity of the Aurelian Steps (*Gradus Aurelii*), the precise location of which is not certain, though they were undoubtedly in or close to the Roman Forum, where all major trials were held.[1] The chief prosecutor was the youthful Decimus Laelius,

---

[1] The *gradus Aurelii*, also known as the *tribunal Aurelium*, were, according to the most recent archaeological opinion, near the public speaker's platform (*rostra*). See Giuseppe Lugli, *Monumenti minori del Foro Romano* (Rome, 1947), 76; cf. S. B. Platner, *A Topographical Dictionary of Ancient Rome* (London, 1929), 539 f. The spacious semicircle of steps, erected by an Aurelius Cotta, would have been well suited for the assembling of the large crowd of interested spectators. In an earlier speech (*Pro Cluentio* 93) Cicero had complained of a prosecutor who took advantage of the physical arrangement of the

while Flaccus was defended by Quintus Hortensius and Marcus Tullius Cicero, the two leading orators of the time. A large crowd of spectators, many of them Jews, thronged the space around the tribunal. Cicero was the final speaker for the defense, as was his custom when there was more than one defending lawyer. The great orator, a consummate master of every technique of appeal to a jury, whether in creating sympathy for his client or stirring prejudice against the opposing side, [1] made use of all the tricks of his profession in ridiculing the prosecutor, Laelius, and his supporters. Cicero's words are worth quoting *in extenso*, since they not only offer a typical instance of the superb art which made him Rome's most effective pleader but also present significant information about the status of the Jews at that particular time:

We come now to the libel involving the gold, the Jewish gold. This is obviously the reason why the present case is being tried close to the Aurelian Steps. It is because of this particular charge that you have sought out this location, Laelius, and that mob. You know how large a group they are, how unanimously they stick together, how influential they are in politics. I will lower my voice and speak just loudly enough for the jury to hear me; for there are plenty of individuals to stir up those Jews against me and against every good Roman, and I don't intend to make it any easier for them to do this. Since gold was regularly exported each year in the name of the Jews from Italy and all our provinces to Jerusalem, Flaccus issued an edict forbidding its exportation from Asia. Who is there, gentlemen of the jury, who cannot sincerely commend this action? The exportation of gold had been forbidden by the Senate on many previous occasions, and most strictly of all during my consulship [four years previously]. Furthermore, that Flaccus opposed this barbarous superstition [*i.e.*, Judaism] was a proof of his strong character, that he defended the Republic by frequently defying the aggressiveness of the Jewish mobs at political gatherings was an evidence of his high sense of responsibility. But, we are told, when Gnaeus Pompey captured Jerusalem, the victorious commander touched not a thing in that shrine. This was a typically shrewd act

Aurelian Steps to bring in a noisy crowd that made it difficult for the defense to present its case.

[1]) See H. J. Leon, "The Technique of Emotional Appeal in Cicero's Judicial Speeches," *Classical Weekly*, 29 (1935), 33-37.

on his part. In a state as suspicious and as slanderous as ours, he left his detractors no room for criticism. I surely do not believe that the distinguished general was deterred by the religion of the Jews, who were our enemies besides, but it was rather his scrupulous honesty which deterred him. Now where does that leave the accusation, since you make absolutely no charge of embezzlement, you approve the edict, you admit that there was due process of law, you do not deny that the whole procedure was carried on openly and publicly, and the fact reveals that men of the highest prominence had a part therein? (*Pro Flacco* 66-68).

After naming the Asiatic cities involved[1] and indicating the amount of gold confiscated in each, Cicero continues :

The gold is fully accounted for; the gold is in the public treasury; there is no charge of embezzlement. The motive of the charge is to arouse prejudice. The prosecutor turns his argument away from the jury and directs the flow of his words toward the surrounding mob. Every country has its own religion, Laelius, we have ours. Even while Jerusalem was still standing and the Jews were at peace, their religious rites were repugnant to the glory of our Empire, to the prestige of our name, to the institutions of our ancestors. This is all the more true now that that race has demonstrated its attitude toward our Empire by taking up arms against us, and it has proved how dear it is to the immortal gods in that it has been conquered, deprived of its autonomy, reduced to slavery. (*Pro Flacco* 69)

A certain caution is, of course, necessary in evaluating the arguments of a lawyer, especially of a Cicero, who on another occasion (*Pro Cluentio* 139) admitted frankly that his words spoken before a jury should not be interpreted as representing his own conviction and that when pleading a case he was like an actor playing his role with a view to producing a desired effect. It was a regular part of Cicero's method to weaken the charges of the prosecution by belittling its supporters. In his defense of Flaccus, Cicero skillfully worked on the natural prejudice of the Romans against a people who had been subdued by Roman arms only a few years previously. Even the device of pretended fear was used by the orator on another conspicuous occasion (*Pro Milone* 1-2). Still, while

---

1) These were Apamea, Laodicea, Adramyttium, and Pergamum.

we can make liberal allowance for the lawyer's exaggerations and distortions, it is obvious that his words would have had little point were it not a fact that the Jews of Rome were already a rather large and politically influential element of the Roman population. One may, accordingly, safely assume that the Jewish community had been building up for some time, probably for several decades, to have attained the importance implied in Cicero's words.

As for Flaccus, thanks to the masterly defense by Hortensius, whose speech is not preserved, and especially by Cicero, he was acquitted and escaped a merited punishment.[1] Although his confiscation of the Jewish gold was vindicated in this trial, there is no evidence that the ban on the export of this gold was applied further, and we may assume that the Jews of Rome, Italy, and the provinces continued to make their annual contributions to the Temple.

From the tone of Cicero's aspersions it can be inferred that such political weight as the Jews possessed was thrown on the side of the "Populares," the liberal democratic or people's party which was finding a new and powerful leader in Julius Caesar.[2] Especially significant is Cicero's statement that the Jews could be stirred up "against every good Roman" (*in optimum quemque*), which is his usual way of referring to his own political party of the "Optimates," the conservative senatorial group which stood for the retention of the traditional prerogatives of the aristocracy. It is natural enough that the liberal program of the Populares should have appealed to the Jews, the vast majority of whom doubtless belonged to the less privileged classes. While a good many of the emancipated foreigners had become retainers (*clientes*) of aristocratic families and voted on the side of their patrons, there is no evidence that many of the Jews of Rome may be placed in that category.

In the annals of the turbulent decades which preceded the crash of the Republic and the establishment of Caesar's

---

[1]) We know from a later source, Macrobius *Saturnalia* 2.1.13, that the case against Flaccus was a strong one. Macrobius actually calls Flaccus "entirely guilty" (*nocentissimus*) and says that Cicero saved him *de manifestissimis criminibus*.

[2]) On the sympathy of the Jews toward the Populares, see VR, 8.

dictatorship, the Jews of Rome are mentioned only in the Ciceronian speech which has just been discussed. They must have witnessed Pompey's spectacular triumphal procession in September of 61, in which Jewish captives, among others, were degraded by being forced to march among the hordes of prisoners who followed the victor's chariot.[1] What the reactions of the Roman Jews were at the humiliating sight can only be surmised, since no historian has recorded them.

When the disastrous civil war between Pompey and Caesar broke out in 49, the Jews, those not only of Rome but probably of the whole Empire, were wholeheartedly on Caesar's side. It is not difficult to understand why. Pompey was remembered as the general who had slain many Jews in his assault on Jerusalem, who had violated the sanctity of the Temple by entering its Holy of Holies, who had enslaved many Jews and had forced upon Jewish nobles the humiliation of marching in chains behind his triumphal chariot. Besides, Pompey was the head of the aristocratic faction of the Optimates, while Caesar, as leader of the Populares, championed the rights of the common citizen. We know from Josephus that Caesar appointed Aristobulus, the Hasmonaean, commander of two legions to campaign against Pompey's forces in Syria, but unfortunately he was poisoned by his enemies before he could reach his destination (AJ 14. 7. 4. 123-4; BJ 1. 9. 1. 183-4). In Palestine, Caesar received valiant support from Hyrcanus and his minister Antipater, while the Jews of Egypt gave him material aid in their country. It is not unlikely that the Jews of Rome itself were active on Caesar's side, but we have no record of this.

In return for the support which he had received from the Jews, Caesar showed them his favor conspicuously, and his decrees in their behalf, which, fortunately recorded by Josephus (AJ 14. 10. 1-8. 185-216), have been called the Magna Carta of the Jews,[2] were the foundation for the special

---

[1] It may be, as Reinach holds, that an elaborate gold vine, the gift of Aristobulus, was displayed in Pompey's triumph (Textes, p. 283, note 2). Cf. VR, 5, note 7 and p. 6. The gift was set up in the Temple of Jupiter Capitolinus, where it was seen by Strabo (AJ 14.3.1.35-36).

[2] By B. Niese in Hermes, 11 (1876), 488, quoted with approval by Vogelstein (VR, 10).

privileges which the Jews of Rome and the Empire continued
to enjoy for more than three centuries, until the rule of the
Christian emperors. By these decrees they were granted full
freedom of worship. The strict rules governing private associations (*collegia*) were relaxed in the case of the Jews, who
were allowed free assembly for the practice of their cult and
for the holding of meals in common. They were granted permission to raise money for communal purposes and to send
the Temple tax to Jerusalem. Because of their refusal to bear
arms or march on the Sabbath and their insistence on special
foods in accordance with their dietary laws, Caesar exempted
them from compulsory military service. Special Jewish
courts were recognized, so that cases involving only Jews
could be tried by a Jewish tribunal instead of the regular
Roman courts.[1] No wonder that after Caesar's untimely
death beneath the daggers of Brutus and his fellow conspira-
tors, the Jews, above all others, mourned for him. Suetonius
informs us (*Jul.* 84. 5) that for many nights after Caesar's
murder groups of Jews came to weep at the site of his funeral
pyre.[2]

After the death of Caesar, his edicts in favor of the Jews
were renewed by senatorial decree and were reaffirmed by the
commanders of the Roman forces in various parts of the
Empire (*AJ* 14. 10. 9-26. 217-267). In the year 40, during the
Second Triumvirate, the Roman Senate proclaimed Herod
King of Judaea, and many of the Roman Jews may have
seen the solemn procession in which the new king was escorted
by Mark Antony and Octavian to the Temple of Jupiter on
the Capitoline Hill, where a record of the senatorial decree
was deposited and a thank-offering on behalf of the Jewish
ruler was sacrificed to the pagan god (*AJ* 14. 14. 4-5. 385-9;
BJ 1. 14. 4. 284-5).

Caesar's grandnephew and adopted son, Octavian, who

---

[1] On these special privileges, see Juster, II, 110-116.

[2]) Suetonius' word is *bustum*, which seems to refer here to the place
where Caesar's body was actually burned, *i.e.*, in the Roman Forum
at the spot where the Altar of the Deified Julius, subsequently erected
there, may still be seen. Since *bustum* may also mean "tomb," the
reference may be to the site of the family tomb of the Julian *gens*
in the Campus Martius, where the pyre intended for the cremation
of Caesar's body had been raised.

became the ruler at Rome under the title of Augustus, was no less favorable to the Jewish citizens of Rome than his great predecessor had been. For this period our historical sources are more abundant, since substantial information is available from Philo, Josephus, and Suetonius, while references to the Jews in such writers of the time as Horace and Ovid testify to the growing importance of the community. Not only were Caesar's edicts renewed by Augustus himself and by his son-in-law, Marcus Agrippa, and other officials (*AJ* 16. 6. 1-7. 160-73), but the Jews were granted the additional privilege that, when the free distribution of grain and other commodities or largesses of money to the poorer citizens fell on the Jewish Sabbath, the portion allotted to the Jews was reserved for them so that it could be claimed on the following day (Philo, *Legat.* 158). Philo points out that the Jews occupied a large section of the city in the area across the Tiber (the Transtiberinum; see below, pp. 136 f.) and that Augustus in no way interfered with their religious and communal activities or with the collection and sending of funds for the Temple at Jerusalem (*Legat.* 155-7). The Emperor further demonstrated his good will toward the Jews by adorning the Temple at Jerusalem with costly gifts and commanding that a burnt offering be made there daily in perpetuity at his expense as a token of his homage to the supreme God of the Jews (*Legat.* 157).[1] Agrippa also showed his favor in various conspicuous ways (*AJ* 12. 3. 2. 125-6; 16. 2. 5. 60; 16. 6. 4-7. 167-73). On a visit to Jerusalem, after being received with acclaim by the populace, he entertained them with a grand banquet and had a hecatomb sacrificed in the Temple on his behalf (*AJ* 16. 2. 1. 14-15). It is, accordingly, reasonable to assume that the Roman congregations of the Augustesians and the Agrippesians (see below, pp. 141 f.) were named, respectively, for the Emperor and his son-in-law, whom he was grooming to become his successor.

That the Jewish community of Rome was attracting notice

---

[1] On the other hand, he refrained from showing himself too friendly to the Jews, since he commended his grandson, Gaius, for not offering prayers at the Temple, presumably during a visit to Jerusalem (Suet., *Aug.* 93). Curiously, Vogelstein (VR, 11) substitutes Claudius for Gaius in citing this detail.

in the aristocratic circles of the Augustan era is clear enough
from allusions in the writers of that time. The good-natured
satirist, Horace, playfully alludes to their proselytizing
activity. If his critic, he says, will not allow him to indulge
his minor vice of writing verses about human conduct, a
large band of poets will come to his aid and, like the Jews,
will force the dissenter to join their throng (*Sat.* 1. 4. 140-3).
Horace jests at the superstitions of the Jews. Commenting
on a miracle performed in a temple of Gnatia, a town on the
Adriatic coast of Apulia, where incense was said to liquefy
without the application of fire, he remarks, "Let the Jew
Apella believe that; I won't." He adds that he believes that
the gods do not concern themselves with human affairs and
he contrasts the easy-going Epicurean gods with those stern
deities (presumably like the austere God of the Jews) who
send miracles down from heaven (*Sat.* 1. 5. 97-103). Who
Apella was we do not know, but Horace has chosen the name
as that of a typical Jew.[1] A third reference in Horace gives
us some indication that the observance of the Jewish holy
days may have been rather prevalent even among the Roman
upper classes. While trying desperately to tear himself loose
from a persistent social climber, who wanted Horace to introduce him to his wealthy patron, Maecenas, the poet caught
sight of a friend, Aristius Fuscus, and with gestures intimated
to him that he wanted to be released from his unwelcome
companion. The amusing incident took place just beyond the
Sacred Way (Sacra Via) near the Temple of Vesta at the
entrance to the Roman Forum.[2] The following dialogue ensued:

> HORACE. Wasn't there something you wanted to talk to
> me about in private?
> FUSCUS. Oh yes, I remember, but I'll talk to you at a
> more favorable time. Today is the thirtieth Sabbath. You
> don't want to insult the circumcised Jews, do you?
> HOR. But I don't have any religious scruples.
> FUS. Well, I do. I'm sort of weak that way, like most
> people, you know. So excuse me. I'll talk to you some
> other time. (*Sat.* 1. 9. 67-72).

---

[1] Among the several hundred Jewish names on the catacomb
inscriptions the name Apella does not appear.

[2] For some strange reason Vogelstein places this episode in the
Jewish quarter of the Transtiberine region (VR, 37, and again in

While the reference to the "thirtieth Sabbath" (*tricesima Sabbata*) remains an unsolved puzzle, despite the scholarly effort which has been exerted in trying to explain it,[1] the passage shows clearly enough that Jewish practices had penetrated into pagan Roman circles, perhaps even into the higher social orders.

Especially frequent at this time are the references to the observance of the Sabbath as a sacred day, though there is no further allusion to any "thirtieth Sabbath." The amorous poet Tibullus implies that "Saturn's sacred day" (*Saturni sacram diem*), *i.e.*, the Sabbath, is an unfavorable day for starting on a journey (1. 3. 18). There is a similar allusion in Ovid to this superstition that the "foreign Sabbath" (*peregrina Sabbata*) is a bad time to leave on a trip (*Remed. Am.* 219-220). The same poet twice indicates that the holiday on the Jewish Sabbath is a favorable time for courting a girl, referring once to the "seventh-day rites observed by the Syrian Jew" (*Ars Am.* 1. 76) and once to the "seventh-day festival observed by Syrian Palestine, a day unsuited for ordinary business affairs" (*Ars Am.* 1. 415-6).

Somehow there existed among the Romans the idea that the Jews observed the Sabbath as a fast day. The historian Pompeius Trogus, who lived in the time of Augustus, explains the custom as going back to Moses, who ordained that the Jews should observe the seventh day by fasting because that day marked the end of their arduous march through the Arabian desert, when they went for seven days without food (Justin's *Epitome* 36. 2. 14). Even the Emperor Augustus seems to have thought that the Jews fasted on the Sabbath. In a letter to his stepson Tiberius, who was to become his successor, he writes:

> Not even a Jew, my dear Tiberius, observes the Sabbath fast as faithfully as I did today. It was only after the first night hour that I took two mouthfuls of food at the bath before my rubdown was started (Suetonius, *Aug.* 76. 2).

Augustus' misconception about the Jewish observance of

Jews of Rome, 19 f.), despite Horace's specific references to the Sacred Way and the Temple of Vesta.

[1] See the interesting discussion in Radin, *Jews Among the Greeks and Romans*, 399-402.

the Sabbath is somewhat surprising, since he seems to have had ample opportunity to acquire at least some acquaintance with Jewish customs. Apart from the minor circumstance that his wife Livia had a Jewish handmaid named Acme (*AJ* 17. 5. 7. 141; *BJ* 1. 32. 6. 641), he was well acquainted with Herod and certainly knew the several sons of Herod who were educated in Rome and spent many years there during Augustus' regime. Asinius Pollio, a man prominent in the political and social life of Rome, was a friend of Herod[1] and at his house Alexander and Aristobulus, the sons of Herod and Mariamne, who were later executed at their father's order, lived during their long stay in Rome (*AJ* 15. 10. 1. 342-3). Antipater, another of Herod's sons, spent at least two periods in Rome (*AJ* 16. 3. 3-4. 1. 86-7; 17. 3. 2. 53; *BJ* 1. 29. 2. 573), and Antipas, Archelaus, and Philip, also sons of Herod, received their education in the same city (*AJ* 17. 1. 3. 20; *BJ* 1. 31. 1. 602). One may, of course, question to what extent these Romanized sons of the Jewish ruler observed the customs of their forefathers, at least during their stay at Rome.

While we have no information as to whether these Jewish princes had any contacts with the members of the Jewish community in Rome, it is clear that at least Alexander and Aristobulus, the sons of Mariamne, were beloved by them. After the execution of these two brothers the charlatan who pretended that he was Alexander was acclaimed by the Roman Jews, who jubilantly thronged to meet him and escorted him in regal style through the streets of Rome, thanking God that the reports of the murder were false (*AJ* 17. 12. 1. 330-1; *BJ* 2. 7. 1. 105). There is no indication that the other sons of Herod enjoyed a similar popularity at Rome. In fact, when an embassy of fifty men came to Rome from Palestine a few months after Herod's death (4 B.C.E.) to petition Augustus that Archelaus, who had succeeded to the throne of Judaea, be deposed and they were granted a hearing in the Temple of Apollo on the Palatine, the Jews of Rome, re-

[1] The friendship between Herod and Pollio may, as some have recognized, provide a clue to the Old Testament echoes in Virgil's Fourth (Messianic) Eclogue, which was written to glorify Pollio's consulship. On the Jewish connections of Pollio see L. H. Feldman, "Asinius Pollio and his Jewish Interests," *TAPA*, 84 (1953), 73-80.

presented by more than eight thousand men, indicated their enthusiastic support of this petition (AJ 17. 11. 1. 300-1; BJ 2. 6. 1. 80-1). That the community could produce so large a number of men for this occasion is, unless the figure is materially exaggerated by Josephus, an indication of a considerable Jewish population, perhaps 40,000 or even more (see below, pp. 135 f.). Several years later another embassy came to Rome with a similar petition, complaining bitterly of Archelaus' misrule. This time Archelaus was deposed by Augustus and sent into exile at Vienne in Gaul (AJ 17. 13. 2. 342-4; BJ 2. 7. 3. 111). While it is likely that the Roman Jews actively supported this embassy also, there is no record of the fact. During the reign of Augustus, other Jewish embassies came to Rome, as for instance those from the Jews of Cyrene and of Asia Minor (AJ 16. 6. 1. 161), but our sources say nothing of their contacts with their coreligionists in Rome.

We have seen from the allusions in the writers of the period that the Jews were aggressive in securing converts to their religious views and practices. Among the proselytes we should perhaps include the distinguished writer, Caecilius of Cale Acte (or Calacte), the most important rhetor and literary critic of the Augustan Age next to Dionysius of Halicarnassus, whose friend he was. He was of servile origin, a native of Cale Acte in northern Sicily, and originally bore the name of Archagathus. He was later freed, taking the name of Caecilius. Of his extensive writings only fragments have come down to us, but they had a material influence on later writers in the field of literary criticism. According to the tenth-century Suidas lexicon, which reflects earlier sources, Caecilius was "Jewish in religion" (τὴν δόξαν Ἰουδαῖος), an indication that he was a proselyte. Although some scholars have questioned this testimony, there seems to be no valid reason for refusing to accept it, since the lexicographer would hardly have invented such a detail. It is interesting that another Caecilius, a generation or two earlier, is also alleged to have been a proselyte to Judaism. Plutarch, in his biography of Cicero (7. 5), makes this assertion with reference to Quintus Caecilius Niger, who was quaestor in Sicily during the administration of the corrupt Roman governor Verres (73-71 B.C.E.). The biographer mentions this detail in order to explain a jest by

Cicero, who in his prosecution of Verres had occasion to denounce Caecilius. Since the Latin name Verres means "hog," Cicero is said to have remarked of Caecilius, "What has a Jew to do with a hog?"[1] While scholars have rightly pointed out that a Jewish freedman could not at that time have risen to the office of quaestor, a position which led to a seat in the Senate, and have therefore assumed that Plutarch has confused the two Caecilii, it is entirely possible that the quaestor Caecilius was actually a "Judaizer," that is, one who had accepted monotheism and adopted such Jewish practices as observance of the dietary laws and the Sabbath (see below, pp. 250-53). In any case, the pun certainly has the true Ciceronian flavor.

Augustus died in 14 C.E., after a long and successful rule, during which the city and the Empire enjoyed, in the main, both peace and prosperity. Thanks to the Emperor's encouragement of literature and art, the Augustan Age became proverbial as a Golden Age, producing such poets as Virgil, Horace, Ovid, Tibullus, and Propertius, the great prose historian Livy, and such artistic masterpieces as the Altar of Peace. The Jews had ample reason to be grateful to Augustus, because he not only continued the favorable policies of Julius Caesar toward them but went even further in establishing their special privileges.

Under Tiberius, Augustus' successor as *princeps*, the Jews fared less well, although the Emperor himself is now known to have been a high-minded and capable ruler, despite the unfavorable picture which historians both ancient and modern have transmitted to us.[2] The evil influence as regards the Jews appears to have been Aelius Sejanus, in whom Tiberius, as he later learned to his sorrow, placed too great confidence, not only appointing him to the powerful office of praetorian prefect, but leaving him virtually in charge of affairs in Rome during the Emperor's self-imposed exile from the capital city. Philo informs us (*Legat.* 24. 159-160) that Sejanus,

---

[1] Τί 'Ιουδαίῳ πρὸς χοῖρον. The Latin equivalent would probably be *Quid Iudaeo cum verre* ? See Th. Reinach, "Quid Iudaeo cum Verre ?" *REJ*, 26 (1893), 36-46. Reinach thinks that the joke is probably a post-Ciceronian invention.

[2] See, especially, F. B. Marsh, *The Reign of Tiberius* (London, 1931).

desirous of destroying the Jews, invented calumnies against them, and in another passage (*Flac.* 1. 1) he alludes to him as a persecutor. Latin writers, as Eusebius (*Hist. Eccles.* 2. 5. 7), citing Philo as their source, make of Sejanus a second Haman, who sought to wipe out the entire Jewish people.[1]

The immediate occasion for Tiberius' action against the Jews may have been the scandal recorded by Josephus (*AJ* 18. 3. 5. 81-4). According to the Jewish historian, a noble Roman lady named Fulvia, wife of the senator Saturninus,[2] who was a friend of the Emperor, was victimized by four Jewish charlatans, one of whom was a fugitive from Palestine, where he had a criminal record. Taking advantage of the fact that Fulvia had become a proselyte to Judaism (προσεληλυθυῖαν τοῖς 'Ιουδαϊκοῖς), he pretended to give her instruction in the wisdom of the Laws of Moses, and the four of them persuaded her to contribute money and costly draperies for the Temple at Jerusalem. Upon learning that she had been swindled, the disillusioned and indignant Fulvia induced her husband to report the matter to Tiberius, who, because of the act of these four scoundrels, ordered the banishment of the Jews from Rome.

It is not always easy to decide how far to trust the accuracy of Josephus, but in this instance the fact of the banishment, at any rate, is attested by the Roman historians who deal with the period. Our most reliable source, Tacitus, informs us (*Ann.* 2. 85. 4) that in 19 C.E. action was taken to expel the Egyptian and Jewish rites and that the Senate decreed that four thousand of the freedman class infected with this superstition (*ea superstitione infecta*) and of suitable age (*i.e.*,

---

[1] The sterner policy in Judaea at this time is perhaps to be connected with the influence of Sejanus in the Roman government. It was when Sejanus was nearing the height of his power that Pontius Pilate was made procurator of Judaea. E. Stauffer has pointed out, in *La Nouvelle Clio* 1/2 (1950), 507 f., that Pilate's issuing of coins bearing Roman cult symbols indicates a contempt for Jewish feelings. These issues no longer appear after the death of Sejanus.

[2] This Roman senator may perhaps be identified with Gaius Sentius Saturninus, who was consul in 4 C.E., or with Lucius Sentius Saturninus, who appears to have been this man's brother. Groag (Pauly-Wissowa, *RE, s.v.* SENTIUS, col. 1528) suggests that since Josephus, just before his account of the Fulvia episode, has described another scandal involving a certain Paulina, whose husband was named Saturninus, there may be a confusion of name in one or the other instance.

of military age, about eighteen to forty-five) should be sent to Sardinia for police duty against bandits. Tacitus adds the cynical observation that if they were to perish there because of the bad climate, it would be a small loss. In addition, the senatorial decree required that the others leave Italy unless they abandoned their profane rites by a certain date. Suetonius, probably employing the same source, also states (*Tib.* 36) that Tiberius repressed the Egyptian and Jewish rites, forcing the followers of "this superstition" to burn their religious vestments and all their paraphernalia (this would seem to refer only to the worshipers of Isis) and sending the Jewish young men, ostensibly under the terms of military service, to the provinces with the worst climate, while the other members of the race and the followers of similar practices were required to leave Rome under the penalty of life-long slavery if they failed to obey.

From these two versions plus the statement in Josephus that because of the swindling of Fulvia all the Jews were banished from Rome and that four thousand of them were drafted into the army and sent to Sardinia, it is apparent that many Jews were forced to leave Rome and perhaps other parts of Italy, although of our three sources only Tacitus mentions an expulsion from Italy.[1] Since many of the Jews must have been Roman citizens, we may well doubt that they could have been banished without a formal trial and conviction for violating the laws of Rome. The practice of Judaism was no crime in Rome at that time nor, indeed, at any time under the pagan emperors; and Tiberius, as has

---

[1] It has been suggested, *e.g.*, by A. Momigliano in his *Opera dell' Imperatore Claudio* (Florence, 1932), 62, note 1, and in his *Claudius the Emperor* (Oxford, 1934), 96, that some of those expelled from Rome went to Ariccia (some twenty miles away) and other places near the city, as indicated by the scholiast on Juvenal 4.117; but one may wonder why, if they were permitted to return to Rome soon afterward, some were still there in Juvenal's time, about sixty years later. Schürer (III, 63) thinks that the Jews who went to Ariccia were those dislodged from Rome by Claudius, but that these soon returned to Rome. There would still remain the question of why these were still there when Juvenal wrote. The beggars of Ariccia were notorious, since Martial also refers to them (2.19.3; 12.32.10). Some of these beggars may have been Jews, but there is no reason whatever for thinking that they were remnants of those expelled by either Tiberius or Claudius.

been convincingly established, was a strict observer of the Roman law.[1] It is not unlikely that Sejanus, taking advantage of the activity of the Jews in gaining proselytes at a time when the Emperor was trying to strengthen the traditional religion of Rome, and profiting by the scandalous Fulvia episode, persuaded Tiberius to expel from Rome those Jews who could be so treated under the Roman law. Hence, probably only foreign Jews and freedmen, who did not enjoy the full rights of citizenship, were the victims of the senatorial decree. As for the four thousand men of military age who were sent to Sardinia, Tacitus states definitely that they were of the freedman class (*libertini generis*).[2] The additional statement in Suetonius that they were sent ostensibly under the terms of military service (*per speciem sacramenti*) probably means that the normal exemption of Jews from military conscription was not applied in their case, so that they were drafted into the army as a means of getting them out of Rome. Many of these, as we learn from Josephus (*AJ* 18. 3. 5. 84), were punished because they refused to violate their ancestral laws in connection with the requirements of military duty.[3] While we do not know just how extensive the banishment under Tiberius was, we can be sure that it was of brief duration.[4]

---

[1]) See Radin, *Jews among the Greeks and Romans*, 308 f. and especially R. S. Rogers, *Criminal Trials and Criminal Legislation Under Tiberius* (Middletown, Conn., 1935).

[2]) It is not certain whether these were actually freedmen, as was maintained by Radin, who added the assumption that "most, if not all, of these men were freedmen of other nationalities who were converts to Judaism" (*op. cit.*, 308), or whether *libertini generis* refers to both actual freedmen and descendants of freedman, as was argued by E. T. Merrill in *CP*, 14 (1919), 365-374. Philo states (*Legatio* 23.155) that most of the Jews of Rome were freedmen, but this must be an exaggeration. For a while during the Republic the term *libertinus* was used of sons of freedmen, as we know from Suet. *Claudius* 24.1 (cf. Isidore *Origines* 9.4.47), but by the time of Suetonius the term was restricted to actual freedmen. It is not impossible, however, that the phrase *libertinum genus* may refer to freedman stock rather than to actual freedmen.

[3] There is evidence that there were Jewish groups in Sardinia during the Roman period, but there is no way of telling whether any of these went back to the young Jews who were sent there by Tiberius. Some Jewish tombs and inscriptions have been found at Sant' Antioco (ancient Sulcis). See *Jüdisches Lexikon*, s.v. SARDINIEN, and *CII* 657-660.

[4] Probably to be linked with these events is an episode in the life

Upon the sudden overthrow and death of Sejanus in October of the year 31, Tiberius, realizing that an injustice had been done the Jews because of the slanders of that evil minister,[1] restored all their rights and, we may reasonably assume, allowed the exiles to return.

During the regime of Tiberius (14-37) the Jewish prince Agrippa, grandson of King Herod, and his mother Berenice lived in Rome and were closely associated with the royal household. Berenice was a dear friend of Antonia, the sister-in-law of Tiberius, while Agrippa was on intimate terms first with Drusus, the Emperor's son, and after his death with Gaius, the Emperor's grandnephew, who was to become the next emperor (AJ 18. 6. 1. 143; 18. 6. 4. 166-7). Agrippa, however, fell into disfavor with Tiberius toward the end of his reign and was actually imprisoned for several months (AJ 18. 6. 6. 188 ff.). It is not improbable that the influence of Antonia, to whom Tiberius was obligated for exposing the treachery of Sejanus (AJ 18. 6. 6. 180-2) and who cherished the memory of the deceased Berenice,[2] helped toward restoring the favorable position of the Jews; but this is mere speculation. Certain it is that by the beginning of the reign of Tiberius' successor, Gaius, the Jews formed a large element in the population of Rome and were again in full enjoyment of their well established rights.

In the brief and irresponsible rule of Gaius (37-41), better known by his nickname of Caligula, the status of the Jews in the city seems to have remained unchanged. They must have been interested in the embassy of Alexandrian Jews, headed by Philo, who came to Rome to complain before the

---

of Seneca (*Epist. ad Lucil.* 108.22). He tells us that in his youth, that is, during the early years of Tiberius, he was so far influenced by the tenets of Epicureanism that he abstained from the flesh of animals. In view of the prejudice against such foreign religious practices at a time when alien rites were being driven out of Rome, his father persuaded him to return to a normal diet.

That the chief motive of Tiberius' action against the Jews was religious is cogently argued by E. Mary Smallwood, "Jews Under Tiberius," *Latomus* 15 (1956) 314-329. She demonstrates that the Emperor was attempting to check Jewish proselytism, particularly among the higher nobility.

[1] See Philo, *Legatio* 24.160.

[2] For Antonia's devotion to the memory of Berenice, see *AJ* 18.6.4.165. Cf. VR, 16.

Emperor of the abuses inflicted upon the large Jewish community of Alexandria by the Greeks of that city. The Jewish
philosopher has left us a vivid account in his *Embassy to Gaius*
(*Legatio ad Gaium*) of the humiliations to which the envoys
were exposed by the eccentric Emperor, who received them
in his gardens on the Esquiline, leading them in a merry
chase from building to building on the pretext of making a
tour of inspection, while their Greek adversaries mocked them
and jeered and charged them with disloyalty before the
Emperor. Every now and then Gaius recognized the presence
of the Jewish envoys by asking them such questions as why
the Jews did not sacrifice to him as a god and why they
abstained from the flesh of swine, all this amid unrestrained
glee on the part of the Greeks, who lauded the Emperor's
brilliant wit. At last, when Philo and his companions were
completely despondent and exhausted, Gaius took pity on
them and dismissed them with the humane comment that
those who did not believe in his divinity were not so much
wicked as unfortunate and stupid (*Legat.* 44-45. 349-367).

The trouble caused in Jerusalem by Gaius' insistence on
having his statue set up in the Temple had no effect in Rome,
as far as we are aware. Agrippa, who had been imprisoned by
Tiberius, was released by Gaius and made king over a portion
of his grandfather Herod's dominion (*AJ* 18. 6. 10. 237).
Later, while in Rome, he appealed to the Emperor not to
insist on having his statue erected in the Temple and did,
in fact, succeed in getting the decree rescinded. Soon afterward, on a fresh impulse, the irresponsible Gaius reaffirmed
it, and serious trouble was averted only through the deliberate
delay of the Roman governor Petronius, who was legate of
Syria, and the timely assassination of the hated ruler (*AJ* 18.
8. 7-8. 297-301; Philo, *Legat.* 35-42. 261-337).[1]

The reign of Claudius (41-54 C.E.) began auspiciously
for the Jews. It was, in fact, the Jew Agrippa who helped
materially to establish Claudius on the throne by guiding
him through the critical and exciting hours following the
murder of Gaius and by persuading him to accept the princi-

---

[1] E. Mary Smallwood, "The Chronology of Gaius' Attempt to
Desecrate the Temple," *Latomus* 16 (1957) 3-17, offers a full chronology
of this episode; her account is based on Philo rather than Josephus.

pate as he wavered indecisively (*AJ* 19. 4. 1-2. 236-245). The new Emperor promptly rewarded Agrippa, not only for these services but also out of regard for his old friend and schoolmate, by adding Judaea and other territories to his kingdom, thus making him the ruler of an even greater realm than his grandfather Herod had controlled (*AJ* 19. 5. 1. 274-5; *BJ* 2. 11. 5. 215). Josephus alludes to the celebration in the Roman Forum as Agrippa entered into a formal treaty with the Roman people (*AJ* 19. 5. 1. 275). The text of the donation of the territory, inscribed on bronze tablets, was solemnly set up in the Capitoline Temple (*BJ* 2. 11. 5. 216). Agrippa himself received the consular insignia and presented his thanks before the Senate in an oration in Greek (Dio 60. 8. 2-3).

Among the earliest official acts of Claudius' regime was the issuance of edicts addressed to various parts of the Empire affirming the special rights and privileges of the Jews, disclaiming the oppressive acts of Gaius, and emphasizing the Emperor's high regard for the brother kings, Agrippa and Herod, and his confidence in the loyalty and friendship of the Jews toward the Roman people. Because of renewed riots between Jews and Greeks in Alexandria—this time the Jews seem to have been the aggressors[1]—Claudius dispatched sharp instructions to the government of that city to restore order and respect the rights of the Jews, at the same time warning both factions to keep the peace (*AJ* 19. 5. 2-3. 279-291).

Thanks to the fortunate discovery of a papyrus at the site of the Egyptian town of Philadelphia in 1920 or 1921, we have the text of a letter sent by Claudius to the Alexandrian authorities in reply to a petition which was presented to him by a delegation from that city. The papyrus, which is now in the British Museum,[2] reveals that while confirming the rights

---

[1] So *AJ* 19.5.2.278.

[2] *Pap. Lond.* 1912; lines 73-104 deal with the Jews. The letter, first published by H. I. Bell, *Jews and Christians in Egypt* (London, 1924), promptly evoked a considerable literature: *e.g.*, H. Willrich, "Zum Brief des Kaisers Claudius an die Alexandriner," *Hermes*, 60 (1925), 482-489; M. Radin (review of Bell) in *CP*, 20(1925), 368-375; R. Laqueur, "Der Brief des Kaisers Claudius an die Alexandriner," *Klio*, 20 (1926), 89-106; M. Engers, "Der Brief d. Kais. Claud. an d. Alex.," *Klio*, 20 (1926), 168-178 (reply to Laqueur); A. Neppi Modena, "A proposito del P. Lond. 1912.73-104," *Aegyptus*, 7 (1926), 41-48; H. Stuart Jones, "Claudius and the Jewish Question at Alexan-

of the Jews in carrying on their worship and observing their traditional customs, Claudius strongly reprimands both parties and threatens them with severe punishment if the peace should again be broken. He reserves his sharpest language for the Jews, rebuking them for sending two embassies[1] and warning them to show appreciation of the rights which they enjoy by peacefully minding their own affairs. The unexpected severity of the Emperor's reprimand of the Jews is significant in connection with an action which he seems to have taken soon afterwards.

Suetonius, in his biography of Claudius (25. 4), as part of a list of actions involving foreigners, informs us with tantalizing brevity that the Emperor "expelled from Rome the Jews who persisted in rioting at the instigation of Chrestus" (*Iudaeos impulsore Chresto assidue tumultuantis Roma expulit*). These few words have produced an extensive literature in a controversy which concerns mainly the following points: (1) Was there actually an expulsion of the Jews under Clau-

---

dria," *JRS*, 16 (1926), 17-35; H. Janne, "Lettre de Claude aux Alexandrins et le Christianisme," *Annuaire de l'Inst. de Philol. et d'Hist. Orientales et Slaves*, 4 (1936) = *Mélanges Franz Cumont*, 273-295. See also V. M. Scramuzza, *The Emperor Claudius* (Cambridge, Mass., 1940), 64-79 and notes. The text, accompanied by a translation, is available in Bell, *op. cit.*, and in the Loeb Series *Select Papyri* II (1934), No. 212 (the part dealing with the Jews is on pp. 84-87). The text alone is published in M. P. Charlesworth, *Documents Illustrating the Reigns of Claudius and Nero* (Cambridge, 1939), pp. 3-5.

[1] The text seems to indicate that the Greeks sent one embassy, while the Jews sent two. Claudius' statement that the sending of two embassies was unprecedented would hardly make sense if these represented the two major factions in a dispute. In fact, a Greek and a Jewish embassy had come to Gaius from Alexandria only a few years before, when Philo was head of the Jewish group (see above, p. 21). In the present instance the two sets of Jewish envoys represented two opposing points of view, perhaps that of the native Jewish citizens of Alexandria and that of the immigrant group, or the more conservative and the more liberal factions, respectively. That there were two Jewish embassies is the view of sundry scholars, including M. Radin (*CP*, 20 [1925], 368-375), A. Momigliano (*Opera di Claudio*, 64 and *Claudius the Emperor*, 97), Willrich (*Hermes*, 60 [1925], 483), Stuart Jones (*JRS*, 16 [1926], 28), and S. Davis in *Race Relations in Ancient Egypt* (London, 1951), 108. That there was only one Jewish embassy was held by Bell (*op. cit.*, 29) and Scramuzza (*op. cit.*, 255, n. 51) and the translator in the Loeb edition (p. 87). More recently, Bell has accepted the view that there were two Jewish embassies (*Cults and Creeds in Graeco-Roman Egypt* [Liverpool, 1953], 44).

dius? (2) If there was an expulsion, did it include all the Jews or only the rioters? (3) Did the episode, whatever its character, occur in the first year of Claudius or several years later? (4) Do the words *impulsore Chresto* indicate disputes in the Jewish community with regard to the new Christian gospel or do they simply refer to the leading troublemaker, one named Chrestus?

Let us take these up briefly, point by point:

(1) As though in deliberate contradiction of any allusion to an expulsion of the Jews under Claudius, the third-century historian Cassius Dio (60. 6. 6) asserts that Claudius did not expel the Jews, because their numbers had become too great for an expulsion, but that, while permitting them to continue to observe their traditional way of life, he forbade them to hold meetings. Josephus, in his detailed account of the history of the Jews during that period, does not refer to any expulsion, nor does Tacitus in his narrative of the latter half of Claudius' reign (his account of the first six years of Claudius is lost). On the other side, in addition to the positive statement in Suetonius, there is the evidence of *Acts* 18. 2, where we learn that when Paul came to Corinth, he found there the Jew Aquila and his wife Priscilla, who had recently arrived there from Italy, because Claudius had ordered all the Jews to leave Rome. Statements in later Christian writers, as, for example, Eusebius in the fourth century (*Hist. Eccl.* 2. 18. 9) and Orosius in the fifth (*Adv. Paganos* 7. 6. 15-16) seem to have no independent value in this connection.

(2) The language of Suetonius can be interpreted as meaning that only those Jews who rioted were expelled. If this is what Suetonius meant, then Dio's statement offers no contradiction, since he denies only that there was a general expulsion of the large Jewish population. The writer of *Acts*, however, says definitely that all (πάντας) the Jews were ordered out of Rome.

(3) Dio's statement occurs in his account of the earliest acts of Claudius' reign. There is no indication of date in Suetonius, since that historian observes no chronological arrangement. Orosius definitely places the expulsion in the ninth year of Claudius, which would be 49 C.E. He cites Josephus as his source; but, as we have seen, the text of

Josephus has no reference whatever to an expulsion under Claudius. Since Orosius is notoriously inaccurate, his unsupported testimony has little if any value. Neither Tacitus nor Dio mentions such an expulsion in the account of the year 49, and we should have expected Tacitus, at least, to have some reference to an act so drastic as the driving out of so large a group. The statement in Acts that Aquila and Priscilla had lately (προσφάτως) arrived in Corinth from Italy has been taken as confirming the date 49 for the expulsion, since Paul's visit to Corinth belongs to 51 or 52, when Gallio was proconsul of Achaea. It need not, however, be assumed that this couple went to Corinth immediately after leaving Rome. They may well have spent several years elsewhere in the interim,[1] so that the first year of Claudius, 41, is not necessarily excluded.

(4) The most baffling of the problems is raised by Suetonius' two words, *impulsore Chresto*. Radin, among others, suggests that we have here the name of a Jewish agitator, Chrestus, a fairly common name at the time.[2] In reply it has been pointed out[3] that, if some otherwise unknown person were referred to, Suetonius would have used the qualifying word *quodam*, "a certain," as is his wont. If the allusion is, as most scholars believe, to Jesus as the Christ, the spelling variant offers no difficulty, since *Christus* and *Christianus* were commonly written with *e* instead of *i* at this time.[4] The question is complicated by doubts as to whether the Christian group was substantial enough by that time, especially if the episode occurred in the first year of Claudius, to have occasioned turbulent controversies in the Jewish community. If Janne is right in holding that a Christian group was established in Rome as early as the year 40,[5] the difficulty is resolved. In that case, we may suppose that Suetonius, misinterpreting

---

[1] That Aquila and Priscilla traveled about a good deal after Paul saw them in Corinth is evident from subsequent references to them. Later they were in Ephesus (Acts 18.19, 1 Cor. 16.19), in Rome (Rom. 16.3 ff.), and again in Ephesus (2 Tim. 4.19).

[2] Actually, the name Chrestus does not appear among the several hundred known names of Roman Jews.

[3] By H. Janne in *Mélanges Bidez* (1934), 540.

[4] For examples, see Janne, *op. cit.*, 541 f.

[5] *Op. cit.*, 547.

his source, as he not infrequently did, apparently thought that Christus (or Chrestus) was there in person to stir up trouble. There is, of course, the possibility that the text of Suetonius has been garbled in transmission; but all our manuscripts are in agreement on the reading.

Amid the welter of few facts and many conjectures, the following reconstruction of the relation between Claudius and the Jews in the first year of his rule may be justified. At the beginning of his reign, Claudius, because of his own liberal attitude and the influence of his friend Agrippa, issued edicts reaffirming the rights of the Jews throughout the Empire. This reaffirmation was especially needed after the unfriendly attitude of Gaius had encouraged the enemies of the Jews to abuse them, notably in Alexandria. In the Jewish community of Rome bitter controversies had arisen through the missionary activities of a group from Palestine, who sought to win converts to the new gospel of Jesus as the promised Messiah. In the efforts of the more conservative elements to expel from their congregations those who accepted this gospel, serious riots arose which caused the authorities deep concern. Claudius, in his letter to the Alexandrians, reflected his impatience over the turbulence of the Jews at home by his use of sharp language warning the Alexandrian Jews to show appreciation of their special privileges and not "to stir up a general plague throughout the world."[1] As the rioting in Rome continued, becoming even worse, Claudius decided on drastic action. Since the Jewish group was too large for a general expulsion and the Emperor's sense of fairness and his respect for the laws of Rome would have deterred him from punishing the majority, who were peaceful and law-abiding, he expelled only those who had a prominent part in the disturbances and banned the rest from holding assemblies, for fear that new

---

[1] Some scholars interpret the word νόσον (see the bibliography in Scramuzza, *Emperor Claudius*, 285-286, n. 19) as referring to the "plague" of Christianity. This seems to me quite improbable, since Christianity had not yet become so prevalent as to justify such concern. Claudius is apparently alluding to no more than the troublesome riots (perhaps caused by the earliest attempts to introduce the new gospel) which were occurring among the Jewish groups not only in Rome and Alexandria but presumably in other parts of the Empire as well.

trouble would start. Among those expelled was Aquila, who was a leader of the faction that had accepted Jesus as Christ. Since this police action did not affect the community as a whole, Josephus did not consider it important enough to mention in his account of the period. Suetonius misunderstood his source, and Dio, finding the statement that all the Jews were expelled from Rome by Claudius, took special pains to refute it. As for the statement in Acts that all the Jews were expelled, we must regard it as an error, since it is at variance with the other indications. That there was no expulsion of Jews in the latter part of Claudius' reign, despite the statement in the late and unreliable Orosius, may be concluded from the failure of both Tacitus and Dio, as well as Josephus, to mention an event which, if it had occurred, would have involved some tens of thousands of individuals and would surely have been included by these historians in their detailed chronicle of the period.[1]

The son of King Agrippa, who was to become Agrippa II, was brought up at Rome in the household of Claudius. Because of his youth (he was about 17) at the time of his father's death in 44, he succeeded to only a part of Agrippa I's kingdom (*AJ* 19. 9. 2. 360-2). As various embassies came to Rome from Judaea, Claudius seems to have been influenced by young Agrippa in his replies to them. In one document he refers to him as "my own Agrippa, whom I have reared and kept with me, a most loyal person" (*AJ* 20. 1. 2. 12). Agrippa appears also to have enjoyed the favor of the Empress Agrippina (*AJ* 20. 6. 3. 135).

Although Nero's acts of tyranny and extravagance affected some elements of the population, the fourteen years of his reign (54-68) seem to have been tranquil for the Jewish

---

[1] On the entire problem of Claudius and the Jews there is a considerable bibliography. The following list cites some of the more significant treatments, apart from those dealing with the Alexandrian letter, which have been cited above in the notes to pp. 22 and 23: Schürer, III, 61-63, especially note 92; Vogelstein in VR, 19-20, and *Jews of Rome*, 55 f.; E. T. Merrill in *Essays in Early Christian History* (London, 1924), 102-108; A. Momigliano, *L'Opera dell' Imperatore Claudio*, 61-76, and *Claudius the Emperor*, 29-38 and notes; H. Janne, "Impulsore Chresto," *Mélanges Bidez* (1934), 531-553; A. D. Nock in *Cambridge Ancient History*, 10 (1934), 500 f.; V. M. Scramuzza, *The Emperor Claudius*, 151-152 and note 20 on pp. 286-287.

group in Rome. We have, at any rate, no evidence to the contrary. From Josephus we infer that Nero's second wife, Poppaea, was partial to Judaism and may even have been a convert,[1] and while the adherence of this corrupt woman (if we may trust what the Roman historians tell of her) is hardly a credit to Judaism, she used her influence with Nero to win favor for the Jews. Josephus himself, coming to Rome in 64 with a petition, was introduced to Poppaea by the Jewish actor Alityrus, who was a favorite of Nero, and was aided in his mission by the Empress. The great fire of 64 did not touch the principal Jewish quarter across the Tiber, since the river was an effective barrier against the spread of the flames. Nero's brutal persecution of the Christians soon after the fire was directed only toward that sect, which the authorities appear now for the first time to have differentiated from the Jews. It may be remarked here that the opinion expressed by some writers[2] that this persecution was instigated by the Jews is supported by not a particle of evidence. The outbreak in 66 of the great Jewish insurrection in Palestine seems in no way to have affected the status of the Jews in Rome itself.

How the Roman Jews fared during the chaotic year and a half between the violent end of Nero and the accession of

---

[1] Josephus calls her "god-fearing" (*AJ* 20.8.11.195). For her kindness to Josephus see his *Vita* 3.16. B. W. Henderson, *Life and Principate of the Emperor Nero* (London, 1903), 467, thinks that Poppaea was not actually a proselyte, since Josephus would have been more specific about it if she had been, but that she merely followed the fashionable mode of observing certain Jewish practices; *i.e.*, she was a "Judaizer."

[2] *E.g.*, Paul Styger, *Juden und Christen im alten Rom* (Berlin, 1934), 37-44. This writer, while insisting that the function of historical research is to present the truth uprightly and impartially (p. 63), reflects the anti-Jewish bias of the German government at that time by not only blaming the Jews for the Neronian persecution, with not a single positive citation to support his view, but also attributing the subsequent persecutions of the Christians to Jewish calumnies. Most other Christian scholars, however, have been more objective in evaluating the evidence. *Vide* A. Bludau, *Der Katholik*, 83 (1903), 131-132; R. Wilde, *Treatment of the Jews in the Greek Christian Writers of the First Three Centuries* (Washington, 1949), 144. On the innocence of the Jews in connection with the later persecutions of the Christians, see G. F. Hardy, *Studies in Roman History* (London, 1906), 47-49; J. E. Seaver, *Persecution of the Jews in the Roman Empire* (Lawrence, Kansas, 1952), 7-18.

Vespasian in December of 69 is completely unknown. Nor do we have any record of how they reacted to the siege and capture of Jerusalem and the destruction of the Holy City and its Temple in 70. Those Jews who, like Josephus, could tolerate the sight, witnessed the magnificent triumphal procession with which mighty Rome's victory over tiny Judaea was celebrated in grand style. To Josephus we owe a detailed account of the procession, in which the spoils of the Temple were displayed, seven hundred of the tallest and handsomest of the Jewish captives marched as prisoners, and the leaders of the revolt, Simon Bar Giora and John of Giscala, walked in chains (*BJ* 7. 5. 3-6. 118-157).[1] On the majestic Arch of Titus, which was not completed until more than a decade later, when Titus was already dead and had been made a god, one can still behold the sculptured record of the occasion: prince Titus riding proudly in his four-horse chariot, while the goddess Victory places the wreath of laurel on his head; the Roman soldiers bearing aloft the sacred implements of the Temple, notably the golden table, the silver trumpets, and the golden candelabrum of the seven branches. The trophies were solemnly deposited in Vespasian's newly dedicated Temple of Peace. Commemorative coins were struck, bearing on their reverse a towering palm tree, symbolic of Palestine, flanked by allegorical figures of a mourning Jewess and a Jew with his hands tied behind his back, and displaying the proud legend, *IVDAEA CAPTA*.[2] Later, in 80, a triumphal arch was raised, probably at the east end of the Circus

---

[1] Vogelstein (VR, 21, 25) states that Cenedaeus and Monobazus, Jewish princes of Adiabene, were among the captives brought to Rome in order to march in Titus' triumph; but we know from Josephus (*BJ* 2.19.2.520) that these princes had been killed early in the war.

[2] Many specimens with the head of either Vespasian or Titus on the obverse are extant. The Jewish Museum in New York City has a fine copy. See the illustration in *JE*, 12.426. For the various issues, with descriptions and illustrations, see H. Mattingly and E. A. Sydenham, *The Roman Imperial Coinage*, II (London, 1926), 68, 73 f., etc. (head of Vespasian), 127, 131 (head of Titus) and Pl. 2.29; also H. Mattingly, *Coins of the Roman Empire in the British Museum*, II (London, 1930), describes and illustrates many specimens; *e.g.*, pp. 115-118, 131-132, Pl. 20.5-10, Pl. 57.4. Other issues commemorating the event have the inscription *IVDAEA DEVICTA* or only *IVDAEA* with representation of a mourning Jewess; see *op. cit.*, II, 62, 74, 79 and Pl. 13.8, 9.

Maximus, on which was carved an inscription recording that it was set up

> By the Senate and the People of Rome to the Emperor Titus Caesar Vespasianus, son of the Deified Vespasianus, Augustus, Pontifex Maximus, ten times invested with the Tribunician Power, seventeen times proclaimed Imperator, eight times Consul, Father of his Country, their Leader, because by his father's teachings, counsels, and auspices he subdued the nation of the Jews and destroyed the city of Jerusalem, which all commanders, king, and nations before his time had either vainly assailed or left entirely untouched.[1]

The statement has been made by modern writers[2] that, because of the expansion of the Roman Empire by the conquest of Judaea, the official boundary (*pomerium*) of the city of Rome was extended by Vespasian, as was customary when the bounds of the Empire were enlarged. That Vespasian actually extended the *pomerium* in the year 75 is attested by the inscriptions of four of the boundary stones which have been found in Rome,[3] but it is unlikely that this action was intended to commemorate the victory over Judaea. In reality, the Jewish War added no territory to the Empire, since Judaea had been transformed by Augustus into a Roman province under a procurator in 6 C.E. After the brief rule of Agrippa I from 41 to 44, it had again been converted into a procuratorial province. The conquest by Vespasian and Titus could have been viewed only as the suppression of a revolt. Actually, between the fall of Jerusalem in 70 and the extension of the *pomerium* in 75, Rome had added some territory to its Empire (notably Syria Commagene in 72 and some portions of Britain and Germany), so as to justify extension of the city boundaries.

---

[1] Neither the arch nor the inscription is extant. The text of the inscription, which was found in the Circus Maximus, was copied before the ninth century and is preserved in the Einsiedeln Itinerary (*CIL* 6. 944).

[2] *E.g.*, Vogelstein in VR, 23.

[3] *CIL* 6.31538a, b, c and *Notizie degli Scavi*, 1933, 241. Cf. C. Hülsen, *Hermes*, 28 (1887), 615 ff. T. Mommsen, *Römisches Staatsrecht*, III (Leipzig, 1887), 735, n. 3; H. E. Newton, "The Epigraphical Evidence for the Reigns of Vespasian and Titus," *Cornell Studies in Classical Philology*, 16 (1901), 5; R. Weynand in Pauly-Wissowa, *RE*, *s.v.* FLAVIUS, 2666.

While the national status of the Jews, dependent though it had been, was now completely destroyed, the privileges which they had enjoyed in both the city and throughout the Empire were not diminished. The only significant change was the transformation of the Temple tax, which the Jews had paid annually for the Temple at Jerusalem, into a poll tax, called the *fiscus Iudaicus*, which was to go instead to the Temple of Jupiter Capitolinus. This tax, which, as before, came to two drachmae (or denarii) a person per year (approximately one dollar in purchasing power), was required of all those who followed the ancestral practices of Judaism (Dio 66. 7. 2) and presumably included full proselytes as well. The handling of the tax was apparently administered through an imperial official at Rome whose title was *procurator ad capitularia Iudaeorum* (*CIL*, 6. 8604). That Vespasian did not intend this tax as a special penalty directed against the Jews is clear from the institution of a similar tax for Alexandrians (*fiscus Alexandrinus*) and for Asiatics (*fiscus Asiaticus*).[1] Finding the national treasury exhausted by the extravagance of Nero and the civil wars which followed his death, the shrewd Emperor used such poll taxes as an effective means of bringing in substantial revenues. In the case of the Jews it involved no new tax, but simply the continuation of an old one with a change of objective. The several million Jews of the Empire, plus the millions of others who were similarly taxed, contributed substantially in this way to Vespasian's much praised rebuilding of the state finances. This tax continued to be imposed upon the Jews for nearly three centuries under both pagan and Christian emperors until it was abolished in 361 by the Emperor Julian, who had the tax lists burned so that the tax might not be reimposed.[2]

The end of the Jewish War must have produced a large increase in the Jewish population of Rome. Many who came as war captives were doubtless freed from slavery either through the aid of their fellow Jews or through their own efforts. Among the more distinguished Jews who settled in

---

[1] See Rostowzew (= M. Rostovtzeff) in Pauly-Wiss., *RE*, *s.v.* FISCUS, 2403 f.

[2] Julian, "Letter to the Jews," *Epist.* 25. 397a (= *Epist.* 51 in the Loeb edition of W. C. Wright, Vol. III, p. 78). For a study of this topic see M. S. Ginsburg, "Fiscus Iudaicus," *JQR*, 21 (1931), 281-291.

Rome at this time was King Agrippa II, who had remained in Rome during the war and as a reward for his loyalty was given the rank of praetor (Dio 66. 15. 3-4). Agrippa's sister, Berenice, lived in the palace on the Palatine as Titus' mistress, fully expecting, according to Dio (66. 15. 4), to become his wife, despite the displeasure of the Romans, who did not take kindly to seeing their prince, the heir apparent to the imperial power, consorting with a foreign princess who might some day become the Empress. Berenice was some twelve years older than he and had been married three times; she was the mother of two children, and there was gossip about improper relations between her and her brother Agrippa. Nevertheless, Titus seems to have been genuinely in love with her; but as the hostility of the people increased, he reluctantly forced her to leave Rome, a separation difficult for both of them, as indicated by Suetonius' expressive *invitus invitam* (*Titus* 7. 1, 2).

Another noteworthy Jew who made his residence in Rome was the historian Josephus, who had deserted to the Romans during the war and had been brought to Rome by Titus. Receiving lodging in the house where Vespasian had lived before he became Emperor, he was rewarded with Roman citizenship and a pension and was granted a large tract of land in Judaea (*Vita* 76. 423, 425). He was even given the honor, if we may trust Eusebius (*Hist. Eccl.* 3. 9. 2), of having his statue set up in Rome and his books placed in the public library. In recognition of this generous patronage, he prefixed to his Jewish name the family name of his benefactors, becoming Flavius Josephus. Under the successive rules of the sons of Vespasian, Josephus continued to enjoy the favor of the Flavian house (*Vita* 76. 428-9) and, released from most material cares, wrote those historical works which, whatever we may think of the moral fiber of their author, have been an invaluable contribution to our knowledge of his people.

The accession of Titus at his father's death in 79 had no effect, so far as we know, on the Jewish population. The magnificent games which attended the opening in 80 of the vast Flavian Amphitheater, better known to us as the Colosseum, did not affect the Jews any more than the others, nor do we know whether Jewish war captives had a part in its construction, as has sometimes been asserted.[1] Berenice returned to Rome in the hope that her former lover, now the all-powerful Emperor, might make her his wife; but Titus, concerned about public opinion, gave her no encouragement (Dio 66. 18. 1). The fact that she was now over fifty years old, while he was thirty-nine, may have been a contributing consideration.

The death of Titus at the age of forty-one, after only two years of rule, was regarded by the Jews as divine punishment for his destruction of the Temple, and fanciful tales about his death have come down in Jewish tradition.[2] His liberality to the point of extravagance, in strong contrast to the frugal regime of his predecessor, had made him beloved of his people, so that his death caused genuine sorrow throughout the Empire. His younger brother, Domitian, who succeeded him in 81, was a sternly efficient ruler, whom history has recorded as a tyrant. In his relationship to the Jews he is remembered for his unreasonably rigorous enforcement of the collection of the *fiscus Iudaicus*. Vexed by the many evasions of the tax on the part of those who, though born Jews, concealed their origin and those who, having become proselytes to Judaism,[3] failed to register on the tax rolls, he went to extreme measures to discover the delinquents. Suetonius relates that when he was a mere youth, he personally witnessed the shameful spectacle of a procurator examining a ninety-year-old man in the presence of a crowded court to see if he was circumcised. (*Domit.* 12. 2).

Some indication that Domitian may have taken drastic action in punishing Roman proselytes to Judaism has been found in the episode of Flavius Clemens and his wife, Flavia Domitilla. Clemens, as the son of Vespasian's elder brother, Flavius Sabinus, was Domitian's first cousin. Clemens' wife was probably the daughter of Domitian's sister, also

---

[1] *E.g.*, by Vogelstein (*Jews in Rome*, 65), who says: "The gigantic structure of the amphitheater was built by the forced labor of the Jewish captives in a phenomenally short time."

[2] See *JE*, *s.v.* TITUS.

[3] There seems to be no reason for holding that these latter were Christians, as does J. Janssen in his edition of Suetonius' *Vita Domitiani* (Groningen, 1919), 59 f. The words *qui vel improfessi Iudaicam viverent vitam* are perfectly clear, and by the time of Domitian there was no confusion, as Janssen thinks, between Christians and Jews, at least not in official circles.

named Flavia Domitilla. Since Domitian had no son, he had
designated the two oldest sons of Clemens and Domitilla as
his heirs and successors. By combining the account in Suetonius (*Don.it.* 15. 1) with that in Dio (67. 14. 1-2), we learn
that in 95, the year in which Clemens was Domitian's colleague
as consul, the couple was convicted of atheism (ἀθεότης) and
the practice of Judaism.[1] Clemens was executed and his wife
was banished to the island of Pandateria, off the coast of
Campania. Although Dio's statement that they were accused
of going over to Jewish practices (ἐς τὰ τῶν Ἰουδαίων ἤθη
ἐξοκέλλοντες) is quite specific,[2] Christian tradition has made
of Clemens and Domitilla martyrs in a persecution of the
Christians by Domitian, a view which is often repeated and
accepted by modern scholars.[3]

The oldest testimony for such a view is that of Eusebius
(*Hist. Eccl.* 3. 19, 20) who, writing some two centuries after
the event, makes Domitilla the niece of Clemens instead of
his wife and states that she was punished for being a Christian
and banished to the island of Pontia.[4] The earliest statement
that Clemens also was a Christian is found in the eighth-century
Byzantine writer Syncellus (1. 650. 19).[5] Because of the

---

[1] The Jews were commonly accused of being atheists, since they
would not recognize the Roman gods and had no images of their own
deity. See E. T. Merrill, *Essays in Early Christian History*, 156.
Strangely contradictory is the statement by Stein (Pauly-Wiss., *RE*,
s.v. FLAVIUS CLEMENS, 2538) that while the charge of "atheism"
normally applies to Judaism, in this case it is practically certain that
it applies to Christianity.

[2] Because Dio never refers to the Christians or to Christianity, he
has been accused of an anti-Christian bias, *e.g.*, by E. G. Hardy,
Studies in Roman History, 67. This charge is effectively answered by
E. T. Merrill in *Essays in Early Christian History*, 86-96.

[3] For a recent example see L. Hertling and E. Kirschbaum, *Le
catacombe romane e i loro martiri* (Rome, 1949), 28-30. Here the strange
remark is made (p. 29) that Suetonius and Dio speak of Clemens'
execution in such language "that there can remain no doubt that the
cause was the Christian religion." The same point of view is expressed
by Leclercq in *DACL* III (1914), 1868 f. and even in Schürer, III,
168, n. 57 (with bibliography); cf. *ibid.*, 64, n. 97. For a discussion
of the problem with bibliography see Stein in Pauly-Wiss. *RE*, *s. vv.*
FLAVIUS CLEMENS and DOMITILLA.

[4] Jerome (*Epist.* 108.7 = Migne 22.882) states that Pontia was
celebrated as having been Domitilla's place of exile when she was
banished by Domitian as an adherent of Christianity. He makes her
the daughter of Clemens' sister.

[5] In a garbled version of Eusebius' *Chronicle*, Clemens seems to be

contradictory statements about Domitilla, some modern scholars have held that two different women, each named Flavia Domitilla, are involved and that both were persecuted as Christians. That the well-known Christian catacomb of Domitilla was dug on the private estate of a certain Flavia Domitilla is an unquestioned fact. Still, the definite statement in Dio, a historian who surely knew the difference between Judaism and Christianity, seems to compel the conclusion that Clemens and Domitilla were convicted as Judaizers. It is, of course, entirely possible that Domitilla returned from exile after Domitian's death and was subsequently converted to Christianity. In that case, we have an explanation of her connection with the catacomb and her place in Christian tradition. It has been pointed out by E. T. Merrill[1] that Suetonius' account of the episode implies that the real reason for Clemens' downfall was Domitian's fear that he was conspiring to overthrow him. In any case, however, the fact that Clemens could be convicted on the ostensible charge of practicing Judaism would suggest that some effort was made to check Jewish proselytizing activity. We have, at any rate, an indication here that Judaism was penetrating into the highest aristocratic circles of Rome. For a persecution of the Christians by Domitian, despite the much repeated modern view, there seems to be no evidence at all.[2]

It was in the time of Domitian that four distinguished Jewish scholars came from Palestine on a visit to the Jewish

---

referred to as a Christian, but the reading is too confused to be of value; see Merrill, *Essays*, 164.

[1] *Essays*, 149. Merrill points out that the "contemptible unaggressiveness" which characterized Clemens is not a proof of his being a Christian, as is often asserted, but Suetonius' method of indicating that the fear of conspiracy in his case was quite unfounded, since he was conspicuously, even reprehensibly, free of political ambition.

[2] Combining the mention by Suetonius (*Domit.* 10.2) and by Dio (67.14.3) of an Acilius Glabrio whom Domitian executed (probably as a Judaizer), and the fact that a Christian cemetery was dug on the estate of a family of that name, some modern scholars have assumed that Glabrio was another martyr in a Domitianic persecution. All that one may reasonably concede is that at some later time members of the family of the Acilii Glabriones became Christians; cf. Hertling and Kirschbaum, *Le catacombe*, 31-33. Those who speak of a persecution of Christians by Domitian can cite no "martyrs" other than Clemens and Glabrio. See the discussion in Merrill, *Essays*, Ch. VI (pp. 148-173), "The Alleged Persecution of Domitian."

community of Rome. These were the celebrated Patriarch, Rabban Gamaliel, and three other rabbis: Joshua ben Hananiah, Eleazar ben Azariah, and Akiba. During their stay, they preached in the synagogue and held discussions with Christian and pagan scholars, discussions which have left traces in the talmudic tradition.[1] Vogelstein's assumption that their visit had some connection with the Flavius Clemens episode appears to have no basis.[2]

Vogelstein has characterized the reign of Domitian as "a period of horror" for the Jews of Rome, adding that "the Jews of the entire Empire were threatened, during this reign, with serious danger."[3] Apart from the rigorous enforcement of the *fiscus Iudaicus*, which may well have been motivated only by the desire to secure the greatest possible revenue from that source, and the prosecution of certain Judaizing nobles, of whom Clemens is the chief example, there is no indication that Domitian treated the Jews harshly.

Domitian's reign came to an abrupt end with his assassination in 96, and the benign senator Cocceius Nerva succeeded him. Nerva promptly instituted a more liberal policy in administering the *fiscus Iudaicus*, commemorating the occasion by issuing a special coin which bore the legend *Fisci Iudaici Calumnia Sublata* (abolition of the unjust enforcement of the Jewish tax) and displayed a palm tree as a sort of symbol of Judaism, somewhat similar to that on Vespasian's *Iudaea Capta* series.[4] Nerva further showed his liberal attitude by putting an end to accusations for impiety[5] and for following the Jewish mode of life (Dio 68. 1. 2).

Nerva, who died after only sixteen months of rule, was the first of a series of five enlightened rulers who gave Rome and the Empire an efficient and liberal government for almost

---

[1] See *JE*, 5.560.

[2] VR, 29. There seems also to be little reason for his suggestion that these rabbis stayed at the home of Josephus. Cf. also Vogelstein, *Jews in Rome*, 68 f.

[3] *Op. cit.*, 68.

[4] Mattingly and Sydenham, *Roman Imperial Coinage*, II (1926), p. 227, no. 58; p. 228, no. 80, and Plate VII.124. These are of the years 96 and 97.

[5] Dio's ἀσέβεια may, however, mean disloyalty to the majesty of the Emperor (*i.e.*, treason) in this passage. If so, it is the equivalent of the Latin *maiestas*.

a century (96-180). About the internal history of the Jewish community in Rome during this period we know distressingly little. There is no evidence that the community was affected by the great Jewish revolts in the reigns of Trajan and Hadrian, a time during which scores of thousands of Jews lost their lives in a desperate struggle to cast off the rule of Rome; important Jewish communities were wiped out, and even the pitiful ruins that were left of the city of Jerusalem after the sack by Titus' army were virtually obliterated. On the site of the Holy City the Emperor Hadrian built a pagan city, naming it Aelia Capitolina both for himself (Aelius was his family name) and for Capitoline Jupiter, and strictly barring all Jews from the area.

Hadrian's law forbidding circumcision, whatever its motive, was not directed exclusively against the Jews, but also affected other peoples of the Empire who practiced this rite. Still, this law was the first in a series of legislative acts which affected the Jews adversely. Hadrian has his place in history as one of the ablest and most enlightened of all the rulers of Rome, yet because of his crushing of the Bar Kokhba rebellion, his desecration of the site of the Temple with a shrine of Jupiter and replacement of the Jewish city with a pagan one, and his attempt to ban the rite of circumcision, he is in Jewish tradition[1] perhaps the most hated of the Roman emperors.

The Jewish scholar Theudas appears to have been in Rome during the reign of Hadrian. He is said to have introduced among the Roman Jews the practice of including in the meal on the eve of Passover a roast lamb in commemoration of the paschal lamb which had been sacrificed in Jerusalem.[2] He seems also to have brought aid to teachers of the Law who had been displaced during the revolts and to have secured financial support for Jewish schools.

Such decrees as Hadrian had issued restricting Jewish religious practices were either rescinded or modified by his

---

[1] Cf. *JE*, *s.v.* HADRIAN; M. Simon, *Verus Israel* (Paris, 1948), 127; E. Mary Smallwood, "The Legislation of Hadrian and Antoninus Pius Against Circumcision," *Latomus* 18 (1959), 334-347.

[2] On this matter and the protests from Palestine see E. R. Goodenough, *Jewish Symbols*, I, 14 f. and S. Zeitlin's criticism in *JQR*, 45 (1954), 72. For Theudas see VR, 70 and *JE*, *s.v.*

successor, Antoninus Pius, who relaxed the ban on circumcision by permitting Jews to practice this rite, but only on their own children (*Digest* 48. 8. 11). If performed on non-Jews, the act was subject to the penalty for castration. It was under Antoninus that Rabbi Simeon ben Johai and Rabbi Eliezer ben Jose came to Rome, where they persuaded the Emperor to take a friendly attitude toward the Jews. They lectured in the schools and synagogues and made decisions on ritual matters. At this time the leading rabbi and the spiritual head of the community appears to have been Matthias ben Heresh, who had recently come to Rome from Palestine and set up a school (Beth Midrash) in Rome. The disasters which plagued Rome under Antoninus and Marcus Aurelius, such as flood, fire, pestilence, and famine, must assuredly have affected the Jews, especially the poorer elements among them, along with the rest of the city's population; but no specific data can be cited.

The fairly frequent references to the Jews in the post-Augustan literature of Rome, while attesting that they attracted notice in the more intellectual circles, give us a picture distorted by misinformation and prejudice. The attitude is generally one of amused contempt at the exotic and seemingly absurd Jewish customs. The philosopher Seneca, who wrote in the time of Claudius and Nero, objects to the observance of the Sabbath because thereby the Jews give up a seventh part of their lives to idleness and are handicapped by not being permitted to perform even urgent tasks on the Sabbath day.[1] He is annoyed by the smoking lamps of the Sabbath and would have them forbidden on the ground that "the gods have no need of light nor does the smoke give pleasure to man" (*Epist.* 95. 47). Seneca's younger contemporary, the satirist Persius, including Judaism among superstitions which enslave the individual, alludes to the Sabbath as "the days of Herod" and scornfully describes the violet-wreathed lamps belching greasy smoke as they are set out at the besmeared windows, the large tunny fish with coiling tail swimming in fish sauce on the platter of red clay,[2] the white flask swollen with wine, the awed prayer of silently

---

[1] Quoted in Augustine, *De Civ. Dei* 6.11.
[2] The cheap Arretine earthenware is probably meant here.

moving lips on the "circumcised Sabbath" (5. 179-184).

The reason for the Jewish abstinence from pork puzzled the Romans. Some, like the satirist Petronius, thought it was because the Jews worshiped the pig.[1] Plutarch, the biographer and philosopher, who flourished during the time of Trajan and Hadrian, devoted a whole treatise to a discussion of this weighty problem.[2] There are frequent, usually contemptuous, references to the practice of circumcision.[3] Martial, the witty epigrammatist of the time of Domitian, included in a catalogue of unpleasant smells the odorous breath of fasting Jews (4. 4. 7), and among the unendurable noisemakers of the city the Jewish mendicant, "taught to beg by his mother" (12. 57. 13). He makes merry about a circumcised poet who not only maligns and plagiarizes Martial's poems, but, although born in the heart of Jerusalem, satisfies his lust with Martial's slave boy (11. 94). Martial has, or pretends to have, a circumcised Jewish slave (7. 35. 3-4).

Cornelius Tacitus, Rome's greatest historian, writing during the reign of Trajan, prefixes his narrative of the destruction of Jerusalem at the hands of Titus with an account of the origin and customs of the Jewish people (*Hist.* 5. 2-5). This normally careful historian, following inaccurate and biased sources (he does not seem to have known the writings of Josephus), presents a fantastic version of the early history of the Jews and their religious practices. Only the more striking details of Tacitus' account need to be brought out here:

The Jews, according to one view, came originally from Crete, their name being derived from that of Mount Ida by corruption of *Idaei* to *Iudaei*. Fleeing from Crete, they settled in Libya at about the time that Jupiter drove Saturn from his celestial kingdom. According to other theories, they were originally Egyptians or Ethiopians or Assyrians or even the Solymi who are celebrated by Homer, a name which they incorporated in that of their chief city, Hierosolyma. They settled for some time in Egypt, whence they were expelled

---

[1] F. Buecheler, *Petronii Saturae*, ed. 6 (Berlin, 1922), Frag. 37.
[2] *Quaestiones Convivales* 4.5.
[3] Petronius, *Frag.* 37 (Buecheler); Martial 7.30.5, 7.35.3-4, 11.94; Tac. *Hist.* 5.5.2; Juvenal 14.99.

by King Bocchoris, who sought, on the advice of an oracle, to cleanse his realm of a plague of skin eruption by driving out this people "hated by the gods." Moses, who was their leader in the exodus through the desert, sought to strengthen his hold upon the people by establishing new religious rites which differed from those of all other peoples. Everything that is sacred to the Romans is profane to the Jews, while what the Romans regard as impure is permissible among the Jews (5. 4. 1). They consecrated the image of an ass in their shrine[1] because a herd of wild asses showed them a spring of water as they were perishing of thirst in the desert. They abstain from the flesh of the pig because they themselves once suffered from the skin infection (*scabies*) which is common to that animal. Their frequent fasts commemorate their long period of hunger in the desert, while the use of unleavened bread is a reminder of the grain which they stole when they fled from Egypt. They are idle on the seventh day because this day marked the end of their painful trek through the desert. The leisure of the Sabbath has proved so attractive to them that they also devote every seventh year to indolence.

Most of their other rites are depraved and disgusting. They have induced the vilest elements everywhere to scorn their own religions and pay tribute to the Jews, thus increasing their wealth. While loyal and charitable among themselves, they cherish hostility and hatred toward all others. They will not eat or sleep with non-Jews, and, though lustful without restraint, they have no relations with alien women. They have adopted the rite of circumcision in order to distinguish themselves from other peoples, and they require all converts to submit to this rite. Such proselytes are taught first of all to scorn the gods, to cast off their fatherland, to hold cheaply their parents, children, and brothers. They stress increase of their numbers, not killing any surplus infants, as do the Romans.

They have no fear of death, since they regard the souls of those who die in battle or by execution as eternal. They

---

[1] On the curious but widespread belief among the ancients that the Jews worshipped an ass, see S. Krauss, *JE*, *s.v.* Ass-Worship. The early Christians also were accused of ass-worship.

imitate the Egyptian custom of burying their dead instead of cremating them (5. 5. 3). Their ideas about the after-life are like those of the Egyptians, but while "the Egyptians worship various animals and graven images, the Jews worship with the mind only and recognize but one divinity. They consider it profane to fashion images of the gods in human shape with perishable materials. The supreme, eternal being, they believe, is not capable of being represented and is imperishable. Accordingly, they set up no images in their cities, much less in their temples. Such flattery is paid to no kings, nor such honor to the Caesars (5. 5. 4)." Tacitus concludes this discussion by rejecting any connection between the Jewish rites and those of Liber (Bacchus), since "the rites of Liber are festive and gay, while those of the Jews are absurd and mean."

It is noteworthy that along with the unfavorable picture which Tacitus presents of the Jews there seems to be a touch of admiration for their supreme, unrepresentable Deity and for their stubborn refusal to set up images of kings or of the Caesars. He may have had in mind the episode of the statue of Gaius (see above, p. 21). The historian seems, however, to have overlooked the fact that his allusion to the consecration of the figure of an ass in their shrine is at variance with their ban on the worship of any image.

While the tone of most Roman writers in their references to the Jews is that of amusement or of lofty scorn, Juvenal, the foremost of the Roman satirists, who wrote in the reigns of Trajan and Hadrian, is stirred to bitter invective. A conservative Roman in most matters, he reacted with violence to the influx into Rome of foreign elements, which he looked upon as corrupting the wholesome moral environment of the city. Greeks, Syrians, and Jews come in for special attack, although no foreigners are spared. He presents an unsavory picture of a horde of beggarly Jews camping in the once beautiful grove of Egeria with a basket and a bundle of hay [1] as their household equipment (3, 12-16). Synagogues are the haunts of beggars (3. 296). Jewish beggar women, leaving their basket and their hay, play on the credulity of Roman

---

[1] The hay has been variously interpreted as used for bedding or to keep the Sabbath food warm on the principle of the fireless cooker.

matrons by telling their fortunes and whispering in their ears an interpretation of the Solyman laws. For a very small fee those Jews will interpret your dreams for you to suit your taste (6. 542-547). Palestine is a land "where kings with bare feet observe the Sabbath and a traditional clemency indulgently allows pigs to die of old age" (6. 159-160). Most of all, the satirist rages against those Romans who adopt the rites of Judaism and influence their sons to do likewise. He condemns the Roman father who fears the Sabbath and whose sons, going beyond their father, worship no god but the clouds and the sky and do not distinguish between the flesh of pigs and of human beings and even submit to circumcision. Taught to scorn the laws of Rome, they memorize and follow and fear the Jewish law, "which Moses handed down in a mysterious scroll," and which commands them not to point out the way to any but followers of the same rites and to direct to a spring of water only the circumcised. Juvenal holds the father to blame as one who devoted every seventh day to idleness and abstinence from all the ordinary duties of life (14. 96-106).

It is evident from this passage in Juvenal's Fourteenth Satire that the success of the Jews in winning converts was regarded as especially detrimental to the moral fiber of the Romans. Earlier, Seneca had complained that "the practices of this damnable race have already prevailed in every land. The vanquished have given laws to the victors."[1] As we have already seen, it was this phase of the activity of the Jews of Rome that was probably the basic reason for the repressive measures adopted by the authorities from time to time.

The regime of good government with which Rome had been blessed since the accession of Nerva in 96 was ended with the death in 180 of the noble idealist and Stoic philosopher, Marcus Aurelius. His son, Commodus, was a self-indulgent, capricious ruler, whose reign was violently terminated by assassination in 192. It was probably during the reign of Commodus that Callistus (or Calixtus), who was a slave at that time but who was later to become Pope and for whom the well-known Christian catacomb on the Via Appia is named, weary of life, broke into a synagogue in Rome and disrupted

---

[1] Quoted in Augustine *De Civ. Dei* 6.11.

the Sabbath service.[1] For this act of violence he was sentenced by the praetor to forced labor in the mines of Sardinia. This tale, which is related by an opponent of the papacy, probably Hippolytus, may, however, be apocryphal.

Under Septimius Severus and his dynasty (193-235) the attitude of the administration toward the Jews continued to be favorable. Jews were expressly made eligible to hold public office and were at the same time exempted from such official duties as might interfere with their religious practices (*Digest* 27. 1. 15. 6; 50. 2. 3. 3). The only known act detrimental to the Jews was a decree of Septimius Severus forbidding conversion to either Judaism or Christianity (Spartianus, *Severus* 17. 1),[2] but it does not seem to have been rigorously enforced.[3] The degenerate Elagabalus (218-222), himself a worshiper of the sun-god Elagabal, from whom his nickname was derived,[4] took a lenient view of all religions and intended to have the worship of Judaism, along with that of Christianity and other religions, transferred to a temple on the Palatine Hill close to his palace (Lampridius, *Antoninus Heliogabalus* 3. 4-5). He even underwent circumcision and abstained from pork (Lampridius 7. 2; Dio 79. 1).

The last of the dynasty, Alexander Severus (222-235), was so friendly toward the Jews that his detractors referred to him scornfully as the "Syrian archisynagogus" (Lampridius, *Alex. Sev.* 28. 7),[5] much as the epithet "rabbi" might now be used derisively under the circumstances. His biographer, Aelius Lampridius, records the fact that he reaffirmed the special privileges of the Jews (22. 4). His admiration for Abraham was such that he kept a bust of him in the shrine of his palace, along with portraits of Christ and other distinguished figures of the past (29. 2). His high regard for both

---

[1] See VR, 32.

[2] *N.B.*, Spartianus and the other biographers of the later emperors are included in the collection known as *Scriptores Historiae Augustae*.

[3] See M. Platnauer, *Life and Reign of the Emperor Septimius Severus* (Oxford, 1918), 153.

[4] His real name was Varius Avitus. When he became Emperor, he assumed the title of Marcus Aurelius Antoninus.

[5] A. Momigliano, "Severo Alessandro Archisynagogus," in *Athenaeum*, N.S., 12 (1934), 151-153, discusses the meaning of this epithet, presenting the unlikely theory that Severus may actually have founded a Jewish synagogue at Rome.

the Jews and the Christians is further indicated by his avow-
edly following their example in announcing beforehand the
names of those he intended to appoint to important posts,
with the exhortation that any unfavorable information about
them be lodged with the authorities before the appointment
was confirmed (Lampridius 45. 6-7). Vogelstein, on the basis
of a reference in a twelfth-century commentary, thinks that
the Roman Jews named one of their synagogues for Alexander
Severus, and Frey has tried to identify this with the synagogue
of Arca of Lebanon, to which he thought he found a reference
in an inscription from the catacombs.[1] This question will be
discussed in a later chapter (see p. 163-65).

In the disastrous half century which followed the assassination of Alexander Severus in 235, the Jews of Rome must
have suffered along with the rest of the population, but there
is not a solitary reference to the Jewish community during
that period. With the accession of Diocletian in 284, Rome
ceased to be the capital of the Empire. Whether this change
affected the Jews is completely unknown. There is no evidence
that the persecutions of the Christians in the latter half of
the third century and the first decade of the fourth involved
the Jews. With the reign of Constantine, Christianity became
the dominant power, and the emperors after Constantine,
with the sole exception of Julian, were Christians. While
the Jews of Rome were, of course, affected by the many laws
restricting Jewish proselytism, barring intermarriage of Jews
with Christians, forbidding Jews to possess Christian slaves,
and similar adverse legislation, such as we find recorded in the
Theodosian Code, the written sources offer no data applying
specifically to the community in Rome.[2]

[1] VR, 34; *CII*, pp. LXXIX ff.
[2] On the treatment of the Jews by the Christian emperors to the
end of the Western Empire see Vogelstein in VR, 113-127; P. Rieger
in *Jüdisches Lexikon*, s.v. KAISER, RÖMISCHE, STELLUNG ZU DEN
JUDEN; M. Simon, *Verus Israel*, 155-162. On the anti-Jewish legislation, see especially J. E. Seaver, *Persecution of the Jews in the Roman
Empire* (Lawrence, Kansas, 1952), 300-438. Vogelstein pays special
attention to the relations of Julian with the Jews (pp. 119-121),
notably his abolition of the *fiscus Iudaicus* after it had existed for
nearly three centuries. A good account of Julian's attitude toward
the Jews is offered by Michael Adler, "The Emperor Julian and the
Jews," *JQR*, 5 (1893), 591-651.

Briefly reviewing the four centuries surveyed in the preceding pages, we find that a Jewish community was established in Rome during the early decades of the first pre-Christian century. Thanks to the favorable attitude of Julius Caesar, the Jews were granted many special privileges, which were retained and even expanded under the pagan rulers of Rome. During the early Empire, the Jewish community became a large element in the population of the city. While dissidence within the group and excessive zeal in winning converts sometimes brought forth repressive measures by the authorities, especially under Tiberius, Claudius, and Domitian, these were only ephemeral exceptions to what was otherwise a consistently friendly and tolerant policy on the part of the Roman rulers. The existence of the community was at no time interrupted, and it continued to flourish as long as Rome itself was the prosperous capital of a great Empire.

CHAPTER TWO

THE JEWISH CATACOMBS OF ROME

A. Discovery of the Catacombs

Our information about the Jewish community of Rome, apart from the relatively scanty historical data available from the literary sources, is based upon the materials yielded by the catacombs. That the Jews of Rome, as well as the Christians, buried their dead in those underground cemeteries which are called catacombs[1] became known some three and a half centuries ago, when Antonio Bosio, famed as the "Columbus of the catacombs," first came upon a Jewish catacomb on December 14, 1602. This was not long after the sensational discovery in 1578 of a Christian catacomb on the Via Salaria, an event which started an enthusiastic hunt for these memorials of the early centuries of Christianity.

It is perhaps not inappropriate to remind the reader that the catacombs were neither intended nor employed as places for refuge and concealment during periods of persecution, but that they were the normal cemeteries of the Jewish and Christian communities of that ancient period and continued to be used as such until they were superseded by the open-air type of cemetery in the fourth or fifth century. The

---

[1] The original meaning of the word "catacomb" is not known. In the fourth century C.E., and perhaps earlier, it was used to designate a region on the Via Appia between the second and third mile, where the road dips down before rising toward the tomb of Caecilia Metella. See Hülsen in *RE* III, 1782 f. The Circus of Maxentius, which lies to the left of the highway (as one goes away from the city), was referred to as being *in catacumbis*. This expression, as well as *ad catacumbas*, was used also for the Basilica of St. Sebastian and its subterranean cemetery, in which, it is supposed, the bodies of Saints Peter and Paul were kept for a while. It is presumed that from the use of the phrase in connection with this cemetery, the word *catacumba* was later extended (probably by the ninth century) to apply to other similar subterranean cemeteries. Attempts to link the word etymologically with Greek κύμβη or τύμβος or with Latin *cumbo* (found only in compounds, such as *decumbo*) have not been convincing. For the use of the word "catacomb" in English, see *New English Dictionary*, *s.v.*

very fact that they were excavated entirely beneath the surface of the earth, so that their existence was ultimately forgotten, accounts for their preservation, whereas the cemeteries which succeeded them, exposed as they were to the abuses of invading armies, common vandalism, and changes in the ownership of property, have so completely disappeared that even their locations are unknown. On the ground under which the catacombs lie, crops now grow and in some instances there stand houses in which people live, perhaps hardly aware that beneath their homes lie the melancholy graves of the ancient dead. One cannot help but wonder whether Benito Mussolini, during his years of residence at the Villa Torlonia, felt any emotion at realizing that some thirty feet below the mansion in which he lived, the gardens in which he strolled, stretched the bleak, grave-lined corridors of an ancient Jewish cemetery, the resting place of a people whom he denounced as strangers in Italy!

Bosio's fortunate discovery was made in a vineyard near the Via Portuense about a mile and a quarter beyond the present Porta Portese,[1] on the south slope of the Janiculum, in what is now the populous district of Monteverde Nuovo. The site is a quarter of a mile west of the present Trastevere railroad station. Bosio's own account of his experience is interesting enough to be worth quoting.[2] After apologizing for including an account of a Jewish cemetery in his work on "sacred" cemeteries and thus mixing things profane with things sacred, he hastens to assure his readers that the "sacred" cemeteries of the Christians were never profaned or contaminated by bodies of Jews, since the latter had a cemetery of their own. He offers a brief survey of the literary evidence for the presence of Jews in ancient Rome and then relates the circumstances of his discovery of a Jewish cemetery

---

[1] It must be remembered that the Porta Portese of Bosio's day was not the same as the present one, but was 453 meters further south on the Via Portuense behind the site of the old Trastevere railroad station of Piazza Ippolito Nievo. The old gate, the ancient Porta Portuensis of the year 403, was destroyed in 1643 by Pope Urban VIII, who built the present gate as part of his new fortifications against the threat of French invasion.

[2] Antonio Bosio, *Roma Sotterranea*, I (Rome, 1632), 141-143.

while exploring the vineyards along the Via Portuense:[1]

On Saturday, the 14th of December in the year 1602, having passed through the afore-mentioned gate [Porta Portuense], accompanied by the Marchese Giovan Pietro Caffarelli, a noble Roman, and Giovanni Zaratino Castellino, a cultivated gentleman, we turned into the first branch road on the right, ascended the afore-mentioned Colle Rosato, and entered a vineyard which had once belonged to Bishop Ruffino but was at that time owned by the children of one Mutio Vitozzi. At the extremity of this vineyard, which faces the Tiber, we found a cave opening, which was narrow, difficult, and dangerous, on the side of a steep cliff, beneath which lies a valley containing large tufa quarries under the cemetery. Entering through this opening with bodies bent, we penetrated into the cemetery, which is excavated in the tufa (this is very infirm in some places) and is of moderate extent, since we apparently explored the whole of it in the two hours that we remained there. We observed, however, that there were other entrances and passages choked with earth, which may possibly extend much further. This cemetery, like the others, has its graves cut into the walls and in some places has trenches and tombs excavated in the pavement. We did, however, observe there one feature differing from the other cemeteries, in that for the most part these tombs are closed not with tiles and marble slabs, but with stucco-covered bricks, on which the epitaphs were in nearly every instance inscribed in red letters. Some of these were even engraved in the stucco, and we found many such examples. These inscriptions were all in Greek and in a damaged condition, since the graves had been opened by curious and greedy excavators, so that portions of the bricks and stucco bearing the inscription had been destroyed, with the consequence that no inscription offers a complete sense and only the first words are visible, these being, in almost every case, ΕΝΘΑΔΕ ΚΙΤΕ ΕΝ ΕΙΡΗΝΗ. On one tomb there still remained entirely preserved in red letters the name ΑΣΑΠΡΙΚΙΙ.

After a discussion of the use of Greek by both the Romans and the Jews of that time[2] and a comment on the word εἰρήνη (peace), he resumes his description of the catacomb:

---

[1] The present version is more complete and somewhat more literally rendered than that which I offered in *HUCA*, 5 (1928), 299 f.

[2] He thought that the Jews of Rome used Greek for their epitaphs in preference to Hebrew in order that they might be understood by all and so survive to future generations; or possibly because these particular Jews were natives of Greece.

It is very crudely and roughly constructed, containing only two private chambers (*cubicoli*) and even these are very small and mean, as is the entire cemetery, since not even a fragment of marble can be seen there nor any painting nor any mark of Christianity. One sees only, on practically every grave, the seven-branched candelabrum, either painted in red or imprinted on the stucco, a practice peculiar to the Jews and even persisting to our own time. . . . Notably, at the head of a dead-end corridor there can be seen a large candelabrum painted in red over the graves in the following manner. [An illustration is offered.] We found there also many rough lamps, crudely made of terracotta, all of which were broken with the exception of one which was intact and had imprinted thereon the above-mentioned candelabrum, which has the following shape [illustration]. Inside one tomb we found a metal medallion which was so badly corroded by age that no part of it could be made out. From the fact that we found no sign of Christianity in the cemetery and that we read on the fragment of one inscription the brief word ΣΥΝΑΓΩΓ, *i.e.*, Synagogue, and from the other details described above, we have decided and firmly believe that this was the particular cemetery of the ancient Hebrews. We are, however, ready to yield to any saner and better judgment.

Bosio died in 1629 before publishing the results of his catacomb discoveries. In 1634, five years after his death, his work, entitled *Roma Sotterranea*, appeared, though it bore the date 1632. We hear no more of this Jewish catacomb until the middle of the eighteenth century, when various archaeologists claimed to have visited it.[1] Noteworthy is the visit at that time by Gaetano Migliore, who described his adventure in colorful language. After giving some information about the catacomb according to the observations of Bosio and Giuseppe Bianchini, he continues:

Finally, not to have to rely on the descriptions of others, I decided a few years ago that I would personally enter this crypt of the Jews across the Tiber, so that, if at all possible, I might prepare a plan of what was left of the Jewish ceme-

---

[1] Among these were Giuseppe Bianchini, Cardinal Domenico Passionei, Gaetano Migliore, and possibly Ridolfino Venuti. For details and bibliography see my discussion in *HUCA*, 5 (1928), 302 f. The following description by Migliore is found in a Vatican manuscript (Cod. Lat. 9143, f. 127). The Latin text is conveniently available in *CII*, I, 206-207.

tery and thereby gain the favor of scholars. Crawling as far
as I was able, in view of the imminent danger and the crevi-
ces in the ground, I examined with my own eyes the remains
of the vaulted structure with its crumbling wall and the
perpendicular cinèrary recesses in the walls, and I did indeed
fancy that I saw here and there, trampled under foot, the
fragments of Hebraic emblems. But as I was making an
effort to decipher the characters on the walls, faded as
they were through age and barely visible in the dim light
within the bowels of the earth, the insecurity of the stony
fabric and the rocks threatening at every moment to come
tumbling down upon my head from all directions persuaded
me with saner counsel to take my feet to the outdoors.

Migliore concludes the passage with an indignant protest
at the disgraceful neglect which makes it impossible to visit
such "precious treasures of antiquity" without endangering
one's life.

For nearly a century thereafter this Jewish catacomb seems
to have been entirely neglected, so that even its site was
forgotten. We hear of futile efforts to find it on the part of
Father Giuseppe Marchi in 1843, of the celebrated Christian
archaeologist, Mariano Armellini in 1879, of Nikolaus Müller,
whose name was to figure largely as an investigator of the
Jewish catacombs, in 1884, and again in 1888, and of the
French archaeologist, Seymour de Ricci, in 1900 and in 1904.[1]
In October of 1904, the Commissione di Archeologia Sacra in
Rome was notified that laborers, while quarrying stone in
Monteverde, had broken into some ancient tombs. The task of
investigation was assigned to Nikolaus Müller, who positively
identified the cemetery as the lost catacomb which had been
discovered by Bosio more than three centuries earlier. Excavation was pursued intermittently in 1904, 1905, and 1909,
after which the work was discontinued because of the lack
of funds.[2] Since the area had been weakened by the quarrying
of building stone, the catacomb soon collapsed entirely. The
inscriptions and other significant objects which could be
removed were placed in the Lateran Museum, where a special
Jewish Room (Sala Giudaica) was set up under the direction
of Müller. In 1913 and again in 1919, other portions of the

[1] See *HUCA*, 5 (1928), 306-307, and the footnotes.
[2] N. Müller, *Die jüdische Katakombe am Monteverde zu Rom* (Leipzig, 1912), 18-20.

catacomb were found and the inscriptions were removed to the safety of museums (see below, p. 72).

Meanwhile, on May 1, 1859, a second Jewish catacomb was found in what was then the Vigna Randanini (now Vigna San Sebastiano) on the old Appian Way (Via Appia Antica) close to the branch road, Via Appia Pignatelli. This site is, accordingly, about midway between the catacomb of St. Calixtus and the church and catacomb of St. Sebastian. This large and important catacomb was explored and described by Father Raffaele Garrucci, one of the leading Christian archaeologists of that day.[1] Many of the numerous inscribed marble plaques which were found there have disappeared from the catacomb, some to reappear in various public and private collections (see below, pp. 70 f.). Those remaining, with few exceptions, have been affixed to the walls arbitrarily with no effort to set them near the place where they were found. Some have even been placed upside down or sideways. In only a few cases do they remain on the original closures of the graves.

Not long after the discovery of the catacomb in Vigna Randanini, a small underground Jewish burial place was found in 1866 in the vineyard of Conte Cimarra, situated on the Vicolo di San Sebastiano, a little beyond the church of St. Sebastian. It was discovered by laborers who were digging in that area in connection with some work in the vineyard. The place was explored by Giovanni Battista de Rossi, the outstanding Christian archaeologist of the nineteenth century, who was the first to develop what may be called the science of Christian archaeology. De Rossi's brief exploration was followed by an equally brief notice.[2] His promise of a plan and full description to be published within a year was never carried out. The site of the catacomb (if the term may be applied to a hypogeum of such small extent) is now in the area of the Vigna Limiti, which has been cut up into building lots for suburban villini.

---

[1] In his *Cimitero degli antichi Ebrei scoperto recentemente in Vigna Randanini* (Rome, 1862). Additional details are offered in his "Descrizione del cimitero ebraico di Vigna Randanini," in *Dissertazioni archeologiche di vario argomento* II (Rome, 1865), 168-178.

[2] In *BAC*, 5 (1867), 16.

Later, in 1882, another Jewish catacomb was found on the Via Casilina (formerly Via Labicana), about a mile and a half outside Porta Maggiore, also in a vineyard, Vigna Apolloni. Discovered accidentally by workmen who were reopening an old pozzolana quarry, it was explored by De Rossi's disciple and later successor, Orazio Marucchi,[1] who on his first visit took it to be Christian, but subsequently, upon discovering a seven-branched candelabrum scratched on a stucco closure, realized that it was Jewish. Excavation was not attempted until two years later and then for only a few days with but three workmen. Marucchi stresses the fact that he conducted this exploration with "true risk of life" in view of the ruinous condition of the terrain. Unfortunately, no further excavation was attempted, and now even the exact site of the catacomb is not entirely certain. At any rate, the widening of the Via Casilina (Fig. 1) has apparently destroyed whatever traces may have been left of this catacomb.[2]

Soon afterward, in the spring of 1885, some men digging in a pozzolana quarry found a small catacomb on Via Appia Pignatelli, which branches left from the Via Appia just before the site of the Jewish catacomb of Vigna Randanini. The catacomb lay a short distance beyond the well-known Christian catacomb of Praetextatus. It was promptly examined and partly excavated by Nikolaus Müller, who identified it as Jewish, although none of the few inscriptions and decorations which he mentions would make such an identification certain.[3] Regrettably, the detailed description of the catacomb

[1] O. Marucchi, "Di un nuovo cimitero giudaico sulla Via Labicana," *Dissertazioni della Pontificia Accademia Romana di Archeologia*, ser. II, vol. II (1884), 499-532. The account is reproduced in Marucchi's *Catacombe romane* (Rome, 1903), 279-297 (plan on p. 281), and appears much abridged in the posthumous revised edition of this work (Rome, 1932), 678-681.

[2] Frey states (*CII*, I, p. 46) that he made several unsuccessful attempts to penetrate the catacomb and actually entered some isolated galleries in that area. In 1951 even these traces had disappeared.

[3] N. Müller, "Le catacombe ebraiche presso la Via Appia Pignatelli," in *Römische Mittheilungen*, 1 (1886), 49-56. Müller decided that the catacomb was not Christian because he discovered none of the usual symbols of Christianity. It seemed to him to be Jewish because it was separated from the Jewish catacomb of Vigna Randanini only by the highway (Via Appia Pignatelli), and the closures of the loculi resembled those of the Jewish catacombs rather than the Christian. Paintings of palm trees also were interpreted as a Jewish motif. The

which Müller promised to include in his proposed work on the ancient Jewish cemeteries of Italy never appeared, since he died (in 1912) before this work was completed. At the present time no trace of the catacomb is to be seen in the cultivated ground which covers the area.

The last Jewish catacomb to become known, and one of the most important, was discovered, also accidentally, in 1919, by workmen digging foundations for a new stable on the grounds of Villa Torlonia on Via Nomentana, in the northern part of the city, only a half mile outside Porta Pia, just beyond the intersection with Via Lazzaro Spallanzani.[1] The first investigators were the archaeologist Roberto Paribeni and the architect Italo Gismondi. The former published a brief description accompanied by texts of the inscriptions and a plan by Gismondi.[2] The present writer twice explored this catacomb in 1922 and found a number of inscriptions which had been overlooked by Paribeni. The first thorough investigation was that of H. W. Beyer and Hans Lietzmann, who published the results, along with the texts of the inscriptions, photographs of the tombs and decorations, and an improved plan, in 1930.[3]

Thus, up to the present time, six ancient Jewish burial, places (if we include the doubtful one on Via Appia Pignatelli) have been discovered in the area of Rome. Three of these were of very small extent and yielded only scanty materials. Of the three large catacombs, the one at Monteverde is entirely destroyed; the other two, on the Via Appia and the Via Nomentana, respectively, are still available for study.

---

scarcity of inscriptions and other materials was due to the catacomb's having been thoroughly ransacked at some ancient period. Goodenough (*Jewish Symbols*, II, 34 f.), though with some hesitation, regards this as probably a Jewish burial place.

[1] It is an interesting detail that, as far back as 1865, De Rossi had predicted that a Jewish cemetery might be found on the Via Nomentana or Via Tiburtina (*BAC*, 3 [1865], 95). He based his prediction on the reference in an inscription to a synagogue near the *agger* of the Servian Wall (this is *CII*, 531).

[2] "Catacomba giudaica sulla Via Nomentana," *N. Sc.*, 1920, 143-155.

[3] *Die jüdische Katakombe der Villa Torlonia in Rom* (Berlin and Leipzig, 1930).

B. Description of the Catacombs

It may seem rather strange to us that the Jews of ancient Rome should have put their cemeteries entirely beneath the surface of the earth. The pagan Romans, who normally cremated their dead, placed the ashes in tombs above ground. There were, however, some Roman families which practiced inhumation, entombing the remains in chambers which were hollowed out in caves or beneath the ground. The best known of such family inhumation tombs is that of the Scipios, which lies on the Via Appia just inside the Porta Appia (Porta San Sebastiano), by which the highway passes through Aurelian's Wall. It may be recalled here that the Etruscans also placed their dead in cemeteries consisting of separate subterranean family tombs, notable examples of which are to be seen in the great necropolises of Cerveteri and Tarquinia to the north of Rome.

As for the Jews, it seems likely that they transferred to Rome and adapted to the Roman terrain the Palestinian custom of making use of natural caves for burials or cutting artificial caves in the cliffs of the area.[1] Finding no appropriate cliffs in the campagna around Rome (burials within the limits of the city were forbidden by law), they burrowed into the volcanic tufa which lies beneath the surface. This stone, which is soft enough to be cut rather easily, yet firm enough to hold together, was ideally adapted to the construction of underground chambers and corridors. While the Palestinian Jews placed their dead in private tomb-chambers by families, the Jews of Rome, living crowded together in the slum quarters of a great city and possessing no private estates outside the city proper, found it necessary to develop community cemeteries. The early Christians of Rome, as well, were constrained to employ the same type of cemetery, and it is not

---

[1] An old classic on Jewish burials is Joh. Nicolai, *De Sepulchris Hebraeorum*, Lugduni Batavorum (Leyden, 1706). It is still quoted. See *JE, s. vv.* Burial and Cemetery and the chapter on "Begräbnisplätze" in S. Krause, *Talmudische Archäologie* (Leipzig, 1910-1912), II, 71-82. For a detailed treatment of the tombs which have been found in Palestine see E. R. Goodenough, *Jewish Symbols in the Greco-Roman Period* [hereafter referred to as Goodenough], I (New York, 1953), 61-177, with extensive bibliography and fine illustrations (in vol. III).

unlikely that they learned the catacomb method of burial from their Jewish neighbors. As is well known, many of the earliest Christians of Rome were Jews in origin, so that it is natural to infer that they simply continued the burial technique which was familiar to them.[1]

It will have been noted that all six of the Jewish burial places, like those of the Christians, are to be found within a mile or two outside the limits of the ancient city, close to major highways. Thus there is one to the north by the Via Nomentana, one to the east by the Via Labicana (now Casilina), three to the southeast close to the Via Appia, and one to the south a few hundred yards from the Via Portuense. The catacomb of the Via Nomentana is now covered by the Villa Torlonia; that of the Via Labicana is marked by a vineyard and an old pozzolana quarry; that of Via Appia Pignatelli by a cultivated field; that of Vigna Cimarra by suburban villini; that of the main Via Appia is beneath a farmhouse and cultivated ground; and that of Monteverde has been displaced by large modern apartment houses.

At the entrance to the underground cemetery there appears normally to have been a sort of vestibule or forecourt open to the sky. Only at the Appia catacomb may such a vestibule be seen at the present time. Müller testifies that he found remains of a vestibule at the Monteverde catacomb and some traces of what he identified as probably those of a similar vestibule at Via Appia Pignatelli.[2] It is entirely possible that further excavation at the Nomentana catacomb would reveal some kind of forecourt, since the original main entrance has not been located. At the other two sites so little excavation was done that not even a hypothesis as to a vestibule is warranted.

---

[1] Jewish catacombs have been found in various other parts of the Mediterranean world, the most important being in the south Italian city of Venosa (H. J. Leon, "The Jews of Venusia," *JQR*, 44 [1954], 267-284). Others have been discovered in Sicily at Syracuse (P. Orsi in *Römische Quartalschrift*, 14 [1900] 190-198) and Noto Vecchio, the ancient Netum (Orsi in *N.Sc.*, 1897, 89-90); in Sardinia at Sant' Antioco, the ancient Sulcis (A. Taramelli in *N.Sc.*, 1908, 150-152); and at Malta (see the references in Goodenough, II, 57). For the Jewish cemeteries in North Africa, notably at Alexandria and at Gammarth near Carthage, see Goodenough, II, 62-68.

[2] *Jüd. Kat.*, 22 f.; *Röm. Mitt.*, 1(1886), 50.

The vestibule of the Monteverde catacomb, as described by Müller,[1] was a vaulted structure, long and narrow, with brick walls. The Appia vestibule, to which one descends by seventeen modern steps (the ancient entrance has disappeared), is a large rectangular atrium, measuring 88 feet by 18 feet, 7 inches, with its long axis running east and west (Fig. 2). It was divided by a transverse wall into east and west sections, and the east section was in turn divided by a wall running lengthwise down the center. In the north wall of the west portion there were two niches, originally painted blue (one is no longer visible), and in the south wall there were two shallow apses. The pavement was in a black and white mosaic of about the first half of the second century C.E., but this is now entirely covered over.[2] In the west wall there are two doorways, of which the one on the right, a low passageway, leads by five steps into a small room originally containing a well, which is not visible now; the other leads by six steps into a sort of antechamber communicating with the well room by a door in the wall to the right. From this antechamber one passes into the catacomb proper. At a later period the west end of the outer atrium was vaulted over (the vaulting is no longer to be seen), and against the original north wall there was constructed an inner wall, pierced by triple superimposed rows of low arches (Fig. 3). Further to the east the arches form only a double row and finally a single row. Similar arches in double rows were constructed against both faces of the longitudinal dividing wall. On the middle portion of the south wall of the atrium there are similar arches in a single row.

The earliest portions of the atrium are in reticulate masonry (*opus reticulatum*), probably of the first part of the second century, thus contemporary with the mosaic floor. The later portions are constructed of rows of tufa blocks alternating with a thin line of narrow bricks in a single layer, a type of masonry common in the latter part of the third century (Fig. 4). At a still later period the arched areas, which somewhat resemble the vaulted tombs called arcosolia, were used for burials, although they seem not to have been built originally

[1] *Jüd. Kat.*, 22-23. The vestibule was not excavated, so that no fuller description is available.
[2] See the illustration in *CII*, p. LIX.

for this purpose. Portions of terracotta sarcophagi are still to be found in the niches (Fig. 5). It should be noted that most of what is now visible in the vestibule is a modern reconstruction based on the remnants of the original masonry. The original arched niches are 6 feet 6 inches wide, 2 feet 2 inches high, and 1 foot 9 inches deep (Fig. 3). The modern replacements are somewhat larger.

Scholars are not agreed as to the use which was made of these vestibules. Some, following an original suggestion by Garrucci,[1] have thought that they were synagogues, but for this view there is no evidence whatever. Müller offered the suggestion that they may have been intended as a place for the pallbearers and the bier, a view in which he had been anticipated by Garrucci, who had changed his earlier view.[2] The Appia vestibule, at any rate, is much larger than would be needed for such a purpose. It seems probable that the vestibule was intended as a space for a funeral service, similar to the modern ceremony at the graveside.[3] The corridors inside the catacomb itself were too narrow to permit any kind of function, so that most likely the appropriate ceremony was performed in the large antechamber before the body was borne down into the dark passages to be placed within the grave niche, which lay open and ready.

From the vestibule one ordinarily descends into the cemetery proper by steps varying in number according to the terrain. As has been stated above, the galleries with their graves were carved out of the volcanic tufa. The Monteverde catacomb was excavated in a reddish tufa which, according to the geologist De Angelis d'Ossat,[4] has been wrongly called

---

[1] *Cimitero* 6. Later (*Diss. Arch.* II, 150) Garrucci revised his view and suggested that the outer edifice came to be used partly for sepulture and partly as an atrium where the bier could be laid down before being carried inside.

[2] *Jüd. Kat.*, 23, and see the previous note.

[3] Goodenough (II, 15 f.) also favors the view that the antechamber "served for some ritualistic function in connection with burial," but he goes on to maintain that the ritual included a funerary banquet, without offering any satisfactory evidence to support such a hypothesis. He holds also that the well is to be connected with some sort of purification rite.

[4] Gioacchino de Angelis d'Ossat, *La geologia delle catacombe romane* (Vat. City, 1939), 25; cf. *Roma* 13 (1935), 367 f.

granular tufa. This material was perfectly adapted for the wide corridors and high ceilings which characterized this catacomb, differentiating it especially from the Christian ones. The collapse of the catacomb was, therefore, not due to its having been constructed in an inferior quality of tufa, as has been repeatedly stated by Müller[1] and others, but was caused by the fact that the stratum of lithoid tufa, which lies beneath the catacomb level, was at various times removed in the process of quarrying for this excellent building material, the so-called *tufo di Monteverde*, the *saxa rubra* of the ancient Romans. Because of the extensive quarrying in this region there have been many collapses of the upper strata, sometimes with disastrous results to existing buildings. The destruction of the catacomb was completed when the hill was cut back to make room for new streets and an extensive development of large, middle-class apartment houses (Figs. 6 and 7).

Since there is a full description of the Monteverde catacomb in Nikolaus Müller's monographs[2] and no part of it remains on the site, a brief description, which is necessarily derived from Müller, will suffice here. The interior, which was reached by a short flight of six steps, showed a variety of architectural arrangement. The subterranean corridors were generally wider than those of the Christian catacombs. The horizontal grave niches (*loculi*) cut in the walls on both sides of the corridors were arranged in tiers of from four to eight, one above the other, and in one gallery more than twelve superimposed loculi were found. There were fewer tomb chambers (*cubicula*) than in the other catacombs. Müller found only four of these. He describes eleven different types of grave. In the earlier portions of the catacomb, graves sunk below the floor level of the corridors were employed. These included both single and double tombs. Most numerous were the niche graves, the loculi, which are the prevailing type also in all the other catacombs, both Jewish and Christian. Their openings were generally sealed with masonry consisting of pieces

---

[1] E.g., *Jüd. Kat.*, 22: *ein Grundstück ... dessen Tuffqualität von schlechtester Beschaffenheit ist.*

[2] *Die jüdische Katakombe am Monteverde zu Rom* (Leipzig, 1912) and in the posthumous "Il cimitero degli antichi Ebrei posto nella Via Portuense," *Dissertazioni della Pontificia Accademia Romana di Archeologia.* Ser. II, 12 (1915), 207-318, Pl. IX-XII.

of tufa combined with mortar, the exterior face being covered with stucco or a smooth layer of mortar. In some instances plaques of tile together with other materials were used as closures. The epitaphs were either painted (*dipinti*) or scratched (*graffiti*) on the stuccoed closure of the grave or were carved on a marble slab which was affixed to the closure. Only one example was found of the arcosolium type of grave, *i.e.*, an arched niche with one or more graves excavated below the baseline of the niche. There seems to have been no instance of a painted tomb chamber, such as one finds in the Appia and Nomentana catacombs. A number of sarcophagi were found, some of terracotta, very few of stone. Müller thought that such marble sarcophagi as were there originally had been carried off, since various marble sarcophagi bearing Jewish symbols and inscriptions, though only fragments in some instances, have turned up in Rome.

The catacomb of the Via Appia may be entered either from Via Appia Antica by a steep stairway of thirty-four steps, a modern reconstruction on the original foundation, or on the side toward Via Appia Pignatelli by six steps from the open-air atrium, where the original main entrance was. The cemetery is for the most part excavated in a fine quality of tufa known as *pozzolanella* at a depth of some thirty feet below the surface.[1] The lower portions, which are in the less coherent *tufo terroso*, have partially collapsed and are inaccessible. On the whole, the galleries are fairly wide, varying from about five to seven feet. Their height is about six feet, with minor variations. Two light wells (*luminaria*) opening to the exterior admit light to a limited area (Figs. 8 and 9).

The ground plan is very irregular,[2] an indication that the cemetery was developed haphazardly. The loculi, the closures of which, thanks to the activities of ancient grave robbers, have with few exceptions disappeared entirely, are ranged in three or four superimposed tiers, fewer accordingly than in either the Monteverde catacomb or, as we shall see, the Nomentana catacomb. The dimensions of these loculi, which are by far the most common type of grave, are more or less

---

[1] On the geology of this catacomb see G. de Angelis d'Ossat, *La geologia delle catacombe romane*, 176-178.
[2] See the plan by Frey in *RAC* 10 (1933), 184.

as follows: length six feet, height one foot three inches, depth one foot eight inches. Besides the loculi and the familiar arcosolia, there are burial shafts sunk slightly beneath the floor level and, in the west portion near the Via Appia entrance, numerous graves of the type called *koki:n* (כוכים) in the Mishna.[1] These *kokim*, which are found here alone among the Jewish catacombs of Rome, are cut into the wall at right angles to the gallery somewhat below the floor level and usually have an arched ceiling instead of the flat ceiling found in the loculi. Many more tombs of this *kokim* type could be cut into a given length of corridor, since the wall was pierced by the narrow end, which measures about two feet,[2] instead of the six-foot length of the normal loculus (Figs. 10 and 11).

In the walls of the galleries and of the private chambers as well, small niches for lamps, averaging six by four inches, were cut at irregular intervals. Some of the arcosolia have openings for two graves, others have space for a sarcophagus sunk beneath the floor level, and, in fact, portions of sarcophagi are occasionally to be seen in them (Fig. 12). There are many small loculi for children and even for tiny infants, and in some areas there are clusters of these children's graves. On the front of one *kok* there is carved a finely-shaped *ascia*, the ax used by the diggers (*fossores*) to cut the corridors and tombs out of the tufa.[3]

There are some thirty tomb chambers, cubicula, three walls of which are usually pierced by loculi. Four of these rooms have fairly well preserved frescoes on the doorway, walls, and ceiling. While these paintings, which will be described in a later chapter (pp. 204-06), show no exclusively Jewish motifs, with the exception of a Menorah painted on the wall of one room (Fig. 12), there is no compelling reason for thinking that any of them were pagan hypogea which were later taken over by the Jews and absorbed into the catacomb. Two connecting cubicula, which are elaborately decorated

---

[1] S. Krauss, *Talm. Arch.*, II, 72. This is the prevailing form in Palestine. See especially Goodenough, I, 66.

[2] The normal dimensions of a *kok* are as follows: width 2′, height 2′, depth 5′3″. Since the last dimension corresponds to the length of the body, it seems that some bodies must have been inserted with difficulty.

[3] See the illustration in Goodenough, III, fig. 791.

with human, animal, and floral figures (Figs. 13-16),[1] were entered from the galleries containing the *kokim* and clearly form a part of the original catacomb.[2] At the threshold of this pair of interconnecting rooms there is now a marble step which, on closer inspection, proved to be the reversed lid of a sarcophagus bearing on its front edge a Greek inscription almost entirely covered with plaster (Fig. 17). When the plaster was scraped off, the inscription was revealed as that of the child archon Iocathinos, which had been published by Garrucci in 1863 and had since disappeared.[3] Each of these cubicula has two arcosolia, one in each side wall (Figs. 13, 15, 16). In the inner room a loculus was cut above each arcosolium and on the right side of the rear wall.

The epitaphs were usually engraved on marble slabs set into the mortar of the closures, but in some instances they were scratched or painted on the stucco of the facing.[4] Unfortunately, the inscriptions on marble have not been kept at the places where they were found, so that very few of the inscriptions can be connected with specific tombs. The walls of the catacomb show numerous scribblings by modern visitors, who in some places have not scrupled to deface inscriptions and even frescoed surfaces (Fig. 15). Some

---

[1] The dimensions of these two rooms are as follows: The first is 11' by 8'4" with a height of 7' at the center of the vaulted ceiling. The inner room, which is smaller but somewhat higher, is 7'5" by 7'3" by 7'9".

[2] That these rooms were separate hypogea was the opinion of Garrucci (*Diss. Arch.*, II, 156 f.). Marucchi (*Cat. Rom.* [1903], 246) suggested that this portion of the catacomb was originally pagan and was later combined with the Jewish cemetery. Frey insists that the frescoes must be of pagan origin and that the two painted rooms originally had a separate entrance, but were later connected with the catacomb galleries, which are about one meter higher (*Biblica*, 15 [1934], 285; *CII*, p. CXXIV). It may be observed that a similar situation is found in the Nomentana catacomb, where the frescoed room and the arcosolia, which are unquestionably Jewish in origin, are found at a different level from the other parts of the catacomb and were probably reached by an entrance not yet discovered.

[3] H. J. Leon, "Two Jewish Inscriptions of Rome Rediscovered," *RAC* 29 (1953), 101 ff. The photograph on p. 101 is reversed, showing the inscription right side up. For the original publication of the inscription see Garrucci in *Civiltà Cattolica*, II, (1863) p. 111, no. 12. It is no. 120 in Frey's *CII* and in our Appendix of Inscriptions.

[4] Most of these *graffiti* and *dipinti* were discovered and first published by Frey in *RAC* 10 (1933), 27-50.

damage was done also during the war period of 1943-1944, when this catacomb, like some of the Christian catacombs, was used as an air-raid shelter. Further, and more serious, damage is being caused, particularly to the frescoes of the painted rooms, by the seeping through of water from the irrigation of the vegetable farm which lies above the catacomb. Several of the galleries and cubicula which had once been cleared are now so choked with earth that access to them is difficult and in some places even impossible. Some areas have recently been reinforced with brickwork to prevent further collapse.

The entrance to the Via Nomentana catacomb is in the grounds of Villa Torlonia near the corner of Via Nomentana and Via Lazzaro Spallanzani (Figs. 18, 19).[1] The catacomb lies in a stratum of volcanic tufa of the variety known as *tufo terroso*.[2] One descends by six modern steps followed by fifteen ancient ones cut out of the tufa (Fig. 19). The wall of the ancient stairway is constructed of double rows of tufa blocks alternating with single rows of narrow brick, all held together by thick layers of mortar, a type of construction commonly used during the third century. Some portions of the heavy stucco covering of this wall are still in place. The plan of the catacomb[3] shows some attempts at regularity, which were not entirely successful. Galleries which were intended to be parallel almost run into each other. In one instance, where a corridor was dug from opposite ends, the two sections failed to meet.[4] Operating underground in the dim light of oil lamps, the *fossores* found it difficult to keep their orien-

---

[1] For an excellent detailed description of the catacomb see H. W. Beyer and H. Lietzmann, *Die jüdische Katakombe der Villa Torlonia in Rom* (Berlin, 1930), 1-14 (hereafter referred to as *BL*).
[2] At least in the opinion of De Angelis d'Ossat, *La geologia e le catacombe romane*, I (Rome, 1930), 286. This geologist, stating that he was unable to study this catacomb because it is so badly preserved as to be inaccessible, assumes reasonably that it is dug in the same kind of tufa as the catacombs of St. Nicomedes and St. Agnes, between which it lies. It was, to be sure, inaccessible at the time when Mussolini, occupying the Villa Torlonia, had that entire area heavily guarded, but actually the catacomb is well preserved and can be studied with reasonable comfort.
[3] The best plan is that in *BL*, Taf. 31.
[4] On the *BL* plan, see the corridors running east from the north-south gallery CF.

tation, as any person who merely tries to walk among the already constructed galleries can well appreciate. One portion of the catacomb, that containing the frescoes, is not at so deep a level as the rest and appears to have been dug independently at an earlier time. It must surely have had another entrance, which might be revealed if there were further excavation. At present one can pass from the lower to the higher section by climbing up a heap of earth at the point where the two meet.[1]

According to Paribeni[2] the total length of the galleries explored is some three thousand feet, comprising an area of about five acres. The galleries vary in size, but are for the most part narrower and higher than in the Appia catacomb (Fig. 20). The width is generally about three feet, though ranging from two feet four inches to three feet six inches. The height of the galleries varies from around five feet four inches to as much as ten feet, the norm being somewhat over six feet. Some areas which had collapsed, or threatened collapse, were reinforced in 1946 by the Commissione di Archeologia Sacra, which has commemorated its work by a plaque affixed to the gallery wall near the painted room.

The forms of the graves show less variety than in the other two Jewish catacombs, nearly all being of the loculus type. There are some sixteen arcosolia, built to hold either one or two bodies, and five chambers containing arcosolia and loculi.[3] The loculi of the galleries are ranged in several tiers, which vary in different portions of the catacomb from three to ten. The usual number is five to eight. While there are many small niches for children, one finds a few instances of a full-sized loculus which has been divided in the middle by a vertical partition of brick and mortar so as to hold the bodies of two children, an indication that some graves were cut before the actual need for them.

---

[1] Point M in the *BL* plan. For a discussion of the two levels, which appear to belong to two separate catacombs, see *BL*, p. 6.

[2] *N. Sc.* 1920, 143.

[3] The average dimensions of the loculi of this catacomb are length 6', height 1' or slightly over, depth 1'6", thus not differing materially from those in the Appia. The two arcosolia of the painted room measure, respectively, length 6', height 4'3", depth 5', and length 6', height 3'11", depth 4'4". The room itself is 8'2" square and 7'2" high. See the detailed diagram in *BL*, p. 10.

There are, occasionally, small niches for lamps (Fig. 21) and in a few spots traces of a round, flat vessel, about six inches in diameter, which had been affixed to the exterior of a loculus, probably as a means of identification. At several points, chiefly at the intersections of galleries, geometric patterns have been painted in white on the vaulted ceiling, presumably for purposes of orientation in those dark passages where everything bears the same aspect (Fig. 21). The cubicula have vaulted ceilings with simulated supports consisting of corner pillars carved out of the tufa (Figs. 22, 23). One of these rooms in the earlier and higher part of the catacomb has richly painted decorations on the walls and ceiling and on the vaults and back walls of the arcosolia. The paintings of this room and of the arcosolia in the corridor nearby will be described in another chapter (pp. 207-09).

Every one of the graves was broken into by marauders at some time in late antiquity, so that usually there is little or no trace of the closure, which consisted of a wall of brick or pieces of tufa joined by thick layers of mortar, with often a smooth stucco finish on the exterior. If the grave was identified by an epitaph, this was either painted in red (*dipinto*) or, less frequently, scratched with a sharp instrument (*graffito*) on the facing of the loculus. Nearly all of the inscriptions are to be found in the northern (and later) portion, where many of the closures have been partly preserved. Representations of the menorah, painted or scratched, are to be seen here and there, sometimes not accompanied by any epitaph (Fig. 24). The fact that the inscriptions are for the most part briefly and crudely scrawled (Fig. 25) and the indications that many of the graves had no epitaph whatsoever attest to the comparatively low economic level of the congregations which made use of this catacomb. There were, to be sure, several inscriptions on marble, which have been removed from the catacomb, so that there is no way of knowing in what areas they were found. These few instances of the use of marble for the epitaphs, the presence of the cubicula and the painted decorations, and the discovery of several sarcophagi point to the existence of at least some wealthy families amid their less prosperous coreligionists who buried their loved ones in this cemetery.

The Nomentana catacomb is somewhat damper than the Appia, and in some areas the moisture has slowly filtered through, forming a white lime deposit on the walls (Fig. 21). The skeletal remains, which are still abundant inside the graves, are gradually crumbling away in the moist environment. It creates a strange impression to read on a loculus the fragmentary epitaph with the name of the deceased, as follows: "Here lies Julia R. . . In peace be her sleep" (No. 35), and at the same time within the partly open niche to see Julia's moldering skull and bones (cf. Fig. 25).

Since the other three ancient Jewish burial places which were found in Rome, those of Via Appia Pignatelli (if this is, indeed, Jewish), Via Labicana, and Vigna Cimarra, are no longer extant and were, in any case, of small extent with few remains of interest, there is no need to repeat here the descriptions published by those who explored them before their disappearance.

Various attempts have been made to assign dates to these catacombs, but unfortunately there are few reliable criteria for dating them. We have seen that the earliest portions of the open-air vestibule of the Appia catacomb appear, from the reticulate masonry and the pattern of the mosaic pavement, to go back to the first part of the second century C.E., while the latest portions probably belong to the third century. The masonry of the entrance stairway of the Nomentana catacomb indicates third-century workmanship. In all the catacombs stamped bricks and tiles, which were used in the closures, may offer some basis for dating. These brick stamps, which bear the name of the manufacturer, can usually be dated with a considerable degree of accuracy. The question with reference to the catacombs is whether the bricks are contemporary or whether second-hand materials, possibly dating from a much earlier period, were employed. It seems reasonable that new materials were used to a large extent, so that where a number of stamps belonging to a certain period are found in a catacomb, a possible criterion for dating is available The first to make a systematic study of the brick stamps of the Jewish catacombs was Father Frey,[1] who found

---

[1] See his *CII*, just before the texts of the inscriptions of each catacomb.

that those of the Nomentana are of the second century, though a few are earlier; those of Via Appia Pignatelli are of the first and second centuries; those of the Appia are of the second or early third; those of Monteverde, which are more numerous than elsewhere, range from the beginning of the first to the end of the third century.

Combining these data with other less tangible criteria, such as the names (see below, pp. 110, 116) and the artistic decorations, we may assume with a fair degree of confidence that the Monteverde catacomb was the earliest, perhaps going back to the first century B.C.E., when the Jewish community was first established in Rome, and that it continued in use at least to the end of the third century; that the Appia catacomb was used from the first century C.E. to the end of the third century; that the Nomentana also was used in the first to third centuries. It seems that at the end of the third century, or early in the fourth, the Jews of Rome abandoned the custom of burying in catacombs and began to use open-air cemeteries.

In many respects the Christian catacombs resemble those of the Jews, so that most scholars assume that the Christians adopted the catacomb method of burial from the Jews. This is a reasonable assumption, since the earliest Christians of Rome, as is well known, originated from the Jewish community and the Jewish catacombs seem to antedate the Christian ones. The most notable differences between the two are that in the Christian cemeteries the galleries are for the most part narrower and more regular; the Christians closed the loculi with large tiles, usually in groups of three, instead of building them up of bricks or tufa blocks and mortar, as did the Jews; the Christians introduced more cubicula for family groups; the Christian catacombs are in many instances constructed on more than one plane, so that one descends from one level to other groups of galleries lying directly underneath (the catacomb of St. Calixtus, for example, has six such levels), while the Jewish catacombs are all on one plane, though there are minor differences of level in different sections of each catacomb. It may be added that the Christian catacombs usually contain chapels for memorial services to the martyrs who were entombed in them, whereas the Jews, observing no such custom, had no similar chapels in their burial places.

CHAPTER THREE

THE JEWISH INSCRIPTIONS OF ROME

Of the material objects yielded by the catacombs the most important are the several hundred inscriptions, the brief and frequently pathetic epitaphs which marked the individual graves. Some afford us no more than the name of the deceased, with perhaps a wish for his peaceful repose; others reveal also the name of a parent or child or husband or position held in the congregation; while not a few have survived in so fragmentary a state as to yield only tantalizing remnants of words which challenge the ingenuity of a restorer. It is from these inscriptions that we are able to glean a considerable body of data on the language which the Jews of Rome spoke, the names which they bore, the names of their congregations, the titles of their officials, the organization of their communities; some indications, though sadly inadequate, of their religious ideas, the extent to which they had adopted the mores of their Gentile neighbors, and a few scraps of vital statistics, such as age at marriage, age at death, size of family. Many bear symbols and decorations which throw some light on their cult objects and artistic attainments.

Two Jewish inscriptions of Rome were known some years before the discovery of any Jewish catacomb. Philippe de Winghe, a Fleming of the sixteenth century (died 1592), includes them among the inscriptions recorded in a manuscript of the Royal Library of Brussels.[1] They are the Latin epitaph of Beturia Paulla (*CII* 523)[2] and that of Zosimus in Greek (503). The same two are found in a Vatican manu-

---

[1] Cod. 17872-3, according to A. Ferrua, *Epigraphica*, 3 (1941), 38. For a more detailed account of the discovery of the inscriptions, with full bibliography, see my article, "The Jewish Catacombs and Inscriptions of Rome," in *HUCA*, 5 (1928), 299-314.

[2] The numbers identifying these inscriptions are those in J. B. Frey's *Corpus Inscriptionum Iudaicarum* (abbreviated *CII*). The texts of most of these may be consulted, under the same numbers, in the Appendix of Inscriptions in the present volume (pp. 264-346).

script of Claude Menestrier (died 1639)[1]. Whether he copied them directly from the originals, which have since disappeared, or got his texts from de Winghe is not certain, but the latter is more likely.[2] The inscription of Beturia Paulla is found also in a sixteenth-century copy[3] by Alonso Chacón (also called Ciacconius, Ciacconio, and Ciaccone), a Spanish padre who lived from 1540 to 1599 and was one of the earliest explorers of the catacombs.

In the course of more than a century after Bosio's discovery of the Monteverde catacomb in 1602, eight other inscriptions were found,[4] and they were assumed, not always with adequate reason, to be from that catacomb, since no other was known. Apparently the earliest to publish any of the Jewish inscriptions was Jacob Spon of Lyons, who, in 1685, included three of them in his *Miscellanea*.[5] Among these are the two which were copied by de Winghe and Menestrier, to which Spon added the inscription of Julianus, gerusiarch of the Calcaresians (504). The ten Jewish inscriptions which were known during this time are to be found scattered in various works of the end of the seventeenth and the first half of the eighteenth century.[6] Only two of these ten are known to be in existence at the present time, one in the Terme Museum (283) and another (509) in the Sala Giudaica of the Lateran Museum. Of the other eight, only one is mentioned as having been seen after the eighteenth century and even that has now apparently disappeared.[7]

An important decade in the discovery of Jewish inscriptions was that between 1740 and 1750, during which time some sixteen were found[8], mostly at or about the site of the Monte-

---

[1] Cod. Lat. 10545, fol. 150 and 239, respectively.

[2] This is also the opinion of Ferrua, *Epigraphica*, 3 (1941), 38.

[3] Frey cites a Ferrara codex, f. 40, which, according to Ferrua (*l.c.*), is a wrong citation.

[4] These are Nos. 1, 283, 284, 504, 507, 508, 509, 512.

[5] *Miscellanea eruditae antiquitatis*, Lugduni (= Lyons), 1685, p. 371, nos. 118-120. He calls them *hucusque inedita*.

[6] For a full list see *HUCA*, 5 (1928), 301, notes 6-13, and Frey's introductory notes, sometimes incomplete, to the inscriptions involved.

[7] No. 504 was seen by Garrucci near the church of Santa Chiara before 1862 since he alludes to it in his *Cimitero degli antichi Ebrei* (38 f.), which was published in that year.

[8] Nos. 307, 327, 349, 368, 372, 380, 381, 382, 385, 416, 458, 460, 472, 480, 481, 510.

verde catacomb. This was the time when the catacomb was visited by Migliore and probably by others. At least five of these inscriptions[1] seem to have come to light in the year 1748. Copies are found in the unpublished notes of various epigraphists of the period, notably Migliore, Marini, and Raponi, whose manuscripts are preserved in the Vatican Library, and in sundry works published between 1748 and 1862.[2] By the end of the eighteenth century the number of known Jewish inscriptions found in Rome had grown to thirty-four.[3] These attracted a good deal of attention among scholars, whose attempts at interpreting them often seem amusing to us with our fuller understanding of the subject, thanks to the subsequent discoveries.[4] Twenty-two of these are still extant, distributed as follows: four are in the Sala Giudaica of the Lateran, four are in the Terme Museum, two are in the Conservatori Museum on the Capitoline, four are in the Lapidary Museum of the monastery of St. Paul's Outside the Walls, and eight were last noted as being in the National Museum of Naples, to which they were taken after being kept for some time in the Borgia Museum at Velletri.[5]

---

[1] Nos. 368, 416, 460, 472, 480.

[2] For details see *HUCA*, 5 (1928), 304 f., notes 24-35.

[3] These are Nos. 1, 3, 283, 284, 296, 307, 312, 327, 349, 351, 368, 372, 380-382, 385, 397, 401, 416, 458, 460, 472, 480, 481, 510-504, 507-510, 512, 523.

[4] Thus, J. W. Burgon, in *Letters from Rome to Friends in England* (London, 1862), 169, thought that the six Torah scrolls shown in the Ark (327) are loaves of Passover bread. Reinesius (cited in J. G. H. Greppo, *Notices sur les inscriptions antiques tirées de quelques tombeaux juifs à Rome* [Lyon, 1835], p. 8) called the Agrippesians (503) a guild of Christian merchants. Antonio Lupi, in *Dissertatio et animadversiones ad nuper inventum S. Severae Martyris epitaphium* (Palermo, 1734), 51, took the ΚΑΛ of Καλκαρησίων (504) as an abbreviation for Καλήβων, which he interpreted as meaning *circumcisorum*. Some of these earlier scholars were not aware that the menorah was a Jewish symbol; *e.g.*, Greppo, *op. cit.*, 27, on our No. 458; E. Corsini, *Notae Graecorum* (Florence, 1749), Diss. II 130, on No. 507. Even modern scholars have fallen into droll errors. Thus Vogelstein, misinterpreting a description of No. 460, with its shrine (*Aron*) and Torah scrolls, stated that it bore a portrayal of the High Priest Aaron holding the rolls of the Torah in his arm (*VR*, 52: *auf einer anderen die Gestalt des Hohenpriesters Ahron mit Torahrollen im Arme*).

[5] Those in the Lateran are Nos. 3, 382, 385, 509; in the Terme, 283, 481, 502, 510; in the Conservatori, 296, 381; at St. Paul's, 349, 351, 397, 401; at Naples, 312, 327, 368, 372, 380, 416, 460, 480. This

With the discovery of the catacomb in the Vigna Randanini on the Via Appia in 1859, the number of Jewish inscriptions was increased many fold. Father Garrucci, the chief explorer of this catacomb, published 130 in 1862 and 1865,[1] and Marucchi added five in 1883.[2] In 1933, Father Frey published thirty-nine previously overlooked inscriptions which had been painted and scratched on the closures of the grave niches.[3] Although most of this last group are too brief to be of value, a few are significant, especially in adding to our list of proper names (see pp. 95-107). Frey, in his *Corpus*, also published for the first time good photographs of the Appia inscriptions and added a number which, though seen by previous observers, had never been published.[4]

All told, the Appia catacomb has yielded 195 inscriptions.[5] While the *dipinti* and the *graffiti* are still *in situ*, the marbles, as has been stated above, have been set up on the walls with no system and no attempt to place them near the points where they were found. Some are lying on the ground; many are affixed to the walls of the two underground antechambers which one enters from the outer vestibule (Figs. 26, 27); many have been broken, and in some instances portions of the same stone are to be seen in different parts of the catacomb; a few have been set up sidewise or upside down. A number which were entire and in their proper places when Garrucci and Marucchi saw them are now fragmentary and scattered. Whole plaques and portions of plaques have been

---

last group could not be located at the Naples Museum in the summer of 1951, despite a search.

[1] *Cimitero degli antichi Ebrei* (Rome, 1862), 23-69; "Nuove epigrafi ebraiche di Vigna Randanini," in *Diss. Arch.* II (Rome, 1865), 153-167; and "Epigrafi inedite di Vigna Randanini," *ibid.*, 178-185.

[2] *Cronichetta Mensuale*, ser. III, vol. II (1883), 188 ff.

[3] "Nouvelles inscriptions inédites de la catacombe juive de la Via Appia," in *RAC* 10 (1933), 27-50.

[4] In my explorations of this catacomb during 1922, I copied nineteen inscriptions which had not been published up to that time and included the texts in my unpublished Harvard dissertation, *De Iudaeorum antiquorum sepulcretis Romae repertis* (1927).

[5] Frey's 108 and 251, which are included among the Appia inscriptions, do not belong there, since there is no evidence that they were found in that catacomb, or that the latter is even Jewish. On the other hand, we should include Frey's 11* (*CII*, p. 540), which he rejected as pagan, though found in the Appia catacomb.

carried off. When the vineyard was sold, some time after Marucchi's visit in 1884, many of the inscriptions had already been taken away, but some were replaced afterward.[1] In 1904 Seymour de Ricci found 136 inscriptions in the catacomb;[2] in 1922, I counted 122; Frey in the 1930s counted 119, and a number of these were gone when I studied the catacomb again in the period from April to June of 1951. It may be that some stones were carried off while the catacomb was used as an air-raid shelter in the war years of 1943 and 1944. Among those inscriptions which were removed from the catacomb the present locations of several are known. Four are in the Terme Museum; one is in the Conservatori Museum; one is in the museum at the church of St. Sebastian on the Via Appia; seven are in the Wilshire Collection at Pusey House in Oxford;[3] two were seen in Bergamo; half of one is among the Greek and Latin inscriptions at Columbia University, while the other half remains in the catacomb;[4] three somehow got to the Jewish Museum in New York. One stone, which was thought missing, is still in the catacomb, where I found it turned upside down and used as a threshold at the entrance to the two painted rooms.[5]

The discovery, in 1866 by de Rossi, of the small catacomb in Vigna Cimarra added five more inscriptions (277-281), while Marucchi's find of the catacomb on the Via Labicana in 1882 yielded but three (75-77), none of these being of particular value, and the uncovering of a catacomb on Via Appia Pignatelli in 1885 by N. Müller added only two in-

---

[1] O. Marucchi, *Catacombe romane* (Rome, 1903), 234, n. 2.

[2] *JE*, IX, 481. De Ricci was to publish a corpus of Jewish inscriptions in Greek and Latin, but this never appeared.

[3] The Terme Museum has Nos. 95, 136, 228, 262; the Conservatori, 130; San Sebastiano, 202; Pusey House at Oxford, 118, 125, 141, 143, 151, 159, 210. On the Oxford group see T. B. L. Webster, "The Wilshire Collection at Pusey House in Oxford," *JRS*, 19 (1929), 150-164. The first to identify these as from the Appia catacomb was L. Robert in *REJ* 102 (1937), 121; cf. *idem* in *Hellenica*, 3 (1946), 97.

[4] No. 101; see H. J. Leon, "A Jewish Inscription at Columbia University," *AJA*, 28 (1924), 251 f. Those seen in Bergamo, and possibly still there, are 135 and 153; those in the Jewish Museum are 208, 217, and *CII* 200.

[5] No. 120; see *RAC* 29 (1953), 101-103. See also p. 61, above, and Fig. 17.

scriptions to the collection (79-80), and these are to be regarded as Jewish only if the catacomb itself was Jewish.[1]

Not until the rediscovery of the Monteverde catacomb in 1904 was there any large accretion to the collection of Jewish inscriptions. This catacomb has proved to be the richest source of all, since it has produced 206 countable inscriptions.[2] Those taken from the catacomb in the period from 1904 to 1914 (see above, p. 50) are now kept in the Sala Giudaica of the Lateran Museum. Of the twenty-five inscriptions found at the ruins of this catacomb in 1919, all but one (314), which has disappeared, are in the Terme Museum.[3] The *dipinti* and *graffiti*, with the exception of a few which could be removed and were taken to the Lateran, perished in the catacomb.[4] At present the Monteverde inscriptions are distributed as follows: 135 are in the Lateran Museum; 25 are at the Terme Museum in one of the storerooms; 2 are in the Conservatori Palace on the Capitoline; 5 are in the Lapidary Museum in the monastery of St. Paul's; 7 are in the Naples Museum; 28 were

---

[1] On these discoveries see above, pp. 51-53 and notes. The inscriptions from the Via Labicana numbered 73 and 74 in *CII* are entirely useless, since they are only vague scrawls which Marucchi took for Hebrew letters.

[2] After Nikolaus Müller died in 1912, the inscriptions from Monteverde were finally published by his disciple, Nikos A. Bees: *Die Inschriften der jüdischen Katakombe am Monteverde zu Rom* (Leipzig, 1919). Bees' additions to Müller's notes are far from satisfactory.

[3] No. 314 was apparently lost soon after its discovery. Although the other inscriptions found by Paribeni at this time are listed in the inventory of the Terme Museum, this one alone is missing from the list. This group of inscriptions was published by Paribeni in *N. Sc.* (1919), 60-70.

[4] Frey includes 204 Jewish inscriptions as from this catacomb (*CII* 290-493). Of these, four (367, 380, 479, 482) must at present be rejected, since there is no evidence which justifies attributing them to the Monteverde catacomb. Six, however, of those which Frey rejects as pagan (24*, 30*, 31*, 32*, 33*, 35*) should be considered as Jewish on the principle that inscriptions found in a Jewish catacomb and having no definite non-Jewish indications are to be regarded as Jewish. It is not unlikely that nos. 494, 495, 496, 503, 504, 510 also belong to the Monteverde group, since they were either found in the Trastevere region or refer to congregations known to have used that catacomb. In addition, as I have demonstrated elsewhere ("The Jewish Community of Ancient Porto," *HTR* 45 [1952], 165-175), at least three (535, 537, 543) and most probably others of the inscriptions of Porto should be included here.

destroyed with the catacomb; while the fate of 4 is unknown.[1]

The next and last substantial addition to the collection was occasioned by the discovery, in 1919, of the catacomb on Via Nomentana, which has yielded a total of sixty-eight items.[2] Of these, fifty were originally painted on the loculi, three are *graffiti*, and fourteen are on marble slabs which had been moved from the catacomb and temporarily placed in the stable which lay above it. One, which had been overlooked, is inscribed on a large sarcophagus which stands on the grounds of the Villa Torlonia (Figs. 28, 29).[3]

Besides the inscriptions known to come from specific catacombs, scattered discoveries at various times have yielded thirty-three additional items.[4] To these should be added the thirteen which have hitherto been listed as found at Porto, but which almost certainly were carried there from Rome.[5] In addition, there are nine inscribed gold glasses from Rome which should be included in the total.[6] When all are added together, we have a grand total of 534 inscrip-

---

[1] The four of unknown fate are 307, 314, 458, 472. The twenty-five at the Terme Museum include, besides the twenty-four added by Paribeni, one (350), which was found at the site of Monteverde catacomb about 1911.

[2] To the 66 in *CII*, add the inscription of the Caelia Omnina sarcophagus (35a), which I published in *JQR*, 42 (1952), 413-418, and a Hebrew *graffito* which I saw on a loculus and which read, apparently, שלום על ישראל.

[3] See the preceding note. In May of 1951 I saw in the catacomb a number of *dipinti* and a few *graffiti*, all so damaged or indistinct that they seemed hardly worth the effort of copying. They showed traces of names and formulas, but not a complete word. Several were in the last accessible cubiculum (VI on the plan in *BL*), which is reached with some difficulty, and in a few of the comparatively unexplored galleries, *e.g.*, the corridor T-Z, west of the painted room.

[4] To those in *CII* [*N.B.* nos. 732 and 733 in Frey's Appendix, pp. 597-598] add the inscription of Benedicta, first published by A. Vaccari in *Biblica*, 19 (1938), 340-342 and now in the museum of the Pontificio Istituto Biblico (no. 733a in the Appendix of Inscriptions in the present volume); that of Marta, published by A. Silvagni in *Inscriptiones Christianae*, II (Rome 1935), no. 5791, and now in the Lapidary Museum of the monastery of St. Paul's (Appendix, no. 733b); and that of the Caelia Omnina sarcophagus at the Villa Torlonia (Appendix, no. 35a).

[5] See my article on Porto, cited p. 72, note 4, above.

[6] These are *CII* 515-522 and 732 (on p. 597). The 231 brick stamps listed by Frey, while of value in estimating the date of the catacombs, are rightly not counted as Jewish inscriptions.

tions from the Jewish congregations of ancient Rome, distributed as follows:[1]

Monteverde	206
Via Appia (Vigna Randanini)	195
Via Nomentana (Villa Torlonia)	68
Vigna Cimarra	5
Via Labicana	3
Via Appia Pignatelli	2
Porto (probably from Monteverde)	13
Of uncertain or unknown provenience (most being probably from Monteverde)	33
Gold glasses	9
Total	534

[1] Of the inscriptions published in *CII*, I believe that the following ought not to be included among the Jewish inscriptions of ancient Rome: nos. 5, 285, 500, 524, 529, which are the epitaphs of "god-fearers" (*metuentes* or θεοσεβεῖς), who are not properly regarded as Jewish and were not interred in Jewish cemeteries (see below, pp. 253, 256); no. 287, which refers to Jews but is not Jewish; no. 288, which was not found in a catacomb and has no Jewish indications; no. 499, which belongs to the early Middle Ages; no. 514, an amulet of unknown provenience; no. 526, a probably spurious item from Cagliari in Sardinia (see A. Ferrua in *Epigraphica*, 3 [1941], 41); no. 527, a verse inscription, which is more probably Christian than Jewish (see Ferrua in *Civ. Catt.* 1936, IV, 309); no. 528, the Jewish connection of which is highly dubious; no. 531, which is that of a pagan fruit vendor whose place of business was near a synagogue. Besides, nos. 73 and 74, the allegedly Hebrew scrawls of the Via Labicana, should be thrown out as being of no value whatsoever. Sundry others, though showing too few letters to be of much use, may still serve as items in assembling statistical data on language.

CHAPTER FOUR

THE LANGUAGE OF THE JEWS OF ROME

It is a familiar fact that the Jews of the Diaspora were to a large extent Greek-speaking. By the beginning of the third century B.C.E., following the conquests of Alexander the Great, Hellenism had spread widely over the Mediterranean world, and Greek had become not only a sort of lingua franca, but actually the vernacular of many of the peoples in that part of the world; and the Jews were no exception. It is, in fact, clear from references in the contemporary literature and from the epigraphical evidence that Greek was extensively used even in parts of Palestine.[1] A glance at the Jewish inscriptions from Palestine in the second volume of Frey's *Corpus*[2] will reveal to how great an extent those in Greek outnumber those in Hebrew or Aramaic, and this is particularly true of the sepulchral inscriptions, which best indicate the language of the common people. The fact that the Hebrew Bible had to be translated into Greek is in itself an evidence that for many of the Jews Hebrew had become virtually an unknown tongue. After the destruction of Jerusalem by Titus in 70 C.E., the use of Hebrew continued to lose ground in favor of Greek, so that even in the synagogues the Greek language was employed for the ritual and the Torah readings. It should occasion no surprise, therefore, to discover that the Jews of Rome also were Greek speakers.

The inscriptions from the catacombs represent virtually our only source of information concerning the language spoken by the Roman Jews. That they were predominantly a Greek-speaking community in a Latin city is immediately obvious from the fact that a large majority of the inscriptions are in the Greek language. An examination of the inscriptions

---

[1] On the use of Greek in Palestine see S. Liebermann, *Greek in Jewish Palestine* (New York, 1942), especially pp. 30, 37-39. On the use of Greek by Diaspora Jews see R. Gottheil in *JE*, III, 185 f.; Schürer, III, 140-142; Goodenough, *Symbols*, II, 123 f.; A. Neubauer, "On Non-Hebrew Languages Used by the Jews," *JQR*, 4 (1891), 9-19.

[2] The Palestinian inscriptions are on pp. 113-339.

will give some indication of the extent to which the Jewish
population used other languages, such as Latin and Hebrew
or Aramaic. A closer study will reveal something of the level
of literacy of these Jews and how correctly they used the
languages which they spoke. While many of the 534 inscriptions enumerated in the preceding chapter are so fragmentary
as to have little importance, the survival of even a single
letter will generally identify the language in which the
inscription was written, so that such inscriptions have, if
nothing else, at least a statistical value in a study of the
language.

To start with the over-all picture, the 534 inscriptions
break down by language as follows:

Greek		405
Latin		123
Hebrew		3[1]
Aramaic		1
Greek and Latin bilingual		1
Aramaic and Greek bilingual	1

by percentages:	Greek		76%
	Latin		23%
	others	about	1%

In round figures, we may say that three-fourths of the
inscriptions are written in Greek and one-fourth in Latin,
while those in Hebrew and Aramaic are so few as to be almost
negligible. It should be noted, however, that several inscriptions have the Hebrew word שלום or ישראל or the phrase
שלום על ישראל added at the end,[2] an indication that the
knowledge of Hebrew was not completely absent. It is a
curious fact that seventeen of the Latin inscriptions are
written in Greek letters, while three are Greek inscriptions

---

[1] The unintelligible scrawls which have been listed as Hebrew
inscriptions (CII 73, 74, 294, 295) are not counted here. Of the three
indubitably Hebrew inscriptions, two (292, 293) are fragments inscribed
on stucco-covered tiles from Monteverde and probably in each case
the concluding formulas of an inscription in Greek or Latin. The other,
unpublished, is a two-line inscription scratched in irregular and indistinct letters on the stucco of a loculus in the Nomentana catacomb.
The second line is almost certainly the common formula, שלום
על ישראל.

[2] These are 283, 319, 349, 397, 497, and perhaps 296, the Semitic
characters of which are called Nabataean by Chwolson (Corp. Insc.
Heb., 147).

in Latin letters.[1] Besides, several of the Latin inscriptions close with a common Greek formula, which usually is written in Greek letters, but is occasionally transliterated into Latin characters.

A separation of the inscriptions by the catacombs in which they were found reveals certain striking differences in the language habits of the users of these catacombs. The following table will bring out these differences:

Language of Inscriptions by Catacombs

Catacomb	Greek	Latin	Semitic	Bilingual	Totals
Appia	124	71	0	0	195
Monteverde	161	41	3	1	206
Nomentana	63	4	1	0	68
Others	57	7	0	1	65
Totals	405	123	4	2	534

By Percentages

Catacomb	Greek	Latin	Semitic	Bilingual
Appia	63.6	36.4	0	0
Monteverde	78.2	19.9	1.4	0.5
Nomentana	92.6	6.0	1.4	0
Others	87.7	10.8	0	1.5

It is immediately apparent that those Jewish congregations which buried their dead in the Appia catacomb were definitely the most Romanized, since they show by far the largest percentage (36.4) of Latin inscriptions, while the least Romanized were the users of the Nomentana catacomb, whose language was almost exclusively Greek. In fact, there is not a single Latin inscription among the epitaphs painted or scratched directly on its loculi. The only Latin epitaphs from this catacomb were found on four marble plaques (68-71), an indication possibly that these Latin speakers were somewhat more prosperous than most of their fellows, since they could afford an epitaph on marble. As for the Monteverde catacomb, about one-fifth of its users represented the more Romanized element, insofar as we may judge

---

[1] At Venosa there is one inscription (*CII* 595) in which the Greek words are written in Hebrew characters, but no such phenomenon appears in the Roman inscriptions. For a comparison between the language of the Jews of Venosa (ancient Venusia) and those of Rome see *JQR*, 44 (1954), 273 ff.

from the language of their inscriptions. Since nearly all of the Semitic inscriptions, few though they be, come from this catacomb, as well as those which show a Hebrew word or phrase at the end, we may infer that an acquaintance with Hebrew was kept alive, albeit in feeble fashion, among this group alone.

Even the most cursory scanning of the texts of the inscriptions reveals that a large proportions of them are marked by glaring errors in spelling and grammar. A further look at the photographs in Frey's *Corpus* shows that the letters are in very many instances crudely formed, sometimes so awkwardly scrawled as to be hardly decipherable. There are, however, many epitaphs which are correct or nearly so in their language and not a few in which the letters are attractively shaped by a practiced hand. We may conclude, accordingly, that all levels of literacy were represented among the Jewish population of ancient Rome, but that there must have been a distressingly large percentage of individuals with little or no education. We must, of course, bear in mind that the inscriptions themselves were not, in most instances, done by the hand of a member of the family of the deceased. At least those inscribed on marble must have been the work of stonecutters, even though the texts were probably supplied to them. Still, it is not probable that a well-educated family would have permitted an almost illiterate epitaph or one with poorly-formed letters to mark the grave of a beloved child or parent. We may safely assume that in general the language and form of the inscriptions are an approximate measure of the level of literacy of the families concerned.

It is precisely the inscriptions with misspellings and other errors which give us some conception of how the Jews spoke their Greek and Latin.[1] In the absence of phonetic transcrip-

---

[1] It is necessary, however, to distinguish between genuine linguistic phenomena and careless slips by the person who inscribed the epitaph. Thus we often find Λ for Α or Δ and C for E and vice versa, because the horizontal stroke was carelessly omitted or inserted, and there are many similar slips which offer no evidence about pronunciation. We should, accordingly, not follow N. Müller, who regarded such spellings as EIOYAIA and IOYAEIOC as not slips of stonecutters but genuine dialectical peculiarities ("nicht als Fehler des Steinmetzen, sondern als dialektische Eigentümlichkeit ansehen," in *MB*, 97).

tions of their speech, such as are available to linguists who study modern dialects, our only criteria for a reconstruction of the spoken language of the Jews of ancient Rome are the errors in spelling, particularly those caused by the confusion of similar sounds. For example, the numerous instances of the substitution of ι for ει and the reverse indicate clearly that these had the same sound.

Without an enumeration of all the details, which I treated with some fullness in a separate study some years ago,[1] the aberrations from correct Greek in the Jewish inscriptions reveal the following facts about how the Greek was pronounced:

The original diphthong αι was indistinguishable in pronunciation from the simple vowel ε. This is clear from the following examples:[2]

κε (391, 511) for καί; Εβρεος 354) and Αιβρεος (370) for Ἐβραῖος; Ιουδεα (296) for Ἰουδαία; αιν (93, 363) for ἐν; αιτων (88, 380) for ἐτῶν; ενθαδαι (536) for ἐνθάδε; παρθαινος (381) for παρθένος; and, most commonly, κειτε for κεῖται.

In the last mentioned word the second syllable is wrongly written with ε about four times as often as with the correct αι.

Similarly, ει and ι were pronounced alike, as is proved by these forms:

δεικεα (363) for δικαία; Δωρεις (536) for Δωρίς; ουδις (314, 401) for οὐδείς; βειωσας (9, 118) for βιώσας; θαρι (380) for θάρρει; ιρηνη (very frequent) for εἰρήνη; ις (86) for εἰς; and the extremely common κιται or κιτε for κεῖται.

The i of Latin names is often represented by ει in Greek transcriptions instead of the usual ι:

e.g., Αγριππεινου (322), Ακυλεινα and Προκλεινα (389) for Aquilina and Proculina; Κρισπεινα (132), Σαβεινος

---

[1] "The Language of the Greek Inscriptions from the Jewish Catacombs of Rome," *TAPA*, 58 (1927), 210-233. Although the number of inscriptions which I used for this study was 494, as compared with the 534 available at the present time, the data presented are still valid, since the additional inscriptions simply offer further instances of the phenomena already described.

[2] Since the inscriptions themselves show no accents or breathings, these are also omitted here, except that in representing the correct equivalents the customary marks are used. The numerals given in the parentheses are those in Frey's *Corpus* and in our Appendix of Inscriptions. The citations are, for the most part, only *exempli gratia* and not intended to be a complete listing of instances.

(398, 402), Καιλερειναι (215) for *Celerinae*; also in common Latin words, such as φειλιε (248) for *filiae* (dative); βιξει αννεις (215) for *vixi annis*.

It should be noted here that both αι and ει had by the time with which we are concerned lost their diphthongal pronunciation and were identical in sound with ε and ι, respectively, in the speech of both educated and uneducated alike.[1] In educated circles, however, the traditional spellings were used, just as in our day a properly educated person would not confuse the spellings of *sail* and *sale*, though he pronounced them alike.

The only other Greek diphthong whose pronunciation had changed materially was οι, which the Roman Jews apparently did not distinguish from simple υ, a pronunciation which had become prevalent in the Greek-speaking world by the early part of the common era.[2] This is clear from the many occurrences of the spelling κυμησις or κυμισις for κοίμησις, a word which is used in the most frequent of all the sepulchral formulas, ἐν εἰρήνη ἡ κοίμησίς σου or αὐτοῦ. In the Latin transcriptions of this word the forms *cymesis* (224, 262) and *cymisis* (523) are found, but never *coemesis*, which would have been expected if the οι had retained its earlier pronunciation. Since the vowel υ seems still to have kept its ancient sound, which approximated that of modern French *u* or German *ü*,[3] we may conclude that οι also had this pronunciation.

As for the simple vowels, ε and η represented, respectively, the short open and long close *e*-sounds (approximately as in English *ten* and *they*). The fairly frequent erroneous interchange of ε and η

e.g., ην (509) for ἐν; νεπιος (97, 138) for νήπιος; ητη (102) for ἔτη; ηνδηκα (102) for ἔνδεκα (but this last inscription shows eight examples of η for ε)

is an indication that to some extent the quantitative and qualitative distinction between these vowels tended to be obscured. In a few inscriptions, in which the numerous errors betoken a low level of literacy, one finds a confusion between η and ι:

---

[1] See E. H. Sturtevant, *The Pronunciation of Greek and Latin* [2] (Philadelphia, 1940), 40, 49.

[2] *Ibid.*, 52.

[3] *Ibid.*, 43 f.

δης (391) for δίς; ανιρ (314) for ἀνήρ; *autis* (523) for αὐτῆς; ιτις (102) for ἥτις; νιπιους (349) for νήπιος

The rather numerous instances of the spellings κοιμισις and κυμισις for κοίμησις are to be explained as vowel assimilation, since the middle syllable, placed as it was between an *ü*-sound and an ι, easily tended to be assimilated to these sounds. Thus the word κοίμησις, which was pronounced, approximately, *kymisis*, was often written phonetically. If the examples pointing toward an ι- sound of η are examined carefully, it becomes clear that this pronunciation was found only among the least literate classes and that in general the vowel η had retained its *e*-sound.[1] On the other hand, in the Jewish inscriptions of Venosa, a century or more after the latest of the Roman ones, there are indications that η was already pronounced like ι,[2] but the process had apparently only just begun in the inscriptions from the Jewish catacombs of Rome. The other vowels, α, ι, o, ω show no important spelling variants which would indicate a change from their traditional sounds.[3]

The Greek consonants still seem to have retained their classical pronunciation, with the exception of φ, which in earlier times had been pronounced like a *p* followed by an aspiration, so that the Romans transcribed it as *ph*.[4] The Roman Jews, however, pronounced it like our *f*, as is evident from the fact that Latin *f* is always transcribed by φ, and Greek φ is rendered by *f*, only once by *ph*:

e.g., Φαβια (413), Φαυστινα (283), φηκιτ (215, 257, 263, 266) for *fecit*, φιλιους (264) for *filius*, Ρουφος (145); *Afrodisia* (220, 232), *Eufraxia* (237), *Dafne* and *Daph(n)e* (223).

There is plenty of evidence that θ and χ were true aspirate mutes, pronounced *t-h* and *k-h*, respectively, as in English *hothouse* and *backhand*.[5] The consonant β seems not yet to have

---

[1] See *TAPA*, 58 (1927), 214-216 and cf. Sturtevant, 37 f.
[2] Leon in *JQR*, 44 (1954), 275.
[3] Sporadic slips, such as α for ε (ανθαδε 391), o for ε (μοτα 150), may be dismissed as due to carelessness on the part of the writer or the stonecutter.
[4] Sturtevant, 80.
[5] See *TAPA*, 58 (1927), 228. On the pronunciation of the Greek aspirates cf. Sturtevant, 76-82.

acquired the sound of the spirant *v*, as in modern Greek.[1]
The one example of a Latin transcription of β is by *b* and not
by *v*:

theosebes (228)

Conversely, however, Latin *v*, which already had approximately the sound of the same letter in English,[2] was always
transcribed by β, which represented the closest Greek approxi-
mation to this sound:

 e.g., Φλαβια (172, 361), Φλαβιος (172, 417), Σεβηρους (264),
Βικτρω (102) for *Victor*

There are occasional indications that some individuals,
like the modern Cockney, had trouble with their initial aspirates. This is discernible only in Latin transcriptions of Greek
words, for the Greek aspirate was not written, since the use
of the so-called "rough breathing" sign belongs to a much
later period. Thus we find the feminine definite article ἡ
transcribed in Latin without an *h* as *ae* (224), *au* (523), and *e*
(262). On the other hand, an *h* is wrongly prefixed in *hirene*
(262) for εἰρήνη.[3] There seem to have been many who had
trouble with the pronunciation of the aspirated consonants
θ and χ, sometimes leaving off the aspiration so that τ and x
are used in their place, or wrongly attaching the aspirate to a
"smooth" mute, so that we find θ instead of τ and χ instead
of x:

 e.g., ενταδε (374, 377), παρτενος (320), *mellarcon* (284, a
Greek inscription in Latin letters); κιθε (377) and χιτε (391)
for κεῖται[4]

In some instances the confusion is due to a false assimilation
with a preceding or following aspirate:

ενθαδε χειθε εθων (277) for ἐνθάδε κεῖται ἐτῶν, where the x
and τ of the verb and the τ of the noun wrongly acquire
an aspirate because of the preceding θ, and Ευθυχιανο (110)
for Εὐτυχιανός, where the τ is wrongly aspirated because
of the following χ. Other similar examples: ενθαδε κειθαιν
(384), ενθαδε εκειθεν (397), ανθαδε χιτε (391)

 [1] Sturtevant (p. 88 and note 95) thinks that β may have become
a spirant by the second century C. E. Cf. *TAPA*, 58, 227 f.
 [2] Sturtevant, 143.
 [3] Two instances of μεθ εμου (299, 302) for μετ' ἐμοῦ are also
examples of a misapplied aspirate.
 [4] For more examples see *TAPA*, 58, 228.

In other instances we find metathesis or transfer of the aspirate, in that the aspirated mute loses its aspirate, but this aspirate is attached to one or more following smooth mutes, somewhat as though one were to say: "An orrible haccident hoccurred." All errors of this sort are found in the ἐνθάδε κεῖται formula:

ενταδε κιθε (377), ενταδε χειθε (416), ειταδε χειθε (403), ενταδε εκιθεν (405)

That this particular type of confusion occurred only among the comparatively uneducated is indicated by an examination of the inscriptions in which such errors are found. Of the nine examples cited above, six are in inscriptions which show many errors of spelling or grammar, whereas three (377, 397, 416) seem, from the shapes of the letters and the types of errors, to be the work of the same stonecutter, apparently a person who, like Arrius in Catullus' 84th poem, had trouble with his aspirates.

It is worth noting that the pronunciation of the Greek among the common people at this time, at least as it is revealed among the Jews of Rome, had gone only a small part of the way toward the itacism of the modern Greek, in which the letters and combinations η, ι, υ, ει, οι, and υι all have acquired the same sound, that of our long e (as in be). As we have seen, only ι and ει generally had this sound, while η was tending in that direction, at least in the mouths of the comparatively illiterate. In addition, αι and ε were already identical, as they are in modern Greek, and φ had the sound of f; but the other letters show no sign of a trend toward the modern pronunciation.[1]

The inflection of Greek nouns and adjectives shows only occasional variations from the classical norm. It should be noted that in the dative singular the "iota subscript" never appears on our inscriptions, nor, in fact, is there a single

---

[1] Three misspellings of the word γερουσιάρχης might point toward a *y*-sound of γ before ε, as in modern Greek: ιερουσιαρχη[ς] (405), ειερουσαρχης (408), and ιερευσαρχων (504). These are to be attributed rather to a confusion with the word ἱερεύς. Müller (in *MB*, 5) rightly calls this phenomenon *Volksetymologie*. The spelling γιερουσαρχη (95) may well be due to a stonecutter's error. In Latin transcriptions of Greek names γ appears as g even before ε: *Protogenia* (217), *Archigenia* (35*).

instance of this letter, which had long since ceased to be pronounced.[1] Masculine names with nominative in -ας have a genitive either in -α or in -ατος:

Τουβια (497), Γαδια (510); Ιουδατος (12), Γαδιατος (535)

Masculine names which would ordinarily end in -ιος show a very frequent variant in -ις:[2]

e.g., Αλυπις (502), Αναστασις (364), Ευσεβις (119, 332, 333) and many others.

but the genitive of such names ends regularly in -ιου and the dative in -ιω:

e.g., Γελασιου (25); Αστεριω (95).

By analogy with the Latin nominative in -us, one finds the ending -ους instead of -ος in words, mostly proper names, of the second declension:

Επιγενιους (323), Σαλπινγιους νηπιους (162), Σελευκους (52).

Some datives of this declension end in -ο instead of -ω, probably also on the analogy of Latin:

Ευθυχιανο (110), σινβιο (110) for συμβίῳ.

The noun υἱός shows a unique genitive variant:

υιους (543).[3]

Those third declension nouns which normally end in -ευς show also nominatives in -εος and -εους:

γραματεος (142), γραμματεος (53, 149), γραμματεους (99, 148), ιερεους (346).

---

[1] Sturtevant, 57. Garrucci, followed by Frey, reads ANΔPIAI, for ἀνδρείᾳ, in 118, an inscription from the Appia now at Pusey House, Oxford; but the correct interpretation is undoubtedly ἀνδρί (dative of ἀνήρ) followed by an adjective, probably ἀϊμνήστω. See T. B. L. Webster in *JRS*, 19 (1929), 151, no. 9, and L. Robert in *Hellenica*, 3 (1946), 97.

[2] So elsewhere; see A. Thumb, *Die griechische Sprache im Zeitalter des Hellenismus* (Strassburg, 1901), 154.

[3] Instead of TOY YOYC AYTHC, Frey reads TOY YIOY CAYTHC, interpreting the last word as an error for ἑαυτῆς; but this longer form of the reflexive occurs only twice in these inscriptions (169, 391), each time without the article. See my discussion of this detail in *TAPA*, 84 (1953), 68, n. 4.

In the genitive, besides the correct form in -εως, we find also a single form in -εος:[1]

[γραμμα] τεος (67)

In the dative, γραμματεω (149) occurs instead of the correct γραμματεῖ, but this is natural enough in an inscription which has γραμματεος for the nominative form.

Among the pronouns the only noteworthy variants from the standard are found in the use of the indefinite relative for the simple relative:

e.g., οστις (299) for ὅς, ἥτις (136b, 141, 151, and frequently) for ἥ;

and the interrogative τις in place of the relative, whether masculine or feminine:

τις masculine (99, 148, 152); τις feminine (159, 377).

Examples of variants in the conjugation of verbs are comparatively few, since, apart from κεῖται, ἔζησεν, and ἐποίησεν, verbs appear infrequently on these sepulchral inscriptions. The augment is very rarely omitted in secondary tenses:

θηκεν (153), ποιησεν (314).

In two examples the verb κεῖται is supplied with a false augment and otherwise garbled:[2]

ἐκιθεν (405), εκειθεν (397)

The few other inflectional variants which occur are not worth recording, since they are found only in single examples and cannot be regarded as indications of general usage.

A comparatively uneducated people would be expected to make errors in syntax, especially in using a language like the Greek with its rich variety of cases and moods. We find,

---

[1] In *CII* 24 Ευοδου του γραμματευς is probably genitive, although Frey takes it as nominative, transcribing the name as *Euodoutos* (strange name!) and conjecturing that the preceding lacuna contained the formula ἐνθάδε κεῖται. The actual space, however, leaves no room for this formula. Ferrua, in *Epigraphica*, 3 (1941), 32, more plausibly, regards the words as genitive depending on a missing υἱός.

[2] The verb κεῖται shows a large variety of spellings, some due to the confusion between spelling and pronunciation, some to the intrusion of the aspirates χ and θ, some to inexplicable ignorance or carelessness. Besides the common κειται, κειτε, κιται, κιτε, we find κιτεν (349), κειτι (314), κειτη (367), κετι (543) κιτει (410), κιετε (415), εκειθεν (397), εκιθεν (405), χιτε (391), κιθε (377), χειθε (277, 403, 416), and the anomalous form κικε (56).

accordingly, sundry instances of the misuse of cases; e.g., genitive for dative:

συν τη συμβιου αυτου (333), αιν ειρηνης (363) for ἐν εἰρήνῃ

genitive for accusative:

εζησεν ετων (359, 384, 397), apparently due to confusion with the descriptive genitive, which would be used without ἔζησεν;

dative for nominative:

ενθαδε κειτε Ευθυχιανο αρχοντι (110), again a mixing of two formulas, since the dative was often used to express the name of the deceased, but of course without κεῖται;

accusative for nominative:

εν ειρηνη κοιμησην (277), εν ειρηνη κομησιν (358);

accusative for genitive:

ετων ενεα κε μηνας ενεα (391), ετων ... [και μ] ηνας ζ' (427). Note that in each instance the correct genitive is followed by an incorrect accusative.

Appositives sometimes fail to agree in case with the substantives to which they refer:

θυγατηρ Μηνοφιλου πατηρ συναγωγης (537),
Ειρηνα ... συμβιος Κλωδιου ἀδελφος Κουντου (319),
κομησιν αυτου Ιουστον νηπιον (358).

Adjectives and participles do not agree with their nouns:

ητη μεια (102) for ἔτος ἔν, in an inscription in which nearly every word has one or more errors; ετη τρεις (418), although the same inscription also has ἔτη τρία correctly; Ρεβεκκα ... ζησας ετη (392);[1] Νωτω ιδιω θρεπτω καλως αντιζωσας (144).[2]

Once a singular verb is used with a plural subject:

ενταδε κιτε θυγατερες δυο (535); here apparently the writer has thoughtlessly used the common formula with the more or less stereotyped singular form of the verb.[3]

---

[1] The reading in *CII* is incorrect, while that in *MB*, no. 33, is right, despite Frey's objection, as a close examination of the stone itself clearly reveals.

[2] In the opinion of Ferrua, *Epigraphica*, 3 (1941), 33, the stonecutter carelessly wrote ΑΝΤΙΖΩCΑC instead of ΖΩCΑΝΤΙ, displacing the ΑΝΤΙ.

[3] The person of the pronoun is sometimes misused. We find one example of second person for third: ενθαδε κιτε Ευπορι μετα του υιου σου (329); and in one instance there is a shift from the second to the third person of the pronoun, then to the first person of the verb: ειτε σε Ιουστε ... κομησιν αυτου ... ενθαδε κειμε[for κεῖμαι] Ιουστος (358).

Since the Latin inscriptions are less than one-third as numerous as the Greek, and, as we have seen, the users of Latin were probably more prosperous, on the whole, and therefore better educated than those who used Greek, we find far fewer examples of aberrations from correct Latin pronunciation and grammar.

That *ae* was pronounced like *e* is clear enough from the many instances of confusion between the two. To cite a few examples:

Elius (456) for *Aelius*, *Iudea* (250), *Iudeus* (68), *que* (217, 230, 237, 267, and often) for *quae*, nominative singular feminine of the relative pronoun.

In the ending of the dative singular of the first declension, simple *e* is very frequently substituted for *ae*:

Asteri filie (213), *Quintille matri karissime* (217), *dulcissime proselyte* (222), *Eulogie matri dulcissime* (230), *coiugi sue* (237).

Sometimes the correct form in *-ae* is found alongside of a form in *-e*:

Gargilie Eufraxiae (237), *Valeriae filiae dulcissime* (267), *Benedicte Mariae vere benedicte* (459), *Isie filiae* (30*).

Much less often *ae* is written in place of *e*:

baenemerenti (234), *nominae* (523) for the ablative.

In the many Greek transcriptions of Latin, *ae* usually appears as αι, but sometimes as ε:

φειλιε καρισσιμε (248) for *filiae carissimae* (dative), Σεβηρε ματρι δουλκισειμε (264) for *Severae matri dulcissimae*, Κεσαρεως (25), Εμιλια (123).

This confusion is not surprising, since in the second century C.E. the pronunciation of *ae* was already becoming identical with that of *e*.[1]

From Greek transcriptions it is clear that the distinction between short and long *e* was generally observed, since the former is nearly always reproduced by ε, the latter by η:[2]

e.g., βενεμερεντι φηκιτ (266).

---

[1] Sturtevant, 128.

[2] To cite a few typical exceptions, αι is used for *ĕ*: βενεμερ αιντι (257), Καιλερειναι (215) for *Celerinae*; η for *ĕ*: Γημηλλινη (102) for *Gemellina*, in an inscription which has η instead of ε eight times; ε for *ē*: Βερεγονδος (97) for *Vērēcundus*, [Κρ]εσκεντινα (278); ι for *ē*: Φιλικεισιμα (415). In connection with this last example, it may be noted that *filix* for *felix* is not uncommon in Latin inscriptions of the period; see the citations in *Thes. Ling. Lat.*, VI, 434, lines 83 ff.

Latin *i* was transcribed in Greek by either ι or ει, a further indication of the identity of these two in Greek:

δισκειπουλειναι (215) for *discipulinae*, κονιουγι (235).

For Latin short *i*, Greek ι is usual,[1] while for long *i*, either ι or ει is employed, the former prevailing.[2] Similarly, short and long *o* appear as ο and ω, respectively:[3]

e.g., Φορτουνατος (418) Δωνατος (318),

The vowel *u* is rendered in Greek by ου, regardless of length:[4]

e.g., κουν (215) for *cum*, κονιουγι (235), φιλιους (264); Λουκιος (155), Ιουλιαι (124).

Variations from these practices are sporadic and of slight significance.

The consonantal *i* seems ordinarily to have been given its standard pronunciation as a semivowel (like our *y* in *yet*), but two Greek transcriptions with ζ may indicate that in some mouths it resembled *dz* as in *adze* or *j* as in *jelly*:[5]

κοζουγι (215, twice) for *coiugi*, Προζεκτω (286) for *Proiecto*.

---

[1] In exceptional instances, *ī* is rendered by ει: δισκειπουλειναι (215) for *discipulīnae*, δουλκισειμε (264) for *dulcissimae*, Μαρκεια (44), Μαρκειε (43) for dative *Marciae* (the same inscription also has the correct form Μαρκια), Πριμειτιβα (385) for *Prīmītiva*, Φιλικειωιμα (415); *ī* is rendered by η: Νωμητωρα (381) for *Numitora*, ρεκεσητ (460) for *recessit*: and once by ε: Στατωρεα (54) for *Statoria*.

[2] Sometimes both are used in the same inscription: βιξει (215) for *vīxī*.

[3] In Latin inscriptions written with Greek characters, when a letter-for-letter method is used, the *o* appears as omicron regardless of quantity. This occurs notably in the dative singular of the second declension: *e.g.*, φιλιο (269), Σαβατιο φιλιο (263). Occasionally one finds omicron for Latin long *o* in purely Greek inscriptions: Προβινκις (130) for *Prōvincius*, Ονορατος (149) for *Hŏnōratus*, but otherwise Ονωρατος (145, 146, 150.).

[4] Rarely is υ used for *u*: ποευει (484) for ποσυει = *posui*, and twice in rendering the name of the synagogue of the Volumnesians: Βολυμνησιων (343) and Βολυμνησων (417) but Βολουμνησιων (402). The Latin nominative ending -*us* regularly appears as -ος, according to normal usage, but there are three instances of an abnormal use of omicron for *u*: Βερεγονδος (97) for *Verecundus*, Αυγοστησιων (368), ανουρο (460) for *annorum*. The congregation named for the Subura is always Σιβουρησιοι, the reflection probably of a popular pronunciation.

[5] The fact that διὰ βίου appears sometimes as ζαβιου (416, 417), with a Latin equivalent as *Iabiu* (480), would also point in this direction.

Consonantal *v*, which in classical usage was pronounced like our *w*, was already a spirant with either the labio-dental sound of our *v* or the bilabial sound which *b* and *v* have acquired in Spanish. This is clear both from the confusion in spelling between *b* and *v*:

> *e.g.*, *bixit* (206, 254, 260, 456, 523) for *vixit*, *venemerenti* (213, 462), *Flavia Datiba* (234), *Beturia* (523);

and from the fact that in Greek, *v* is always reproduced by β (see above, p. 82), which represented the nearest equivalent sound, regardless of whether β had itself already become a spirant. If *v* were still a semivowel, it would have been rendered by ου, as is usual in Greek transcriptions from the classical period (*e.g.*, Ουεσπασιανος), but this spelling does not occur in our group of inscriptions.[1] Evidences that this changed sound of *v* was replacing the earlier semivocalic pronunciation in the Roman world generally is to be found in inscriptions as early as the first century C.E.,[2] so that the pronunciation used by the Jews was similar to that which prevailed in their Roman environment, especially among the less well educated. The instances cited above of confusion between *b* and *v* may perhaps indicate that *b* also was becoming a spirant, a development of which there are some traces by the first century C.E.[3]

The other Latin letters, both vowels and consonants, seem to have represented their traditional sounds among the Roman Jews. There is, at least, no significant evidence to point to a different conclusion. The letter *c* was pronounced like *k* in all positions, as is confirmed by Greek transcriptions of Latin words and names:[4]

> *e.g.*, φηκι (239) and φηκιτ (215 and often), Λουκιλλα (135), Λουκιος (155), Καιλια (363), Καιλιος (364), Πρισκιανος (411).

---

[1] That Latin *qua* and *quae* are transliterated as κουα (215) and κουαι (257), respectively, is a further indication that a semivocalic *v* would have been reproduced as ου rather than as β.

[2] Sturtevant, 142 f.

[3] Sturtevant, 174. If, however, a single example may be regarded as significant, the abbreviated transcription of κοίμησις by *cybis* (206) would perhaps indicate that *b* was sounded as a mute rather than as a spirant. Conversely, Latin *m* is rendered by β in a wretchedly written inscription: βενεβερενδι (239) for *benemerenti*.

[4] One poorly written inscription shows Βερεγονδος (97) for *Verecundus*.

The *g* apparently had the so-called hard sound, even before *e* and *i*. It regularly appears as γ in Greek inscriptions or Latin inscriptions written in Greek characters:[1] *e.g.*, Αγεντι[α] (81), Γημηλλινη (102) for *Gemellina*, κονιουγι (235, 266).

The few examples of the loss of the nasal *n* before *s* represent a phenomenon already common in classical Latin:[2] *mesis* (260), μησις (268), and *meses* (523) for *mensis* and *menses*, *quostituta* (523) for *constituta*; *Cresces* (68), Κωσταντις (92).

The omission of *n* before *t* is due to careless pronunciation or writing:

benemereti (457), βενε[μ]ερετει (484); *posuerut* (260); *fecrut* (273) for *fecerunt*.

The word *coniunx* shows both its full form and the variants *coniux* and *coiux*, which are common elsewhere.[3]

In the inflection of nouns and adjectives very few departures from correct form are to be found. In the first declension the dative singular often ends in *-e* instead of *-ae* because these were pronounced alike. An isolated second declension accusative form in *-un* is found on a crudely carved tablet:

virginiun sun (242) for *virginium suum*

A verse inscription, written in formal style, has the archaic accusative *aevom* (476, line 6). Two words which properly belong to the third declension received genitive plurals of the second declension:

nepotorum (13*), *omniorum* (210).

One adjective has an incorrect superlative form:

carimo (231) for *carissimo*.

---

[1] An exception is κοικι (239) for *coiugi* in an inscription with many other errors of spelling. The form *cogiugi* (236), where the first *g* replaces a consonantal *i*, might be taken as an indication that in the mouths of some persons the *g* had become palatalized (as in our *gem*), but this isolated instance is probably of no more significance than the spelling *colugi*, also for *coiugi*, which occurs in one inscription (468).

[2] Sturtevant, 153 f. The names of synagogues with Latinized forms in-*ensis* always appear without a nasal: Αγριππησιων. Αυγουστησιων, Σιβουρησιων, Καμπησιων, etc.

[3] See the examples in *Thes. Ling. Lat.*, *s.v. coniux* (IV 341). Isolated variants are *coiiux* (221), *cogiugi* (236), *colugi* (468), κοζουγει (215, twice), κοικι (239).

Syntactical errors are equally few. Twice the preposition *cum* governs the accusative instead of the ablative:[1]

> *quae fecit cum Celerinum* (262), *fecit cum Virginiun sun* (242).

Extent of time, especially in expressions indicating the age of the deceased, is rendered by either the accusative or the ablative, more commonly the latter. Either construction was admissible in classical usage, especially after the time of the Republic. The hesitation between the two was such that in three of our inscriptions both are found:

> *qui vixit ann. tres dieb. viginti tres* (71); *que vixit annis XVIII dies III ... que vixit annis III dies III* (242); *bixit annis LXXXII mesisX* (260).

There is one example of wrong agreement between participle and noun:

> *Stafylo archonti ... omnibus honoribus fuctus* (265) for *functo*;

and one of a plural verb with singular subject:

> *Aellia benemerenti Procle posuerut* (260).

Here, however, the stonecutter seems to have left out a second nominative by mistake, since he added *Almas posuit*.

There are also a few inscriptions in which there is confusion between the first and third persons:

> *Cocotia ... fecit ... fratri meo* (206) instead of *fratri suo*; Σεμπρωνιους ... κοζουγει ... κουν κουα βιξει ... φηκιτ (215) for *coiugi ... cum qua vixi ... fecit*, Ειουλια Αλεξανδρα φηχι κοικι σουω (239) for *feci coiugi suo*.

The reflexive pronoun is misused in only one instance, in a metrical inscription, in which metrical convenience may have determined the form:

> *haec ... secum transsegerat annum* (476, line 3), *secum* being used instead of *cum eo*.

In the same inscription the classical norm of verbal construction is violated by the use of *quod* and the subjunctive

---

[1] This construction is common in vulgar Latin from the first century C.E. on. See Stolz-Schmalz, *Lateinische Grammatik*, ed. 5, by M. Leumann and J. B. Hofmann (Munich, 1928), 532.

with *sperare* instead of the accusative and infinitive, but this construction became normal in late and mediaeval Latin:

> *sperare potest ideo quod surgat in aevom | promissum* (476, lines 6 f.).

To sum up, this survey indicates that neither in their pronunciation of the Greek and Latin nor in their grammatical usage did the Jews of Rome differ in any demonstrable way from the other less educated Greek-speaking and Latin-speaking groups of the Mediterranean world of the second and third centuries. There is no evidence whatever of a Judeo-Greek or Judeo-Latin in any respect comparable with the Yiddish or Ladino of later times. The Jews formed no linguistic island in ancient Rome.

CHAPTER FIVE

THE NAMES OF THE JEWS OF ROME

It was the great Jewish scholar Leopold Zunz who observed that "the names of a people are its annals in cipher," implying that he who finds the key has the entree to a rich treasure of historical and cultural information. Especially is this true of the annals of the Jewish people. A study of the names borne by the Jews throughout their vicissitudes both as a nation and as a people scattered among the nations brings out significant facets of their political and cultural fortunes.

Zunz and other scholars have traced the changes in the names of Jews throughout the ages, demonstrating the succession of Persian, Babylonian, Aramaic, Greek, and Roman influences in antiquity and the effects of Jewish contacts with the various European nations throughout the Middle Ages into modern times.[1] Such a study of the names is of particular interest in determining the cultural associations of an immigrant group which has become rooted in an alien environment. Gradually, as such a group adapts itself to its surroundings, it accepts, among the customs of the adopted country, the names current in that country. This phenomenon, which has been too familiar throughout the history of the Jewish Diaspora to require illustration, is notably exemplified among the Jews of ancient Rome.

---

[1] The fundamental study is that of Leopold Zunz, *Namen der Juden* (Leipzig, 1837), included also in his *Gesammelte Schriften*, II (Berlin, 1876), 1-82. For other studies on Jewish names see Joseph Jacobs in *JE*, s.v. Names (Personal); T. H. Gaster in *Universal Jewish Encyc.* s.v. Names of the Jews; H. Loewe in *Juedisches Lexikon*, s.v. Namen der Juden (post-Biblical part). Neither of the last two pays any attention to the epigraphical sources. Juster, *Les juifs dans l'Empire Romain*, devotes a chapter (II, 221-234) to the Jewish names in the Roman world. When Juster wrote, most of the names from the Monteverde inscriptions had not yet been published and the Nomentana catacomb had not been discovered. Besides, those names that were available were in many instances based on incorrect transcriptions and interpretations. Why Juster limited his lists to the Latin names borne by the Jews, ignoring the Greek and Semitic ones, is not apparent.

Of the Jews who arrived in Rome as immigrants, many were already Hellenized, having come to regard Greek as their native speech, much as many Jews in recent times came to regard a Germanic dialect, Yiddish, as the proper Jewish tongue, reserving Hebrew as the "sacred language" of the Bible and the ritual. Thus in our day purely Germanic names, such as Goldblatt, Rosenblum, Greenbaum, have come to be especially associated with Jews. As we examine the names of the Jews of ancient Rome, we shall find a strikingly similar situation. It will be of interest to determine the extent to which the Jews of Rome kept the names of their Semitic forefathers, to what degree their use of the Greek language of the general Hellenistic milieu was accompanied by the adoption of Greek names, how far their adaptation to the immediate Roman environment influenced them to give Latin names to their children. It will be interesting also to note such matters as whether there was a tendency to use the same names in families, where family names are traceable, whether sons and daughters might be named for their parents, whether Greek-speaking and Latin-speaking groups used names corresponding to their respective vernaculars, whether there was any significant difference in policy with regard to naming boys or girls. An additional point of interest with reference to the Jews of Rome in particular, in view of their division into a number of congregations residing in different sections of the city, would be to discover whether there was any notable difference in the use of names as between the different groups.[1]

As the primary source for finding answers to such questions as these, I list here all the identifiable names appearing on the inscriptions, arranged according to the language of the name,[2]

[1] The present study supersedes my former one, "The Names of the Jews of Ancient Rome," *TAPA*, 59 (1928), 205-224. At that time I had a total of 517 names as compared with the present 551.

[2] In some cases, where a name is based on a word that may be classified as either Greek or Latin, such as Hilarus or Margarita, it is difficult to decide in which language category to place it. In these and other doubtful instances arbitrary decisions had to be made, but such cases are so few, comparatively, that the statistical results will not be materially affected and the conclusions not at all. It should be noted here that Frey's index is of little value in classifying the names, since he lists under "Noms Propres Grecs" all names written

and alphabetically within each language category, with additional grouping according to the name's single or multiple structure. All names are presented in Latin characters and in the normal Latin spelling,[1] although, as we have seen above, the great majority of the inscriptions containing them are written in Greek. Each name is given in the nominative form, regardless of the case which is used in context. Where one or more letters are missing and can be supplied with reasonable certainty, the lacuna has not been indicated. Errors in spelling are ordinarily not reproduced, but when the spelling on an inscription differs materially from the normal form, that spelling is added in a parenthesis. Each name is followed by the number of the inscription in which it appears, according to the numbering in Frey's *Corpus* and that in our Appendix of Inscriptions. Should the reader wish readily to identify the catacomb in which each inscription was found, he may note that the Nomentana inscriptions involve numbers 6 to 72, the Appia 81 to 285, the Monteverde 290 to 493. The others are either of unknown provenience or from the small catacombs which have yielded only scanty data. Disagreements with Frey's allocations to the several catacombs are indicated in each instance.

LATIN NAMES (254 examples)

I. SINGLE NAMES (202 examples)

Abundantius 206	Amabilius 361
Aelia 260	Annia 87, 300
Aelianus 139	Annianus 88, 310 (perhaps
Agrippinus 322	also ... ΝΙΑΝΟΥ 39)
Adiutor 7 (Αιουτωρ)	Annius 301

in Greek characters, regardless of their language, and under "Noms Propres Latins" those written in Latin characters. Thus, many purely Latin names, such as Claudius and Marina, appear in the Greek list, and such Greek names as Agathon and Eulogia may be found in the Latin list, while a common Latin name like Aurelius appears in both lists. There is no category of Semitic names, and such names are listed under either Greek or Latin according to the language of the inscription in which they appear.

[1] Thus the Greek nominative in-ος appears in our lists as -*us*, υ as *y*, ει as *i*, ου as *u*, 'Αλέξανδρος as *Alexander*, etc.

Antonina 236
Aper 304
Aquilina 389
Aurelius 218[1]
Bellula 458[2]
Benedicta (733a, not in CII)[3]
Caelius 365
Cara 535 (probably from Monteverde)[4]
Castricius 124, 221
Castus 128, 230
Celerinus 262
Centullia 129[5]
Claudius 37
Clodius 319 (Frey lists as Monteverde, but provenience uncertain)
Cocotia 206 (masc.)

Constantius 92 (Κωσταντις), 507[6]
Cossutius 131
Crescentina 39, 96, 278
Crispina 126, 132 (both of the same person)
Damnata 475
Dativus 416
December 224
Digitius 17
Domnus 20, 494
Domi [tius?] 19[7]
Domitia 105
Donatus 318
Dulcia 227
Dulcitia 106, 141, 226
Faustina 283, 419
Faustinus 171

[1] This is probably part of a multiple name, the stone being fragmentary. If a single name, it is our only example of Aurelius not used in combination with another name.

[2] *Bellula* appears to be the diminutive adjective from *bella* (pretty). Compare other feminine names in our inscriptions indicating personal characteristics; *e.g.*, Dulcia, Dulcitia, Felicissima, Felicitas, Iustissima, Pietas.

[3] On a stone now in the museum of the Pontificio Istituto Biblico in Rome.

[4] I have demonstrated that the KAPA of the inscription is a proper name; see "The Daughters of Gadias," *TAPA*, 84 (1953), 67-72, and especially p. 70.

[5] Vogelstein (*VR*, 471, no. 87) comments that this name (written Κεντουλια) is an error for *Quintilia*; Frey, following Garrucci, regarded it as a "popular deformation" of *Centuria*; Ferrua (*Epigraphica*, 3, 33) prefers to equate it with *Getulia*. No such conjectures are needed. Centullia's father, Ursacius, migrated to Rome from Aquileia (see No. 147), among the inscriptions of which town the name Centullius occurs (*CIL* 5. 1121).

[6] Frey prefers *Constantinus*. Since the stone is no longer extant and the most reliable of the epigraphists who copied it read only ΚΩΝΣ-ΤΑΝΤ and the name Constantinus does not otherwise occur in our onomasticon, it seems preferable to call the name Constantius.

[7] A lacuna is indicated by Frey, but actually only ΔΟΜΙ was scratched on the stucco of the loculus. No letters have been lost. It appears that the scribe stopped, for some reason, before finishing the name.

strategic plan (now w…
plan.

Task Forces

Task forces were assigne…
ATS. Work of the task forces is …
proactive work by the committee
process.

Assignments

- #1 McMahan,
- #2 Widbin, Jer
- #3 Widbin, Fel
  involvement in
- #4 Felmlee, Je
- #5 Jennings –
  budget proces
- #6 Schroeder,
  expansion
- #7 Barkatt, Sc
- #8a Complete
  investment ma
- #8b McMahar
  through aggre

Meeting schedules

- Tuesday, May 1 11:0
- Tuesday, May 22 C…

Felicianus 11* (from the Appia; Frey lists as pagan)[1]

Felicissima 339, 415

Felicitas 462

Felix 30* (from Monteverde; Frey lists as pagan)

Flavia 361

Flora 69

Fofotis 464[2]

Fortunatianus 240

Fortunatus 418

Fostinus (variant of Faustinus 56[3]

Fronto 307[4]

Gaius 100, 101, 236, 263[5]

Gaudentia 314, 315

Gaudentius 316[6]

Gemellina 102

Germanus 242

Honoratus 145, 146, 149, 150 (only two different persons)

Impendius 466

---

[1] This inscription, although found in the Appia catacomb, is rejected by Frey and placed in a group of "Inscriptions Probablement Païennes." Frey gives the same treatment to sundry other stones found in the Jewish catacombs if he fails to discover some positive indication that they are Jewish. If this criterion were to be followed consistently, many an additional inscription would have to be rejected. It seems much more reasonable to assume that the inscriptions in a Jewish catacomb are Jewish unless they have definite non-Jewish indications, such as the pagan formula *Dis Manibus*, in which cases one may infer that the stone was used for some such purpose as a filler to close a loculus.

[2] Fofotis is a peculiar name. It appears in the dative form *Fofoti*, from which Frey derives a nominative *Fofos*. Possibly the name is a corruption or variant of the common Roman name Fufidius, or Fufius.

[3] Frey, following Paribeni and Lietzmann, reads ΦΟ..ΙΝΟΥ and interprets the name as *Photinos* (?). Depite Frey's confident assertion that there is a lacuna, the inscription clearly shows ΦΟΣΤΙΝΟΥ, a reading which I verified in 1951. For Fostinus as a variant of Faustinus, cf. the familiar Clodius and Claudius, Plotius and Plautius.

[4] Since the letters ΕΠΟ precede ΦΡΟΝΤΩΝ, some interpreters, including Frey, read the name as *Epophronton*. It appears better to regard the ΕΠΟ as a stonecutter's slip for ΕΤΟ, *i.e.*, ἐτ(ῶν) ο′ = aged seventy years. So also Vaccari in *Biblica*, 19 (1938), 342. The inscription is that of an apparently aged woman, Aurelia Zotice, whose grandson, named Fronto, set up the stone to her memory. Unfortunately, the accuracy of the readings cannot be verified, since the stone is not extant.

[5] *CII* 57 is recorded as ΓΑΙΙΟ (after Lietzmann), but these traces of letters on a piece of tile in the Nomentana catacomb are much too uncertain to justify inclusion of the name.

[6] The name Gaudentius occurs also on a stone in the atrium of Santa Maria in Trastevere. The inscription is very possibly Jewish, since it shows a bird and an object that looks much like a shofar, as it is represented on our inscriptions (cf. 254, 283, 545). Frey, however, thinks that is probably Christian; see his illustration and comment in *CII*, pp. 583 f, no. 86*. Because of the uncertainty I have not included the inscription in this study.

---

[1] On a Jewish sarcophagus from the Nomentana catacomb (Figs. 28, 29). See *JQR*, 42 (1952), 413-418 and below, pp. 214 f.

[2] The reading is uncertain and since the inscription was on the closure of a loculus destroyed together with the Monteverde catacomb, the text cannot be verified. The name may have been Margarita.

[3] Although the word *margarita*, which means "pearl," is of Greek origin, the proper name was Roman rather than Greek.

[4] The stone was counted among the Porto inscriptions by Frey and his predecessors. I have shown in *HTR* 45 (1952), 172-174 that it is one of a group which probably came from the Monteverde catacomb.

[5] Orstorius seems a peculiar name, but W. Schulze in *Zur Geschichte lateinischer Eigennamen* (Berlin, 1904), 334, cites such Roman names as Obstorius, Opstorius, Ostorius.

[6] Frey gives no reason for including this among the Appia inscriptions. Actually, its provenience is unknown. It may be from the Monte-

Plotius 49
Polla 241
Pomponius 384
Prima 361
Primitiva 385
Priscianus 411
Probus 152
Proca 386
Procla (= Procula) 260, 387, 388
Proclina (= Proculina) 389
Proclus 390
Proculus 391
Proiectus 286
Quintiana 506
Quintianus 368
Quirinus 367 (provenience uncertain; Frey lists as Monteverde)
Regina 476
Reginus 207
Renatus 153
Restituta 265
Rufinus 79[1]
Rufus 145, 146 (both of the same person)
Sabina 158, 159
Sabinus 230, 398
Salvius 161
Salutia 478
Salutius 122, 374
Severa 264
Severus 264
Silicius? 511 (Σειλικες)

Simplicia 166, 167
Sossianus 235
Statoria 54
Successus 53
Telesinius or Telesinus 479 (provenience uncertain; Frey lists as Monteverde)
Ursacia 147
Ursacius 129, 147, 167 (all three of the same person)
Ursus 148
Valentiano 310 (fem.)
Valeria 267
Valerius 247, 267
Venerosa 268
Verecundus 97 (Βερεγονδος)
Vernaclus (= Vernaculus) 35* (from Monteverde; Frey lists as pagan)
Veriana 12, 27 (both of the same person)
Vibia 156
Victor 98, 102, 312, 313
Vindicianus 483
Vitalio 13, 99
Vitalis 522

2. Double Names (49 examples)

Aelia Patricia 266
Aelia Septima 208
Aelius Aprilicus 456
Aelius Primitivus 457
Agentia ... ana 81

---

verde catacomb, as Ferrua has suggested (*Civ. Catt.*, [1936] IV, 135), since it was at one time in the Velletri collection, nearly all the stones of which are known to have come from Monteverde.

[1] This is from the small catacomb of Via Appia Pignatelli. Since we cannot be quite certain that the catacomb itself was Jewish, there is similar uncertainty about this inscription and the name.

Aninius Sabinianus 299
Annius Genialis 9[1]
Aurelia Auguria 209
Aurelia Celerina 215
Aurelia Flavia 216
Aurelia Quintilla 217
Aurelius Bassus 83
Aurelius Crescens (or Crescentius) 218
Caelia Omnina (35a, from the Nomentana; not in CII)[2]
Caelius Quintus 505
Claudia Marciana 461
Claudia Prima 366
Claudius Provincius 130
Cresces Sinicerius 68
Domitia Felicitas 212
Faustula Provincia 233
Flavia Antonina 416
Flavia Caritina 234
Flavia Dativa 234
Flavia Flaviana 299

Flavia Iuliana 172
Flavia Vitalinis 235[3]
Flavius Constantius 463
Flavius Iulianus 172
Flavius Sabinus 417
Iulia Aemilia 123
Iulia (Ιολεια) Marcella 34
Iulia Rufina 31* (from Monteverde; Frey lists as pagan)
Iulia R ... 35
Iulia Severa 352
Iulus (= Iulius?) Sabinus 468
Iunius Iustus 357
Lucius Maecius 470
Lucretia Faustina 247
Maecia Lucianis 470
Rufilla Pietas 262
Sabina Palma 160
Siculus Sabinus 402
Ulpia Marina 257
Veturia Paulla 523[4]

---

[1] Lietzmann (in *BL*, 36) derives the name, which appears as Ανεις, from חנניה. Since the second name seems to have been Genialis (ΓΕ[.]ΕΙΑΛΗΣ, was preserved on the fragments of the stone), the first name more probably represents the Roman name Annius, and we have the regular combination of gentile name followed by cognomen. The combination of Hebrew name plus Latin cognomen has no parallel in our group of inscriptions. It is, of course, possible that Annius in this instance is a Latinization of a Hebrew name. The same may be said of the feminine name Annia, listed above.

[2] The name is found on a sarcophagus from the Nomentana catacomb. See p. 98, n. 1, above.

[3] The second name appears as Βιταλινι, in the dative. Frey takes it as an erroneous form for *Vitalinae* from a nominative *Vitalina*, but ι for *ae* would be decidedly abnormal. Ferrua (*Epigraphica*, 3, 34) prefers the name *Vitalis*, the normal dative of which would, however, be *Vitali*. Since all the names of the inscription are Latin and the inscription itself is in Latin, though written in Greek letters, one would hardly expect a Hellenized inflectional form such as *Vitalini* from a nominative *Vitalis*. In any case, *Vitalis* is a masculine cognomen, hardly appropriate with a feminine *gentilicium*. Hence I have preferred to take the name as *Vitalinis*.

[4] Some early copiers of the inscription read the name as *Beturia Paulina*, others as *Beturia Paucla* (apparently for *Paulla*). Since the

..... a Marcella 33* (from Monteverde; Frey lists as pagan)
..... ia Felicitas 414
..... ia Marcella 496 (probably Monteverde)
..... ia Sabina 242

3. Triple Names (3 examples)

Gaius Furfanius Iulianus 465
Lucius Maecius Constantius 470
Lucius Maecius Victorinus 470

GREEK NAMES (175 examples)

Aetetus 325 (Ετητος)
Agathon 6
Agathopus 209
Alexander 84, 85 (two persons), 92, 140, 210, 370, 501
Alexandra (or Alexandria) 501
Alexandria 8
Alexe 171 (fem.)
Alypius 502 (two persons)
Amachius 86
Amarantus 339 (Ημαραντος)
Amelius 1 (two persons)
Ammias 296 (fem.)
Amni . . . 179 (sex uncertain)
Anastasia 298, 732
Aphrodisia 232
Archigenia 35* (from Monteverde; Frey lists as pagan)
Asias 90
Asclepiodote 91, 92
Asteria 94

Asterias 93
Asterius 95 (two persons), 305
Athenion 82
Calandio 127
Chrysas 286
Chrysis 222 (fem.)
Chrysius 170
Cyrias 11* (fem., from the Appia; Frey lists as pagan)
Cyrillas 310[1]
Cyrus 133
Daphne 15, 223
Daphnus 16
Delphinus 4
Deuterus 103, 225
Dionysias 104 (masc.)
Dionysias 256 (fem.)
Diophatus 18
Doris 536 (probably Monteverde)
Epagathus (733b; not in CII)[2]

stone has long been lost, no check is possible. This woman was a proselyte, who took the name Sara when she adopted Judaism. See below, p. 254.

[1] Ferrua (Epigraphica, 3, 36), less probably, regards Κυρυλλα as nominative and therefore a feminine name. I prefer to agree with Frey that the deceased is Valentiano (he errs in calling her Valentiniano), the daughter of Κυρυλλας, i.e., Cyrillas, which is a masculine name.

[2] The inscription, not included in CII, was found in 1897 near St. Paul's and is now in the Lapidary Museum of the monastery attached to that church. Since Epagathus was a gerusiarch, the inscription is certainly Jewish. See Silvagni, Inscriptiones Christianae Urbis Romae, II, 5991.

Eparchia 228

Epigenius 323

Epiphania 130

Eucarpus 111

Eudoxius 109

Eugenia 326

Eugraphius 55

Euhodia 391 (two persons)

Euhodus 24[1]

Eulogia 230, 327, 328

Eulogius 112,[2] 231

Euphranticus 12, 27 (both of the same person)

Euphrasius 335, 336

Euphrenon 385

Eupore 329[3]

Eupsychus 337

Eusebia 330

Eusebis 25 (fem.)

Eusebius 26, 113, 114, 119, 331, 332, 333

Eutropius 418

Eutyches 232

Eutychianus 110

Eutychis 334 (fem.)

Eutychius 412

Eutychi . . . 115 (sex uncertain)

Gelasius 25, 317

Helles 322

Hermia 26

Hermione 108 (provenience uncertain; Frey lists as Appia)

Hermogenes 324

Hilara 342

Hilarus 238, 343

Himerus 239

Iaso 341 (sex uncertain)

Iason 32, 289

Iocathinus 120

Ionius 362

Irene 21, 319, 320, 333

Irenes 240 (fem.)

Irenaeus 69

Isia 30* (from Monteverde; Frey lists as pagan)

Isidora 291[4]

Isidorus 229[5]

Istasia 361

---

[1] Frey prefers to call the name *Euodoutos*, but, as has been shown above (p. 85, n. 1), he has wrongly taken the TOΥ as part of the name, whereas it is the definite article going with the following word.

[2] According to Frey the name is *Eulogistos*, but here again the letters TΩ must surely go with the following ιδιω τεκνω since the definite article is regularly used with ἴδιος.

[3] Frey is in doubt whether the form Ευπορι is a vocative from Εὐπόριος or a nominative form of the feminine name Εὐπόρη. The latter is decidedly preferable. See *TAPA*, 59 (1928), 211, note 39.

[4] The inscription is a bilingual, Greek and Aramaic, the only one of this kind. The name appears as אסודרה in the Hebrew characters.

[5] The stone reads ESIDORVS ETERVS, which Frey and others have regarded as a double name. There is, however, no other example in these Jewish inscriptions of a person having two Greek names. Since the inscription is Greek, though written in Latin letters, ETERVS most probably represents the Greek ἑταῖρος = *colleague*. This suggestion was, in fact, made by Garrucci in his *Cimitero degle antichi Ebrei*, p. 7. Similarly, in No. 207, which is, conversely, Latin written in Greek characters, we find ΚΟΛΑΗΓΑ (*sic*), apparently for *collega*.

Leontia 369

Leontius 134 (two persons)[1]

Leus 157[2]

Macedonius 370

Melitium 141 (fem.)

Menander 3

Menophilus 537 (probably Monteverde)

Monimus 379

Musaeus 474

Nicander 511

Nicetes 256

Nicodemus 380 (provenience uncertain; Frey lists as Monteverde)

Numenius 142, 143, 305

Pancharius 48, 106, 509

Pancratius 28

Pardus 159

Paregorius 497

Philippus 334

Plane 258

Poemenis 151 (fem.)

Polycarpus 96

Poly[me?]nius 383[3]

Procopius 126, 132, 137 (all three of the same person)

Rhodion 173[4]

Salpingius 162[5]

Seleucus 52

Sirica 168, 213

Socus (= Σωκος) 231

---

[1] Since only the letters ΛΕΟΝΤΙ are preserved of one of the names and the inscription is very fragmentary, it is possible that the incomplete name is that of a woman, Leontia, daughter of Leontius.

[2] The name is given in the genitive as Λεου. This could be a Hellenized form of *Levi*, as Frey and others have suggested.

[3] Müller (*Jüd. Kat.*, 140), followed by Frey, filled the name out as Πολυ[μ]νις, *i.e.*, *Polymnis* (= *Polymnius*), a common enough Greek name, but the lacuna requires at least two letters. This name should, accordingly, be rejected in favor of such possibilities as Polymenius, Polyxenius, Polyaenius, Polychronius, Polygonius, Polysthenius, all of which are known Greek names and would more suitably fit the space.

[4] Frey insists that the letters ΡΟΛΙΩΝ represent part of the name of a synagogue, that of the Herodians, but it seems certain that the name of a person is involved. See Leon, "The Synagogue of the Herodians," in *JAOS* 49 (1929), 318-321, and Frey's discussion in *CII*, pp. 124-126. More recently, Ferrua also has argued effectively that this cannot be the name of a synagogue (*Epigraphica*, 3, 34). See also below, pp. 159-62. Since the word in question is preceded by an upright stroke which may be part of an "H", the name could be Herodion, a name which occurs in the New Testament as that of a Christian in Rome (*Rom.* 16.11). This name is, however, spelled 'Ηρωδίων, and in an inscription as beautifully carved as the one in question (see Fig. 30) an error of spelling is quite unlikely. Hence the name should be taken as Rhodion, which is a known Greek name (*CIG* 1608, which reads ΡΟΔΩΝΟΣ wrongly for ΡΟΔΙΩΝΟΣ, according to Pape-Benseler, *Wörterb. d. griech. Eigennamen, s.v.* 'Ρόδων).

[5] The inscription is embellished with a pair of trumpets, obviously as a pun on the name, since the Greek *salpinx* is the word for trumpet (Fig. 55).

Sophronia 511	Theophilus 119 (two persons)
Sophronius 55, 135	Trophime 169
Staphylus 265	Trophimus 169
Stephanus 404, 405	Tryllis 112
Straton 406	Tychicus 412
Symmachus 408, 409	Xanthias 70
Syrus 410	Zenon 116
Thalassa 28	Zosimus 51, 503
Theodora 30	Zotice 117
Theodorus 31	Zoticus 118, 338[1]
Theodotus 358	

SEMITIC NAMES (72 examples)

Abas 371	Eli 30
Almas 260[2]	Gadias 510, 535 (probably
Aster 213, 306, 732, 733[3]	Monteverde; both of the
Badiz? 308[4]	same person)
B?]alsamia 309[5]	Iacob 340
Beniamin 376	Ionathan 216, 277
Besula 460[6]	Ioses 126, 347

[1] Although the fragment shows no more than ZΩT, the name is most probably Zoticus. Frey reads only the first two letters of the name, but a trace of the T is clearly visible.

[2] Frey prefers to read *Alumas* because a figure like the letter *U* appears above the *L*. The Hebrew equivalent of *Almas* may be עלמה or עלמת. It would not be unreasonable to classify *Almas* as Greek, since there is a Greek name Ἄλμος.

[3] This must be regarded as a Hellenized form of Esther. The name is actually spelled Aσθηρ in two of the inscriptions (732, 733). Perhaps illogically, the names Asteria, Asterias, and Asterius have been classified here among the Greek names, the justification being that these are frequent Greek names, whereas *Aster*, a common noun meaning "star," is rare as a Greek proper name, and even then is a masculine name, whereas all our examples are feminine.

[4] The inscription is so hopelessly garbled that the name is uncertain.

[5] So the name is usually restored. Frey connects it with בעלשמם "Baal of Heaven" and comments that the Jews of Rome did not think of the origin of the name. Both name and explanation must be regarded as uncertain.

[6] The name appears as Βεσουλες for Βεσούλης, a genitive. It could represent בתולה, although one would expect a θ or τ rather than a σ to reproduce Hebrew ת. Frey calls the name *Vesula* and Ferrua (*Epigraphica* 3, 37) makes it *Bessula*. The latter is, to be sure, a Roman name, but a masculine one, whereas in our inscription the form of the genitive shows that it is feminine.

Isaac 282

Iudas 12, 33, 121, 122, 345,
346, 347, 348, 349, 350, 351

Lazar 321[1]

Mara 41, 372

Maria 1, 12, 96, 137, 252, 374,
375, 511

Marta (733b; not in *CII*)[2]

Mniaseas 508

Rebecca 261, 392

Sabbasa 396

Sabbatia 153

Sabbatis (fem.) 155, 156, 157

Sabbatis (sex uncertain)
373, 391, 394, 395[3]

Sabbatius 263, 329, 397, 477

Salo 510 (probably Monte-
verde)

Samuel 399, 401

Sara 12, 400[4], 543 (probably
Monteverde)

Simon 163, 165, 176[5], 403

Simonis 267 (fem.)

Zabuttas 269 (two per-
sons)[6]

Zortas[ius?] 44

Double Name

Tubias Barzaharona 497

---

[1] Only the letters ZAP remain on the stone. Frey prefers *Eleazar*, but the space will not allow more than two letters for the missing portion of the name.

[2] From the inscription referred to on p. 101 n. 2, above.

[3] The *Sabbatis-Sabbatius* names are variously spelled. For the variants see *TAPA*, 59 (1928), 214. When the name appears with the *-tis* ending, one cannot tell, unless there is some indication in the context, whether the name is intended for the feminine Sabbatis or the masculine Sabbatius, since, as has been noted, the normal *-ius* masculine ending often appears as -ις.

[4] The name is followed by the letters OYPA, which Frey interprets as the Latin name *Ursa*. This seems very improbable, nor is there any other instance of a Hebrew name followed by a Latin one.

[5] The surviving letters of what appears to be the name are ΕΙΜΩΝ, so that the conjecture of Frey and others that the name was Σείμων is quite plausible.

[6] Vogelstein (*VR*, 67, note 15) connects the name with זבדיה, the normal Greco-Latin form of which is *Zebedaeus*. Frey links it with the same root, זבד, from which various names were derived. Juster, however (II, 230, n.1), regards it as a variant of *Sabbatius*, a most unlikely conjecture, since so common a name would hardly have been corrupted to that extent. It may be noted that the name *Zabda* occurs in a few inscriptions found in or near Rome, but none of these can be accepted as Jewish. One, indeed, that of M. Abenna Zabda, is actually in the Jewish catacomb of the Via Appia, but it was found outside the catacomb near a pagan columbarium (according to C. L. Visconti, *BICA*, [1861], 22). Frey is quite right, therefore, in rejecting the inscription (*CII*, pp. 537 f). The tombstone of a certain L. Valerius Zabda, one of three freedmen with Jewish cognomina (the others are Baricha and Achiba), is conspicuous on the Via Appia, some five miles out (*CIL* 6, 27959 and *CII* 70*).

LATIN AND GREEK NAMES (35 examples)

1. Double Names (30 examples)

Aelia Alexandria 208
Aemilia Theodora 83
Agrius Euangelus 207
Alexandria Severa 144
Aurelia Althea 214
Aurelia Helenes 219
Aurelia Protogenia 217
Aurelia Zotice 307
Aurelius Alexander 219
Aurelius Hermias 220
Aurelius Olympius 24* (from Monteverde; Frey lists as pagan)
Caelia Euhodus 363
Caelius Anastasius 364
Cattia Ammias 537 (probably Monteverde)
Claudia [Bere?]nice 461
Fabia Asia 413[1]
Gargilia Eufraxia 237

Iulia Alexandra 239
Iulia Alexandria 470
Iulia Aphrodisia 220
Marcia Tryphera 43
Marcia Zenodora 43
Naevia Cyria 47
Pompeius Eutyches 259
Sempronius Basileus 215
Tullius Irenaeus 266
Tyrisia Profutura 243[2]
Varia Zotice 311
Aemi?]lius or Iu?]lius Anteros 302
Iu?]nia Antipatra 303

2. Triple Names (5 examples)

Atronius Tullianus Eusebius 72[3]
Iulia Irene Arista 72
Marcus Quintus Alexus 284
Quintus Claudius Synesius 319
Tettius Rufinus Melitius 480

---

[1] On the stone the name appears in the genitive, Φαβίας Ασια[ς]. Frey calls the name *Fabia Cassia* as a result of wrong division of the two words and carelessly misinterpreting the Greek lunate sigma (C), the regular form in these inscriptions, as Latin C. In his index (p. 617) he records the name as Φαβία Κασσία.

[2] Abnormally, the Greek name precedes the Latin. (In such a name as Alexandria Severa, the former had become quite Latinized, and there is the association with the name of the Emperor Alexander Severus.) It may be that PROFVTVRA is no name at all, but the future participle; thus, *profutura fecit* would mean "set up this stone in a spirit of good will," or the like, but there is no parallel to such an expression in our inscriptions. The name Profutura is, however, found on a Christian inscription of the Catacomb of Priscilla (Marucchi, *Catacombe romane*, 490). The name Tyrisia also is peculiar. It may possibly represent a Greek form Τειρεσία.

[3] It is by no means certain that *CII* 72 is Jewish. The inscription is on a sarcophagus which was found at the Church of Sant' Agnese on the Via Nomentana and is now in the cortile of the Palazzo Spada (Fig. 31). It is usually regarded as Jewish because the deceased Iulia Irene Arista is lauded for her devotion to the Law (*iuste legem colenti*).

LATIN AND SEMITIC NAMES (12 examples)

1. Double Names (10 examples)

Appidia Lea 212
Aurelia Maria 96
Aurelius Ioses 209
Benedicta Maria 459
Claudius Ioses 538 (probably Monteverde)

Fabia Mauria (= Maria?) 413
Flavia Maria 457
Pompeius Ionata 259
Pticia Aster 468
Titinia Anna 411

2. Triple Names (2 examples)

Lucius Domitius Abbas 212
Lucia Maecia Sabbatis 470

DOUBTFUL NAMES (3 examples)

Oproman (Οπρωμαν) 382[1]
PMOΛNOC AMEM? 154[2]

Suc[ca? or cessa?] (COYK..) 248[3]

From a study of these 551 names, the first fact of interest which appears (Table I) is that, although the community

TABLE I

Language of Name

Latin only	254	46.1%	Some Latin ...	301	54.6%
Greek only	175	31.8%	Some Greek ..	210	38.1%
Semitic only	72	13.1%	Some Semitic..	84	15.2%
Latin and Greek .	35	6.4%			
Latin and Semitic	12	2.2%			
Language doubtful	3	0.5%			
Total....	551				

was fundamentally a Greek-speaking one, the purely Latin names surprisingly not only outnumber all the others but are

---

[1] The name Oproman does not fit into any of our language categories. A name *Opramoas* is cited from Rhodiopolis in Lycia (*CIG*, 4324).

[2] The wretchedly formed letters make the reading very dubious. Frey reads PMOANOC AMCM, interpreting the first word, with hesitation, as the name *Romanos* and the second, also with hesitation, as an abbreviation of the adjective ἄμεμπτος = irreproachable, a not implausible conjecture.

[3] Frey, after Garrucci and others, suggests that the name should be filled out as Σουκ[κεσσα], *i.e.*, *Successa*. The missing portion, however, despite Frey's assertion to the contrary, could not have contained more than two or three letters. I have suggested the name *Succa* (*TAPA* 59, 209, note 21), which might be either a Semitic name or, more probably, the feminine counterpart of the name *Socus* (231).

more than equal to the Greek and Semitic names combined. Further, if names made up of two language elements are considered, it will be seen that more than half (54.6 %) of all the persons whose names are known had at least one Latin name.

Apparently, then, the Roman Jews had accepted the Latin names of their Roman neighbors to a much greater extent than they had adopted the Latin language. It was a familiar parallel in our own time that Yiddish-speaking parents give their children names current in the non-Jewish environment.

Distributing the names according to the languages spoken by the individuals (or their families) as indicated by the language of the inscription (Table II),[1] we find that Latin speakers show an overwhelming preference for Latin names in that 77.6% have some Latin element, while Greek speakers also prefer

TABLE II

Language of Name by Language of Inscription

	In Greek Inscriptions	In Latin Inscriptions	In Greek Inscriptions	In Latin Inscriptions
Latin name only ...	161	93	41.1%	59.6%
Greek name only ...	142	24	38.7%	15.4%
Semitic name only ..	60	11	15.3%	7.1%
Latin and Greek-name	15	20	3.8%	12.8%
Latin and Semitic name	4	8	1.0%	5.1%
Totals[2]	392	156		
Some Latin	180	121	45.9%	77.6%
Some Greek	167	44	42.6%	28.2%
Some Semitic	64	19	16.3%	12.2%

Latin names, though by only a small margin over Greek names (45.9% *vs.* 42.6%). Semitic names, which comprise only 15 % of the total, occur somewhat more frequently among the Greek speakers than the Latin speakers (16.3% *vs.* 12.2%).

---

[1] The Latin inscriptions written in Greek characters are considered as Latin, and vice versa.

[2] The three doubtful names are not included here.

It is, accordingly, clear from Table II that those who spoke Greek showed a slight preference for Latin names over Greek names and used Semitic names in less than one-sixth of all known instances; of Latin speakers more than three-fourths used Latin names, much less than one-third used Greek names (often combined with a Latin name), and only about one-eighth used any Semitic name at all.

If the names are examined from the point of view of the sex of the bearer (Table III), it is discovered that a girl was more likely to receive a Latin name than was a boy.

TABLE III

Language of Name by Sex of Bearer

	Masc.	Fem.	Masc.	Fem.
Latin name only	142	110	44.0%	51.2%
Greek name only	121	50	37.5%	23.3%
Semitic name only ..	43	25	13.3%	11.6%
Latin and Greek name	13	22	4.0%	10.2%
Latin and Semitic name	4	8	1.2%	3.7%
Totals[1]	323	215		
Some Latin	158	140	48.9%	67.0%
Some Greek	134	72	41.5%	33.5%
Some Semitic	47	33	14.6%	15.1%

As appears from the foregoing Table, more than five-eighths (67%) of the females but less than one-half (48.9%) of the males had at least one Latin name. While a boy had a better chance than a girl of receiving a Greek name, Latin names were preferred for boys also. With regard to Semitic names there appears to be no significant difference in percentage as between males and females.

The usage with regard to the language of the name varies also according to the catacomb in which the inscription was found. As will appear from Table IV, users of both the Appia and Monteverde catacombs show a strong preference for

---

[1] The totals exclude not only the doubtful names but those of ten persons whose sex cannot be identified from the inscriptions.

Latin names, with the Appia leading somewhat in this respect, while in the Nomentana catacomb the Latin and Greek names are found in almost equal number.

Proportionately, almost twice as many Semitic names are found among the Monteverde communities as in either of the other two groups. To express the facts differently, the Appia catacomb shows a larger percentage of Latin names than any

TABLE IV

Language of Name by Catacomb

	Appia	Monte-verde	Nomen-tana	Appia	Monte-verde	Nomen-tana
Latin name only	116	95	26	50.2%	45.5%	43.3%
Greek name only	73	59	24	31.6%	28.2%	40.0%
Semitic name only	21	35	7	9.1%	16.7%	11.7%
Latin and Greek name	16	13	3	6.9%	6.2%	5.0%
Latin and Semitic name .	5	7	0	2.2%	3.3%	0.0%
Totals[1]	231	209	60			
Some Latin	147	115	29	63.6%	55.0%	48.3%
Some Greek	89	72	27	38.1%	34.3%	45.0%
Some Semitic ...	26	42	7	11.3%	20.1%	11.7%

other (63.6%), the Nomentana the largest percentage of Greek names (45%), and the Monteverde the largest percentage of Semitic names (20.1%). These data will fit in with other evidence pointing to the conclusion that the Appia group included the most Romanized congregations, the Monteverde the most conservative, and the Nomentana the most Hellenized and least Romanized.

The use of single and multiple names also shows certain noteworthy differences as between speakers of Greek and Latin, between the sexes, and between the different catacombs.

---

[1] In addition, there are 48 names in inscriptions of miscellaneous and unknown provenience. These are distributed as follows: Latin 17, Greek 19, Semitic 9, Latin and Greek 3. I have classified as from Monteverde those inscriptions which mention synagogues associated with that catacomb. The Porto inscriptions have been allocated to Monteverde.

While single names include some five-sixths of all the known names, Table V demonstrates that Greek speakers preferred single names in a ratio of about nine-to-one, whereas Latin speakers preferred them by less than two-to-one.

TABLE V

Single and Multiple Names by Language of Inscription

	In Greek Inscrip-tions	In Latin Inscrip-tions	In Greek Inscrip-tions	In Latin Inscrip-tions
Single names........	351	97	89.5%	62.6%
Double names.......	39	50	9.9%	32.3%
Triple names........	2	8	0.5%	5.2%
Totals[1]	392	155		

Double names were used more than three times as often by the Latin speakers as by the Greek speakers. Only two instances of a triple name are found in the Greek inscriptions and one of these is written in Latin characters (284).

An examination of the single and multiple names as used for the two sexes (Table VI) produces the rather unexpected result that girls were three times as likely as boys to receive

TABLE VI

Single and Multiple Names by Sex of Bearer

	Masc.	Fem.	Masc.	Fem.
Single names....... ..	285	153	88.2%	71.2%
Double names....... .	30	60	9.3%	27.9%
Triple names........	8	2	2.5%	0.9%
Totals[2]	323	215		

a double name (27.9% *vs.* 9.3%), although single names were much more commonly used for both sexes. Of the ten triple names, eight were borne by males.

Since we have seen above that girls were more likely than

---

[1] The doubtful names and the bilingual inscription (497) are not included.

[2] The doubtful names and those of doubtful gender are not included.

boys to receive Latin names and it now appears that many more girls than boys had double names after the Roman fashion, it is obvious that many Jewish families followed the practice, not unfamiliar in modern times, of giving their daughters current, fashionable types of name, while reserving the more traditional single Greek names for their sons.

With regard to the three major catacombs (Table VII), the Appia and Monteverde show approximately the same ratio of single and double names, but the Monteverde has six triple names, while only one comes from the Appia. This divergence is somewhat mitigated, however, in that three of Monteverde's triple names belong to members of a single family, the Maecii (470).

TABLE VII

Single and Multiple Names by Catacomb

	Appia	Monteverde	Nomentana	Appia	Monteverde	Nomentana
Single names ...	187	167	52	81.0%	79.9%	86.7%
Double names ..	43	36	8	18.6%	17.2%	13.3%
Triple names ...	1	6	0	0.4%	2.9%	0.0%
Totals	231	209	60			

In the Nomentana catacomb close to nine-tenths of the names are single, another indication that this catacomb represents the least Romanized group.

We may stop to consider at this point the extent to which the Latin names conform to normal Roman practice. As is well known, Roman citizens generally bore three names, consisting of praenomen, gentile name (*nomen gentile* or *gentilicium*) and cognomen, familiar examples being Gaius Julius Caesar, Marcus Tullius Cicero, Titus Flavius Vespasianus. We have seen that very few of the Roman Jews had the three names, and these did not always follow the Roman practice. Entirely Roman in form are such names as Gaius Furfanius Iulianus, Lucius Maecius Victorinus, Quintus Claudius Synesius, Lucius Domitius Abbas. On the other hand, Marcus Quintus Alexus exhibits the abnormality of two praenomina and a cognomen; Tettius Rufinus Melitius has a gentile name followed by two cognomina. It should not be forgotten, however, that by the third century C.E., to which most of our inscriptions probably belong, the Roman customs as regards names had been altered materially from those which prevailed during the Republic and early Empire. When the Roman Jewish male bore two names, these were usually of the type of gentile name plus cognomen, *e.g.*, Aelius Aprilicus, Aelius Primitivus, Aurelius Bassus. Some variants may be noted. In Caelius Quintus we find a *gentilicium* followed by a praenomen; Siculus Sabinus had two cognomina; in the case of Cresces Sinicerius the gentile name and cognomen were reversed, a not uncommon practice among Romans. This last man, however, was a proselyte, so that he received his name before he became a Jew. The single Latin masculine names are in some instances of the type of praenomen (Gaius, Lucius); often they have the *-ius* ending of the gentile name (Caelius, Castricius, Cossutius, Maevius); most often they are of the cognomen type (Aper, Castus, Donatus, Fronto, Maro). Where the compound name consists of a Latin plus a Greek or Semitic element, the Latin regularly precedes (Aurelius Hermias, Caelius Anastasius, Pompeius Eutyches, Claudius Ioses, Lucius Domitius Abbas).

Very few of the women of the Jewish community bore three names, as we have already seen, and the same is true of Roman women, who usually had one or two names, but rarely three. A Roman woman's name was regularly the feminine equivalent of her father's gentile name (*e.g.*, Julia, daughter of Julius Caesar) with or without a second name. The only Jewish women of Rome for whom we have three names are Lucia Maecia Sabbatis (470) and Iulia Irene Arista (72), and we cannot be completely certain that the latter was Jewish. The double names of women, which, as has been demonstrated, are more abundant than those of males, show for the most part the normal form of gentile name in *-ia* as the first element (Aelia Septima, Aurelia Celerina, Claudia Marciana). Sometimes the second name is also of the *gentilicium* type (Aelia Patricia, Aurelia Flavia, Iulia Aemilia). If the woman's other name is Greek or Semitic, it always follows her Latin name (Aelia Alexandria, Aurelia Zotice, Appidia Lea, Aurelia Maria, Titinia Anna). Our only example of a double name both elements of which are non-Latin is that of a man, Tubias Barzaharona (497), whose second name is obviously a patronymic.

The question will naturally arise whether parents tended to give their children names of the same general type as their own. An examination of the names with this point in mind yields the data of Table VIII.

It is apparent that if the father bore a Greek name, the son was more likely to receive a Greek name than any other, while the daughter's name might be in any of the available

TABLE VIII

Language of Father's Name by Language of Childs Name

Name of Father	Name of Son				Name of Daughter			
	Gk.	Lat.	Sem.	Lat.-Gk.	Gk.	Lat.	Sem.	Lat.-Gk.
Greek	10	0	3	1	3	2	2	1
Latin	3	11	3	0	3	7	2	0
Semitic	1	1	1	0	1	2	3	0
Latin and Semitic	0	0	0	1	0	0	0	0

languages; if the father bore a Latin name, the child, whether son or daughter, would more likely receive a Latin name; if the father's name was Semitic, no preference appears in the few available examples. While there are some instances in which the child's name resembles that of the mother, as will be shown below, an examination of the instances in which we have the names of both mother and child reveals no significant data. Where the name of a child and those of both parents are preserved, the child's name, whether of son or daughter, is more likely to resemble the father's name than the mother's. This again is similar to the Roman practice.

It has long been a Jewish custom, still observed among certain groups,[1] not to name a child for a living person and

---

[1] Natalie F. Joffe points out in *The American Family* (published by the National Council of Jewish Women, 1954) p. 16, that the practice of not naming a child for a living relative is observed by East European Jews, but not by those of southern Europe and the Orient.

particularly not for his own father. That the Jews of Rome observed no such rule is apparent in that there are ten instances in which the son's name was identical with his father's:

Amelius (1), Alexander (84), Alexander (85), Asterius (95), Theophilus (119), Castricius (124, 221), Leontius (134), Zabuttas (269), Alypius (502), Iulianus (504)[1]

It is perhaps of incidental interest that in five of the ten cases where the son was named for the father, either the father or both the father and son are recorded as having been officials of their respective synagogues. The daughter's name is the feminine form of her father's in six instances:

Ursacius-Ursacia (147), Trophimus-Trophime (169), Flavius Iulianus-Flavia Iuliana (172), Marcellus-Marcella (248), Valerius-Valeria (267), Alexander-Alexandra (501)

In two cases the son's name is the masculine form of his mother's:

Petronia-Petronius (149), Severa-Severus (264)

It seems noteworthy in these eighteen instances in which the name of the child is identical with or differs only in gender from that of the parent that all are from the Appia catacomb with the exception of four the provenience of which is not known (1, 501, 502, 504). Among the nearly three hundred inscriptions of the Monteverde and Nomentana catacombs there appears not a single certain example of this practice. This may accordingly be reasonably interpreted as an additional indication that the users of the Appia catacomb were more inclined to follow the customs of the Romans, who named sons and daughters for their fathers, than were their correligionists in other parts of the city.

In a few instances, where the father had two names, the son or daughter was given the father's gentile name, as was the Roman usage, but generally with a different cognomen:

---

[1] That of Julianus is probably from the Monteverde catacomb, since both father and son were officials of the Synagogue of the Calcaresians, the members of which used that catacomb.

FATHER	SON	DAUGHTER
Flavius Iulianus (172)		Flavia Iuliana
L. Domitius Abbas (212)		Domitia Felicitas
Pompeius Ionata (259)	Pompeius Eutyches	
L. Maecius (470)	L. Maecius Constantius	Maecia Lucianis
	L. L. Maecius Victorinus	L. Maecia Sabbatis

In four examples the daughter has a first name like her mother's but a different second name:

> Aelia Septima-Aelia Alexandria (208)
> Aurelia Quintilla- Aurelia Protogenia (217)
> Fabia Asia- Fabia Mauria (413)
> Claudia [Bere?]nice — Claudia Marciana (461)

Just one example appears of a boy named for his grandfather:

> Honoratus (146, 145)

Unfortunately, the scarcity of instances of names through three generations prevents our knowing whether or not this was a common practice.[1]

There emerges a rather curious fact in connection with the citing of parents' names on the inscriptions in that, while the Monteverde inscriptions are slightly more numerous than those from the Appia, yet the names of either or both of the parents appear in only half as many instances in the former as compared with the latter. Table IX shows the facts with regard to the three catacombs: (see p. 117)

Just why the users of the Monteverde catacomb should generally have refrained from giving the name of a parent even on the epitaphs of small children is not apparent. It may be that the more Romanized users of the Appia catacomb were imitating the Roman practice of citing the father's

---

[1] The only other inscription which reveals the names of both grandfather and grandson is No. 140, in which Maronius is recorded as the grandson of Alexander.

TABLE IX

Citing of Parents' Names, by Catacombs

	Appia	Monteverde	Nomentana
Both parents	11	3	0
Father only	19	12	4
Mother only	11	6	2
Totals	41	21	6

name. In the Nomentana catacomb, where the inscriptions are usually very brief, the name of the parent is rarely found. As would be expected, when the name of only one parent is given, it is more frequently that of the father. When only the mother's name is cited, it may probably be inferred that the father was already dead.

Besides the name given them at birth, some individuals later acquired an additional name, known as a *signum*.[1] Such a surname may be designated by the term *signo* or, most commonly, by the expression ὁ καί, rendered in Latin as *qui et*. In one instance the Greek term for *signo*, ἐπίκλην, is found, in its usual accusative form. A list of the ten examples from the Roman Jewish community follows.[2] All examples are given in the nominative, regardless of the form which they show in the inscriptions:

Θεοδώ[ρα] ἡ καὶ Γοργόνεις 30
Νεβια Κυρια ἡ καὶ Μαπλικα 47[3]
Ἀμάχις ὁ καὶ Πριμος 86

---

[1] Important articles on the *signum* are Th. Mommsen, "Sallustius = Sallutius und das Signum," *Hermes* 37 (1902), 443-455; E. Diehl, "Das Signum," *Rheinisches Museum* 62 (1907), 390-420; M. Lambertz, "Zur Ausbreitung des Supernomen oder Signum im roemischen Reiche," *Glotta* 4 (1913), 78-143, 5 (1914), 99-170; Kubitschek in Pauly-Wissowa, *RE*, s.v. Signum, cols. 2448-2452.

[2] If Frey's conjecture is correct, the name Isaac in No. 282 is a *signum*. The inscription is, however, so incomplete that one can hardly be sure that the KAI preceding the name is part of the expression ὁ καί, as Frey took it. It may well be the conjunction linking the names of two persons.

[3] Paribeni's reading of the inscription, from a tile found on the floor of the Nomentana catacomb, is not too reliable. In any case, the name Maplica is a very dubious one.

'Ερμειόνη . . . η ινι (= ἡ ἦν or ἥτινι?) ἐπίκλην ΒΑRШΕΟDΑ
108¹
Μαρωνις ὁ κὲ [. . .] ητος 140
'Αλέξανδρος ὁ κὲ Μαθειος 140²
Cocotia qui et Iuda 206
'Ιώνιος ὁ κὲ 'Ακονε 362³
Μόνιμος ὁ καὶ Εὐσαββάτις 379
Leo nomine et signo Leontius 32*⁴

There are two cases in which a proselyte assumed an additional name after adopting Judaism:

Beturia Paulla . . . proselyta . . . nomine Sara 523
Felicitas proselita . . . NVENN (= nomine?) Peregrina 462

These examples of additional names are pretty well distributed among the catacombs. No particular type of name, as far as can be inferred from these few examples, seems to have been favored. Of those cited above, Primus and Peregrinus are Latin; Gorgonis and Leontius are Greek; Matheius, Iuda, Sara, and probably Acone, are Semitic; Eusabbatis is Hellenized Hebrew; Maplica is of dubious reading and interpretation; Barsheoda is garbled and apparently Semitic.

An examination of the individual names shows that the most common single name among males is Judas, which

---

¹ Although Frey, without stating a reason, includes the inscription among those from the Appia, the provenience is not known. The girl's surname is very curious, being written with a mixture of Greek, Latin, and Hebrew characters (see Fig. 32 No. 14). Frey's transcription of the letters of the name is incorrect and his text of the inscription has other errors, although the stone itself was, and is, readily available on a wall of the Sala Giudaica in the Lateran Museum. The letters of the name seem to represent *Barsheoda*, an extraordinary name for a female! Could it be a corruption of Bathsheba? If so, the errors are hard to explain. Frey compares the name *Barsados* on a Palmyraean inscription.

² The *signum* is written ΜΑΕΙΟΥ (genitive), which is presumably the stonecutter's error for ΜΑΘΙΟΥ, probably a Hellenized form of Matthew. The usual form is Ματθαῖος or Μαθθαῖος. In Pape-Benseler's *Woerterbuch der griechischen Eigennamen* the forms Μαθεῖος and Μαθῖος are recorded as appearing on inscriptions.

³ Juster (II, 229) suggests that Ακονε might be either a transcription of הקנה (better הקנא) = the Zealot, or, with more likelihood, it seems to me, some modification of the word *Cohen*.

⁴ For no good reason Frey regards this Monteverde inscription as pagan.

occurs eleven times; a good second is Iustus with nine or ten occurrences;[1] then follow Alexander and Sabbatius (a few of these may be feminine forms) with eight each, Eusebius and Iulianus with seven each. The most frequent feminine name is Maria with eight instances; then come four examples each of Aster and Irene. In the compound names we find Aurelius and Aurelia appearing fifteen times,[2] Flavius or Flavia ten times, Iulius or Iulia nine times, Claudius or Claudia six times, Aelius or Aelia five times. These are all familiar Roman gentile names, particularly associated with the imperial families of the first three centuries of the Empire.[3] One might compare the popularity of *Fürstennamen*, such as Augusta and Charlotte, among the German Jews of the nineteenth century. It is interesting that the name Flavius was favored, although it was the family name of Vespasian and Titus, the conquerors and destroyers of the Jewish nation.[4] There is, however, not one instance of either Vespa-

---

[1] No. 469, a fragment, has IVST [..], which could be either *Iustus* or *Iusta*.

[2] The count will be sixteen if the first Aurelius of the fragmentary No. 218 is part of a double name, as seems likely, since the other name on the inscription, possibly that of this man's son, is Aurelius Crescens.

[3] The view has been expressed (*e.g.*, by Vogelstein, *VR*, 59, and by Juster, II, 221) that such names stemmed from a period when the Jews who first bore them were freedmen who had taken the gentile names of their former masters, as was the custom among the Romans. Thus the name Flavius would go back to freedmen of the imperial house of Flavius, *i.e.*, to prisoners from Palestine after the disaster of 70 C.E. (so Suzanne Collon in *Mélanges d'archéol. et d'hist. de l'École Française de Rome* 57 [1940], 91). This explanation is far from satisfactory, since it seems that several generations separate the period of our names from the time when there were many Jewish slaves in Rome. Besides, it is noteworthy that most of the names of this type are feminine. The best explanation seems to be that the Roman Jews used such names, and especially for their daughters, because they were popular in the Rome of that day. Juster also makes the improbable suggestion that when Caracalla granted Roman citizenship in 212 to the subject peoples throughout the Empire, many Jews took his family name of Aurelius and that this accounts for the frequency of this name among Jews of that time.

[4] One is reminded that the historian Joseph (or Josephus, as he is better known), when he was emancipated by Vespasian, assumed his patron's gentile name of Flavius, prefixing it to a Latinized form of his Jewish name. It is interesting that Josephus (*Vita* 76, 426-427) gave the name Hyrcanus, a name with a good Jewish tradition, to a son by his first wife, but that his two sons by his second wife, whom

sianus or Titus as a name among the Roman Jews. Such a name as Alexandria Severa (144) would most naturally be linked with the time of the Emperor Alexander Severus, who reigned from 221 to 235 and was friendly toward the Jews, but how much reliance one may reasonably place on such names as criteria for dating the inscriptions is hard to determine and will be discussed in a later chapter.

The patriarchal names, which have been favored among Jews of all periods and places, were used very little by the Roman community. It is noteworthy that not one of the some 550 Roman Jews whose names are preserved was named Abraham[1] or Israel, and that we have only one example each of Isaac and Jacob. The name Moses also is entirely absent, unless one regards Museus (474) as a Hellenized equivalent.

While the incidence of Semitic names is small in comparison with the Greek and Latin ones, it is apparent that some names originally Semitic were adapted or even translated so as to conform to the familiar Roman and Greek types. Thus Aster, Mniaseas, Museus, Annia, Sabbatius and Eusabbatis are probably adaptations of Esther, Manasseh, Moses, Anna (Hannah), and Shabbetai, respectively. Such Hellenized forms as Ioses for Joseph and Iudas for Judah were already common even in Palestine. In any case, it is clear that our contemporary process of transmuting Isaac to Irving, Judah to Julius, Moses to Mervin, Rebecca to Rose, and Sarah to Sylvia or Shirley had its close parallel in ancient Rome.

It is quite possible, though far from certain, that names like Dativus and Donatus are translations of Nathan;

---

he took after he settled at Rome, received the pagan names Justus and Simonides, which are Latin and Greek, respectively. The latter acquired in addition the *signum* Agrippa. It should perhaps be observed that the name Justus was common among Jews, while Simonides was the name of one of Josephus' ancestors and can be a patronymic associated with the Hebrew name Simon as well as with the familiar Greek name.

[1] Ferrua (*Civ. Catt.* [1936] III, 471) cites an inscription copied at St. Paul's by Margarini in the seventeenth century which seems to show the name Abraham, but the text is so garbled and incomplete that little can be made of it. If we may trust Frey's index, the only occurrence of the name Abraham among the ancient inscriptions from Europe is on a Greek epitaph from Macedonia (*CII* 693).

Gaudentius, Gelasius, and Hilarus of Isaac; Theodotus and Theodorus of Jonathan; Iustus and Probus of Zadok; Vitalio, Zosimus, and Zoticus of Chayim; Theophilus of Jochanan; Irene and Irenaeus of Shelomith and Solomon, respectively; Regina of Malcah; Dulcitia and Dulcia of Naomi; while Felicissima and Felicitas may even represent Simchah. In view, however, of the general ignorance of Hebrew in the community, it may well be that most Jewish parents who gave their son a name like Theodotus or called their daughter Irene had no Hebrew equivalent in mind. There is, in fact, no evidence that the custom which still prevails among Jews of assigning to a child a Hebrew name from which the official name is supposed to stem was practiced among the Jews of Rome.

It may seem a trifle amusing that a monotheistic group should have tolerated names associated with pagan deities. Obviously those Jewish parents who gave their children such theophorous names as Aphrodisia, Asclepiodote, Dionysias, Diophatus, Hermias, Hermogenes, Iovinus, Isidora, and Zenodora gave little or no thought to the literal meanings of these names. They used them because they were the mode in that environment. Similarly, modern Jews who name their children Gregory, Jerome, Lawrence, Stephen, Barbara, Patricia, or Catherine do not connect these names with the Christian saints from whom their popularity springs.

Our analysis of the names makes it quite apparent that in this respect, at least, the Jews of ancient Rome had gone far toward integration with their pagan neighbors. The preference for good Latin names, the adoption of compound names after the Roman manner, the naming of sons for their fathers, even the use of names associated with pagan gods, all indicate an adaptation to the mores of the majority group. It is clear also that girls in particular were given names fashionable in the non-Jewish environment, and that the users of the Appia catacomb were the most Romanized in their names as well as in their language and in other matters.

CHAPTER SIX

THE SEPULCHRAL FORMULAS AND EPITHETS

A cursory reading of the epitaphs reveals that most of them begin and end with standard formulas which recur in an almost unvarying uniformity. This is true especially of the Greek inscriptions, which regularly begin with a "Here lies" expression and end with the formula "In peace be his (her, their, your) sleep." It will be desirable to examine these formulas closely, in order to see what variants are offered and to discover any significant differences that may appear in connection with the several catacombs.

The standard opening formula is ἐνθάδε κεῖται with its variant spellings.[1] Instead of ἐνθάδε there are four instances of ἔνθα and twelve of ὧδε. Occasionally the third person of the verb is replaced by the first person (κεῖμαι).[2] Once the verb κατάκιτε is found instead of the simple verb (382).[3] In several instances the formula appears at or near the end of the inscription instead of at the beginning.[4]

The closing formula is normally ἐν εἰρήνη[5] ἡ κοίμησις αὐτοῦ (αὐτῆς, αὐτῶν) with the not infrequent variant in the second person (σου).[6] Often the article ἡ is omitted, probably by haplography, since the preceding word εἰρήνη ends in "H", so that one "H" was unintentionally left out. Sometimes the final genitive is omitted, usually because not enough space

---

[1] See above, Chap. IV, p. 85 and note 2.

[2] Examples of ἔνθα: 296, 501, 513, 733b; of ὧδε: 25, 37, 55, 79, 120, 129, 147, 167, 357, 502, 510. 537; of κεῖμαι: 37, 118, 358.

[3] Perhaps also in the fragment, *CII* 426, where the letters TAK are regarded by Frey (and also by Müller) as part of this verb.

[4] At the end: 45, 47, 298, 324, 348, 502, 537; near the end: 37, 358.

[5] Actually, the iota subscript never appears in these inscriptions, but the transcriptions are presented with the standard classical forms except where it seems desirable to reproduce the exact spellings of the inscriptions themselves.

[6] In the Jewish catacomb of Venosa, which is a century or two later than those of Rome, we find this formula expressed in its Hebrew equivalent as שלום על משכבו (see *JQR*, 44 [1954], 282).

was left for it. Lack of space also accounts for the abridgment of the formula to a simple ἐν εἰρήνῃ.

Although many of the more than four hundred Greek inscriptions are in such condition that either the beginning or the end or even both are lost, I have counted 294 which show one or both of these formulas, and of only 34 can we be certain that they had neither formula. The number of inscriptions showing both is 112, as compared with 88 of which we can say with confidence that they had one without the other. The following list will make the distribution clear:

Total usable inscriptions	328
ἐνθάδε κεῖται	239
ἐν εἰρήνῃ	167
Both formulas	112
ἐνθάδε κεῖται without the other	72
ἐν εἰρήνῃ without the other	16
One or both formulas	294 (239 + 167 − 112)
Neither formula	34

It appears that of the 328 Greek inscriptions which are well enough preserved to be counted in this connection, about three-fourths begin with the standard "Here lies" formula, while a lesser number, slightly over half, end with the "peace" formula. Close to nine-tenths have either or both formulas, leaving hardly more than one in ten that have neither.

While the general pattern for the community in the use of these sepulchral formulas has been established, a separation by catacombs reveals certain differences in usage, whatever may be the significance of these differences. The following Table presents the data:

Use of Formulas by Catacombs

	Appia	Monte-verde	Nomen-tana	Others
Total usable inscriptions	101	138	49	40
ἐνθάδε κεῖται	49	120	40	30
ἐν εἰρήνῃ	68	64	17	18
Both formulas	32	57	12	11
ἐνθάδε κεῖται without the other	6	46	11	9
ἐν εἰρήνῃ without the other	15	0	0	1
One or both formulas	85	127	45	37
Neither formula	16	11	4	3

The curious fact is revealed that, although users of the Monteverde catacomb omitted the opening formula in only one-eighth of the instances, the Appia users omitted it more than half the time. On the other hand, while more than half of the Monteverde epitaphs left off the closing formula, fewer than one-third of the Appia epitaphs failed to include it. In fact, such was the preference of the Monteverde users for the first of these formulas that while they might often omit the second one, they seem never to have omitted the "Here lies" formula, that is, if they used any formula at all. Why the Appia users, who represented the more Romanized and perhaps more liberalized elements of Roman Jewry, should have been much more partial to the wish that the deceased should sleep peacefully, whereas the more conservative Monteverde groups stuck to the opening formula and were not so particular about the other, is hardly evident. It may be that the conservative members tended to adhere to the traditional pattern for commencing an epitaph. Among the even less assimilated users of the Nomentana catacomb, with its fewer inscriptions, the results resemble those from Monteverde. Fewer than one-fifth omitted the opening formula, but nearly two-thirds left off the closing one. In many instances this may have been due to lack of space, since the epitaphs were painted or scratched on the limited area of the closure of the loculus, a factor which would not apply at Monteverde, where marble slabs were generally used. It is at Monteverde, incidentally, that we find the largest proportion of inscriptions with both formulas and the smallest with neither, perhaps an additional indication of both conservatism and sufficiency of space. The Appia, on the other hand, shows the largest number omitting both formulas. The group of miscellaneous inscriptions, mostly of unknown source, shows a distribution similar to that of Monteverde, an indication that most of these probably originated in that catacomb, as has already been noted, rather than in the Appia. Very few, if any, of them are likely to be from the Nomentana, since its inscriptions were, as we have seen, with few exceptions executed directly on the stuccoed closures.

In this connection, the Appia inscriptions show another strange departure from the practice elsewhere in that they manifest in the concluding formula a strong preference for the second person of the pronoun over the third, as the following brief tabulation will demonstrate:

	Appia	Monte-verde	Nomen-tana	Others
Third person (αὐτοῦ, αὐτῆς, αὐτῶν)	21	40	8	12
Second person (σου)[1]	34	3	2	1

In the Appia the second person prevails by a proportion of more than three-to-two, whereas elsewhere the third person is preferred by ten-to-one (60-to-6).

Besides the two common formulas which have been discussed, others appear sporadically. Two (365, 390) end in the imperative verb form κοιμάσθω (= let him sleep) instead of the usual noun construction with κοίμησις. There is a single (124) substitution of κοίτη (= bed) for κοίμησις. In seven cases the wish is expressed that the deceased will rest among the just or pious, probably representing the Hebrew עם הצדיקים. This phrase is rendered in Greek either as μετὰ τῶν δικαίων (110, 118, 150, 193, 281) or as μετὰ τῶν ὁσίων (55, 340). It is sometimes substituted for ἐν εἰρήνῃ in the closing formula (110, 118, 340); twice it is preceded by the expression καλῶς κομοῦ (150) or κοιμοῦ (281), both for κοιμῶ, with the meaning "sleep well." In a unique instance (193) the preceding expression is μιμησω πατερ, in which the strange verb form is perhaps meant as a passive imperative or a future passive of μιμνήσκω, producing the meaning "be remembered (or, you will be remembered), father, among the just."[2] In one inscription (55) the phrase μετὰ τῶν ὁσίων is appended to the complete ἐν εἰρήνῃ formula, so that it becomes a prayer that the deceased will sleep in peace among the pious. Peculiar is προσεύχοιο ἐν εἰρήνῃ τὴν κύμησιν αὐτοῦ (126 = "may you pray that in peace be his sleep").

---

[1] Once (92) the plural ὑμῶν occurs, also in an Appia inscription.
[2] Ferrua (*Epigraphica* 3 [1941], 34), following Vaccari (*Biblica* 19 [1938], 342), thinks that μιμησω is for μνήμη σου (may your memory be..."), while Frey (*ad loc.*) suggests the imperative μέμνησο with *active* meaning ("souviens-toi"). There is a lacuna between πατερ and των δικαιων. It would be easy to supply μετά, were it not that the final letter of the gap looks like a trace of an "N" rather than an "A." Frey proposes [μετὰ παντω]ν.

The word for "blessing," εὐλογία (= ברכה) is found five times in various combinations. One Nomentana inscription (25) ends with the isolated word ευλογιαν, there being no room for a complete phrase.[1] Twice in the Appia catacomb (173, 204) we find εὐλογία πᾶσι, (a blessing to all).[2] The biblical aphorism, "The memory of the righteous shall be for a blessing" (Prov. 10.7, זכר צדיק לברכה) appears twice (86, 370) as μνήμη (or μνεία) δικαίου εἰς εὐλογίαν. In the former instance the quotation is followed by οὗ ἀληθῆ τὰ ἐνκώμια (the praises of whom [i.e., the righteous] are truthful).

The word μνήμη or its variant μνεία (usually written μνια) is found also in other combinations. The passage from Proverbs cited above is rendered once (201) as μνήμη δικαίου σὺν ἐνκωμίῳ. This rendering is closer to the Septuagint version, which reads μνήμη δικαίων μετ᾽ ἐγκωμίων, whereas the other is a reproduction of the version of Aquila. Twice (148, 343) the word μνεία is followed by a genitive and nothing further, intended perhaps as an abbreviated form of the full phrase with εἰς εὐλογίαν. In No. 119 the incomplete MNIA ΣΟ represents either the abridged expression (i.e., μνεία σοῦ) or the first part of the complete formula. There is no way of telling how much is lost.

Quaint to us is the formula θάρσει οὐδεὶς ἀθάνατος = "Be of good courage; no one is immortal." It is found not only in pagan and Christian epitaphs[3] but also on five inscriptions of the Jews of Rome. The dead Gaudentia, nineteen-year-old daughter of Oclatius (314), is thus encouraged by her bereaved but unnamed husband. The same formula comforts the "innocent youth" Nicodemus, archon of the Siburesians, who died, beloved by all, at the age of thirty (380). The words are especially pathetic as applied to the infant Samuel, whose life ended at the tender age of one year and five months (401),

---

[1] Frey failed to see the final two letters, which stand beneath the last two letters of ΕΥΛΟΓΙ.

[2] In No. 204, ευλογεια πασιν is interpreted by Frey as εὐλογεῖ ἄπασιν, in which he takes the first word as a verb and interprets the expression as meaning "He (i.e., the deceased) wishes a blessing to all," a curious distortion of a familiar phrase.

[3] For a full discussion of this formula see Marcel Simon's "Θάρσει οὐδεὶς ἀθάνατος. Étude de vocabulaire religieux," Rev. de l'hist. des religions 113 (1936), 188-206.

and to the child Euphrasius, aged three years and ten months (335).[1] Samuel's epitaph, crudely carved and marred by misspellings, is embellished with a representation of the Ark of the Law flanked by two Menorahs (Fig. 34),[2] an indication possibly of the faith of his parents that this infant, though not exempt from mortality, would live again in the light of Judaism. The same spirit of encouragement in the face of the tragedy of death is shown by the use of single words of cheer, as θάρσι (123 = be of good courage),[3] εὐψύχι, εὐφρόνι (303 = be of good spirit, be of good cheer), this to a child of two years and four months, and εὐψύχι followed by μετὰ τῶν δικέων (110 = be of good spirit among the righteous).[4] One inscription (337) starts with the comforting idea that the grave is the "house of eternity" (οἶκος αἰώνιος = בית עולם).

Occasionally, in addition to the more-or-less standardized formulas, one encounters individualized expressions of devotion or sorrow. The devoted husband of Julia Aemilia, who died at forty, after appealing to her to be of good courage (θάρσι), adds "You lived a good life with your husband. I am grateful to you for your thoughtfulness and your soul" (123). Lucilla, a faithful wife, is described as "the glory of Sophronius, a woman highly praised" (135).[5] Quite unique in our collection is the epitaph which Theodotus set up to his four-year-old foster son, Justus (358). In a poetic style, which shows traces of dactylic rhythm, he pours forth his affections: "Would that I who reared you, Justus, my child, were able to place you in a golden coffin. Now, O Lord, vouchsafe in Thy righteous judgment that Justus, a peerless child, may sleep in peace."

---

[1] The only other example of this formula is in the fragment of a marble slab (450) of which hardly anything is left except for the formula. Incidentally, the verb of the formula appears either as θαρρει (335, 380, 401) or as θαρσει (314, 450), each with variant spellings.

[2] See also *CII*, p. 310 and Goodenough, *Jewish Symbols*, III, 706.

[3] Possibly the חזק of Hebrew epitaphs represents the equivalent of θάρσει (cf. *CII*, II, 1397).

[4] The verbs εὐψύχει and εὐφρόνει are found elsewhere instead of θάρσει in the combination with οὐδεὶς ἀθάνατος. *Vid.* Simon, *op. cit.* (above, p. 126, n. 3), 188.

[5] In T. B. L. Webster's virtually certain reconstruction of No. 118, a grieving wife alludes to her dead husband as ἀτμνηστος, "ever to be remembered." *Vid. JRS*, 19 (1929), 151.

As is usual in sepulchral inscriptions, there are various adjectives denoting affection. Such are ἀγαπητός, beloved (43, 125, 137); γλυκύς, sweet (358, 379), with its very frequent superlative γλυκύτατος (1, 84?,[1] 85, 96, 141, 145, 155, 169, 358, 424); and once (126), with the same meaning, ἡδύς. There are numerous allusions to the uprightness, piety, and other praiseworthy qualities of the deceased, expressed by such epithets as ἄξιος, worthy (36, 96, 110); σπουδέα, virtuous (132); ἄμεμπτος (93, 154?)[2] and ἄμμωμος (1), without reproach; ἀμίαντος, without stain (193); ἀσύνκριτος, without peer (130, 149, 358); ἀβλαβής,[3] innocent (380); δίκαιος, righteous (321, 363); and the very common ὅσιος, pious; πᾶσι φειλητός, beloved by all (380); πάντων φίλος καὶ γνωστὸς πᾶσι, friend of all and known to all (118). Besides the frequent ὅσιος there are more emphatic references to piety in such expressions as *theosebes* (Greek word in a Latin inscription), God-fearing (228);[4] and adjectives compounded with φιλο-, as φιλόνομος, lover of the Law (111); and φιλέντολος, lover of the Commandments (132, 203?,[5] 509). Loyalty to the group is expressed by φιλόλαος, lover of his people (203, 509), and φιλοσυνάγωγος, lover of his synagogue (321); and one charitable person is characterized as φιλοπένης, lover of the poor (203).

An individual's good life is often indicated by the phrase καλῶς βιώσας or καλῶς ζήσας (or ἔζησεν), having lived a good life. Cattia Ammias, a grandmother, lived both a good life

---

[1] In No. 84 only the letters ΓΛΥ of the adjective are preserved. The superlative γλυκύτατος seems to have been favored in the Appia, since all but two of the examples are from that catacomb.

[2] In No. 154 the letters appear to be AMEM, which Frey reasonably interprets as an abbreviation of ἄμεμπτος.

[3] The word αβλαβι has been misinterpreted by sundry scholars (including Frey) as a proper name. Since the young man's name was Nicodemus, the word αβλαβι, inserted as it is between θαρι and ουδεις αθανατος, is undoubtedly a vocative from ἀβλαβής. The correct form would, to be sure, be ἀβλαβές, but since the nominative would have been pronounced in less cultivated circles as ἀβλαβίς (see above, pp. 80 f.), the vocative was assimilated to that of words ending in -ις.

[4] Frey strangely takes the word as part of the woman's name, calling her *Eparchia Theosebes*.

[5] In No. 203 only the letters ΦΙΛ..ΟΣ of the word are preserved, but since it comes between φιλολαος and φιλοπενης, the reconstruction φιλ[εντολ]ος is plausible.

and a Jewish one (537: καλῶς βιώσασα ἐν τῷ 'Ιουδαϊσμῷ); and the gerusiarch Julianus lived his life on good terms with everybody (353: καλῶς βιώσας μετὰ πάντων), an enviable record for a synagogue official. Theophilus the gerusiarch not only lived a good life but also had a good reputation (119: καλῶς βιώσας καὶ καλῶς ἀκούσας). The only quotable inscription from the possibly Jewish catacomb of Via Appia Pignatelli is the epitaph of an old soldier, Rufinus (79), who met a good death (καλῶς ἀποθανών) at sixty-nine after a military career.

Devotion to members of one's family, as to one's husband, parents, children, brothers, is most frequently expressed by φιλο- compounds. Examples are φίλανδρος, devoted to her husband (158, 166, 195); φιλοπάτωρ (125, 505) or φιλοπάτορος (152), devoted to his father; φιλομήτορος (152), devoted to his mother; the last two epithets being applied to the child Probus, aged two years, one month, three days, who loved both his father and his mother. Other adjectives of this type are φιλότεκνος (321, 363), devoted to his or her children; φιλαδελφῶν (321, 363) or φιλάδελφος (125), devoted to one's brothers. The ill-fated little boys, Fortunatus and Eutropius (418), who died on the same day, aged three years and four months and three years and seven months, respectively, are pathetically characterized as "little children who loved each other" (νήπιοι φιλοῦντες ἀλλήλους).

The loyalty of a widow to the memory of her deceased husband is indicated in the epithet μόνανδρος (81, 392), wife of only one husband. Father Frey maintained[1] that only on Christian epitaphs does this adjective indicate a widow who did not remarry, whereas in connection with pagans and Jews, among whom divorce was common, the epithet indicates that the woman was not a divorcée, and so had only one husband. This is a thoroughly improbable interpretation, since, in the first place, there is no evidence that divorce was common among the Jews of this period and, in the second place, it would be very unlikely in any case that the fact that a woman was never divorced would be recorded on her tomb as a special virtue. Since it was a common practice

---

[1] "La signification des termes MONANΔΡΟΣ et Univira," *Recherches de Science Religieux* 20 (1930), 48-60. Cf. Ferrua (who disagrees with Frey) in *Civ. Catt* (1936) IV, 302.

among Jews for widows to remarry, it was apparently regarded as a noteworthy mark of devotion to her dead husband if a widow did not take another husband.

In one inscription (319) a certain Irene is described as the παρθενικὴ σύμβιος, virgin wife, of Clodius, an indication that he took her as his bride when she was a virgin. Frey (ad loc.) thinks that the phrase means that it was the first marriage for both parties, who remained together until separated by death, but there seems to be no reason for taking it in this mutual sense. In a fragmentary inscription (81) the epithet παρθενικός (only ΠΑΡΘΕ is preserved) seems to be used of the husband who was married for the first time. This appears also to be the meaning of the word virginiun (for virginio) in a Latin inscription (242).

The Latin inscriptions differ from the Greek in that they show no standard formula at either beginning or end. After the pagan Roman fashion, they normally offer the name of the deceased in the dative case, the name of the survivor who set up the inscription in the nominative, and the verb fecit (e.g., Nikete proselyto digno et benemerenti Dionysias patrona fecit, 256). Sometimes posuit is found instead of fecit[1] and often the verb is omitted altogether. Either the nominative or the dative comes first, the former being preferred. The relationship between survivor and deceased is commonly indicated and there may be a statement of age at death, usually with the words qui (quae) vixit followed by the number of the years. In the Appia catacomb the sequence of nominative of survivor, dative of deceased, followed by fecit, is the commonest pattern, but this form is found in the other catacombs also. The participial adjective benemerenti (literally, "well-deserving," but approximately the equivalent of our "in grateful memory") is often included.

Epithets and formulaic expressions are much less frequent and less varied in the Latin inscriptions than in the Greek. By far the most commonly found is the above-mentioned benemerenti, which occurs at least 36 times. This adjective, which is extremely frequent also in pagan and Christian

---

[1] The following have posuit: 217, 260 (also posuerut for posuerunt,) 484, 489. Occasionally the first person of the verb is found: e.g. feci (270), φηκι (102, 239), ΠΟΕΥΕΙ for ποσυει = posui (484).

inscriptions, had become so stereotyped that it was often abbreviated.[1] The Latin equivalent of ἐνθάδε κεῖται is found in only two instances,[2] once as *hic posita* (228) and once as *hic est positus* (497), the latter being in a Greek-Latin bilingual in which the Latin version is a translation of the Greek. The ἐν εἰρήνῃ type of formula is rarely imitated in the Latin. Once (458) it appears as *quiecet* (for *quiescit*) *in pace*, and once (477) the phrase *in pace* is found without a verb (*Sabbatius in pace*). Usually, however, the *in pace* formula is the mark of a Christian inscription. The concept of sleeping with the righteous which, as we have seen, occurs several times in the Greek inscriptions, appears in four Latin inscriptions, usually in the form *dormitio tua in bonis*[3] (212, 228, 250), but once (210), with transliteration of a Greek word, as *dormitio tua inter dicaeis*.

Of epithets denoting affection the most frequent are *dulcissimus* with seven examples and *carissimus* with four.[4] *Desiderantissimus* (greatly missed), which is fairly common in pagan inscriptions, is found only once (35*).[5] The fine character of the deceased is indicated by such adjectives as *optimus* (218), *incomparabilis* (243, 457), the equivalent of ἀσύνκριτος, and *sanctissimus*, once only (233), though common in pagan

---

[1] These abbreviations occur: B.M. (215, 217, 470), BNM (209), BEN.ME (30*), BENEMERT (208).

[2] The Jews of Venosa (ancient Venusia), on the contrary, generally began their Latin epitaphs with *hic pausat* or *hic quiescit* (or *requiescit*). *Vid. JQR*, 44 (1954), 282. Outside of Rome Jews frequently used the beginning formula *hic requiescit in pace* (e.g., *CII* 558, 559, 644, 645, 646, 670).

[3] At least, this is the form in the only complete example (250). In No. 228 De Rossi claimed to have read *in bono* on a portion of the stone which is now missing. On the basis of this instance Frey reconstructs the missing part of 212 as *in b[ono]*, but in view of 250 and 210 and the use of the plural in the equivalent Greek expression (μετὰ τῶν δικαίων), the plural *in bonis* seems more likely.

[4] Examples of *dulcissimus*: 68 (abbrev. *dul.*), 222, 230, 264, 267, 273, 457; of *carissimus* (sometimes spelled *karissimus*): 208, 217, 231 (*carimo*), 248. It is noteworthy that nine of these eleven examples are from the Appia. Cf. p. 128, n. 1, above, where it is pointed out that nearly all the Greek adjectives of this kind appear in this same catacomb. I can suggest no explanation other than that certain groups preferred certain forms of expression.

[5] Frey lists this as a pagan inscription, but without sufficient reason, since it was found in the Monteverde catacomb.

inscriptions. The butcher Alexander, who died at thirty, is described as "a good soul, the friend of everybody" (210: *anima bona omniorum amicus*); the child Impendius, whose death came a few weeks after his third birthday, was an "innocent soul" (466: *anima innox*); the proselyte Nicetas was both "worthy and well-deserving" (256: *digno et bene-merenti*); Aurelia Celerina was "a good wife and a good pupil" (215, Latin in Greek letters: κοζουγι βοναι ετ δισκειπουλειναι βοναι) in the seventeen years which she lived with her husband, Sempronius Basileus; Marcia is described with eloquent simplicity as "a good Jewess" (250: *bona Iudea*); Abundantius, dead at nineteen, had grown up and worked with (206: *concresconio et conlaboronio*) his bereaved brother, Cocotia; the peerless husband, Aelius Primitivus, archon presumptive, died at thirty-eight after sixteen years of married life "without ever a complaint" (457: *sine ulla querela*), if we may trust the testimony of his loving widow, Flavia Maria. The expression *sine ulla querela* is found so frequently on pagan sepulchral inscriptions as a stereotyped expression that its sincerity may be suspect at times, but in the present instance the epitaph seems to have a tone of genuineness.

If the sarcophagus of Julia Irene Arista, now at Palazzo Spada (Fig. 31), is really that of a Jewess,[1] she was a pious woman "who scrupulously observed the Jewish Law" (72: *iuste legem colenti*). In a few instances the merit of the deceased is brought out by an effective play on words. Benedicta Maria, mother and nurse, is described, with an allusion to her name, as *vere benedicte*, "truly blessed" (459). A grieving husband, whose wife, Gargilia Eufraxia, passed away at nineteen, inscribed an epitaph to her as *bene merenti set sic non merenti*, "deserving well but not deserving this" (237).

Several epitaphs are more distinctive in their sentiments. The grief-stricken mother of the proselyte Cresces Sinicerius (68), who died at the age of thirty-five, gives vent to her sorrow in these words: "His mother did for her sweet son that which he should have done for me" (*mat. dul. flu. suo. fec. qud. ips. mihi deb. facere* ≡ *mater dulcissimo filio suo fecit quod ipse mihi debuit facere*).While this thought is found not

---

[1] See above, p. 106, note 3.

infrequently in pagan epitaphs, it still conveys what seems to be a genuine message of grief. Julia Afrodisia, after memorializing her husband, Aurelius Hermias (220), in the usual stereotyped form, adds these touching words: "And she asks and begs that a place be reserved for her so that she may be placed beside her husband when the time comes" (*et petit et rogat uti loc. ei reservetur ut cum coiuge suo ponatur quam donec*). Veturia Paulla, who became a proselyte to Judaism at the age of seventy and died at eighty-six, is described as "consigned to her eternal home" (523: *domi heternae quostituta* [for *consituta*]), an expression corresponding to the Greek οἶκος αἰώνιος, which was noted above.

Decidedly original is the sarcastic tone of an inscription found in the Monteverde catacomb (32*): "Friends, I await you here. Leo is my name and Leontius my surname." (*Amici, ego vos hic exspecto, Leo nomine et signo Leontius.*) So shocked was Father Frey at the voicing of so ironic and flippant a sentiment amid the consistent solemnity of the Jewish epitaphs that he decided that it must be a pagan inscription which had somehow found its way into a Jewish catacomb. But could there not have been this one Jew who took a cynical view of death and dared to express it on his tombstone? In the same spirit is the recent epitaph of an Englishman bearing the words: "Cheerio. See you soon." (*Time*, July 7, 1952).

In a class by itself is the Monteverde epitaph of Regina (476), whose husband immortalized her memory in a poem consisting of thirteen dactylic hexameter lines, composed with substantially correct meter and syntax[1] and offering the longest and most elaborate of all the inscriptions hitherto found in the Jewish catacombs (Fig. 33). Alluding to their mutual love through more than twenty years of married life, the sorrowing husband expresses his confidence that Regina will live again in the eternal home promised to the worthy and pious and assured in her case by her piety, her pure life, her love for her people, her faithful observance of

---

[1] There are a few minor deviations from good form: In line 3, the reflexive *secum* is wrongly used for *cum eo*; in line 5, the final syllable of *victura* is wrongly to be scanned as long; in line 6, the *quod* clause with *sperare* differs from the classical use of accusative with future infinitive, although the *quod* construction becomes common at a later period.

the (Jewish) Law, her devotion to her husband, and concludes with the assertion that his faith in her immortality is the husband's comfort in his grief.[1]

These sentiments of sorrow and affection, inscribed by Jews seventeen or more centuries ago, give us some insight into their emotions when stricken by the loss of those dearest to them. While most refrained from expressing their feelings on the epitaphs, yet those few who did have left us a touching memorial of devotion and tenderness.

---

[1] For more on this inscription see below, pp. 248 f.

Addendum: In five Greek inscriptions (283, 292, 296, 319, 497) we find the Hebrew word שלום (peace); two (293, 397) have שלום על ישראל (peace on Israel); one (349) has ישראל alone.

CHAPTER SEVEN

THE SYNAGOGUES OF ANCIENT ROME

When the philosopher Philo came to Rome at the end of the brief and arbitrary reign of the crack-brained Emperor Gaius (37-41 C.E.) as the head of an embassy of Alexandrian Jews protesting against the mistreatment of the Jewish community of that city by its Greek inhabitants, he found that Rome had a large Jewish population, occupying a considerable portion of the Transtiberine section (the modern Trastevere), the region on the right bank of the river across from the principal areas of the city (*Legatio* 23. 155). How large the Jewish community was at that time can only be conjectured. From the statement in Josephus (*BJ* 2. 6. 1. 80; *AJ* 17. 11. 1. 300) that eight thousand Roman Jews supported the petition of an embassy of Palestinian Jews to the Emperor Augustus in 4 B.C.E., historians have estimated that there must have been from forty thousand to fifty thousand Jews in Rome at that time in order to produce so large a number of men, presumably all mature and more or less able-bodied.[1] It is, of course, entirely possible that Josephus exaggerated the figure, as ancient historians not uncommonly did, especially when they dealt with thousands, but even so there is much to substantiate the estimate that the Jews of Rome numbered their tens of thousands. The statement in Tacitus (*Ann.* 2. 85. 4) that

---

[1] Vogelstein (*VR*, 38) had estimated the Jewish population of Rome in the early Empire at 40,000, stating that this was a conservative figure (*kaum zu hoch*), but in his more recent work (*Jews of Rome* [Philadelphia, 1940], 17) he reduced this to 20,000 without stating the reason for his change of opinion. Most other scholars accept an estimate of 40,000 to 50,000, while Juster (I, 209) makes it even higher, 50,000 to 60,000 in the time of Tiberius. Recently Solomon Grayzel (*History of the Jews* [Philadelphia, 1947], 140) has concurred with the figure of 50,000. He and others have estimated that the total number of Jews in the Roman Empire at this time was from six to seven million. In addition, there were perhaps a million in Babylonia. While the disastrous revolts under Trajan and Hadrian substantially reduced the Jewish population in the Empire, there was probably no material effect on the numbers of Jews in Rome.

in 19 C.E. some four thousand young men of military age (eighteen to forty-five), most of whom, if not all, were Jews, were sent off for military service in Sardinia would also point to a population of perhaps fifty thousand from which this large number could be drafted. To reinforce these data from the historical sources we have the incontrovertible evidence of the catacombs with their many thousands of tombs, several hundred inscriptions, and, most important, the names of no fewer than eleven different synagogues or congregations.[1]

It may be regarded as reasonably certain that the earliest substantial Jewish settlement was in the Transtiberinum (Augustus' Fourteenth Region) on the right bank of the Tiber and that the bulk of the Jewish population was concentrated in that area throughout the ancient period and even into the Middle Ages. It is the region mentioned by Philo as the Jewish quarter, the chief Jewish cemetery (that of Monteverde) was just outside this area, and some seven Jewish congregations appear to have had their headquarters within its confines.

It is abundantly clear from the literary sources that the Transtiberinum was the chief foreign quarter of the city, a district characterized by narrow, crowded streets, towering tenement houses, teeming with population. References in Martial, Juvenal, and other writers attest to the unsavory character of the area, to the snake charmers, the fortune tellers, the noisy vendors of salt fish, hot peas, and steaming sausages, the peddlers and petty merchants that thronged its streets. Here were the miserable quarters of the poor, unassimilated, immigrant population, wretchedly housed in vast tenement blocks, perhaps hundreds to a building, as in the poorer quarters of Rome or Naples in our day, subject

---

[1] Among the more important discussions of the Jewish community and its synagogues are the following: George La Piana, "Foreign Groups in Rome during the First Centuries of the Empire," *HTR* 20 (1927), 183-403, especially 341-371; J. B. Frey, "Les communautés juives à Rome aux premiers temps de l'Église," *Recherches de Science Religieuse* 20 (1930), 267-297, and in *CII*, pp. LXVIII-LXXXI; Arnaldo Momigliano, "I nomi delle prime 'synagoghe' romane e la condizione giuridica delle communità in Roma sotto Augusto," *Rassegna Mensile di Israël* 6 (1931-2), 283-292; Suzanne Collon, "Remarques sur les quartiers juifs de la Rome antique," *Mélanges d'Archéologie et d'Histoire de l'École Française de Rome* 57 (1940), 72-94.

to the perils of fire, building collapse, and the not infrequent floods of the Tiber. The slopes of the Janiculum, rising from the Transtiberine valley, were occupied by the fine mansions and gardens of the wealthy, offering a vivid contrast to the humble dwellings of those who had to struggle to make their living. We are not to suppose that all the Jews of this quarter lived under such unwholesome conditions. The richly decorated family tomb chambers of the catacombs, the finely carved sarcophagi, the marble slabs engraved by skillful stonecutters, indicate that there were some prosperous Jews who lived under comfortable circumstances. It is a familiar fact that in the Middle Ages there were magnificent palaces of the nobles in the midst of the lowly hovels of this sector, and so it may well have been in ancient times. But on the whole, it seems that the Transtiberine Jews were a humble folk, occupying a low place on the economic ladder.

As the numbers of the Jews in Rome grew—there was probably a large increase after the fall of Jerusalem in 70 C.E.— they began to make their homes in other quarters of the city: the Subura, a crowded district on the slopes of the Esquiline in the eastern part of Rome, and the Campus Martius along the left bank of the Tiber, and doubtless in other areas about which we have no record. From Juvenal (3.12-16) we gather that there was some sort of encampment of Jews in the Grove of Egeria off the Via Appia outside the Porta Capena, but to state, with some of the modern authorities,[1] that this was one of the permanent Jewish quarters seems a mistake, since the satirist clearly refers to a settlement of beggarly vagrants, whose sole household equipment was a basket and a bundle of hay (3. 14: *quorum cophinus faenusque supellex*).

While we may assume that there were Jews who lived outside the three quarters (Transtiberinum, Subura, Campus Martius) about which we may be reasonably certain, it is

---

[1] Vogelstein (*VR*, 48), following a suggestion by Mommsen, went so far as to locate a synagogue there. La Piana (*op. cit.*, 221) thought that the largest Jewish community was that outside Porta Capena, and Momigliano (*op. cit.*, 290) called it one of the largest. P. Romanelli (*Bull. Assoc. Arch. di Roma* 2 [1912], 137) noted that the Jewish quarter of Porta Capena, situated as it was on a major traffic artery, the Via Appia, was favorably located for business.

hardly wise to place them in specific areas on the basis of the doubtful interpretation of perhaps a single inscription or an unverified tradition. Thus a Jewish community has been established on the Caelian Hill in the area of the church of S. Stefano Rotondo because of the epitaph (210) of a certain Jewish butcher, Alexander, at the market (de macello).[1] It seems to me rash to conclude that the macellum mentioned in the inscription must be the Macellum Magnum of the Caelian. Could it not have been some Jewish market the site of which is not known to us? Jews have been conjecturally placed also on the Aventine[2] because of a tradition that the church of S. Prisca is on the site of the house of Aquila and Priscilla (or Prisca), a Jewish couple who became Christians and were faithful followers of Paul (Acts 18. 2; Rom. 16. 3). The discovery in 1880 of the inscription of one Jason (289), twice archon, in the Tiber near the Ponte Sisto has led some scholars to place a synagogue or at least a Jewish community center close to the spot where this inscription was found.[3] In view of the ease with which small stones are moved from their place of origin, conclusions based on such sporadic finds are hardly worthy of serious consideration.

If the situation prevailing in the Middle Ages may be used as a criterion—and ethnic groups tend to remain in their area of concentration until important changes of circumstance produce a dislocation—we may cautiously assume that the chief Jewish quarter of antiquity lay in the sector between the modern Viale di Trastevere and the river, that is, the district around the churches of S. Cecilia and S. Francesco a Ripa, now traversed by such streets as Via Anicia, Via dei Genovesi, and Via dei Salumi. It has been pointed out[4] that

---

[1] By Suzanne Collon, op. cit., 91.

[2] Also by Collon, ibid.

[3] Among others, by Berliner, Gesch. Jud., I, 63; Marucchi, Cat. Rom. (1903 edition), 294; Müller, Jüd. Kat., 120; Collon, op. cit., 83 f.

[4] R. Lanciani, New Tales of Old Rome (Boston, 1891), 249; Romanelli, op. cit., 135. Bosio had expressed the opinion that the ancient Jewish community was centered near the church of S. Salvatore in Corte in this area, since he derived the name of the church from a Latin word for "the circumcised" (curti); but it has since been demonstrated that the name Corte was taken from the quarters of the cohort of the city police and firemen (cohors vigilum), the ruins of which were discovered in 1868 very close to this church.

a street through this area was known in the Middle Ages as Rua Iudaeorum and that the bridge connecting the Tiber Island with the left bank, now known as Ponte Fabricio or dei Quattro Capi, was once called Pons Iudaeorum. It is less likely that the Jewish center was farther north, around the Porta Settimiana above Ponte Sisto, where a Jewish community developed after the dispersion of the Ghetto in the nineteenth century. The discovery of the Jason inscription, which I have mentioned above, seems largely responsible for this view. Strangely, Vogelstein, in both his older work and his fairly recent book on the Jews of Rome,[1] states that the famous encounter between Horace and the Bore and the jesting remark of Aristius Fuscus about the Jews (to quote the latter work) "to be rightly understood, must be thought of as taking place in the Jewish quarter" of Trastevere—this in the face of Horace's specific statement that the incident occurred near the Temple of Vesta by the Roman Forum (*Sat.* I. 9. 35).

The term "synagogue" (Greek συναγωγή, Latin *synagoga*) was used properly of the congregation itself, while the place of worship was generally known as a *proseucha* (προσευχή).[2] This latter term does not occur in the Jewish sepulchral inscriptions of Rome, though it is found not infrequently on Jewish inscriptions outside Rome and appears once in a non-Jewish Roman epitaph of a fruit vendor "at the wall by the synagogue" (*CII* 531: *de aggere a proseucha*). The names of the Roman synagogues are known to us only from the sepulchral inscriptions, and it should be observed that the name of a synagogue is mentioned only in connection with officials of the various congregations and never just for ordinary members.

Since no trace of any synagogue or other Jewish congrega-

---

[1] In *VR*, 37 and *Jews of Rome*, 19 f.

[2] In this study the terms "synagogue" and "congregation" are used interchangeably, since we customarily speak of a person as being a member or official of a synagogue or temple or church when the congregation is meant rather than the structure. For a full discussion of the terms used among the ancient Jews for synagogues and congregations, see S. Krauss, *Synagogale Altertümer*, 1-27 (the Greek terms are treated in pp. 11-17, 24-27). Cf. also Salo Baron, *The Jewish Community* (Philadelphia, 1942), I, 61 f.

tional structure, apart from the catacombs, has been discovered, all attempts to locate any synagogues or congregational centers must, until further discoveries are made, be looked upon as no better than blind guesses. Some modern scholars have attempted, on the basis of completely unfounded assumptions, to indicate the precise areas where certain of these synagogues were located, even to the point of marking the spots on a map.[1] I shall undertake in what follows to present what is actually known, as well as some of the conjectures, about these synagogues or congregations. They are presented, for convenience, in alphabetic sequence.

1. Synagogue of the Agrippesians ('Αγριππησίων).

This congregation was probably located in the Transtiberine district, since two of the three inscriptions (365, 425, 503) bearing the name were found in the Monteverde catacomb and the third very probably came from there, though its provenience is not recorded. Since this inscription (503) was one of the relatively few Jewish inscriptions known to eighteenth-century scholars and most of these certainly came from the Monteverde catacomb, it is most likely that this one also came from there. A slight—but very slight—supporting detail would be the fact that it was once located in the Trastevere church of S. Salvatore in Corte. The three inscriptions refer to (1) Caelius, who was prostates of this congregation,[2] (2) a gerusiarch, whose name is not preserved, and (3) Zosimus, a life archon.

The name of the congregation is generally believed[3] to

---

[1] So Suzanne Collon in her article cited above, p. 136, n. 1. While this study contains much useful material, the author is too ready to accept unsubstantiated hypotheses and add not a few of her own. Her map of Rome marking the Jewish quarters is on p. 74.

[2] For the congregational officers and their functions see the next chapter.

[3] *E.g.*, by Berliner (*Gesch. Jud.*, I, 63), Vogelstein (*VR*, 39 and *Jews of Rome*, 27), Schürer (III, 82), Frey (*CII*, p. LXXII). Momigliano argues, in *op. cit.* (above, p. 136, n. 1), 286, that four synagogues, those of the Agrippesians, Augustesians, Herodians, and Volumnesians, were founded at the same time in the year 7 B.C.E. His argument, though ingenious, is hardly tenable, since there is no good evidence, as will be demonstrated below, that there was a Synagogue of the Herodians and the identity of the Volumnius for whom the synagogue was named is completely unknown.

have been derived from that of Marcus Vipsanius Agrippa, son-in-law of Augustus, who is known to have befriended the Jews (see above, p. 11) and may have been the patron of the congregation and even the builder of its synagogue. While this view is not improbable, it must still remain a conjecture. It has been suggested also[1] that one of the Jewish kings, Agrippa I or Agrippa II, may have been the source of this name. While there is no reference in the historians to any direct contact between the kings Agrippa and the Jewish community of Rome—although both of them spent a great deal of time in Rome (see above, pp. 20-22, 32)—this view also is possible. In the absence of further data, no confident conclusion is justified here. We must, I believe, discard the suggestion[2] that the members of this congregation were originally Jewish slaves or freedmen of the household of Marcus Agrippa, since there is no basis for such a view.

As for the location of the synagogue, all that one can say is that it was most probably in the Transtiberine region. I cannot follow Suzanne Collon[3] in placing it opposite the Campus Martius in the area of Ponte Sisto. She holds that it was perhaps at the head of the Pons Agrippae, a Tiber bridge named for Agrippa, not far from the point where the above-mentioned stone of "Jason twice archon" was found. She suggests that this Jason may have been an official of the Synagogue of the Agrippesians and that the stone, which is only a small block (23 × 20 cm.), actually a normal size for a sepulchral inscription, may have been attached to the community center or synagogue of the congregation to commemorate Jason's having built or repaired the structure at his own expense.[4] All this is the merest speculation with but faint likelihood of being near the truth.

---

[1] Notably by Müller (*Jüd. Kat.*, 108 and *MB*, 6), who thought one of the Jewish Agrippas the more likely source of the name, especially since, he believed, there was a Synagogue of the Herodians named for Herod. Schürer, however (*Gemeindeverfassung der Juden in Rom*, 15), had rejected this possibility and insisted on the Roman Agrippa.

[2] See Schürer, III, 82, Müller *Jüd. Kat.*, 108, Bormann in *Wiener Studien* 34 (1912), 363.

[3] *Op. cit.* (above, p. 136, n. 1), 83.

[4] This suggestion had been made earlier by Marucchi in *Dissert. Pontif. Accad. Archeol.* 2 (1884), 527; also by Müller in *Jüd. Kat.*, 120. Sepulchral stones comparable with the Jason stone in size are Nos.

2. Synagogue of the Augustesians (Αὐγουστησίων, Augustesion).

Six inscriptions mentioning this congregation have turned up (284, 301, 338, 368, 416, 496). Since four of these are known to be from the Monteverde catacomb and the other two may come from the same source,[1] we can properly place this synagogue also in the Transtiberinum, although there is no clue to its precise location. From these inscriptions we learn of (1) Marcus Quintus Alexus, scribe (*grammateus*) and archon-designate (*mellarcon*) of the congregation, (2) Annius, gerusiarch, (3) Zoticus, archon, (4) Quintianus, gerusiarch, (5) Dativus, life archon, (6) [. . .]ia Marcella, Mother of the Synagogue.

It is highly probable that the congregation was named for the Emperor Augustus, who was a true friend of the Jews and may have been the patron of this particular community. It is clear, accordingly, that this must have been one of the oldest of the congregations, since it was presumably founded at some time during the reign of Augustus (27 B.C.E. to 14 C.E.). As in the case of the Agrippesians, we should reject the view that its members originated from slaves and freedmen of the imperial household.[2]

3. Synagogue of the Calcaresians (Καλκαρησίων, Καλκάρησις).

Of the six inscriptions which mention this congregation

---

226 (22 × 20 cm.), 208 (22 × 24 cm.), 217 (28 × 29 cm.) In fact, most of the slabs which marked the loculi were larger than this supposed dedicatory stone, which was much too small for the marker of a building. In any case, the place of its discovery would be no reliable clue to its original location.

[1] Since No. 284 was known in the eighteenth century, it is likely to have come from the Monteverde catacomb, which was probably the source of nearly all the Jewish inscriptions of Rome known prior to the discovery of the Appia catacomb in 1859.

[2] Cf. p.141, n. 2, above. Among the Monteverde inscriptions none can be identified as that of a slave or freedman, nor is there anything to suggest such an origin, so that the theory must remain a hypothesis for which there is not a particle of evidence. One might contrast with the Jewish inscriptions those of the slaves and freedmen of the house of Livia, Augustus' Empress, in *CIL* VI, pp. 878-97, and the epitaph of the three Jewish freedmen on the Via Appia (*CIL* VI, 27959; *CII*, p. 572, No. 70*).

(304, 316, 384, 433, 504, 537) at least four were found in the Monteverde catacomb, so that we may reasonably place this one in the Trastevere group. The two inscriptions of unknown provenience include one (504) which was known before 1700 and may have come from Monteverde, and one (452) a portion of which was carried to Porto early in the nineteenth century, forming one of a group of stones which, as I have demonstrated elsewhere,[1] probably came from the Monteverde catacomb.

We have a fuller list of officers from this synagogue than from any other in Rome. Those mentioned in the inscriptions are, respectively, (1) Aper, archon, (2) Gaudentius, twice archon, (3) Pomponius, twice archon, (4) a grammateus whose name is lost, (5) Julianus, gerusiarch, and (6) his son, Julianus, archisynagogus, (7) Menophilus, Father of the Synagogue.

Valiant efforts have been made both to interpret the name of this congregation and to locate it topographically. From the fact that the Latin word *calcarenses* or *calcarienses* is used of limekiln workers or lime burners, it is most commonly assumed that this was the congregation of the Jewish guild of lime burners.[2] It seems hardly credible that enough Jews were engaged in this occupation to form a separate congregation, nor does it appear to have been a Jewish custom for members of the same occupation to form a separate religious group and to name their congregation for their occupation.[3] It is more likely that the name of the synagogue was derived from the street or section where it was located, *i.e.*, the street or district of the Calcarenses, but there is no good evidence to reveal where this was. On the basis of two non-Jewish inscriptions of the guild of the *calcarenses*, which were found near the Baths of Diocletian, Suzanne Collon[4] places the synagogue in the northeastern part of the city near the Porta

---

[1] In *HTR* 45 (1952), 174.

[2] Among those expressing this view are Schürer (III, 84), Krauss (*Syn. Alt.*, 256), La Piana (*op. cit.* [p. 136, n. 1, above], 352, 370), Collon (*op. cit.*, 89).

[3] Krauss (l.c.) cites a very problematical Synagogue of the Weavers (טרסיים) in ancient Palestine.

[4] *Op. cit.*, 89. The inscriptions are *CIL* VI, 9223, 9224.

Collina, which was a long distance from the Monteverde catacomb, but very close to the Jewish catacomb of Via Nomentana, yet the burial ground for this congregation was in the former place and not the latter. Frey points out[1] that in the eleventh century there was a region called Calcaria in the southern part of the Campus Martius near the Circus Flaminius; but this district also, even if the name went back to ancient times, is far from the Monteverde catacomb. There is, however, no trace of such a name for any area of Trastevere either in the ancient or the medieval period, so that we must remain in the dark with reference to the location of this synagogue. Since one of the inscriptions (537) refers to the synagogue as that of the Carcaresians (Καρκαρησίων) instead of Calcaresians, Derenbourg conjectured[2] that it may have been located near the *carcer* of the Circus Maximus; but it is more reasonable to regard this unique spelling as the result of a stonecutter's error or possibly of some variant in pronunciation.[3]

4. SYNAGOGUE OF THE CAMPESIANS ((Καμπησίων, Campi).

Three inscriptions (88, 319, 523)[4] mention this synagogue. The fact that one of these (88) was found in the Appia would point to this as the burial place of the congregation. Frey places No. 319 among the inscriptions of the Monteverde catacomb; but actually its source is unknown. Neither do we know the provenience of No. 523, which mentions a *Mater* of two synagogues (*Campi et Volumni*), our only example of a person associated with two congregations. Since both 319 and 523 are among those inscriptions which were known before the nineteenth century (No. 523 was known before 1700), these may be from Monteverde, and this is especially likely in the case of the latter because it mentions the Monteverde

---

[1] In *CII*, p. LXXV. Momigliano, *op. cit.* (above, p. 136, n. 1), 289, agrees with Frey.

[2] In *Mélanges Renier* (Paris, 1887), 440.

[3] See *HTR* 45 (1952), 170.

[4] Frey (*CII*, p. LXXIV) includes also No. 433, though with an interrogation. Only the letters KA of the name of the synagogue are preserved; but since the stone was found in the Monteverde catacomb, the synagogue was probably that of the Calcaresians. There is no substantial evidence that the Campesians used the Monteverde catacomb at any time.

congregation of the Volumnesians. It is perhaps reasonable to infer that the congregation at first used the Monteverde catacomb and that later, when the Appia catacomb was developed, it transferred its burial ground to that place.

Scholars are generally agreed that this congregation took its name from the Campus, *i.e.*, the Campus Martius, where its house of worship was presumably situated. This Campus is an extensive plain of some six hundred acres spreading along the left bank of the Tiber between the river and the famous Roman hills. No one seems to have made a serious attempt to locate the synagogue more exactly, since there are no clues either real or imaginary.[1] One can hardly rank this congregation among the earliest in the Jewish community, for the Campus Martius did not develop as a residential area until well on in the period of the Empire. During the Republic much of it was open country, used for a military and athletic training ground, for assemblies of the people, and for sports. Under Augustus and his successors it acquired important public buildings, and subsequently it was built up as a residential district, becoming in the Middle Ages the most crowded part of the city.

The three inscriptions cited above give us scanty information about the congregation. They refer to (1) Annianus, a child archon who died at the age of eight; (2) his father, Julianus, Father of the Synagogue; (3) Quintus Claudius Synesius, Father of the Synagogue; (4) Veturia Paulla, a proselyte taking the name of Sara, Mother of both this synagogue and that of the Volumnesians.

5. Synagogue of Elaea ('Ελαίας, 'Ελέας).

This mysterious congregation is known to us from two inscriptions (281, 509), one from the small catacomb of Vigna Cimarra off the Via Appia, the other of unknown source. On the first of these neither the name nor the title of the synagogue official has been preserved; the second is the epitaph of one Pancharius, Father of the Synagogue of Elaea, who lived to the ripe age of one hundred and ten. The puzzle to

---

[1] Collon, however (*op. cit.*, 87), thinks it may have been near the Saepta, which became a market center.

us is in the significance of the name of this congregation. Despite the numerous conjectures, one must admit that we still do not know. It will be of interest to indicate briefly some of the theories.

Most common, perhaps, is the view that it was named for the olive or olive tree. Schürer, accepting this as absolutely certain (zweifellos),[1] offers as a parallel the "Synagogue of the Vine" (כנישתא דגופנא) in Sepphoris; but it is hard to understand why a Roman congregation should have taken the olive for its symbol. The Christian archaeologist Garrucci[2] suggested that it was named for Elijah. Apart from the fact that the prophet's name, which appears in Greek as 'Ηλείας, could certainly not have been spelled 'Ελέας or 'Ελαίας, we have no parallel of an ancient Jewish congregation named for any human being, not even a prophet. Berliner thought[3] that the name indicated that the congregation was located on the Velia, a spur of the Palatine. Here again the spelling is a prohibiting factor, since Velia would be Grecized in these inscriptions as Βελια or Βελεια, surely not as Ελαια. A number of scholars,[4] perhaps starting with Greppo in the early nineteenth century, have conjectured that the congregation was named for some city from which its members had, at least originally, emigrated. Sundry cities have been proposed in this connection. Greppo cited three possibilities, cities named Elaea in Aeolia, Phoenicia, and Bithynia. M. A. Levy favored a city in Syria, though he conceded generously that the

---

[1] Schürer, II, 524 n. 81 and III, 84. Among others who prefer this interpretation are Müller (Jüd. Kat., 119) and Vogelstein (VR, 40), who hesitatingly (möglicherweise) suggested that the congregation used an olive tree as its emblem.

[2] In Diss. Arch., II, 185.

[3] Gesch. Jud., I, 64. Berliner stated that the linguistic variant Elea-Velia is abundantly attested. He was probably thinking of the Greek city of Elea in Southern Italy which was known in Latin as Velia. This phonetic phenomenon, however, goes back to an early period, when Greek digamma was pronounced, and does not apply to the time with which we are concerned.

[4] The references for those cited here are as follows: J. G. H. Greppo, Notices sur des inscriptions antiques tirées de quelques tombeaux juifs à Rome (Lyon, 1835), 17; M. A. Levy, Jahrb. f. d. Gesch. d. Juden 2 (1861), 315; S. Reinach, Bull. Corr. Hell. 10 (1886), 329 f.; Frey, CII, pp. LXXVII f. Momigliano (op. cit., 289) also favors Reinach's Mysian city.

congregation could have derived its name from the olive or Elijah. Salomon Reinach thought that the synagogue's name should be connected with that of a fairly important harbor city of Mysia in Asia Minor, which had served as the port of Pergamum. Frey, insisting that the name absolutely must be derived from some city or at least a district, suggested six candidates, preferring the Mysian city proposed by Reinach.[1] Until further evidence is uncovered, we must, alas, leave the problem in this unsolved state.

6. SYNAGOGUE OF THE HEBREWS ('Εβρέων).

We have four inscriptions (291, 317, 510, 535) in which this congregation is named. Two were found in the Monteverde catacomb. One (535) was until 1924 in the collection of Cardinal Pacca at Porto and so probably came from the Monteverde catacomb.[2] The fourth inscription (510), referring to the same synagogue official as No. 535, must surely have come from the same source. Hence we may regard it as fairly well established that the Synagogue of the Hebrews was a part of the Monteverde community. No reasonable suggestion has been made, there being no evidence, as to the precise location of its headquarters.[3] The four inscriptions, one of which (291) is a bilingual in Aramaic and Greek, reveal (1) the father of Isidora, an archon whose name is not preserved;

---

[1] Frey's six cities named Elaea are a port in Epirus, a town on the Tyrrhenian Sea, a Phoenician city between Tyre and Sidon, a port in Ethiopia, a city in Bithynia, and one in Mysia, between Smyrna and Pergamum, the last being the same as that proposed by Reinach.

[2] See above, p. 143, n. 1.

[3] We may reject forthwith Suzanne Collon's suggestion (*op. cit.*, 90) that it may have been near the Porta Collina (where she also put the Synagogue of the Calcaresians). Her only argument seems to be that, being Hebrew speakers, they *may* have used the Via Labicana catacomb, where Marucchi thought he read two Hebrew inscriptions (but we have concrete evidence that they used the Monteverde catacomb) and that the Porta Collina is fairly close to that catacomb (actually it is about four kilometers distant). No more acceptable is Müller's view (*MB*, 24) that the members of this congregation were probably not a localized group, but consisted of Hebrew speakers living in various parts of Rome and even in Porto, eleven miles away. On the lack of evidence for a Jewish community at Porto see my article, "The Jewish Community of Ancient Porto," *HTR* 45 (1952), 165-175.

(2) Gelasius, exarchon; (3) Gadias, Father of the Synagogue, mentioned in two inscriptions.

While the location of the synagogue has elicited little or no controversy, there has been no end of discussion in the attempt to explain why this was called the Synagogue of the Hebrews. Several scholars,[1] such as Schürer, Müller, and Krauss, have insisted that it was a Hebrew-speaking group, or that at the least it conducted its religious services in Hebrew. Were this so, we should certainly expect the officers of this congregation to have used the Hebrew language for their tomb inscriptions and those of the members of their families; yet, of the four inscriptions mentioning this congregation three are in Greek and one is a bilingual in Aramaic with Greek translation. Derenbourg's view that this was a Samaritan group has won but little scholarly approval, since he could offer no reasonable arguments to support it; nor can we accept Momigliano's theory that they spoke Aramaic and conducted their services in that tongue. Vogelstein thought that these Jews might have been immigrants who came directly from Judaea, in contrast with those from other lands in the Mediterranean world. Deissmann agreed that this was a congregation of Palestinian immigrants, but insisted that their language was Aramaic and they were not yet Hellenized, a view which hardly harmonizes with the language of the four inscriptions. The suggestion has even been offered that the congregation consisted of Egyptian Jews.[2] More recently Frey[3] has supported the theory that they were immigrants from Judaea and are to be contrasted with the native-born Roman Jews, who called themselves *Vernaculi*.

It seems to me that a much simpler and more plausible explanation of the name is available. It was first offered, to

---

[1] Following are the references for the opinions cited here: Schürer, III, 83 (he says *ohne Zweifel*); Müller, *Jüd. Kat.*, 111 and *MB*, 24; Krauss, *Syn. Alt.*, 56; Derenbourg, *Mélanges Renier*, 439 f.; Momigliano, *op. cit.* (above, p. 136, n. 1), 290; Vogelstein, *VR*, 40; Deissmann in *MB*, 24, n. 1.

[2] See Kirchhoff on *CIG* 9909 (= our 510) and Levy, *op. cit.* (above, p. 146, n. 4), 314. This theory was occasioned by the L-shaped sign framing the numeral denoting the number of years. It was misinterpreted (even by Frey) as representing Λυκάβαντας, which is found on inscriptions from Egypt.

[3] In *CII*, p. LXXVI.

my knowledge, by La Piana,[1] and is a view which, having occurred to me independently, I present as highly probable. The first group of Jews to form a congregation at Rome would naturally have called itself the Congregation or Synagogue of the Hebrews, as different from other religious or ethnic groups. Similarly, there was a Synagogue of the Hebrews in Corinth, as attested by a well-known inscription still to be seen among the remains of that ancient city (*CII* 718), and another of the same name in a town of Lydia in Asia Minor (*CII* 754). As more Jews came to Rome and formed congregations of their own, they adopted appropriate names, while the first congregation retained its original name. This explanation must, of course, remain a conjecture; yet there is nothing in the scant epigraphical data to contradict it and it seems to answer the problem in a satisfactory manner.

In a few inscriptions (354, 370, 379, 505) individuals are designated as Hebrews, and Müller[2] has suggested that all these were members of the Synagogue of the Hebrews. Since, however, it was clearly the practice to designate the name of the congregation only for officials, there is no reason for postulating an exception in these cases. It appears that the adjectives *Hebraeus* ('Εβραῖος) and *Iudaeus* ('Ιουδαῖος) were used interchangeably at Rome, despite Müller's argument to the contrary.

7. SYNAGOGUE OF THE SECENIANS (Σεκηνων).

Only one inscription (7), that of Aiutor (probably for Adiutor), a scribe (*grammateus*), offers the name of this group. We cannot even be sure that it is the name of a congregation, but since in all other instances the genitive following the word *grammateus* is the name of a synagogue, it is a proper assumption that the same is true in this instance. Since Aiutor was entombed in the Nomentana catacomb, we may conclude

---

[1] *Op. cit.* (above, p. 136, n. 1), 356, n. 26, where a summary of the various theories is presented. Momigliano, *op. cit.*, 290, disagrees sharply with this view, arguing that the Synagogue of the Hebrews could not have been the first, since, according to his chronological reconstruction, the earliest congregations were the Agrippesians, Augustesians, Herodians, and Volumnesians, which were initiated simultaneously about 7 B.C.E. On this theory, see above, p. 140, n. 3.

[2] *Jüd. Kat.*, 111.

that the members of the congregation, if there actually was such a congregation, used this catacomb for its burial place.

Accepting the view that there was a Synagogue of the Secenians, we may wonder whence the name was derived. Here there is an abundance of theories. La Piana,[1] following a suggestion by Professor Harry A. Wolfson, proposed a place in Galilee, Sekaneya, the name of which is variously spelled and which is called Sogane by Josephus (*Vita* 51. 265). George Foote Moore, however, rejected this possibility on the ground that the place was never more than a village, that it was destroyed early, perhaps in the war under Hadrian, and that in any case it was never large enough to furnish so great a number of emigrants to Rome as to form a congregation. Frey, with his usual positiveness (here he says *sans hésiter*), derives the name from the harbor town of Iscina, also called Scina, in North Africa, now Medinet es-Sultan, which was designated in a fourth-century map, Tabula Peutingeriana, as *locus Iudaeorum Augusti*. Belisario Manna, believing that the name was derived from some district in Rome, attempted first to connect it with the word σέχος (did he mean σηχός?), the supposedly Greek term for the Servian *agger*, and later with Sicininum, a place on the Esquiline, now occupied by the basilica of S. Maria Maggiore.

Others have attempted to derive the Secenians from some common name rather than a place name. Lietzmann proposed Hebrew *shechenim* (שכנים), which means neighbors. This would make Aiutor the "neighborhood scribe". Lietzmann rightly criticized his own proposal with the objection that Hebrew ‫כ‬ would probably be represented by Greek χ rather than χ. He suggested as an alternative *zekenim* (זקנים) = elders, making Aiutor scribe of the Council of Elders, Here again he noted correctly that Hebrew ‫ז‬ should have been rendered in Greek by ζ and not by σ. This latter proposal should be rejected also on the ground that in every instance the names of official groups within the congregation are designated by Greek terms and never by Hebrew ones. Thus the Elders

---

[1] References for the theories about the Secenians: La Piana, *op. cit.*, 357, n. 27, where he gives the views of Wolfson and Moore; Frey, *Rech. Sci. Relig.* 20 (1930), 292 and *CII*, p. LXXIX; Manna, *NBAC* 27 (1921), 55 and *BCACR* 50 (1922), 215; Lietzmann in *BL*, 31.

would be referred to, not as *Zekenim*, but as *Presbyteri* (πρεσβύτεροι) or as a body forming a *gerusia* (γερουσία). After rejecting his own proposals, Lietzmann accepted, with dubious wisdom, Frey's suggestion of the town of Scina.

All this discussion has led us nowhere. We still do not know whence the Synagogue of the Secenians derived its name. We cannot even be completely certain that there was such a congregation, although it seems very likely that there was. After all, we have only two inscriptions mentioning the Elaea Synagogue, and the Synagogue of the Tripolitans also, as we shall see, is mentioned only twice, so that there is no good reason for rejecting the Secenians because we have only the one reference to them. There may even have been some Jewish congregations in Rome which are entirely unknown to us because they do not happen to be named in any of the inscriptions discovered hitherto.

8. SYNAGOGUE OF THE SIBURESIANS (Σιβουρησίων).

There are five inscriptions which certainly refer to this congregation (18, 22, 67, 380, and 35a, which is not in *CII*),[1] one more is very likely (140), and one is not improbable (37). If all these are accepted, then we have more references to this synagogue than to any other in Rome. Since five of the seven are from the catacomb of the Via Nomentana, we may be confident that this was the usual burial place for the congregation. Yet one inscription (140), on which (though part of the stone is lost) the name of this synagogue has been plausibly reconstructed, was found in the Appia catacomb. We are forced, accordingly, to concede that some of the members of the congregation were entombed on the Via Appia. Since the congregation probably existed through several generations, it is possible that at one period of its history it used the one catacomb, later transferring to the other. We have seen above that the same may have been true of the Campesian synagogue. One of the seven inscriptions (380) is of unknown provenience. Quite without justification, Frey placed it among the inscriptions from the Monteverde

---

[1] It appears on the sarcophagus of Caelia Omnina; see *JQR*, 42 (1952), 413-417.

catacomb. His sole ground seems to have been that it was once included among the stones in the Borgia collection at Velletri, most of which came from Monteverde. As I have pointed out elsewhere,[1] the history of this inscription is different from that of the others in the collection.

The group of inscriptions referring to the Siburesian congregation reveals the following officers: (1) Diophatus, grammateus; (2) an archon whose name is not preserved; (3) Julianus, archon; (4) a Claudius, who may have been an officer of this congregation if the proposed restoration is correct; (5) a grammateus whose name is lost; (6) Maronius, archon of this synagogue, if the restoration is correct; (7) Nicodemus, archon.

It is practically certain that the congregation derived its name from the Subura, a thickly populated district occupying the valley between the Viminal, the Esquiline, and the Imperial Fora and continuing up the west slope of the Esquiline. This district, inhabited by laborers and small shopkeepers, was, like the Transtiberinum, crowded, noisy, dirty, and rather disreputable, although it did not have the foreign flavor of its counterpart across the Tiber. A stroll up Via Cavour, continuing along Via Giovanni Lanza and Via dello Statuto to the vast Piazza Vittorio Emanuele, will take one through the heart of what was the ancient Subura. Just where in the Subura the synagogue was located can only be guessed at. Some[2] have used the evidence of the epitaph of a pagan fruit vendor "from the wall by the synagogue" (*CII* 531: *de aggere a proseucha*) as a proof that the Siburesian synagogue was near that stretch of the Servian Wall which was called the *agger*. This ran from the Porta Esquilina on the Esquiline to the Porta Collina on the Quirinal. If the synagogue mentioned in the inscription was actually that of the Siburesians, it would have to be placed at the Subura end of the *agger* within a few blocks of the present Piazza Vittorio Emanuele. The evidence is, however, of doubtful value, and all we can say is that the theory is a possible one. In the opinion of Suzanne Collon, this view[3] is reinforced by a reference

---

[1] *Op. cit.* (previous note), 416, n. 7.
[2] *E.g.*, Marucchi, *Cat. Rom.* (1903 edition), 295-297; Collon, *op. cit.*, 88.
[3] *Op. cit.*, 89.

in Juvenal (6. 588) to the presence of fortune-tellers at the *agger*. Stating, curiously, that fortune-telling was the chief occupation of the Jewish colony, she uses the Juvenal reference as additional proof that the Siburesian synagogue was located at the *agger*, as though fortune-tellers must have been Jews and must have carried on their occupation close to the place where they lived or worshiped.

We have seen that this congregation made use of the Nomentana catacomb; perhaps later—since this catacomb, on the evidence of the brick stamps, seems not to have been used long after the year 200—the congregation's burial ground became the Appia catacomb.[1] The one on the Via Nomentana would have been much the nearer. Marucchi insisted that the Siburesians used the catacomb on the Via Labicana (the one he discovered), because, as he thought, it was the nearest one to the Subura. He even proposed naming the catacomb "il cimitero dei Siburensi." These statements were, to be sure, published before the discovery of the Nomentana catacomb, but two inscriptions mentioning the Synagogue of the Siburesians were already known at that time and neither was from the Via Labicana.

9. SYNAGOGUE OF THE TRIPOLITANS (Τριπολειτῶν).

This congregation was unknown to us prior to the rediscovery of the Monteverde catacomb in 1904. Only two inscriptions (390, 408) attest to its existence, one referring to an archon named Proclus, another to a gerusiarch named Symmachus.

That this was one of the Transtiberine congregations may be assumed without hesitation. It may also be accepted that the name of the congregation was derived from the city of origin, at least of its founding members. The only question, therefore, is which of the cities named Tripolis is the right one. Only two cities of that name were sufficiently prominent in antiquity to justify consideration here: one in Phoenicia, now

---

[1] Suzanne Collon (*op. cit.*, 81), misled by Frey's erroneous inclusion of the Nicodemus inscription (380) among those from Monteverde, thought that, after the Nomentana catacomb was abandoned, the Siburesians used the Monteverde catacomb. For Marucchi's opinion see his *Cat. Rom.* (1903 edition), 296 f.

Tarabulus esh Sham in Lebanon, the other in North Africa. The latter was actually a group of three cities, Oea, Lepcis Magna, and Sabrata, though the name came ultimately to be attached to Oea alone and still survives as the name of the modern city on the site.

There seems to be no way of deciding which of these two cities was the source of the Tripolitan congregation of Rome. Proponents of the African city[1] include La Piana, Clermont-Ganneau, Collon, Frey, and Momigliano; while Paribeni, Schneider-Graziosi, and Müller thought the Phoenician city the more likely. Those who prefer the African city point out that it had an important Jewish community and maintained extensive commercial contacts with Rome. Suzanne Collon, pointing to a medieval reference to a synagogue of Severus in Rome, surmises that the Emperor Septimius Severus may have brought the Jewish colony to Rome from North Africa, with which he had close connections. On the other hand, the Phoenician city was no less important and it, too, had a Jewish community. In view of the references in the catacomb inscriptions, though they are scant, to Jews coming to Rome from the eastern Mediterranean (see below, pp. 239-40), while there happen to be no references to any from Africa, perhaps a slight preference may be felt for the Asian city. On the basis of the available evidence, however, no decisive opinion is warranted.

10. SYNAGOGUE OF THE VERNACLESIANS ((Βερνάκλων, Βερνακλώρων, Βερνακλησίων).

This synagogue, likewise, was unknown to us prior to the finding of three inscriptions bearing the name (318, 383, 389) in the Monteverde catacomb after its rediscovery in the present century. Subsequently, a fourth inscription (494), most probably from the same catacomb, was discovered by Frey. From the variant forms which the name shows in the inscriptions we may infer that the members of this group called

---

[1] The references for the opinions alluded to in this paragraph are as follows: La Piana, op. cit., 355, n. 24; Clermont-Ganneau, RA, Ser. V, Vol. XI (1920), 366; Collon, op. cit., 85; Frey, CII, LXXXVIII f.; Momigliano, op. cit., 289; R. Paribeni, N. Sc. (1919), 63; Schneider-Graziosi, NBAC 21 (1915), 18; Müller in MB, 105.

themselves Vernacli or Vernaclenses. In the four inscriptions we make the acquaintance of (1) Donatus, grammateus; (2) Poly[me?]nius,[1] archisynagogus; (3) Sabinus, life archon; (4) Domnus, Father of the Synagogue, thrice archon and twice phrontistes. This Domnus displays more titles than any other member of the entire Jewish community hitherto known to us and is the only one thus far revealed as three times archon and twice phrontistes.

This synagogue was apparently among those in the Trans-tiberine district. It is reasonably clear from the name Vernacli that it consisted, at least originally, of native-born Romans. We may conjecture that early in the history of the Jewish community a native-born group formed a congregation of their own to distinguish themselves from the many immigrants. Misled by the fact that the Latin word *verna* means a home-born slave, most authorities have represented the members of this congregation as having been of servile origin. There is, however, nothing in the inscriptions, nothing in the names of the persons involved, to indicate that they were in any degree of less free stock than were the other members of the community whose epitaphs we possess. Besides, a study of the uses of the word *vernaculus* in Latin writers[2] (*vernaclus* is the syncopated form) shows that it regularly means "native" or "indigenous" with no connotation whatever of servitude.

To review some of the theories,[3] Bormann, one of the earliest to discuss this synagogue, advanced the idea that the Vernacli were palace-born slaves of the Emperor. Bees, the editor of Müller's posthumous work on the inscriptions of the Monte-

---

[1] On the possible reconstructions of this name, see above p. 103, n. 3.

[2] The expression *vernacula multitudo* of Tacitus, *Annals* 1.31, is misinterpreted in Harper's Latin Dictionary as meaning "the rabble of slaves." The words actually mean "the city-born rabble," *i.e.*, natives of Rome; see Marsh-Leon, *Tacitus* (New York, 1936), 225 and the various other commentators on this passage. Legions levied from the natives of a province were called *legiones vernaculae*; see Mommsen in *Hermes* 19 (1884), 13. In fact, the word *verna* itself means "native-born" and etymologically has nothing to do with slaves, but it came to be used of slaves born in the house of the master in contrast with those that were purchased.

[3] References for the theories cited here: Bormann, *Wiener Studien* 34 (1912), 365; Bees in *MB*, 98 f; Müller, *Jüd. Kat.*, 111f; Krauss, *Syn. Alt.*, 253; La Piana, *op. cit.*, 352, 355, n. 24; Th. Reinach, *REJ* 71 (1920), 121; Vogelstein, *Jews of Rome*, 16 f.

verde catacomb, taking *Vernac(u)lus* as a diminutive of *verna*, agreed with Bormann (*die richtige Erklärung*), although Müller himself had called this group one which, in contrast to the Hebraei, insisted on adopting native Roman customs.[1] Accepting Müller's view, Krauss also contrasted these "Romanized" Jews with the Hebraei, whom he regarded as conservatives retaining Hebrew as their mother tongue and the language of their divine services. One serious obstacle to such views is that, just as the Hebraei did not use the Hebrew language for their sepulchral inscriptions, the Vernacli did not use Latin: both used Greek.[2] La Piana reverted to the misconception of the meaning of the word *vernaculus* and called this synagogue "an ethnical subdivision, being formed of Jewish slaves born in Rome in the houses of their owners." Similarly, so distinguished a scholar as Théodore Reinach identified the Vernacli as slaves born in servitude and then freed. More recently, Vogelstein also asserted that "the Vernaclesian synagogue comprised the descendants of *vernae*, or home-bred slaves, who had all or nearly all grown up as freedmen." As a parallel he cited the Synagogue of the Libertines, that is, of the Freedmen, mentioned in Acts (6.9) as being in Jerusalem and which, following a frequently repeated but untenable theory, he says "was the synagogue of the Roman Jews who lived in Jerusalem."

The evidence, however, as far as it goes, justifies no such

---

[1] Müller bolstered his view by pointing out that members of this congregation had Latin names and that the genitive form συνγωγη in No. 318 is a transliteration of Latin *syngogae* (for *synagogae*), the η reprenting the Latin *ae*. These arguments will hardly stand up. As for the names, one of the four preserved from this congregation is Greek. The spelling συνγωγη for συναγωγῆς is more easily explained as the error of a stonecutter who also misspelled the name of the congregation (Βερναχλωρω for Βερναχλώρων) by similarly leaving off the final consonant. Besides, as stated in the text, this supposedly "Latinized" group used Greek for its tomb inscriptions.

[2] Momigliano (*op. cit.*, 291), making the Vernaclesians a Latin-speaking group, waves aside any objection based on the language of the inscriptions by stating that Greek was the conventional language of the lapidary style, so that the epitaphs do not reflect the language used by the individuals concerned. If this is so, how else are we to determine what language they spoke? Surely an inference from the name of a congregation is hardly decisive. Besides, as we have seen, Greek was so far from being the conventional language of the epitaphs that about one-fourth are in Latin.

speculations. The inspiration of all these theories about home-bred slaves is the misconception of the meaning of the name of the synagogue. The earliest indication of what I regard as the correct explanation is to be found in Schürer's translation of Vernacli as *die Einheimischen*. Frey also has the right view (*les Indigènes*), but goes too far in suggesting that the group included all the Jews whose native city was Rome.[1] All that we can insist upon is that the Vernacli were a congregation consisting, at least originally, of native Romans and having its synagogue somewhere in the Transtiberinum.

11. SYNAGOGUE OF THE VOLUMNESIANS (Βολουμνησίων, Βολυμνησίων).

Before Müller's rediscovery of the Monteverde catacomb, the Volumnesian synagogue was known only from a single inscription (523), that of Beturia (for Veturia) Paulla, to which we find references as far back as the sixteenth century,[2] so that it may have been the first inscription of the Jews of Rome to become known to scholars. Müller discovered another inside the catacomb (402) and, in later work at the site, two more inscriptions (343, 417) referring to this congregation were found. The names and titles revealed in these four inscriptions are (1) Hilarus, archon; (2) Siculus Sabinus, an infant archon-designate; (3) Flavius Sabinus, life archon; (4) Veturia Paulla, Mother of both the Campesian and Volumnesian synagogues.

In view of the provenience of at least three of these four inscriptions, we may properly include the Volumnesian congregation among those of Trastevere, without attempting, in view of the lack of evidence, to locate it more precisely. It is not so easy, however, to explain whence this group derived its name. Apparently it was named for a certain Volumnius, presumably its patron, so that this congregation would fall into the same category as that of the Agrippesians and Augustesians in that it was named for a patron.

---

[1] Schürer, III, 83; Frey, *CII*, p. LXXVII. That the native-born Vernaclesians used Greek need give us no concern, familiar as we are with American-born groups in our cities whose vernacular is German, Italian, Yiddish, or Spanish.

[2] It was copied by De Winghe, Menestrier, and Chacón; see chap. III, pp. 67 f., above.

Attempts to identify this Volumnius have not been successful. Those scholars who have discussed the matter[1] have
almost unanimously, with degrees of positiveness ranging
from Vogelstein's *vermütlich* and Berliner's *vielleicht*, through
La Piana's "probably," to Frey's *sans doute* and Momigliano's
certamente, fixed upon the Volumnius who is mentioned by
Josephus in connection with certain episodes of Herod's
career. Of this Volumnius we know only what Josephus tells
us: as procurator of Syria he joined with the legate Saturninus
in granting Herod permission to use force against certain
Arabs who had raided his territory (Jos. *AJ* 16. 9. 1, 2. 280,
283). Later, as a member of the advisory council which
deliberated on the fate of Alexander and Aristobulus, the sons
of Herod, he was the first to vote for the death sentence
(*BJ* 1. 27. 2. 538; *AJ* 16. 11. 3. 369). If he had any connection
at all with the Jews of Rome, history is silent about it.
Hence, to link him with the congregation of the Volumnesians
is entirely arbitrary, since there were many Volumnii in
Rome.

An even worse example of the *horror vacui* type of interpretation is Krauss' suggestion that the patron of this congregation may have been none other than the Poly[m]nis,
archisynagogus of the Vernaclesians, whose name is found
on an inscription of the Monteverde catacomb (383). Arguing
that the name is the Greek equivalent of Volumnius (and
criticizing Müller and Bees for not recognizing this), he holds
that this person was either the builder or the patron of a
new synagogue, which was then appropriately named for
him. Apart from the question of why, without any evidence,
one should regard a high official of one congregation as the
founder of a new one, the theory collapses before the fact that
the name Volumnius could not possibly be distorted into the
Greek Πολυ[μ]νις. Latin *v* is always β, never π, in this group
of inscriptions. Besides, a good look at the stone itself or its

---

[1] References for the theories about the Volumnesians: Vogelstein,
VR, 39; Berliner, *Gesch. Jud.*, I, 112; La Piana, *op. cit.*, 355, n. 23;
Frey, *Rech. Sci. Relig.* 20 (1930), 283; Momigliano, *op. cit.*, 285; Krauss,
Syn. Alt., 255; Müller, *Jüd. Kat.*, 108; Dessau in *MB*, 96, n.2; Collon,
op. cit. 84 f. See also Bormann, *Wiener Studien* 34 (1921), 362 f.; he
favors the procurator, but admits that the identification is uncertain.

photograph in Müller-Bees (p. 100) reveals that in the missing part of the name (a portion at the left of the stone is lost), not just one letter, but two or three should be restored, nor is it sure that one of the missing letters is μ. Thus the name was most probably not Polymnis, but perhaps Polymenis (for Polymenius) or Polyxenis or Polysthenis, to suggest a few that would fit the available space.[1] Krauss does not, however, completely reject the procurator Volumnius as a possibility.

More wisely, Müller admitted that the identity of Volumnius is not known, and Dessau insisted that a Jewish congregation would hardly have been named for an official who had had a part in the execution of Herod's sons. Suzanne Collon, while not accepting the identification with the procurator of Syria, thought that the patron of the congregation must have had some intimate connection with the affairs of Syria and Palestine and the house of Herod. One may well wonder why such a connection need be assumed.

To sum up, all that we may reasonably assert of the Volumnesian congregation is that it was probably in the Transtiberine group of congregations and that it was named for a certain Volumnius, who may have been its patron or the builder of its synagogue, but whose identity is entirely unknown to us.

With the Synagogue of the Volumnesians we complete the list of eleven congregations about whose existence we may feel fairly certain. Four other possible synagogues have been named, and in some instances ardently defended, but it seems to me all four must be rejected for lack of sufficient evidence.

The one which has stirred up the greatest amount of controversy is the supposed Synagogue of the Herodians, or Rhodians, according to how a fragmentary inscription of the Via Appia (173) is reconstructed. The surviving fragment is the right portion of a large slab on which three lines of text are inscribed (Fig. 30). Of the first line all that survives is ΓΩΓΗC; of the second, ΙΡΟΔΙΩΝ or ΗΡΟΔΙΩΝ (the upright bar of the first extant letter being either I or the right upright of an H); of the third, ΕΥΛΟΓΙΑ ΠΑCΙ ("a blessing to all").

---

[1] For other possibilities, see above p. 103, n. 3.

Garrucci, the first to publish this inscription,[1] preferred to call the synagogue that of the Rhodians. Vogelstein agreed with Garrucci, insisting that no Jewish congregation would be named for the hated King Herod, whereas there were close trade relations between Rhodes and Rome, so that there might well have been a Jewish group from Rhodes at Rome. Schürer, likewise, favored the Rhodians and rejected the Herodians. Neither Krauss nor La Piana, however, saw any difficulty about acknowledging the existence of a Synagogue of the Herodians. Berliner hesitated between the two, though preferring the Rhodians. The Herodians were unquestioningly accepted by Momigliano, who included this congregation among the four earliest at Rome, the other three being those named for Augustus, Agrippa, and the procurator Volumnius. Passing over the alignment of other scholars in this matter, we come to Father Frey, who argued most vehemently for a Synagogue of the Herodians. Largely in refutation of the present writer, who in two articles had rejected both Rhodians and Herodians,[2] Frey insisted that only the reading Ἡροδίων would fit the epigraphical requirements and that a synagogue named for Herod was quite possible, since Herod, although hated by the Pharisees of Judaea, was highly regarded throughout the Empire because of his lavishness; further, in view of his friendship with Augustus and Agrippa and his several visits to Rome, it is quite conceivable that a Jewish congregation should have made him its patron.

Despite Frey's contention, I feel that the inscription offers us no basis for accepting a Synagogue of the Herodians or even of the Rhodians. It is quite obvious that the greater part of the stone is missing, since it must have borne at least the name of the deceased and his title in the congregation. Frey's suggestion that the inscription was not an epitaph at all, but a plaque marking the area where the members of the Herodian congregation were buried, is not acceptable because

---

[1]) References for the Herodians: Garrucci, *Diss. Arch.*, II, 185; Vogelstein, *VR*, 40; Schürer, *Gemeindeverfassung der Juden in Rom*, 40, n. 37; Krauss, *Syn. Alt.*, 255; La Piana, *op. cit.*, 356, n. 25; Berliner, *Gesch. Jud.*, I, 66; Momigliano, *op. cit.*, 284 ff.; Frey, *CII*, pp. LXXII and 124-126.

[2] "The Synagogue of the Herodians," *JAOS* 49 (1929), 318-321 and in *JQR*, 20 (1930), 305 f.

it would be entirely without a parallel in the Jewish catacombs of Rome. Conjectural restorations must be made on the analogy of the extant inscriptions to be regarded as plausible. We must, accordingly, assume that the greater portion of the inscription has been lost. Since, in all other inscriptions on which the name of a synagogue appears this name immediately follows the word συναγωγῆς or is separated from it only by the article τῶν, whereas here there is a large gap before the alleged name of the synagogue, we are forced to conclude that the last word of the second line cannot be the name of the synagogue and that its name must have been on the missing part of the stone. The word ΡΟΔΙΩΝ should therefore be taken as the name of a person, either the deceased or the relative who set up the inscription. The I which precedes this name is probably the ending of a noun in the dative, such as πατρί or a proper name. On the analogy of other inscriptions from the same catacomb (e.g., 92, 124, 141) and in accordance with the possible space, the inscription may be hypothetically reconstructed as follows:[1]

> ΤΩΑΡΧΟΝΤΙϹΥΝΑ]ΓΩΓΗϹ
> ΚΑΜΠΗϹΙΩΝΜΑΡΩΝ]ΙΡΟΔΙΩΝ
> ΥΙΟϹΕΠΟΙΗϹΕΝ]ΕΥΛΟΓΙΑΠΑϹΙ

τῷ ἄρχοντι συναγωγῆς Καμπησίων Μαρῶνι ‘Ροδίων υἱὸς ἐποίησεν. Εὐλογία πᾶσι.
I.e., To Maron, archon of the Synagogue of the Campesians, his son Rhodion set this stone. A blessing to all. (The names are *exempli gratia*).

To allow room for an inscription of the kind just described would require, according to Frey, a stone of inordinate width. The proposed reconstruction, however, assumes that the surviving fragment is about one-third the width of the original stone. Since the extant portion is 45. 5 cm. high and 60 cm. wide, the requirements would be met by a slab measuring 45. 5 by 180 cm. (= 18 by 72 inches), dimensions by no means out of line with a few other stones, including one still to be seen in the catacomb (140), which is 61 by 188 cm. The

---

[1] This is one of the reconstructions which I proposed in *JAOS* 49 321.

unusual size of the finely cut letters on our stone would be appropriate for a large slab.

As for the name Rhodion, though not common, it is found among the names in Pape-Benseler, *Wörterbuch der griechischen Eigennamen*, and is listed as a proper name in the Suidas Lexicon. Another possibility would be the name Herodion, but since its correct spelling would be Ἡρωδίων, it is less likely as a reconstruction in the present inscription, which is so carefully carved that a misspelling is not to be expected. This fact may also be used as an additional argument against the spelling Ἡροδίων for a synagogue named after Herod, since this name would be correctly written only with an ω (Ἡρώδης-Ἡρωδίων).[1] It may also be pointed out that if the name were formed on the analogy of the other synagogues named for persons (Agrippesii, Augustesii, Volumnesii), we should expect Herodesii, or perhaps Herodiani, as the followers of Herod were called, but not Herodii.

Vogelstein, in his last work on the Jews of Rome, while appearing to accept and explain the Synagogue of the Herodians in his text, agrees with my rejection of the synagogue in his note on the passage.[2] Father Antonio Ferrua also rejects this synagogue and proposes a reconstruction somewhat similar to mine, but requiring more space.[3]

A Synagogue of Severus at Rome is apparently alluded to in David Kimchi's commentary on Genesis I. 31 (כנישתא דאסוירוס). It contained, according to Kimchi, one of the Torah scrolls which Titus had brought to Rome among the spoils of Jerusalem. Those who believe in the existence of this synagogue usually assume that it was named for Emperor Alexander Severus, who was conspicuously friendly toward the Jews.[4] Suzanne Collon suggested that perhaps this synagogue should be identified with that of the Tripolitans, on the supposition that the congregation consisted originally of Jews brought by Septimius Severus from North Africa,

---

[1] This point is made also by Ferrua in *Epigraphica*, 3 (1941), 34.

[2] *Jews of Rome*, 28 f. and 395, n. 5. He regarded my proposed reconstruction of the inscription as "unacceptable," but did not say why.

[3] *Civ. Catt.* (1936) IV, 129 and *Epigraphica*, 3,34.

[4] See Vogelstein, *VR*, 34 and n. 10 and *Jews of Rome*, 27, 86; Krauss, *Syn. Alt.*, 254; Collon, *op. cit.*, 85; Frey, *CII*, p. LXXXI.

where the Emperor was born. Frey tried to link this synagogue with the alleged Synagogue of Arca of Lebanon, discussed in the following paragraph. Since there is no epigraphical evidence for a Synagogue of Severus at Rome and no literary evidence prior to Kimchi in the thirteenth century, we are not justified in including a congregation of this name among those of ancient Rome.

No. 501 of our collection is a portion of an inscription attested only in two eighteenth-century Vatican manuscripts[1] and containing, apparently, a reference to a Roman synagogue. The six-line inscription lacked a portion on the right, so that some two to four letters are lost at the end of each of the first five lines. Where the stone originated, where it was copied, is not stated by either of the scholars who offered its text. We do not even know that it came from Rome or was ever in Rome, since Migliore, whose copy seems to be the earlier, includes it among epigraphic items concerning the Jews of Italy with no indication that it was from Rome (*Excerpta quorum maior pars ad exercitationem epigraphicam de Iudaeis Italicis spectat*). The inscription is the epitaph of an Alexan[dra], daughter of Alexa[nder]. The third and fourth lines, according to the version followed by Frey, read:

ΑΠΟ ΤΗΣ ϹΥΝΑΓ ΑΡΚ....
ΒΑΝΟΥ ΕΝ ΕΙΡΗΝΗ ΚΥ....

The last lines contain the usual "her sleep be in peace" formula and a statement of the age at death (the number of the years is lost). Filling out the missing letters as Ἀρκ[ης[2] Λι]βάνου, Frey discovers that there was a Synagogue of Arca of Lebanon at Rome. Since this city was the birthplace of the Emperor Alexander Severus, he argues that the Emperor's favor attracted many of its citizens to Rome, including

---

[1] Gaetano Migliore in *Cod. Vat. Lat.* 9143, fol. 170b, and Gaetano Marini in *Cod. Vat. Lat.* 9074, p. 940, no. 7. It is likely that Marini's copy is derived from Migliore. Marini indicates that the stone was in Rome, but there is no such indication in Migliore. On the basis of Marini's statement I have included it, though without confidence, among the Roman inscriptions.

[2] In *CII*, p. 366, he wrongly restores Ἀρκ[ου, but has the correct Ἀρκ[ης on p. LXXIX and in his earlier discussions of this topic; see his references on p. 365.

enough Jews to form a congregation. Most probably, asserts Frey, the Emperor built the synagogue, and this synagogue is no other than that which was known as the Synagogue of Severus in the Middle Ages. The fact that father and daughter were named Alexander and Alexandra, respectively, is to him an additional indication that Alexander Severus was patron of the congregation. These names were, however, very common among the Jews of the time, as we have seen.

Although Frey's view is exceedingly attractive[1] and he presents it with such uncompromising phrases as *hors de conteste* and *il n'y a guère de doute*, it will actually not hold up under detailed analysis. First, an examination of Migliore's page at the Vatican shows that he offers two conflicting versions of the inscription side by side. In the one version lines three and four read as indicated above, but in the other version they read:

ΑΠΟ ΤΗC ΠΟΛΕΩC ΑΡΚ. . . .
ΑΝΟΥ ΕΝ ΕΙΡΗΝΗ Η ΚΥ. . . .

The two versions show other minor differences which are of no significance in this connection. Frey cavalierly rejects the alternative version as defective and having no indication of origin. Actually, it is the first of the two versions given by Migliore.[2] While not indicating the provenience of the stone, Migliore states that the second version was copied from the notes of one Montenarius (*e schedis Montenarii*). The important difference between the two is that one reads ἀπὸ τῆς πόλεως 'Αρκ[. . .]ανου and the other ἀπὸ τῆς συναγ. 'Αρκ[. . .]βανου; in other words, the one states that Alexander was of the *city* of (presumably) Arca of Lebanon, the other that he was of the *synagogue* of Arca of Lebanon.

Actually, the version with the word for *city* seems to me to be the correct one, for the following reasons: In the first place, there is not a single instance among the Judeo-Roman inscriptions in which the name of the congregation is given except for an official of that congregation. In the present

---

[1] It has been generally accepted; *e.g.*, by Momigliano, *op. cit.*, 289, and by Vogelstein, *Jews of Rome*, 395, n. 3, where Frey's view that this is the same as the Synagogue of Severus is favored.
[2] Frey (*CII*, p. 365) calls it *une seconde copie*.

inscription there is no indication that Alexander was an official nor is there room to reconstruct a title. Secondly, the word συναγωγή is never found abbreviated on the extant Roman inscriptions. Not that we must insist that it never could be abbreviated; still it is strange that the abbreviation should occur only in this one copy of an inscription. While the preposition ἀπό is found in two instances with the name of a synagogue (343, 416), it occurs twice also with the name of the individual's city of origin (ἀπὸ 'Ακουιλείας 147, ἀπὸ Λαδικίας 296).

Since, therefore, the version in which Arca of Lebanon is the name of a city is no less, perhaps even more, likely to be the correct one than that in which it is the name of a congregation, and since the provenience of the inscription is so completely unknown that we cannot with assurance state that it came from Rome, there is certainly no basis for confidently including a Synagogue of Arca of Lebanon in the ancient Roman community.

Last of the dubious synagogues is that of the Calabrians. It originated with Father Vaccari's very unlikely interpretation of a puzzling Aramaic inscription from the Monteverde catacomb (290).[1] This inscription, which appears to read אניה חתנה דבר כולברוה has not yet been satisfactorily interpreted. Vaccari, reading אַנְיָה חֹתֶנֶת דַּבָּר קלבריה, translated it as "Annia, mother-in-law of the head of (the Synagogue of) Calabria." La Piana,[2] following Vaccari's reading with hesitation, included the Synagogue of the Calabrians in his list of thirteen congregations. While this is not the place to discuss the various and conflicting interpretations of the inscription, there is obviously no firm basis for attributing a Calabrian congregation to the Jews of Rome.

We are, accordingly, left with the names of eleven reasonably certain congregations. There might be some doubt with regard to the Secenians, as indicated above, but the balance of probability seems to be in favor of accepting it. Three of the eleven, the Agrippesians, Augustesians, and Volumnesians,

---

[1] In *NBAC* 23 (1917), 36 ff. and 28 (1922), 47 ff. See Fig. 39. 21.

[2] *Op. cit.*, 352, n. 22. Momigliano, however (*op. cit.*, 285), rejects it, as does Frey (*CII*, p. LXXXI, n. 4). Vogelstein (*Jews of Rome*, 27) is hesitant ("perhaps").

are apparently named for patrons or benefactors; three, the Campesians, Siburesians, and perhaps the Calcaresians, are named for the districts where their synagogues were located; two, the Tripolitans and possibly that of Elaea, for the city from which the founders of the congregation came; two, the Hebrews and Vernaclesians, for some characteristic of the members (Hebrews as opposed to gentiles, native Romans as opposed to immigrants); while the name of the Secenians has not yet received even a plausible explanation.

Since the Jewish community used the catacombs for perhaps three centuries, it is very likely that not all eleven of these congregations existed at the same time. As in modern communities, some congregations disband, new ones are formed, some change their names, some combine. An evidence of such a combination at Rome has been seen by sundry scholars in the epitaph of Veturia Paulla (523), who was Mother of the Synagogues of the Campesians and Volumnesians (*mater synagogarum Campi et Bolumni*). The use of the plural *synagogarum* would seem, however, to indicate that the venerable proselyte was honored by two different congregations. Whatever the process of evolution with regard to this group of eleven congregations may have been, we are in no position to trace the changes, since it is not possible to arrange the inscriptions involving the synagogues in any chronological sequence.

CHAPTER EIGHT

THE ORGANIZATION OF THE ROMAN JEWISH COMMUNITY

We have seen from the foregoing chapter that the large Jewish community of Rome was divided into separate congregations with their respective officers and other dignitaries. While there is no small amount of disagreement as to the number of these congregations and the significance of some of their names, there is an even greater lack of unanimity with regard to the details of their organization.[1] Although the inscriptions reveal in abundance such titles as archon, gerusiarch, archisynagogus, grammateus, they unfortunately fail to give us information about the functions of the officers who bore these titles or their relative importance in the community. This is hardly surprising, since the members of the community obviously knew what the titles meant and the writers of the epitaphs were not concerned about remote posterity. Consequently, in trying to fill the lacunae by bringing to bear analogies from other communities and from talmudic sources, scholars have naturally failed to agree on how far such parallels may properly be applied in determining the organization of Roman Jewry. The present chapter will offer the evidence from the inscriptions and discuss the various views. The reader should not, however, be disappointed if definitive conclusions are not always presented. To a large extent, these are simply not attainable from the fragmentary data which are available to us. If only by some miraculous

---

[1] The more important treatments of the communal organization of the Jews of Rome are the following: E. Schürer, *Die Gemeindeverfassung der Juden in Rom* (Leipzig, 1879); H. Vogelstein in *VR*, 41-48 and *Jews of Rome* (Philadelphia, 1940), 29-33; G. La Piana, *HTR* 20 (1927), 359-363; J. B. Frey, *Recherches de Science Religieuse* 21 (1931), 129-168 and *CII*, pp. LXXXII-CXI. More comprehensive accounts of the ancient Jewish communal organization, including that of Rome, are to be found in Schürer, II, 501-516 and III, 71-96; Juster, *Les Juifs dans l'Empire Romain* (Paris, 1914), I, 413-424 and 450-456 [hereafter cited as Juster]; S. Krauss, *Synagogale Altertümer* (Berlin-Wien, 1922), 112-159 [hereafter cited as Krauss].

discovery we could get possession of a copy of the constitution and by-laws of a single one of these ancient Roman congregations, most of our problems would disappear, but until some such document is turned up, we must reconcile ourselves to large gaps in our information.

Emil Schürer, who in his *Gemeindeverfassung der Juden in Rom* (Leipzig, 1879), was the first to present a systematic treatment of this whole matter, took it for granted that the Roman Jews were organized into their several independent congregations. Finding no evidence of a common organization or *gerusia* (γερουσία), he contrasted the Jews of Rome with those of Alexandria, who had a unified organization headed by an ethnarch and later controlled by a *gerusia*.[1] The Jewish congregations of Rome, however, were, according to Schürer, separate and independent religious *collegia*, organized on the model of communities of the Hellenistic world.[2] In his impressive study on the Jews in the Roman Empire, Jean Juster denied the collegial organization of the Jewish congregations and pointed out that in their essential character they differed from the religious *collegia* and must be regarded as *sui generis*.[3] Juster was apparently the first to maintain that the separate Jewish groups were bound together by a central organization *(sénat central)* called the *gerusia*, with officers and representatives from the several congregations.[4]

This belief in a central council for the entire Jewish com-

---

[1] *Gemeindeverfassung* 15, where the references are cited. Vogelstein earlier (*VR*, 42) agreed with Schürer, but in his more recent work, *Jews of Rome* (p. 32), he thought that the existence of a "united communal organization" was likely. He cites as proof the demonstration of the Roman Jews in connection with the embassies from Palestine after the death of Herod and the existence of a Jewish house of study and court of justice in Rome. These would be evidences that the community could unite on certain projects, as Jewish groups do in our day, but do not prove the kind of central organization reconstructed by Juster and others.

[2] *Op. cit.*, 19 f. He compares the nine archons of Athens as influencing the arrangement of nine archons in the Jewish community of Berenice in North Africa.

[3] Juster, I, 418-424.

[4] I, 420 f., n. 3. He cites Rabbi Matthias ben Heresh as *chef suprême* of the Jewish community of Rome. Actually, he was head of the rabbinic school, not of the community, as Frey (*Rech. Sci. Rel.* 21,137) rightly points out. See *JE*, *s.v.* Mattithiah b. Heresh.

munity was strongly endorsed by Samuel Krauss,[1] who held that in all Jewish communities large enough to have several synagogues there was a Grand Council (*oberster Rat*) with representatives from the various congregations. Calling this Council the *synagoga alti ordinis* or *gerusia*, he cited the organization of the Jews of Alexandria as the prototype. In the reference to an *archon alti ordinis* in one Roman inscription (470) he found a positive indication of the presence of a *synagoga alti ordinis*. The members of this Grand Council were, according to Krauss, the frequently mentioned archons, who were chosen annually, with the exception of those few who were elected for life.[2] A similar view was offered by Professor George La Piana.[3] Insisting that "the evidence of the inscriptions leaves no doubt of the existence in imperial times of officers for the whole Jewish community", he cited, as did Krauss, the *archon alti ordinis*, as well as two archons *pases times* (πάσης τιμῆς) and one archon *pases tessimen* (85, 324, 216), all of whom he regarded as probably officials of this "central organization of government coordinating the activities of the several synagogues, supervising the general administration, and having definite authority in financial and juridical matters." While maintaining that the Roman group probably had no supreme head corresponding to the Alexandrian ethnarch, La Piana believed that this *gerusia* had its presiding officer and a board of archons. More recently, this point of view has been accepted by Charles Guignebert, as also by Dr. Salo Baron, who insists that "the community rather than the congregation was the basic unit."[4]

---

[1] Krauss, 137-140.

[2] Krauss, 152-154.

[3] *Op. cit.* (above, p. 167, n. 1), 361 f. It is strange that nowhere does La Piana cite Juster or Krauss; but he seems to present his views as original.

[4] Guignebert, *Le monde juif vers le temps de Jésus* (Paris, 1950), 280-282; Baron, *A Social and Religious History of the Jews* (New York, 1952), II, 199. In his earlier work, *The Jewish Community* (Philadelphia, 1942), I, 106 f., Dr. Baron had characterized such a general council as loosely organized and interfering little with the internal management of each synagogue. He states also (*Soc. and Rel. Hist.*, II, 199), as did La Piana (*op. cit.*, 363), that the cemeteries were the property of the community as a whole rather than of the separate congregations, but this cannot be attested. At most one may say that a group of congregations probably administered one cemetery

Such theories were energetically opposed by Father Frey, who devoted one whole section of the Introduction to his *Corpus Inscriptionum Iudaicarum* to a refutation of La Piana.[1] Citing the evidence of the inscriptions, he insisted that while each congregation had its own *gerusia*, there was no such body for the community as a whole. He denied that there is any evidence of a supreme head of the community, asserting emphatically, "Le judaïsme n'eut jamais de pape." In his opinion, the sole unifying authority of Roman Jewry was the Law. The reference in Acts (28. 17) to the chief men of the Jews at Rome (τοὺς ὄντας τῶν 'Ιουδαίων πρώτους), which La Piana and others had cited as an indication of an authoritative body of Jewish leaders, Frey reasonably interpreted as referring only to such community leaders as the gerusiarchs of the various congregations. Thus Frey reverted to the original view of Schürer, a view which was endorsed also by Arnaldo Momigliano.[2]

While absolute certainty is not to be expected with the available evidence, it seems that the burden of proof lies on those who argue for a central authority and that they have by no means established their case. The analogy of the Alexandrian community will hardly apply, since the large Jewish group in Alexandria had been an integral part of that city since its foundation and had always played an important role in its affairs, whereas the Jews of Rome had come as immigrants at different times and from different places, forming their congregations as the need arose, and apparently never playing a significant part in the affairs of the great Capital. Accordingly, in the absence of adequate evidence, it is preferable to reject as unproved the thesis of a central *gerusia* with a supreme head and proceed on the assumption that the eleven or more Jewish congregations of Rome were separate and independent entities, each with its own organization and rules, as are the Jewish congregations of large cities in our own day. That the general pattern for the organization of each group was fairly homogeneous may reasonably be assumed.

---

on some sort of co-operative basis; *e.g.*, the Trastevere group of seven congregations which used the Monteverde catacomb.

[1] *CII*, pp. CII-CXI.
[2] *Rassegna Mensile di Israël* 6 (1931-32), 284.

There is general agreement that the head of the congregation or synagogue was, as the title implies, the archisynagogus (ἀρχισυνάγωγος). The inscriptions from Rome afford five examples of this official. Only two of these reveal the name of the synagogue. Poly[me?]nius (383), who was Archisynagogus of the Synagogue of the Vernaclesians, died at the age of fifty-three. The Archisynagogus Julianus (504) was undoubtedly the head of the Calcaresian Synagogue, since we are informed that his son, also named Julianus, was the Gerusiarch of this congregation. In one inscription (282) the name of the synagogue with which the Archisynagogus Isaac was associated was originally on the stone but is now lost. In two others (265, 336) we have only the names of the archisynagogi, Stafylus and Euphrasius, but without mention of the names of their congregations. None of these epitaphs gives us any clue as to the functions of this official.

Since this title had long been used in the Jewish world, it is probable that the duties represented by the office had become more or less standardized.[1] In rabbinic sources the archisynagogus is styled *rosh hakneset* (ראש הכנסת). His was the most honored of all the positions in the congregation, and we may regard him as the spiritual leader of the synagogue.[2] He regulated the divine service, designated the person who would read the portion from the Torah or deliver a homily, and invited strangers to address the gathering. While he did not

---

[1] For examples of archisynagogi see Schürer, II, 510 and notes 23-29. On the functions of this official see especially Schürer, *Gemeindeverfassung*, 25-28 and II, 511; Berliner, *Gesch. Jud.*, I, 69; *VR*, 42 f.; Ginzberg in *JE*, *s.v.* Archisynagogus; Juster, I, 450-453; Krauss, 114 f.; G. F. Moore, *Judaism*, I, 289; Frey, *Rech. Sci. Rel.* 21,152-154 and *CII*, pp. XCVII-XCIX; Baron, *Jewish Community*, I, 103.

[2] Th. Reinach, in *REJ* 71 (1920), 49, made the archisynagogus approximately the equivalent of the modern rabbi. A. Marmorstein, in *Palestine Explor. Fund Quarterly Statement* (1921), 24-26, sharply disagrees, stating that this official was not the spiritual head of the congregation, but only a lay dignitary whose chief qualification was a liberal purse rather than any scholarly attainment or spiritual quality. Juster (I, 450, n. 4), equating the functions of the archisynagogus with those of the rabbi, points out that the title *rabbi* for the spiritual head does not appear until a later time. Baron, in *Jewish Comm.*, I, 103, makes the archisynagogus approximately equal to the modern "church warden," but stresses the high esteem in which he was held in his congregation.

need to be an especially learned man, he must have been well acquainted with the details of the ritual. If the evidence of Jewish inscriptions from other parts of the Mediterranean world may be applied to Rome,[1] the archisynagogus was also charged with the responsibility for the construction and improvement of the synagogue building.

We do not know how the archisynagogus was chosen or how long he held his office.[2] An inscription of Acmonia in Phrygia (*CII* 766) reveals that in a certain congregation an archisynagogus for life (διὰ βίου) and an archisynagogus and an archon combined in restoring its building, presumably the synagogue. The evidence of this inscription points to the likelihood that the archisynagogus was chosen for an indefinite term, holding his office until age, infirmity, or death made the selection of a successor necessary. The venerable retiring official might then be given the honorary title of "life archisynagogus."

From this survey of the possible duties of the archisynagogus, it appears that he was the active leader of the congregation, combining some of the functions which in modern congregations are held by the rabbi and the president, that is, responsibility for the cult and, at least in some communities, for the physical properties. He seems also to have represented the congregation to the community at large. That the Roman authorities looked upon the archisynagogi as the responsible representatives of the Jewish congregations is apparent from the references to them in the Theodosian Code (16.8.4, 13, 14), which, though somewhat later than the time with which we are concerned, probably reveal a situation which had endured through generations. It will be recalled that when Emperor Alexander Severus was mocked for his partiality to Judaism, he was derisively referred to as the "Syrian archisynagogus" (see above, p. 43), a clear indication that the archisynagogus

---

[1] These inscriptions are from the Greek island of Aegina (*CII* 722), Acmonia in Phrygia (*CII* 766), and Jerusalem (*CII* 1404).

[2] Juster (I, 452) states that it was not an elective post, but that the holder was named by the patriarch. How the archisynagogus was chosen when there was no patriarch, he does not say. Frey, on the contrary, holds that the post was elective (*Rech. Sci. Rel.* 21,154; *CII*, p. XCVIII). According to Ginzberg (*JE*, II, 86), the position was normally held for life and was often hereditary.

was the characteristic official of the synagogue. At a later time the term used would have been "rabbi."[1]

Of all the offices of the synagogue the one most frequently mentioned is that of archon. This title is found in no fewer than forty-seven inscriptions of the Roman Jews, well distributed among both catacombs and individual congregations. The Appia catacomb has yielded fourteen instances, the Monteverde eighteen, the Nomentana four, the Vigna Cimarra one; ten references are found in inscriptions whose ultimate provenience is not recorded.[2] In sixteen cases we know the congregation which the archon served, but in most the congregation is not named. Of the sixteen, the largest number, four, are of the Siburesian Synagogue (22, 35a, 140, 380), three of the Calcaresians (304, 316, 384), two each of the Augustesians (338, 416), Vernaclesians (398, 494), and Volumnesians (343, 417), and one each of the Agrippesians (503), Hebrews (291), and Tripolitans (390). Thus of the eleven known synagogues eight are specifically indicated as having had archons, and there is no reason to believe that the other three, the Campesians, Elaeans, and Secenians, lacked such an official, although the capricious chances of discovery have not yet revealed any for them. In addition, there are six instances of mellarchons and two of child archons, which will be considered in due time.

Plentiful though these references to the archonship are, they offer us not the slightest hint as to the duties and responsibilities of the office. While examples of archons are fairly com-

---

[1] It has been pointed out that a person could be both archon and archisynagogus (*e.g.*, Schürer, III, 88), but from the inscriptions cited as evidence (the only Roman one is that of Stafylus, 265) we need not conclude that the two offices were held simultaneously. Since either position was considered important enough to be mentioned on one's tomb, it is probable that in each known instance a man who had been archon was promoted to the higher office. Nor need we be especially concerned over indications that women and children held the title of archisynagogus, since no such instance has come to light at Rome (see Juster, I, 453; Krauss, 118, *CII*, p. XCIX). I regard the Venosa inscription which supposedly refers to a child archisynagogus (*CII* 587) as very dubious; the inscription when copied was in a sadly mutilated condition and is perhaps no longer to be seen. At least, I was unable to find it when I explored the Venosa catacomb.

[2] Since a complete listing of these many examples seems unnecessary, I cite only those on which special comment is made.

mon from other parts of the Jewish world, not only from
Italy, but also from the eastern and western Mediterranean
areas and from Egypt and North Africa,[1] neither these nor
the scant references in literature offer much information.
There has, therefore, as we might expect, been small accord
among scholars on this matter. That the archons were elected
annually is agreed. A homily by a Christian writer of perhaps
the time of Constantine or earlier[2] reveals that the Jews
chose their archons in the month of September during the
Festival of Tabernacles. Since there is no evidence to the
contrary, this statement may reasonably be accepted as
representing a normal practice. That the archons were selected
for a specific term is established also by nine references at
Rome to archons who held the office twice and one to a
three-time archon. There are, in addition, six examples of
life archons (διὰ βίου, ζαβίου, *Iabiu*), a dignity which was
probably honorary rather than involving active service.[3]

In general, there are two main conflicting views as to the
nature of the archonship. Schürer and those others who
believe that each congregation was a completely independent
entity and had its own governing board hold that the archons
were either the individual members of such a board or a small
executive committee of the board.[4] Those who, on the other

---

[1] See the lists in Schürer, III, 85, and notes 37, 38; Juster, I, 444,
n. 2. There seems to have been no such official in the Jewish community of Venosa.

[2] This homily, entitled "De Nativitate Sancti Ioannis Baptistae"
(Frey calls it "De solstitiis et aequinoctiis D. N. Jesu Christi et Joannis
Baptistae"), was falsely attributed to St. John Chrysostom and is
now thought by some scholars to be the work of Pontius Maximus.
See *CII*, p. LXXXVII and the references there; cf. Schürer, III, 86.

[3] Twice archons: 13, 125, 289, 316, 337, 384, 391, 397, 505; thrice
archon: 494; life archons: 266, 398, 416, 417, 480, 503. Although the
title *archon* never accompanies the appellation διὰ βίου, it is almost
universally accepted as referring to this office and nobody now favors
Ascoli's view (*Iscrizioni di antichi sepolcri giudaici* [Torino e Roma,
1880], 112 and note 1) that it represented a prayer for eternal life
(= *ad vitam eternam*, לחיי עולם or לחיי עד or simply לחיים). See the
arguments in Schürer, III, 87, n. 42 and Juster, I, 445, n. 3. Where some
other life office was meant, the title appears to have been specified:
e.g., ἀρχισυνάγωγος διὰ βίου (*CII* 766, Acmonia in Phrygia).

[4] Schürer (*Gemeindeverfassung*, 19) states that the members of the
gerusia were probably known as *gerontes* and *presbyteri* and that the
archons were the bearers of the executive authority of this board, a

hand, maintain that the several congregations were tied together by a communal *gerusia* regard the archons as the administrative officers of this body with each congregation represented by one or more such archons.[1]

There is some indication that a congregation may have had only one archon at a time. This would seem to have been true, at any rate, of the Siburesians, since in at least three of the four instances of archons from this synagogue the definite article precedes the title.[2] The article is found three times also in connection with the expression "twice archon" and once with the "life archon." If each congregation had but one archon, selected annually, with an occasional re-election, this would adequately account for the fact that we have far more

---

view with which Frey emphatically agrees (*CII*, p. LXXXVII, *il n'y a guère de doute*). According to Vogelstein (*VR*, 41 f.) the archons were themselves the members of the governing board, forming a *collegium*, with each archon in charge of a special function.

[1] So Juster, I, 444-446 and Guignebert, *Monde juif*, 281. Juster suggests (I, 446 and n.2) that in some communities the archons may have constituted the entire board, as at Berenice in Cyrenaica, where the Jewish community was governed by a council of nine archons (*CIG* 5361, an inscription of probably the first century B.C.E.). This is also the view of A. Büchler (*JE*, II, 87), who cites, in addition to the evidence from Berenice, the more than thirty-eight archons of Alexandria (there may have been as many as seventy-one) and the situation in Rome, where "there were several communities each with its archon." Krauss (p. 149) adds the point that the archons were both officials of their own congregation and members of the communal *gerusia*. La Piana (*op. cit.*, 361, n. 34), moreover, remarks that where the name of the synagogue is not stated the archon may have been a member of this communal council rather than the officer of a specitic congregation ("archons at large").

[2] These are Nos. 22 (the entire article is legible, despite Frey's indication of a lacuna), 380, and the Julianus inscription(35a), where the article is lost along with a few other letters, but the reconstruction is virtually certain; see *JQR*, 42 (1952), 416. In the fourth inscription of an archon of the Siburesians (26, which is fragmentary) there may well have been an article in the missing portion. Frey (*CII*, p. LXXXVII), in rejecting the possibility of a single archon, regards the article in No. 380 as an error of the stonecutter, stating that this is the sole example. Strangely, he disregards his own interpretation of No. 22, where he restores the article (although, as stated above, no restoration is needed). The addition of the Julianus inscription, which was unknown to him, and the examples of ὁ δὶς ἄρχων (13, 384, 391) and ὁ ζαβιου (416) would completely invalidate Frey's argument. Krauss (p. 148) believes that when the article precedes the title, this archon is simply designated as the congregational representative to the communal *gerusia*.

references to the archonship than to any other office, since the other major officials were chosen for a longer, and perhaps indeterminate, period, as we have seen in the case of the archisynagogus. If, on the other hand, every congregation had a board of archons, the personnel of which changed annually, the number who had served in this capacity would after some years come to be a fairly large portion of the membership of the congregation, and we should expect to find evidence of many more archons than have hitherto been recorded. In fact, the archonship would be too common an office to justify its being recorded on one's tomb. That it was so recorded shows that it was a distinct honor, as it would indeed have been if the congregation had only the one archon in any given year.

As for the functions of the archons, they were probably concerned with secular affairs exclusively, such as business negotiations involving contracts and leases, political connections, and other non-religious matters.[1] Actually, however, there is no positive evidence about their duties. Especially worrisome are the four instances (85, 216, 324, 337) of an archon *pases times* (πάσης τιμῆς)[2] and one (470) of an archon *alti ordinis*. Proponents of a communal *gerusia* point to these as positive indications of the existence of such a council, since they interpret the titles as belonging to the congregational representatives to this *gerusia*.[3] The usual meaning of

---

[1] So e.g., Juster, I, 447, Büchler in *JE*, II, 87.

[2] The *pases tessimen* of No. 216 is manifestly a garbled Latin spelling of the Greek πάσης τιμῆς or perhaps πάσης τῆς τιμῆς, although the latter form is not found.

[3] E.g., Krauss, 137, n. 2, 138; La Piana, op. cit., 362, n. 36. Krauss, in fact, finds traces of the members of this communal body not only in these expressions, but also, as we have just seen, in the use of the article with the title archon, in the inscription of a certain Stafylus (265), an archon and archisynagogus who had held all the honors (*honoribus omnibus fuctus*), and that of an official designated as *exarchon* (see below, pp.188-90). In the last line of No. 470, which has the sole reference to an *archon alti ordinis*, he confidently interprets (p. 258 f.) the small sign resembling an "S", which follows the word *archon*, as the abbreviation of *synagogae* and regards this as the most positive of proofs that there was a higher council. (But why should it be called *synagoga*, which is never used of a council, instead of some term like *gerusia*?) There is, however, no instance of any abbreviation of the word *synagoga*, and since the supposed letter "S" differs materially in form and size from the large, beautifully shaped letters of the in-

the Greek word τιμή is *honor* or *dignity*, so that the expression would seem to designate an archon "of all dignity", that is, some exalted form of that office. This is especially borne out by the epitaph of Eupsychus (337), of whom we learn that he was twice archon, archon *pases times*, and phrontistes. It appears, accordingly, that the archon *pases times* enjoyed a higher dignity than an ordinary archon. Frey, proceeding from the secondary meanings of τιμή as *value, price, evaluation, census*, regards this officer as most probably the financial executive of the congregation charged with collecting the dues, taxes, and other revenues and with making disbursements; in other words, a sort of treasurer.[1] It would seem that if τιμή had so definite a meaning here, it would need to be preceded by the definite article and the expression would be πάσης τῆς τιμῆς; but this phrase does not occur.[2] Possibly the expression *archon alti ordinis* represents the Latin equivalent of the Greek. We must conclude, accordingly, that we have in both these expressions the designation of an archon-

---

scription (see Fig. 33, upper left), it may be regarded as possibly a slip by the stonecutter or a sort of space filler to make the short final line approximately equal to the others. Krauss adds (p. 259) the astonishing explanation that a "cursive" "s" is used in order to indicate that the Greek word συναγωγή is meant. Since the lunate form of the sigma (C) was the only one in regular use at this time, it is hard to understand why a Latin "s", cursive or otherwise, should have been used to represent this letter. Th. Reinach, in *REJ* 71 (1920), 123, regarded this symbol as the sign for *et*, interpreting the phrase as *archon et alti ordinis*, i.e., Maecius was both an archon and a member of the communal council.

[1] *CII*, p. LXXXIX f. In this view he was anticipated by Vogelstein (*VR*, 41 and n. 7). Salo Baron also (*Jewish Community*, I, 102) accepts this interpretation. Krauss, however (p. 165 and n. 1), ridicules the idea (he calls it *komisch*) and insists that the expression denotes an archon "of all honors" who united in his person a combination of offices. Earlier, Schürer (*Gemeindeverfassung*, 22) had suggested that such an archon was probably also an archisynagogus or gerusiarch; but, if so, would not the other office or offices have been mentioned specifically, as they are in the inscriptions of Stafylus, cited above, and others?

[2] Unless there be a trace of it in the garbled *pases tessimen* (see above, p. 176, n. 5). La Piana (*op. cit.*, 362, n. 36), interpreting τιμή as perhaps referring to the communal *gerusia* (its advocates find references to it everywhere), actually inserts the article without warrant. The article would indeed be indispensable if the word were to bear such a meaning. There is, however, no evidence that τιμή ever designated a council of any kind.

ship of high honor, whatever the appurtenances of such an office may have been.

Since the archonship was apparently a position of some importance, we should expect it to be limited to fairly mature persons. In several instances we know the age at death of individuals who had held the office. The life archon Tettius Rufinus (480) attained the ripe age of eighty-five.[1] Pomponius, twice archon of the Calcaresians (384), died at sixty. Three died at thirty-five: Hilarus, archon of the Volumnesians (343); Claudius Ioses (538); Sabbatius, twice archon (397). Still younger were Nicodemus, archon of the Siburesians (380), who lived to be only thirty years and forty-two days, and, if the obscured numeral is correctly read, the archon Zonatha (277, = Jonathan), who died at nineteen. If a fragmentary inscription of the Appia catacomb has been restored rightly (140), it is the epitaph of Maronius, archon of the Siburesians, who lived to the age of twenty-four years and three months. Thus, apparently, relatively young persons of thirty or less, presumably members of prominent families, could attain the archonship. There is one puzzling instance (505) of a certain Caelius Quintus, twice archon, whose age at death may have been only thirteen. His age is indicated on the stone by the non-existent Greek numeral IT, which, were it not for the strangely immature age of a twice archon, would most easily be regarded as a slip for IΓ, the symbol for "thirteen." Frey makes the impossible suggestion (*sans doute*, as usual) that it is an error for IΘ, which would equal nineteen; but while Θ is sometimes interchanged with T in the spelling of whole words, it is inconceivable that such a mistake would occur in the figure of a numeral, where no phonetic confusion is involved. Ferrua reasonably proposed that the figure should be Π, which equals eighty.[2] The obstacle here is that the epithets

---

[1] The numeral is written ⌊XXXV, so that there is the possibility that the "L" is not a part of the numeral but a frame for the numeral, as in the Greek inscription, No. 510. If this is so, the age of Rufinus was thirty-five rather than eighty-five; but the higher figure seems to me the more likely, especially as the frame in 510 is formed somewhat differently.

[2] *Epigraphica*, 3 (1941), 38. Possibly the "twice archon" is to be referred to the boy's father, with the jumbled syntax which occurs in No. 537, where the expression "Father of the Synagogue" is wrongly

φιλοπάτωρ (lover of his father) and παῖς Ἑβραῖος (Hebrew boy) are used of the deceased. Although the word παῖς may represent the Hebrew *ben*, which can be used of adults, we should expect the expression φιλοπάτωρ only in the case of a relatively youthful person whose father survived him (as in 125 and 152). It seems hardly appropriate for a man of eighty. It looks, accordingly, as though we have here an instance of a boy, in his early 'teens', who had twice been archon, however we may explain such a case.

Linked with this problem is that of the child archon (ἄρχων νήπιος), of whom we have two examples at Rome, both from the Appia catacomb. The child archon Annianus (88), the son of Julianus, Father of the Synagogue of the Campesians, died at the age of eight years and two months. The other (120) is the brief epitaph of the child archon Iocathinus. Although his age is not stated, he was evidently only a small child, since the lid of the sarcophagus in which he was buried is hardly more than a meter in length.[1] Obviously the title of archon was conferred on small children as a mark of honor, apparently in view of the distinction of the family. The aforementioned Annianus was the child of a Father of the Synagogue, while the fact that Iocathinus' little body was placed not in an ordinary loculus, but in a marble sarcophagus (the lid, which alone is preserved, is adorned with floral decorations) would indicate that the family was, at least, prosperous.

For what it is worth, one may cite as a parallel the child decurions of ancient Italian towns. Since the Board of Decurions constituted the governing body of a municipality, corresponding to the Senate at Rome, the title of decurion as conferred on children was clearly of an honorary nature in recognition of the high distinction or wealth of their families. The *Corpus Inscriptionum Latinarum* offers at least seven instances of such child decurions, whose ages, where indicated, range from four to seventeen years.[2] In one instance

---

placed in the. nominative instead of the genitive and seems to refer to the daughter instead of the father. There is a similar error in 319.
[1] See H. J. Leon in *RAC* 29 (1953), 103. For a photograph of the sarcophagus lid see Fig. 27.
[2] *CIL* V, 337; IX, 1166, 3573; X, 376, 846, 1036; XIV, 376.

(*CIL* X, 846) the decurions of Pompeii honored N. Popidius Celsinus, a boy of six, by making him a member of their body because of his generosity in repairing from its foundations the Temple of Isis, which had been destroyed by an earthquake (obviously the disaster of 62 or 63 C.E.). In this case, at least, the wealth of the family, liberally used in the public interest, was the reason for the honor shown the child.[1]

In concluding this discussion of the archon, a brief consideration of the mellarchon, archon-elect or archon-presumptive, is appropriate. The Judeo-Roman inscriptions offer six examples of this title, one (85) being from the Appia catacomb and five (284, 325, 402, 457, 483) from the Monteverde. In one instance (85) the mellarchon Alexander was the son of an archon *pases times*, also named Alexander. A certain Marcus Cvyntus (= Quintus) Alexus (284) was both grammateus of the Augustesians and mellarchon at the age of twelve, that is, if the inscription, now lost, was correctly transcribed. Another mellarchon, Aelius Primitivus (457), was thirty-eight at the time of his death. And there is the one surprising case of Siculus Sabinus (402), who, though an infant of only two years and ten months when he died, was already Mellarchon of the Volumnesians. What age he would have had to reach in order to become a full-fledged child archon does not appear. We may gather from these examples that during the period which elapsed between the time of the election of the archon and his assumption of the office he was a mellarchon, and that this title was conferred also on children of prominent families who were presumed some day to become archons, be it active or honorary.

From the existence of the title *gerusiarches* (γερουσιάρχης) we may readily infer that each congregation had a *gerusia*

---

[1] Another parallel has been found in the child *lectores* of Christian communities (Schürer, II, 512, n. 37; Krauss, 118). Victor Vitensis, a Christian writer of the late fifth century, mentions the exile from Carthage of some five hundred Christians, including a number of *lectores infantuli*, during the persecution by the Vandals (*Historia Persecutionis Africanae Provinciae* 3, 34, to be found in *Corp. Scrip. Eccl. Lat.*, VII). A Christian inscription of North Africa is the epitaph of a certain *lector* named Vitalis, who died at the age of five (*CIL* VIII, 453). In this instance the editor, G. Wilmanns, while vouching for the correctness of the reading, suggests that the stonecutter may have made an error.

(γερουσία) or Council of Elders, of which this official was the head, although nowhere in our inscriptions is there any reference to such a *gerusia*.[1] It is not unlikely that its members were called *presbyteri* (πρεσβύτεροι). A fragment of an inscription from Monteverde (378) may have borne the title *presbyterus*, but since only the latter part of the word is preserved (. . . YTEPOC), complete certainty is hardly possible.[2] References to Jewish *presbyteri* in inscriptions outside Rome and in legal documents, such as the Theodosian Code, are of the fourth century and later.[3] It is not surprising that one's membership in the *gerusia* is not mentioned in the inscriptions, since such "Elders," being relatively numerous, were probably not regarded as congregational officers, and it was the custom for only the officers to be recorded as such in their epitaphs.

In the absence of any information it is futile to speculate on the size of the *gerusia*, on how its members were chosen, and for how long a term they served.[4] Nor have we any more definite data with regard to their chairman, the gerusiarch.[5]

---

[1] I. Zoller, *Ricerche Religiose* 8 (1932), 464, finding no evidence of a *gerusia* at Rome, thinks that the gerusiarch was the head of the בית דין, the rabbinical tribunal, a *collegium* of perhaps three rabbis with one presiding, which decided such matters as divorces and release from religious vows.

[2] Frey is positive that the previous letter was a B, but the tiny curve which is visible may be part of a P or even a Θ or O. No. 400 is the epitaph of a certain Sara, who is designated as ΠΡΕCΒΥΤΝC (apparently for πρεσβύτης or more likely πρεσβῦτις). Here the word probably means no more than "elderly woman", comparable to the use of νήπιος and παρθένος, of a child or virgin, respectively, as is pointed out in *MB*, p. 56. Cf. Schürer, III, 90, n. 55. Frey translates *femme âgée*.

[3] The references are listed in Schürer, III, 89, 90, notes 53, 54; Juster, I, 441, notes 2, 3. The three instances from Venosa (*CII* 581, 590, 597) are all of women. There it may be that the wife of a presbyterus is meant, unless this was an honorary title conferred on certain women for distinguished services. It cannot mean "old woman," since one presbytera died at thirty-eight (590).

[4] There is not much point in comparing the large *gerusia* of the Jews of Alexandria, as Frey and others have done. Frey suggests (*CII*, p. LXXXV) that the members may have been elected annually by the general assembly of the congregation.

[5] For a list (incomplete for Rome) of occurrences of this exclusively Jewish title, see Juster, I, 442, n. 7. A marble slab (*CII* 533) found near Castel Porziano, several miles from Ostia, records the official grant by a Jewish community, the name of which has not been preserved (the common restoration of the name of Ostia is purely arbitrary),

Hardly an inkling may be derived from the references to this official in our inscriptions, which have yielded fourteen examples in all, four of which are from the Appia (95, 106, 119, 147), six from the Monteverde (301, 353, 368, 405, 408, 425), one from the Nomentana (9), and three of unknown source (504, 511, and 733b, not in *CII*);[1] of these, however, one (504) may appropriately be associated with the Monteverde catacomb, since it mentions the Calcaresians, who buried there.[2] The synagogue is mentioned in connection with five of these officers.[3] Annius (301) and Quintianus (368) were gerusiarchs of the Augustesians, Symmachus (408) and Julianus (504)[4] were of the Tripolitans and Calcaresians, respectively, and the Agrippesians had a gerusiarch whose name ended in the letter *s* (425).[5] In three instances we have the age at death: Symmachus (408) was eighty, Annius (9) was sixty-five, Quintianus (368) was fifty-four. Thus we have no record of a youthful gerusiarch.

We may infer that the office of gerusiarch was a responsible one, which required ability in the area of public relations, from the fact that three of these officers are praised for their personal qualities. Thus Annius (9), we are informed, lived a good life (καλῶς βειώσας); Theophilus (119), not only lived

---

through three of its officials, one being a gerusiarch, another a pater, and a third whose title is not preserved, of a small plot of land (18 feet by 17 feet) to the gerusiarch C. Julius Justus for a family tomb.

[1] That of Epagathus. See above, p. 101, n. 2.

[2] Frey finds a gerusiarch in No. 355, but he has misread the inscription, which is that of a priest, *hiereus*; see below, p. 192, n. 3.

[3] Krauss (p. 148), adhering to his view that the gerusiarchs were heads of the *gerusia* of the entire community and not of the individual congregations, observes that only the synagogues of the Augustesians and Agrippesians had a gerusiarch of their own, since, in view of the illustrious patrons for whom they were named, they were placed in a separate category and are to be regarded as the mother congregations of Roman Jewry. He should have known better, since the inscriptions revealing gerusiarchs of the Calcaresians and Tripolitans had been known for some time.

[4] Here the title is written ιερευσαρχων, which has sometimes been misinterpreted as two words, meaning "priest archon." That it is only a matter of phonetic misspelling is clear from the forms ιερουσιαρχης (405) and ειεροσαρχης (408). The false analogy with *archon* is seen also at Venosa, where we find the forms γερουσιαρχον (*CII* 600) and *ierusiarcontis* (*CII* 613).

[5] *MB*, p. 5 and Frey have -AC with the conjecture that the name was Judas; but the stone shows no trace of an A.

a good life, but had a good reputation as well (καλῶς βιώσας καὶ καλῶς ἀκούσας); while Julianus (353) left the enviable record of having lived on good terms with everyone (καλῶς βιώσας μετὰ πάντων). One gerusiarch, Ursacius, who came to Rome from Aquileia,[1] buried three daughters, respectively named Centulia (129), Ursacia (147), and Simplicia (167). The record of this unhappy father's tragic loss is still to be seen in the bleak corridors of the Appia catacomb, where the brief epitaphs of the three girls are rather crudely painted on the closures of their graves.

We know nothing more of the gerusiarch's duties than that he was the chairman of the executive board of his congregation. That can be inferred from his title, as we have seen. His position was surely one of high dignity and responsibility, perhaps second only to that of the archisynagogus. The office was entrusted only to mature men and apparently never bestowed in the form of an honorary title to youths and children, as was that of archon. It is probable that, like the archisynagogus, he served for an indefinite term, being replaced only at death or if he became too infirm to carry out the duties of his office. As for the functions of the board over which he presided, we may conjecture, there being no evidence, that it performed duties not unlike those of modern congregational boards, that is, exercising general supervision over both religious and secular matters including the congregational properties, charities, schools, care of the sick, burials, and perhaps assembling the contributions for the Temple at Jerusalem and later for the Patriarch or the imperial treasury.

Second to the title archon in frequency of occurrence on the Jewish inscriptions of Rome is that of grammateus. There are no fewer than twenty-four instances, with the addition of two who are designated as mellogrammateus or grammateus-presumptive.[2] The largest number is to be found in the

---

[1] Frey (*CII*, p. LXXXVI, n.1) unreasonably doubts whether Ursacius was gerusiarch at Rome or at Aquileia. The phrase ἀπὸ 'Ακουιλείας clearly indicates only the man's origin and is not to be combined with the title. Cf. No. 296. In *JE*, V, 642, Krauss makes this Ursacius the president of the communal Roman *gerusia*.

[2] Frey (*CII*, p. XCII) mentions twenty-eight instances (including two mellogrammateis), but an examination of his index of Greek words, on which his total is based, shows that he counts 148 twice, though

Appia catacomb, which has yielded twelve examples plus one mellogrammateus. Five are from Monteverde and seven from the Nomentana. The one other instance of a mellogrammateus was found in the small Vigna Cimarra catacomb. Why there should be relatively more examples of the grammateus from the Nomentana catacomb and so proportionately few from the Monteverde does not appear and it may be the result entirely of chance. The synagogue with which the grammateus was connected is named in six cases: two are from the Siburesian congregation (18, 67), one each from the Vernaclesians (318), Augustesians (284), Calcaresians (433),[1] and Secenians (7).

It seems quite obvious that the grammateus was the secretary of the congregation.[2] The fact that each had its own grammateus and that the dignity was regarded important enough to be recorded on one's tomb is a clear evidence that this was one of the chief offices of the congregation. While there is no indication of the duties, we may properly assume that they did not differ very much from the functions associated with such an office in our day, that is, recording the minutes of the congregational *gerusia* and of the assembly of members, keeping the membership lists up to date, and conserving the records.[3] Quite untenable is the view advanced

---

it has only one reference to a grammateus, and he includes 328, in which no grammateus is mentioned, and 177, which is so fragmentary as not to justify any reconstruction (of the supposed word γραμματεύς only the letters AT are to be seen). On the other hand, Frey omits 31, in the fourth line of which the letters ΓΡΑΜ can be clearly seen. The previous investigators, Paribeni and Beyer and Lietzmann, also missed the fourth line, although the four letters are quite distinct.

[1] Only the letters KA of the name of this synagogue are preserved; but the restoration of the name of the Calcaresians is reasonably certain, since we know that its members used this catacomb. Frey, following Müller (*MB*, p. 6 f.), suggests the alternative restoration Κα[μπησίων], but since the Campesians are known to have buried in the Appia catacomb, such a restoration here is improbable. Müller, recognizing this fact, preferred Κα[λκαρησίων].

[2] He was certainly not secretary of the entire community, as stated by Guignebert (*Monde juif*, 281), who makes him secretary general of the probably non-existent communal *gerusia*. The naming of the individual synagogues with which the grammateus was associated refutes such a view.

[3] This is also the view of Müller (*Jüd. Kat.*, 116), who reasonably compares the grammateus of the Sanhedrin at Jerusalem and of the

by Berliner and by Schürer that the grammateus was the learned scribe (סופר) mentioned in the rabbinical literature, a man skilled in the Torah and a recognized authority in legal matters.[1] Equally unacceptable is the suggestion of Vogelstein that while the grammateus need not be a profound Torah scholar, he was a skilled craftsman who made copies of the Torah scrolls and prepared marriage contracts and other religious documents. When we consider that a Torah scroll lasted for generations and that the special contracts and documents would hardly be needed often enough to require a separate congregational official, we must reject such a view.

Although we have no information about the circumstances of the grammateus' selection and tenure, we may surmise that a properly qualified official held his position for an indefinite period. That the grammateus was usually a mature man is readily inferred from the duties which we must associate with the office. The age at death is given in eleven instances. Honoratus (145) reached the ripe age of seventy years, eight months, twelve days; Judas (351) died at fifty; one grammateus (433) whose name ended in -is (or -ius) died at forty-five; Justus (125) at thirty-seven; Elius Aprilicus (456) at thirty-five; Petronius (149) at twenty-four years, four months, fifteen days; Ursus (148), also a prospective bridegroom, died at twenty-two years, three months. Then we find children on whom the title of grammateus was conferred, probably as a tribute to their families. Such was Marcus Quintus Alexus (284), both grammateus and mellarchon of the Augustesians, although he lived to be only twelve, if the

---

boule of Greek cities. Cf. Juster, I, 448, n. 1; Bees in *MB*, p. 6; and Frey in *CII*, p. XCIII. Krauss (p. 149) makes the grammateus the secretary of both the communal *gerusia* and the individual congregation. More cautiously, Baron (*Jewish Community*, I, 102) states that the grammateus could serve as secretary of the individual congregation or the general community council, his functions varying with the needs of the particular group.

[1] Schürer, *Gemeindeverfassung*, 30 and Berliner, *Gesch. Jud.*, I, 70. For Vogelstein's suggestion see *VR*, I, 47. If the grammateus was usually a scholarly man, then Victor must have been an exception, since the Greek epitaph which he set up for his infant daughter Gemellina (102) teems with errors, showing some misspelling in nearly every word.

transcription of his lost epitaph may be trusted. Still younger were Vitalio (99), aged seven years, fourteen days;[1] Honoratus (146), aged six years, twenty-eight days and actually indicated as "child grammateus" (γραμμα. νήπιος); and a youngster of seven years and some months (180) whose name has not been preserved. Of the two instances of the mellogrammateus, we know the age of one, Judas (121), who lived to be twenty-four. In the case of the other (279) the numeral is so uncertain (the inscription is lost) that one scholar (Silvagni) called it thirteen, another (Frey) made it nineteen, while the letter Π at the end has been interpreted as the numeral eighty (see Frey, *ad loc.*).

Whether the office of grammateus tended to run in certain families is not clear. The incidence of children and of very young men as grammateis would indicate that in some families at least there was a sort of presumptive right to this office, as perhaps also to that of archon. Justus, a grammateus who died at thirty-seven (125), was the son of Maro, who was twice archon. One really noteworthy case is that of the grammateus Honoratus (145) and his descendants. His two sons, Rufus and Petronius, respectively, became archon and grammateus, Petronius dying at the age of twenty-four (149). The son of Rufus, named Honoratus for his grandfather, was a child grammateus (146) and died a few weeks after his sixth birthday.

The title *pater synagogae*, to which there are nine references from Rome (but two refer to the same person) and many from other Jewish communities,[2] seems to have been purely an honorary one, probably involving no active duties. This is, at least, the opinion of most scholars.[3] Berliner, however,

---

[1] Frey, failing to correct Garrucci's miscopying of line three, in which he read ETH·Z·K HMEPAC IΔ, whereas the stone distinctly has the whole word KAI before HMEPAC, has absurdly taken ZK as an inverted numeral representing twenty-seven. Actually, the deceased lad's age is clearly indicated as seven years and fourteen days. Incidentally, the left half of this stone is still in the Appia catacomb, but Frey seems to have overlooked it, since he does not mention the fact and fails to give a photograph.

[2] See the list in Juster, I, 449, n. 2. Variations in the title are found outside of Rome.

[3] *E.g.*, Schürer, *Gemeindeverfassung*, 29; *VR*, I, 43, La Piana, *op. cit.*, (above, p. 167, n. 1) 361, n. 35; Krauss, 166. For Berliner's theory

with no evidence to support his statement, equates the *pater synagogae* with the *parnas* and gives him charge of such matters as care of the sick, distribution of charities, and arrangement of funerals. The pater was associated with a definite congregation, as is obvious from the fact that in seven of the nine instances the name of the synagogue is given. Julianus (88) and Quintus Claudius Synesius (319) were Fathers of the Campesians; Gadias (mentioned twice: 510, 535) was Father of the Hebrews; Menophilus (537) of the Calcaresians; Domnus (494) of the Vernaclesians; and Pancharius (509) of the Synagogue of Elaea. The pious, irreproachable Asterias (93) was Father of an unnamed synagogue; while Mniaseas (508), who is described as a profound scholar (μαθητὴς σοφῶν), is called Father of Synagogues (πατὴρ συναγωγίων), however the plural should be interpreted.

There are indications that the Father of the Synagogue held the position of highest honor in his congregation, although some of the other offices, such as those of archisynagogus, archon, and gerusiarch, were probably invested with greater authority and responsibility. Thus Domnus (494), Father of the Vernaclesians, had been three times archon and twice phrontistes. In No. 319 we are informed that the deceased Irene was the wife of Clodius, who was the brother of Quintus Claudius Synesius, Father of the Synagogue of the Campesians at Rome, certainly a roundabout way to reveal a relationship with a man of distinction. The epitaph of Cattia Ammias (537) bears the information that she was the daughter of Menophilus, Father of the Synagogue of the Calcaresians, and that she had lived as a good Jewess with her husband for thirty-four years, but the husband's name is not mentioned. The father's high dignity, however, was considered worthy of being recorded on his daughter's tomb. That the Father of the Synagogue was a venerable man, probably a sort of elder statesman of his group, may reasonably be surmised. Unfortunately, the age at death is indicated in only one

---

see his *Gesch. Jud.*, I, 69. In a constitution of the Emperor Constantine of the year 331 (*Theodosian Code* 16.8.4) the *patres* are included along with the *archisynagogi* and the *hiereis* among those dignitaries of the Jewish community who were to be exempt from compulsory service of a physical nature.

instance, and there (509) we learn that Pancharius, Father of the Synagogue of Elaea, a man devoted to his people and to the Law, lived a good life to the extraordinary age of one hundred and ten, by far the highest age recorded in our inscriptions of the Jews of Rome.

A similar honor for women is revealed by the title *mater synagogae*, of which there seem to be three instances.[1] The venerable Veturia Paulla (523), who became a convert to Judaism at the age of seventy and died at eighty-six, was Mother of two congregations, the Campesians and the Volumnesians, a unique case in our records of a person associated with two synagogues. Marcella (496) was Mother of the Synagogue of the Augustesians. A faithful wife, whose name was probably Simplicia (166) (the latter half of her name has been lost), seems to have been the Mother of a synagogue, according to the plausible reconstruction of the fragmentary stone. Her surviving husband was a dignitary of the congregation, but his office was mentioned in the lost portion of the stone. It is possible that the Mother of the Synagogue had certain communal duties, such as charitable activities involving women and children; but we have no information.[2] We can, however, feel certain that both the Father and the Mother of the Synagogue were held in high regard, whether or not their positions involved any specific duties.[3]

There are, in addition, four titles which are mentioned only once or twice each in the extant inscriptions. These are the exarchon, hyperetes, phrontistes, and prostates. Since the inscriptions themselves reveal nothing about these offices, the nature of their functions is to be inferred, although with no certainty, from other sources.

We know of two members of the Roman Jewish community who had the title of exarchon: Gelasius (317), who was

---

[1] The *pateressa* mentioned in a Jewish inscription of Venosa (*CII* 606) is often cited as a parallel; but she may have been so called as the wife of a *pater*. The epitaph of a *mater synagogae* of the Jews of Brixia (modern Brescia) was found at Brescia (*CII* 639).

[2] According to Berliner (*Gesch. Jud.*, I, 69) she cared for women, especially the sick and dying.

[3] Frey (*CII*, p. XCV) and others compare the Pater and Mater of the *collegia*, where such titles are known to have been honorary, virtually the equivalent of *patronus* and *patrona*.

Exarchon of the Hebrews, and C. Furfanius Julianus (465), who died at the age of twenty-eight. Frey, accepting a view expressed by Bees and Deissmann, thought that the term *exarchon* is merely the equivalent of *archon*, but it seems most unlikely that there should be an alternative to so familiar and traditional a title.[1] Juster, emphatically seconded by Krauss, took ἐξάρχων as a corruption for, or at least the equivalent of, ἔξαρχος, and, since the latter title, *exarchus*, was used for the chief administrative officer of a province and, in the Church, for the head of a monastery, these two scholars believed that the exarchon was the supreme head of all Roman Jewry. This theory is made improbable by the clear fact that of the two holders of this title whom we know at Rome the one was exarchon of a specific congregation, the Hebrews, while the other lived to be only twenty-eight years old, an unlikely age for so exalted an office.

Müller had suggested that the title designated merely a former archon, a proposal rejected by Bees and ignored by others.[2] This interpretation is at least a plausible one, since the prefix *ex-* seems to have been coming into use to designate a former official, precisely as we use the same prefix in terms like "ex-president." The *Thesaurus Linguae Latinae* cites such words as *exconsul*, meaning a former consul, *exconsularis* with the same meaning, and, in a similar sense, *exduumvir* and *expraefectus*. Although some of these citations belong to a period a century or so later than that with which we are concerned, it seems clear that this type of expression had been in popular use for some time. Somewhat comparable are such Greek words as ἔξαθλος of an older athlete now out of competition and ἔξηβος of a person past his youth. The basic idea of the prefix in both the Latin and the Greek is that of having passed out of a condition or an office. If this view of Müller's

---

[1] For the opinions cited in this paragraph see Frey, *CII*, p. CVII; Bees and Deissmann in *MB*, p. 20; Juster, I, 421 (he incorrectly writes ἐξάρχον, a form which does not occur); Krauss, 138. Baron (*Soc. and Rel. Hist.*, II, 199), disagreeing with Juster and Krauss, but with no apparent evidence, equates the *exarch* with the *archon alti ordinis* and regards this official as a "decorative figure with little real authority." Another scholar who makes the exarchon the head of the whole community is Guignebert (*Monde juif*, 282).

[2] For Müller's theory and Bees' rejection of it, see *MB*, pp. 4, 20.

is the correct one, then Gelasius and Furfanius Julianus were simply ex-archons of their respective congregations. One may reasonably pose the question whether all of the many archons whose epitaphs we have were actually holding this office at the time of their deaths or were already ex-archons, and, if the latter, why was not the term *exarchon* applied to them also, if that is what the word meant? And so we leave this problem with a question the answer to which is not available.

The hyperetes occurs in but one Roman inscription, that of Flavius Julianus (172), who was buried in the Appia catacomb. The epitaph was set up on his tomb by his daughter, Flavia Juliana, who was named for her father. In the New Testament (Luke 4. 20), a hyperetes is mentioned as an attendant in the synagogue at Jerusalem who apparently brought out the Torah scroll to be read at the service and then returned it to its ark. Such an attendant is styled a *hazzan* in rabbinic sources (the term is now used for a cantor). Besides the bringing forth and returning of the sacred scroll, he tended the lamps of the synagogue, proclaimed the beginning of the Sabbath, and may, in general, have performed the duties of a sacristan, now known as a *shammash*.[1] This interpretation of the office of the hyperetes has found general acceptance and seems a very likely one.[2] Each synagogue must have had an attendant of this sort and there is no good reason for thinking that the term ὑπηρέτης, which means "attendant" or "servant", was not used of such an attendant in a Roman synagogue as it was in Jerusalem. From the fact that there is only a single mention of the hyperetes in the inscriptions, although every congregation must have had one, we may perhaps infer that the office was not a sufficiently exalted one to be regarded as ordinarily worthy of mention on one's epitaph.

---

[1] See M. Schloessinger in *JE*, *s.v.* Hazzan, and P. Wiernik in *JE*, *s.v.* Shammash.

[2] See Schürer, *Gemeindeverfassung*, 28; Juster, I, 454; Krauss, 126-128; G. F. Moore, *Judaism*, I, 291; Frey, *CII*, p. XCIX; Baron, *Jewish Community*, I, 102, 104. Frey (*l.c.*) objects, however, to Krauss' suggestion that the Jewish hyperetes was the prototype of the deacons of the early Christians. Krauss (p. 128) equates the hyperetes with the Levites. Baron (*op. cit.*, I, 102) makes him a "salaried assistant" to the archisynagogus.

Although we know of only two instances of the office of phrontistes at Rome, it seems clear that it must have been a post of great responsibility, since in both cases this title is listed at the end of a series of important offices. Thus Eupsychus (337), who died at fifty-five and was buried in the Monteverde catacomb, was twice archon, archon *pases times*, and phrontistes. Domnus (494), whose remains had been placed in a sarcophagus and deposited, most probably, in the same Monteverde catacomb, is styled Father of the Synagogue of the Vernaclesians, thrice archon, and twice phrontistes. Outside of Rome, there was a Jewish phrontistes at Alexandria (*CII* 918) and one at Side in Pamphylia (*CII* 781). The inscription of Side, which belongs to a relatively late period, reveals that the phrontistes of the synagogue made certain repairs and improvements to the building. Since the term *phrontistes* appears in non-Jewish sources as the equivalent of the Latin *procurator* and seems to refer to a sort of supervisor or manager, Frey regarded him as the business manager of the synagogue (*l'administrateur des biens*).[1] Frey would put not only the synagogue building itself, but all the other properties belonging to the congregation, including the cemetery, under his care. From the fact that Domnus was twice phrontistes he surmised that the office was an elective one. All that we can say with certainty, on the basis of our two inscriptions, is that the office was an important one. It is not unlikely, however, in view of the common use of the title elsewhere, that Frey's interpretation is the correct one.

No greater certainty is possible in determining the functions of the prostates. At Rome the only two known holders of this office are Gaius (100), a pious man who died at seventy-two, and Caelius (365), Prostates of the Agrippesians. In the Mediterranean world at this period the term seems to have been used in either of two senses: first, of the presiding officer or leader of a political body, and second, of the patron or representative of some group.[2] In the latter sense it was the

---

[1] In *CII*, p. XCI f. Baron (*op. cit.*, I, 102) agrees with this interpretation.

[2] For the meanings of προστάτης see Liddell-Scott-Jones, *Greek-English Lexicon*. Among the scholars who have regarded the prostates as the *patronus* of the Jewish community are Schürer (*Gemeindeverfassung*, 31 and III, 89, n. 52), Vogelstein (*VR*, 43), Frey (*CII*, p. XCIV f).

equivalent of the common Latin term *patronus*. With reference
to the Jews of Rome, most scholars take it in the second
meaning and interpret the prostates as the official who
defended the interests of the congregation in the community
at large, especially in its relations with the political authorities.
He would then have been a sort of legal representative of
his congregation. This view may well be the right one. Hardly
plausible is the suggestion of Juster, followed by Krauss, that
the prostates was the head of the congregational *gerusia*,[1]
since this position must certainly have belonged to the gerusiarch, and there is no point in regarding the two terms as
synonymous.

There remain a few miscellaneous titles or appellations which
do not, however, designate any specific office in the congregation. Among these is the *hiereus*, or priest, obviously the
equivalent of the Hebrew *cohen*. As in the modern synagogue,
these descendants of Aaron had no official position in the
congregation, but because of their hereditary distinction they
had a minor part in the cult, especially that of pronouncing
certain benedictions.[2] The inscriptions of Rome have revealed
five examples of the *hiereus*: the brothers Judas and Joses
(347), both archons; another Judas (346); and two (355,[3] 375)
whose names are not preserved. There may be some significance in the fact that all these occurrences of the *hiereus*
are from the Monteverde catacomb, the users of which, as has
been demonstrated, tended to be more conservative than those
congregations which buried in the other catacombs. Were
it not for the small number of the instances, one might infer
that the special position of the *hiereus* was recognized only
in the most conservative congregations. That the *hiereus* was
eligible for one of the regular offices in the synagogue is clear
from the case of Judas and Joses (347), who were also archons.

---

[1] Juster, I, 443; Krauss, 145. Both these scholars uncompromisingly
reject the view that the prostates was a type of *patronus*.

[2] This is the generally accepted view. Cf. Frey, *CII*, pp. C-CI.

[3] In No. 355, Frey, misled by the careless application of minium
to the letters, reads ιερου[σιαρ]χων and thinks that this person was a
gerusiarch. But the second line distinctly shows the letters IEPEY
and the following line is so badly weathered as not to be legible. The
photograph is deceptive because the minium does not follow the letters
carved on the stone.

In the fourth century the *hiereis* were listed along with the Fathers of the Synagogues and the archisynagogi as exempt from compulsory service of a physical nature.[1] One woman, Gaudentia (315), is styled a *hierisa*. This is apparently the equivalent of the Hebrew *cohenet* and probably designates the wife (or daughter) of a *hiereus*. It could hardly point to a priestly function for a woman, since no priestesses are to be found in the Jewish worship. Father Frey thought that the title *must* denote a feminine member of the priestly family of Aaron.

A certain Mniaseas (508, = Manasseh) is called a *mathetes sophon* (μαθητὴς σοφῶν), student of the sages, the equivalent of the rabbinic תלמיד חכם, a term applied to scholars of the Law, who were held in special honor.[2] The fragment of an inscription from the Appia (190), which seems not to be extant, bore the word μαθητήν and so may have been the epitaph of another such scholar. Possibly the epithet *nomomathes* (νομομαθής), student of the Law, found on two inscriptions, is a synonymous expression for the same type of scholar. One of these, Eusebius (333), is characterized also as "the teacher" (ὁ διδάσκαλος) and was probably an instructor of Jewish children. The other *nomomathes* (193) is described as "free from stain" (ἀμίαντος), but his name is not preserved.

Thus, in spite of lacunae, we have a reasonably comprehensive picture of the organization of the Jewish congregations of Rome. There is no good evidence for a body exercising supervision over Roman Jewry as a whole or for an officer

---

[1] *Theodosian Code* 16.8.4. See p. 187, note, above.

[2] See I. Broydé in *JE*, *s.v.* Talmid Ḥakam, and cf. *VR*, 46. In No. 239 some have seen a sort of title in the word μουννα; see Frey, *Rech. Sci. Relig.* 21 (1931), 146, n. 46 and *CII*, p. XCII, n. 3 and p. 596, with the references. Since the inscription is an almost illiterate attempt at writing Latin in Greek letters and the stone itself is no longer extant to permit a check of the reading, it seems that speculation about this alleged title is a waste of effort. The same may be said of the word προάρχων, which has been read in *CII* 539, an inscription found at Porto in 1866 and now included among the Jewish inscriptions of the Sala Giudaica in the Lateran Museum. There has been some discussion as to whether or not the proarchon was an official of the Jewish community (thus, Müller, in *MB*, p. 4, thought that it meant "former archon" and so was the equivalent of *exarchon*), but, as I have demonstrated elsewhere, there is absolutely no reason for regarding this inscription as Jewish; see *HTR* 45 (1952), 171-172.

holding authority over the entire Jewish community. Each congregation had as its head an archisynagogus, whose charge was primarily, perhaps exclusively, over the religious activities of the group. His assistant in carrying out the worship was the hyperetes, corresponding to the modern *shammash*. General supervision of the affairs of the congregation was in the hands of a council, probably called a *gerusia*, the president of which was the gerusiarch. An annually-elected official, the archon, was charged with the non-religious activities of the congregation. He may have been the executive officer of the *gerusia*. A grammateus kept the minutes of the meetings of the *gerusia* and, presumably, of the general meetings of the members of the congregation. He would also have been in charge of the archives and membership lists. There was a phrontistes entrusted with the properties and financial affairs and a prostates to take care of legal matters. Besides these there were honorary offices, notably those of archon-for-life and Father (and Mother) of the Synagogue. While this reconstruction is in part conjectural, it offers at least a reasonable picture and is not in contradiction with any of the known facts.

CHAPTER NINE

SYMBOLS AND ART IN THE JEWISH CATACOMBS OF ROME

While the texts of the inscriptions from the catacombs are the most important source of our data about the Jews of Rome, a considerable interest attaches to the numerous examples of symbols and artistic representation which the same catacombs have yielded.[1] These are found carved, painted, or scratched in connection with the inscriptions

---

[1] Apart from the more general treatments of Jewish art which include the materials from Rome, the following deal exclusively or primarily with the objects from the Jewish catacombs:

Antonio Ferrua, "Simbolismo ebraico," *RAC* 30 (1954), 237-243 (a review of Goodenough, *Symbols* I-III)

J. B. Frey, "Il delfino col tridente nella catacomba giudaica di Via Nomentana," *RAC* 8 (1931), 301-314

———, "La question des images chez les juifs à la lumière des récentes découvertes," *Biblica* 15 (1934), 265-300

K. Galling, "Die jüdischen Katakomben in Rom als ein Beitrag zur jüdischen Konfessionskunde," *Theol. Stud. u. Kritiken* 103 (1931), 352-360

E. R. Goodenough, "The Crown of Victory in Judaism," *Art Bull.* 28 (1946), 139-159

———, "The Evaluation of Symbols Recurrent in Time, as Illustrated in Judaism," *Eranos-Jahrbuch* 20 (1952), 285-319

———, *Jewish Symbols in the Greco-Roman World*, Vols. I-VIII (New York, 1953-58) [Referred to in this chapter as Goodenough, except that the illustrations in Vol. III are cited as G followed by the number of the illustration]

———, "The Menorah Among the Jews in the Roman World," *HUCA* 23, pt. 2 (1950-51), 449-492

Hugo Gressmann, "Jewish Life in Ancient Rome," in *Jewish Studies in Memory of Israel Abrahams* (New York, 1927), 170-191

H. J. Leon, ,,Symbolic Representations in the Jewish Catacombs of Rome," *JAOS* 69 (1949), 87-90

A. Marmorstein, "Jüdische Archäologie und Theologie," *Zeitsch. f. d. Neutest. Wiss.* 32 (1933), 32-41

K. H. Rengstorf, "Zu den Fresken in der jüdischen Katakombe der Villa Torlonia in Rom," *Zeitsch. f. d. Neutest. Wiss.* 31 (1932), 33-60

Paul Rieger, "Zu den Fresken in der jüdischen Katakombe der Villa Torlonia in Rom," *Zeitsch. f. d. Neutest. Wiss.* 33 (1934), 216-218

Jacob Zwarts, *De zevenarmige kandelaar in de romeinse diaspora*, Diss. Amsterdam (Utrecht, 1935).

themselves, whether on marble plaques or on the stucco-covered closures of the tombs. In more elaborate form they appear as the decorations of the arcosolia and of the walls and ceilings of the burial chambers. They are seen also on marble sarcophagi and on gold glasses and lamps. In quality they range from ineptly scrawled, almost unrecognizable, attempts at rendering some familiar object to carefully executed representations of no slight artistic merit.

Most frequent by far is the seven-branched candelabrum or menorah. No fewer than 144 of the 534 inscriptions display this symbol in some form or other.[1] The usual form is that of the six curved arms which, along with the upright arm, produce the seven branches ⑂ , but there are such variants as arms which form rectangular elbows ⊔ or which imitate the branches of a tree ⑂ . Occasionally the number of arms is greater or fewer than the standard seven. The base also varies, that with three feet being the most common ⋔ ; but some have no base at all.[2] In addition to its appearance on inscriptions, the menorah is depicted on the closures of tombs otherwise uninscribed and is found in the decorations of arcosolia and tomb chambers, as well as on sarcophagi, gold glasses, lamps, and even on the seals of rings. Other emblems commonly found on the inscriptions include the lulab with thirty-four examples, the etrog with twenty-seven, a flask with twenty-seven, the shofar with fourteen, and six examples of the Aron or Ark of the Law.[3] There are scattering examples of birds (eight instances), chickens, animals such as cows and rams,

---

[1] Frey's *Corpus* fails to indicate the presence of the menorah in the following inscriptions: 17, 31, 44, 159, 355, 391, 410. His index on p. 663 carelessly omits a number of other examples (at least eleven) which are actually visible on his photographs or indicated in his transcriptions. By catacombs, the 144 representations of the menorah are distributed as follows: Appia 46, Monteverde 75 (including four from the Porto collection), Nomentana 10, others 13.

[2] For details of these variations in form see Leon in *JAOS* 69. 87-88.

[3] Distribution by catacombs:
Lulab (34): Appia 10, Monteverde 20, Nomentana 2, others 2
Etrog (27): Appia 9, Monteverde 17, Cimarra 1
Flask (27): Appia 9, Monteverde 17, Cimarra 1
Shofar (14): Appia 3, Monteverde 11
Aron (6): Monteverde 6

trees, scrolls, sundry other objects of doubtful identification, and even one example of a swastika (48).

It may be noted at this point that there has been considerable controversy among scholars with regard to the purpose and meaning of these symbols. While some regard them as representations of cult objects, intended as no more than emblems indicating the Judaism of the deceased, others interpret them as charged with symbolic meaning and as indicating the hope or assurance of immortality. The discussion of this problem will be taken up later in the present chapter.

The most thorough recent treatment of the menorah as a Jewish symbol is by Erwin R. Goodenough.[1] Professor Goodenough points out that, although the rabbis of the Talmud strictly forbade the use of the seven-branched candelabrum in the synagogue,[2] this type of candelabrum was regularly to be found in the synagogues of the Diaspora and is the form reproduced on the inscriptions and paintings of the catacombs and elsewhere in Jewish art. That the menorah represented in the catacombs is not modeled on that of the Temple in Jerusalem will be immediately obvious to anyone who compares it with either the description in Exodus (25. 31-37) or with the famous replica sculptured on the Arch of Titus at the Roman Forum. It may be regarded as certain that the menorah, because of its appearance wherever memorials of the ancient Jews are found, was looked upon as the symbol of Judaism, very much as the six-pointed Star of David (*Magen David*) has become in our modern day and as the Cross has been the symbol of Christianity from ancient times to the present. Goodenough, however, believes that it represents more than a mere religious symbol; that it signifies the God of Judaism and the light which comes from Him into the world, with the seven lamps representing the seven "planets," that is, the sun, moon, and the five actual planets known to the ancients. Thus the menorah came to symbolize God Himself and the hope of eternal life in the world to come.[3]

---

[1] *Op. cit.* (above, p. 195, n. 1), in *HUCA*, 23, 449-492. A revised and abbreviated form of this article appears as chapter four in Goodenough's *Symbols* IV, 71-98.

[2] For the talmudic passages, see *HUCA*, 23, 449, n. 2.

[3] *HUCA*, 23, 466 f., 475. Cf. Goodenough IV, 87.

While it is entirely possible that the menorah originally bore some such symbolic meaning, one can hardly be certain that any such concept motivated the humble Jews who inscribed this emblem on the graves of their dead. To them it had become the symbol of Judaism, and they followed the prevailing mode in using it as such a symbol. Even so, whether or not this emblem had an eschatological significance to its users, it is noteworthy that, common though it is, it appears on fewer than one-third of the inscriptions, and that far more than half of the epitaphs bore no symbol whatsoever.[1]

As for the other symbols, a brief description of them must suffice, since one can only speculate with regard to the significance which they conveyed to their users. As the figures cited above have shown, none remotely compares in frequency with the menorah. The most common of the miscellaneous symbols is the lulab, a conventionalized form of the branch used in connection with the Sukkot ritual.[2] In form it varies from a simple branch to a somewhat more elaborate type indicating the withes which bound the branches together. No attempt is made in the representations on the inscriptions to differentiate the three kinds of branches or twigs (palm, willow, myrtle), but in the more elaborate representations on the gold glasses the lulab is rendered more exactly.

The etrog also, which occurs most commonly in connection with the lulab, is conventionally rendered as a circular or ovoid object, usually with a stem attached. At times, in an attempt at realism, the protuberances of the fruit are indicated

---

[1] It should be noted that a number of the inscriptions are in so fragmentary a state that we cannot know whether or not they originally bore a symbol; but even so, it may be safely asserted that substantially more than half of all the extant inscriptions had no symbol at all. See the Table in *JAOS* 69.90.

[2] See "The Lulab and Ethrog" in Goodenough, IV, 145-166. An account of the appearance of these symbols on the monuments is offered on pp. 145-147. The following inscriptions show clear-cut examples of the lulab: [where no illustration is offered in the present volume, the *CII* number is given, followed in parentheses by the number in Goodenough, III. Those pictured in Goodenough only are designated as G.] Fig. 35, Fig. 36.95, 107, 108, 117; Fig. 38; *CII* 343 (700), 421, 480, and G 770. For the lulab on the gold glasses see *CII* 515 (978), 516 (964, 965), 517 (966), 519 (969, 970), 522 (974), and G 967. To Goodenough (IV, 163) the lulab represents the palm of victory, *i.e.*, victory over death, immortality.

and leaves may be shown. Not uncommon is an object resembling a turnip, which has been variously identified as a mandrake, a horse-radish (a vegetable unknown to Mediterranean lands in antiquity), or as a type of root vegetable and interpreted as representing the bitter herb of the Passover feast. In all probability, this figure is a variant form of the etrog, showing not only the protuberances but also the tapering bottom which characterizes some specimens of this fruit.[1]

Almost as common as the lulab and etrog is the flask, which is seen on no fewer than twenty-seven of the inscriptions. From the fact that it normally accompanies the menorah it has been assumed that it represents an oil vessel; yet there are at least three certain instances of its occurrence without the menorah (*CII* 143, 208, 343 = G 770, 778, 710), so that Gressmann and Goodenough may be right in insisting that a wine flask is always intended. In that case, it would presumably be associated with the sacramental use of wine.[2] The usual form of this flask is that of a two-handled vessel, sometimes elaborately depicted (*e.g.*, Fig. 35). Unique types are seen in the large amphora tapering to a point, as represented on a fragmentary slab from the Monteverde catacomb (Fig. 37, No. 67); the spherical vase carved on a stone from the Via Appia (Fig. 56); and a two-handled chalice, also on a stone from the Appia (G 767) and in the fragment pictured in our Fig. 32. 6. These last instances would favor an association with wine.

Among the frequent representations is the ritual horn or

---

[1] Examples of the simplest form of the etrog, without stem, are seen in 234 (773) and 254 (768). Good instances of the etrog with stem are Fig. 32.15, Fig. 36.107; *CII* 225 (772), 318 (723), 382 (717), 479 (715), 480, 545 (846), G 766. The protuberances appear as spots in Fig. 36.95 and *CII* 299 (702); they are rendered more realistically in Fig. 36.108 and G 721. Clear-cut examples with leaves are Fig. 35, Fig. 36.108, Fig. 56; *CII* 217 (777), 464, G 721. The type resembling a turnip is commonly called a *Rübe*. Examples are Fig. 36.108, Fig. 56; *CII* 234 (773); and G. 721. Marmorstein, *op. cit.* (above, p. 195 n. 1), 41, thinks that the *Rübe* is the symbol of death and resurrection. Rengstorf, *op.cit.* (above, p. 195 n. 1), 58, 60, calls this figure a *Meerrettich* (horse-radish) and takes it for the Passover bitter herb. Frey uses the term *mandragore* (*CII*, pp. CXXVI and 664).

[2] Gressmann, *op. cit.* (above, p. 195 n. 1), 182 f.; Goodenough, I, 96. In I, 30, Goodenough intimates that in his opinion all representations involving wine are to be interpreted as Dionysiac symbolism.

shofar, most probably a reminiscence of that blown at the Rosh Hashanah service.[1] I have counted fourteen instances of this symbol in the inscriptions of Rome. Generally it is found in a simple conventionalized form ⤳ (see Fig. 38); occasionally it is rendered with more attention to the actual appearance of the horn (Fig. 36, No. 108). It is worthy of note that with one exception (Fig. 55), where the two horns are a punning allusion to the name of a deceased child, Salpingius (*salpinx* is the Greek word for horn), the shofar is always found together with other symbols, most commonly the menorah, lulab, and etrog.[2]

On six inscriptions, all from the Monteverde catacomb, there are representations of the Ark of the Law, the *Aron hakodesh*. In each case the ark is topped by a triangular pediment and the two doors are thrown open, revealing the interior.[3] The scrolls of the Torah, seen endwise, are simply represented as circles, the number varying from four to nine. In one instance (Fig. 39, No. 17) six shelves are indicated, but no scrolls. Besides the scrolls in the open shrine, individual scrolls are occasionally engraved on the stones. In three examples (*CII* 193, 225, 361 [our Fig. 36, No. 107] = G 779, 772, 724) the scroll is completely rolled up, appearing as a cylinder,

---

[1] In IV, 167-194, Goodenough devotes a chapter to the shofar. He links the ram's horn with the sacrifice of Isaac and states (p. 193) that it symbolizes the "hope of a life to come." Through the shofar one might gain the mercy of God and the boon of resurrection. To Rieger, however, *op. cit.* (above, p. 195, n. 1), 218, the shofar represents the horn of Elijah proclaiming the coming of the Messiah.

[2] A figure closely resembling the conventionalized form of the shofar appears on the epitaph of a certain Gaudentius, now to be seen in the atrium of the church of S. Maria in Trastevere. The only other figure on the stone is that of a running bird. The inscription may be Jewish, but Frey, without stating his reasons, asserts that it is Christian (*CII*, p. 583 f., no. 86*).

[3] Chapter five of Goodenough, IV (pp. 99-144) is a discussion of the Torah shrine. To Goodenough the shrine with its open doors symbolizes "the cosmic and heavenly place of the Law as a divine symbol" (p. 136), and is a "manifestation of the Shekinah." Rengstorf, *op. cit.*, 53, associating the Ark and the scrolls with the menorah, erroneously states that there is no example of a scroll or the Ark without the menorah. Actually, *CII* 337 and 343 show the Ark without any menorah. Marmorstein, *op. cit.*, 33, interprets the Ark as indicating that the deceased had lived according to the Torah, while the open doors symbolize the effect of the Shekinah on the bones of the dead.

although in one instance, on the epitaph of a grammateus (225), it looks more rectangular than cylindrical. The scroll in 193 is so crudely executed that Frey mistook it for an oil flask. In the third example (361) the knob (*umbilicus*) is indicated at one end. On one stone (*CII* 478 = G 712) the scroll appears with both sides partly rolled up, so that the volume is open at the desired text. An entirely open scroll appears to be represented on the epitaph of a grammateus (Fig. 58), the columns of writing being rendered by parallel vertical lines, so that Goodenough (II, 24) suggests that it may be intended for a ladder, while Frey sees it as a case for holding scrolls. The fact that both this figure and the one mentioned above are on the tombstones of scribes would make it reasonable to see Torah scrolls in both instances. In addition, the scroll of 193 adorns the epitaph of a *nomomathes*, one learned in the Law. A marble fragment, now lost, bore, if we may trust De Rossi's drawing (*CII* 281a = G 805), a grill-shaped object which may have been intended to depict a bundle of scrolls, guarded by a lion, at least as interpreted by Frey.

Besides these symbols, all of which may be regarded as representing cult objects, there is a miscellany of figures which occur in scattered examples. In some instances the identification is far from certain. Representations of birds, not identifiable by species, are seen on nine inscriptions. Particularly interesting—and curious— is *CII* 144 (= Fig. 53), on which the text of the epitaph (that of the devoted foster son of Alexandria Severa, named Notus, who died at twenty-seven) is followed by a row of pictures engraved in primitive fashion. At the right are two cocks with a branch (possibly a lulab) between them. At the left is what may be a dovecote with three small birds moving toward it from two sides and one bird perched at the top. Between the two groups is a small tree and what appears to be a conical hut, resembling a tepee. The whole suggests a possible rural environment for the deceased young man, but what it may mean in the way of religious allusion or eschatology seems beyond conjecture. There is also the attractive stone of Aster (*CII* 306 = G 729 = our Fig. 33, No. 71), the large menorah of which is surrounded by two large birds, one of which seems to be pecking at a bunch of grapes, another small bird, a small tree, and a flask. The epitaph of seven-month-old Judas (Fig. 36, No. 118) has, in addition to two menorahs and two flasks, three birds, two of which stand facing lulabs.

Five of the inscriptions are adorned with figures of animals. *CII* 209 (Fig. 57) has facing heads of a ram and a bovine animal; on *CII* 208 (Fig. 56) the head of a ram is placed between a vase and an etrog; on *CII* 193 (= G 779) a very crudely executed bovine animal is accompanied by a Torah scroll and a menorah. A slab from the Monteverde catacomb (*CII* 24* = G 732), which Frey without sufficient reason regards as pagan, has the standing figure of a bull. For the fifth instance we must rely on the testimony of earlier observers, since the portion of the stone (*CII* 171) which contained the animal figure is gone. Garrucci called it a calf; but De Rossi thought it was a bull.[1] A sixth example may be added on the testimony of De Rossi, who reported that in the small catacomb of Vigna Cimarra he found a marble slab which showed a lion along with a group of other symbols. A reproduction of his drawing may be seen in *CII* 281a (= G 805).

In the catacomb of Via Appia Pignatelli (it is not certain that this catacomb was Jewish) Nikolaus Müller saw an epitaph painted on a frame supported by a pair of nude, wingless cupids (*CII* 79). In the Nomentana catacomb one loculus is adorned with the graffito of a boat with sails and oars (*CII*, p. 44 = G 836). Two baskets of fruit, possibly grapes, are represented on one stone from the Appia (*CII* 213 = G 784), and a similar basket is on a stone from Monteverde (*CII* 299 = G 702). The fruit basket which was on another Appia inscription (*CII* 95) has been broken off and is no longer to be seen. The round objects which appear on two inscriptions (*CII* 343, 361 [our Fig. 36, No. 107] = G 710, 724) are interpreted as representing unleavened bread (matzot). On *CII* 148 (= G 781) the figure of a bird at the right is balanced at the left with what Goodenough (II, 24) calls an *omphalos*, others a beehive.[2] Among the carefully fashioned figures of *CII* 200

---

[1] Garrucci in *Diss. Arch.* II, 173. De Rossi's opinion is cited in *CII*, ad loc.

[2] To Garrucci (*Cimitero* 59) it was a beehive, and Frey lists it in his index (p. 664) as a *ruche d'abeilles*.

(Fig. 35) a knife, perhaps that used for circumcision, may be seen. Frey sees a candle snuffer (*mouchette*) in certain obscure figures on three inscriptions (*CII* 250, 361 [Fig. 36. 107], 484 [Fig. 36. 95] = G 771, 724, 719). What is clearly a shovel of some sort appears on a Monteverde stone (Fig. 37. 66). Goodenough calls it an incense shovel; Gressmann, with the approval of Lietzmann, interprets it as a circumcision knife; to Frey it was a case for holding a scroll of the Torah. Somewhat similar figures, as presented by Goodenough, seem to favor the identification of it as an incense shovel.[1] One inscription with neat lettering (*CII* 300 = G 705) is headed by two facing hand lamps of the familiar Roman type. A "compass rosette," as Goodenough calls it (II, 5f.), appears in a single instance, this also being on a Monteverde stone (*CII* 483 = G 709). A slab built into the wall of the Appia catacomb (G 791) displays the figure of a pickaxe (*ascia*), the type used by the *fossores* who dug the catacombs. Although this figure is common enough in the Christian catacombs, this is the only extant example in a Jewish catacomb.[2]

While the figures painted or carved on the inscriptions, as described above, indicate some attempts, crude though they usually are, at artistic expression among the Jews of Rome, the decorations of the private chambers (cubicula) and of the arcosolia are much more ambitious and are evidently the work of artists of no mean skill. Especially noteworthy are the two painted rooms of the Appia catacomb and the painted room and arcosolia of the Nomentana.

When the painted rooms of the Appia catacomb were discovered, the first reaction was to regard them as of pagan origin, since it was felt that obviously such figures of animals and human beings, including even a nude youth, would hardly

---

[1] See Goodenough, I, 173 f, and II, 5. For his illustrations see III, 873 and the index to volume III, *s.v.* Shovel. In volume IV he devotes a chapter (pp. 195-208) to the incense shovel and discusses the use of incense by the Jews. On pp. 195-97 he describes the form which this shovel takes on the monuments. Since our Roman example differs from the others in that it has a longer handle, Goodenough is not entirely certain (p. 197) that it is an incense shovel. Gressmann's opinion is expressed in *op.cit.* (above, p. 195, n. 1), 189, and Lietzmann endorses it in *BL*, 24, n. 5.
[2] There was a similar figure in the hypogeum of Vigna Cimarra, according to De Rossi, *BAC*, 5 (1867), 16.

have been the work of Jewish artists or used by Jews to adorn a tomb chamber. Even in recent years, Father Frey, despite his acquaintance with the use of similar figures in Jewish synagogues and tombs of Palestine and the Diaspora, insisted that these rooms originally formed a pagan hypogeum which was later absorbed by the expanding Jewish cemetery. This view must by all means be rejected, as has already been demonstrated (above, p. 61), and Goodenough is entirely justified in accepting the decorations as Jewish without hesitation. The paintings were first described and illustrated by Father Garrucci and subsequently, among others, by Th. Roller, Frey, and most fully by Goodenough.[1]

The two rooms, which are off one of the main corridors leading from the entrance at the Via Appia Antica, are interconnected, the first being somewhat the larger.[2] The frescoes adorn the walls, the vaulted ceilings, and the arcosolia, of which there are two in each chamber (Figs. 13-15). The central motif of the ceiling of the first room, contained within the innermost of a series of concentric rings (Fig. 14),[3] is a winged Victory placing a garland on the head of a nude youth.[4] The goddess bears a palm branch in her left hand

---

[1] See above, p. 61, note 2, and the following: Garrucci, *Cimitero* 65-66 and *Diss. Arch.* II, 173-75; Th. Roller, *Les catacombes de Rome* (Paris, 1881), I, 11 f.; Frey, *Biblica* 15 (1934), 284 f. and *CII*, pp. CXXI-CXXV; Goodenough, II, 17-20 and III, 737-56, 762. Cf. also Cohn-Wiener, *Die jüdische Kunst* (Berlin, 1929), 122-24.

[2] For the dimensions of these rooms see above, p. 61, note 1.

[3] In view of Karl Lehmann's demonstration that this pattern of ceiling decoration is often used to represent the dome of heaven ("The Dome of Heaven," *Art Bull.* 27 [1927], 1-27), Goodenough believes (II, 17, 36) that the ceilings in this catacomb and in that of the Via Nomentana are to be interpreted in this way and that the central figure or group represents, in each instance, the inner heaven and "the hope of the devotee for what he will find there." From Lehmann's examples it seems clear that such an interpretation is justified only when the figures involved have celestial associations (*e.g.*, heavenly divinities, signs of the zodiac, and other astronomical symbols). The figures in the Jewish rooms, however, are hardly of that character. It may be that this pattern for decorating a vaulted ceiling developed out of the "dome of heaven" type, but it certainly became a standard technique of ceiling decoration, without any heavenly or eschatological associations. Cf. Ferrua's criticism of Goodenough's interpretation in *RAC* 30 (1954), 243.

[4] Goodenough discusses the symbolism of the crown of victory with much detail in his article, "The Crown of Victory," in *Art Bull.* 28 (1946), 139-59.

and the youth has an object in each hand, some sort of leafy branch and what has been called a quiver.[1] The outer circle has alternating figures of peacocks facing front, with tails spread, and pairs of birds with a basket of flowers between each pair. Outside these are floral garlands, and each of the four pendentives contains a flying bird. The walls of this room are adorned with figures of pegasi, various fowl, peacocks and other birds, and, strangely, a sheep facing a caduceus (Fig. 15).[2]

The central figure in the vault of the second or inner room is the goddess Fortuna holding a cornucopia in her left hand and a shallow libation dish in her right (Fig. 16). In the outer ring are four panels with alternating figures of fish and ducks, and between these are four ovals containing baskets of flowers. Strings of flowers wind around the panels. Outside the ring and below the figure of Fortuna are a hippocampus and two dolphins; on the opposite side, above Fortuna, are a pair of fish. Each of the pendentives contains a floating cupid. The walls of the room are adorned with floral wreaths and birds. The rear wall, now badly damaged, had the figure of a man between two horses, as Roller's sketch of 1881 clearly shows.[3] Attempts have been made to identify the man as Orpheus, and Goodenough cites as a parallel the painting of Orpheus and the beasts in the Dura synagogue. At Dura, however, the animals are obviously the wild beasts which were regularly introduced with Orpheus to represent the power of the musician over wild nature, but the horses of our fresco will scarcely fall within that category.

The Appia catacomb has two other painted rooms, the frescoes of which are so poorly preserved that little can be said about them. One of these rooms still shows a handsome date palm painted in each of its four corners (Fig. 40). Over the sealed children's loculi on the wall at each side of the entrance, huge vases of flowers had been painted, but only

---

[1] By Garrucci in *Diss. Arch.* II, 174.

[2] Goodenough (VIII, 74) interprets this as symbolizing the hope of future life.

[3] *Op. cit.* (above, p. 204, n. 1), Plate IVb, reproduced in Goodenough, III, 740. See Goodenough, II, 19-20 for the discussion. Robert Eisler's sketch of 1915, which is reproduced in Goodenough, III, 762, and shows the man holding a lyre, is not to be trusted. Roller's earlier sketch, which is apparently accurate, shows nothing of the sort.

fragments remain, since marauders have broken into the graves.[1] On either side of the doorway itself is what appears to be a painted *mezuzah*. A fourth frescoed room has a large menorah painted above an arcosolium, which still contains a broken sarcophagus (Fig. 12). The ceiling decorations are too faded to be made out. Crudely painted circles and half ovals contained figures which have entirely disappeared, except that in the four corners there are quarter circles each containing an etrog.[2]

Unfortunately, there has been no attempt to preserve all these paintings against the seeping through of water from rain and the irrigation of the cultivated field under which the catacomb lies. Unless some protective measures are taken soon, the stucco will fall from the ceilings of the two connected chambers, as has already happened in the room with the palm trees. The fine frescoes of these chambers were grievously defaced by the scribbled names of visitors during the period before the catacomb was taken over, about 1946, by the Commissione di Archeologia Sacra.

The painted decorations of the Via Nomentana catacomb differ generally from those of the Appia in that the motifs are readily identifiable as connected with Jewish beliefs and traditions. All these paintings are to be found in what appears to be the earlier portion of the catacomb (see above, p. 64). They involve one cubiculum with its two arcosolia and two other arcosolia in the adjoining corridor. The excavator of the catacomb, Roberto Paribeni, was the first to describe the paintings in some detail. There is a more complete description by H. W. Beyer and Hans Lietzmann in their excellent monograph on the catacomb. A full account, based largely on Beyer and Lietzmann, is offered by Goodenough, who adds acute observations of his own.[3] The interpretation of the frescoes has brought forth a substantial

---

[1] Goodenough, II, 20, and III, 757-58. Goodenough and his predecessors overlooked the *mezuzot*, one of which is barely visible in III, 758 and our Fig. 40.

[2] Goodenough, II, 21, and III, 759-61.

[3] Paribeni, *N.Sc.* 1920, 145; Beyer and Lietzmann, *Die jüdische Katakombe der Villa Torlonia in Rom* [referred to in this chapter as *BL*], 9-27; Goodenough, II, 35-40.

bibliography and a wide divergence of scholarly opinion.[1] The painted chamber, like those of the Appia, has a vaulted ceiling with a central figure encircled by a series of concentric rings, an arrangement which Goodenough sees as representing the dome of heaven.[2] In contrast with the pagan figures of the two Appia rooms, here the central motif is a splendid menorah with its seven lamps ablaze. Four circles, two of which are adorned with tracery, surround the menorah. On the four sides, semicircles enclose identical figures of a dolphin winding around a trident. Between these are smaller circles, three of which enclose an etrog, the fourth a shofar. Amid these circular and semicircular areas there winds a tracery of vines, the whole making a most charming composition.[3]

The arcosolium on the left (north) wall of this room (Fig. 41) was broken into by grave robbers, so that the decorations which covered the loculi in its rear wall have been destroyed. The arch of the arcosolium has a blazing menorah as its central figure, contained within two concentric rings. Left and right within half circles are, respectively, a shofar and a pomegranate.[4] The front wall, below the arcosolium proper, is painted to simulate the front of a strigilated sarcophagus with two

---

[1] Notable discussions of these paintings are to be found in the works by Frey, Galling, Goodenough, Rengstorf, and Rieger, cited above, p. 195, n. 1, and in the following:
Th. Reinach, "Une nouvelle nécropole judéo-romaine," *REJ* 72 (1921), 24-28; R. Wischnitzer, "La catacombe de la Villa Torlonia," *REJ* 91 (1931), 102-107; Cohn-Wiener, *Die jüdische Kunst*, 124.

[2] See above, p. 204, n. 3, and Goodenough, II, 36.

[3] Illustrated in *CII*, p. CXXVII and Goodenough, III, 806. For color descriptions of all the paintings of this catacomb see *BL*, 9-13. A photograph of a detail in color is shown by Frey in *RAC* 8 (1931), 308. Illustrations of the other paintings of this catacomb may be seen in *BL*, plates 3-14, and Goodenough, III, 808-17.

[4] Beyer (in *BL*, 11) mistakenly conjectures that this figure may represent a poppy pod. In the next chapter of the same volume, however (p. 25), it is identified as a pomegranate by Lietzmann. Romanoff (*JQR*, 34 [1944], 307-10), Reifenberg (*Denkmäler der jüdischen Antike* [Berlin, 1937], 51), Zwarts (*op. cit.* [above, p. 195, n. 1], 57), and Goodenough (II, 37) also call it a pomegranate. These are undoubtedly right, since the pomegranate has Jewish associations (see *JE, s.v.*) and is commonly found in Jewish art (see Goodenough, III, Index); but this is not true of the poppy.

lion heads, one on either side, each bearing a large ring in its mouth. The arcosolium on the wall opposite the entrance (east) is similarly decorated (Fig. 42). The rear wall of this arcosolium, though mostly destroyed, still shows the roof of a gabled structure, which Beyer and Lietzmann regard as a Torah shrine, but which others, Goodenough among them, interpret as a temple.[1] On both sides are crescent moons, that to the left shown as waxing, that to the right as waning. The arch of this arcosolium, like the other, has a menorah as its central figure. The half circles contain a pomegranate at left, a closed scroll at right. The scroll shows the knob (*umbili-cus*) of the stick around which it is wound and has a triangular tab (*titulus*) attached to its top, such as was usual with volumes of the period as a means of identification. The front wall is treated like that on the left side of the room so as to resemble a strigilated sarcophagus with lion heads. From the fact that the strigilations are parted at the middle so that those at the left side curve left and those at the right curve right, Goodenough believes that the artist intended to represent curtains drawn apart so as to reveal some sacred object.[2] Unfortunately, any object that may have been painted in the open space has been destroyed. It may have been a menorah, since the menorah is found in a similar location on one of the arcosolia of the corridor, as will be noted below. In both the arcosolia of this cubiculum the decorations are further embellished with floral garlands. There is a figure of a bird in flight above the door of the chamber.

In the wall of the gallery, immediately to the left as one leaves the chamber, there is a third arcosolium (*BL*, Plates 8-11). Little remains of the design of the rear wall. At the left is a portion of a large menorah, flanked by a lulab at its left and an etrog at its right. At the extreme left is a large wine flask represented as partly buried. The few traces of painting at the right of this rear wall show that it also contained a large menorah, balancing that at the left, and a goblet and shofar. The arch of the arcosolium is decorated with eight-sided

---

[1] Illustrated also in *BL*, plates 3, 5; Goodenough, III, 809, 811. For the interpretations see especially *BL*, 21 f. and Goodenough, II, 38, where it is called "some eschatological temple in the heavens."

[2] Goodenough, II, 37.

panels, each containing a star with varying numbers of rays (mostly six to eight). At the base of the arch on either side is a peacock with varicolored plumage, represented as browsing in a flowery field.

Further to the right along the same gallery is the fourth painted arcosolium (Fig. 43). Here the back wall, which is only slightly damaged, shows the Ark of the Torah as a pedimented shrine, its doors wide open so as to reveal six scrolls, seen edgewise, on two shelves. The central part of the Ark has been defaced. Above the shrine is a star and to the left and right of the roof are, respectively, a sun and a crescent moon, each partly covered by clouds. On either side of the shrine there is a large menorah with lights kindled. The menorah at the left has at its left a lulab, at its right a fruit (possibly a pomegranate) and a large two-handled flask. The right-hand menorah has at its left a shofar and at its right what appears to be a knife and a large etrog. Above the entire composition are curtains represented as though pulled back to reveal the group of sacred objects. The vaulted arch of the arcosolium is decorated with a geometric design of rosettes. The base of the vault, which is now largely destroyed, depicted on each side a field with animals contentedly lying down or grazing, a scene which naturally calls forth associations with Paradise (*BL*, Plate 14). On the front wall beneath the arcosolium we again see, as in the two arcosolia of the painted room, a simulated sarcophagus front with strigilations and two heads of lions with ring in mouth. At the middle, where the strigilations are parted, the space is occupied by a small menorah.

These frescoes have elicited many attempts at interpretation, some scholars regarding them as primarily decorative with an emphasis on motifs derived from the Jewish ritual, others finding in them a series of allegories alluding to the blissful life beyond the grave.[1] We have no way of determining which school of interpreters is right. Further discussion of this problem is reserved for the end of this chapter.

---

[1] For example, Goodenough (IV, 128) interprets the paintings of the arcosolium described in the foregoing paragraph as presenting "the saving symbols of Judaism, mystic tokens which, when 'revealed to sight,' opened to the faithful a new world."

The Jewish catacombs contained many decorated sarcophagi, few of which have survived whole, but we do have a number of fragments. It is not possible to say with confidence that all such fragments belonged to coffins used for Jewish burials, since some may have been employed as materials to close the graves. The only ones that we can be completely sure of are those which bear a Jewish inscription or some clearly Jewish symbol.[1] The most complete treatment of the sarcophagi and fragments is that by Goodenough, who offers excellent illustrations. The sarcophagi, which were usually of marble, sometimes of terracotta, must have been relatively expensive, so that those who used them for burials were obviously the more prosperous members of the community. Some of the sarcophagi were without decoration or bore only the conventional strigilations. Only those which were adorned with sculptured figures are of interest here.

The Monteverde catacomb has yielded very few decorated sarcophagi. Most notable is the lid of a child's sarcophagus (now in the Lateran Museum) with the figure of a small boy half reclining on a cushioned couch and holding a bunch of grapes in his left hand, while caressing a tiny dog with his right. Two birds, at the head and foot, respectively, are pecking at grapes.[2] Whether this sarcophagus was a Jewish one and whether the figure is a portrait of the child who was entombed therein are disputed questions. Frey thought that this lid came from a pagan sarcophagus and was part of the debris from a pagan cemetery above and near the site of the Jewish catacomb. Goodenough, while holding that the figure is not a portrait of the deceased child with his pet, believes that it is a Jewish representation of an "eschatological banquet." He suggests that the thirty-inch length of the sarcophagus indicates that it contained the body of a child less than a year old, therefore much younger than that represented on the lid. Since the sarcophagus lid appears to have been

---

[1] So also Ferrua in *RAC* 30,239. Goodenough's treatment of the sarcophagi is to be found in II, 11-14, 25-30, 41-44; for his illustrations see III, 733, 736, 786-89, 795-804, 818-34.
[2] Illustrated in *CII*, p. CXXV, and Goodenough, III, 736. For descriptions and discussions of this sarcophagus see Müller, *Jüd. Kat.*, 39-41; *CII*, p. CXXVI; Goodenough, II, 11-12.

found in the catacomb, one may reasonably presume that it represents a Jewish burial. Still, the fact that the head was found separated from the rest and that there was no trace of the sarcophagus itself lends at least some plausibility to Frey's conjecture that it came originally from outside the catacomb. The whole matter is so uncertain that confidence in either direction is hardly justified. The left portion of a sarcophagus lid found in the same catacomb shows a pair of semi-reclining winged cupids (*putti*), each holding a cornucopia and a basket of fruit, with a large fruit basket on a pedestal between them. This was balanced by a similar pair on the right, now almost entirely destroyed.[1] Another fragment in the Monteverde catacomb had the figure of a swimming dolphin.[2]

A fairly large number of sarcophagus fragments has been found in and about the Via Appia catacomb. Several of these have recently been published and discussed for the first time by Goodenough.[3] There is genuine doubt as to which of these actually originated in the catacomb itself. The best known and most discussed is the "Season Sarcophagus," which is now in the Terme Museum (Fig. 44).[4] All we have left is a portion of the front displaying a large menorah in its central medallion, which is supported by a pair of winged female figures in flowing robes (Cumont and Goodenough call them Victories). Beneath is a wine vat with two spouts in the shape of lion heads. Three children, two of them holding curved

---

[1] See Müller, *Jüd. Kat.*, 41-42; Goodenough, II, 13 f. and III, 733; Cumont, *Recherches sur le symbolisme funéraire des romains* (Paris, 1942), 496 (fig. 104), 497. According to Cumont the four cupids (he calls them *génies*) are the four seasons amid symbols of the fertility of the earth, but these cupids show none of the characteristics which usually differentiate the allegorical representation of the Seasons on sarcophagi.

[2] Müller, *Jüd. Kat.*, 41, Goodenough, II, 14.

[3] Goodenough, II, 28-30; illustrations in III, 795-804.

[4] The fullest discussion is Cumont's "Un fragment de sarcophage judéo-païen," *RA* 4 (1916), 1-16. This article was reprinted with some additions and revisions in his *Recherches sur le symbolisme funéraire des romains*, 484-498. For earlier discussions see especially Garrucci, *Diss. Arch.* II, 155; H. Leclercq, *Manuel d'archéologie chrétienne* (Paris, 1907), I, 523. More recent treatments are to be found in Goodenough, II, 26-27; G. M. A. Hanfmann, *The Season Sarcophagus in Dumbarton Oaks* (Cambridge, Mass., 1951), I, 195.

wands, are inside the vat energetically trampling the grapes. The main theme of the sarcophagus was an allegory of the Seasons, represented by four almost nude, winged male figures. Those to the left, illustrating Spring and Summer, have completely disappeared. To the right the figure of Autumn holds a basket of fruit in his right hand and a pair of dead wild fowl in his left. At the extreme right is a portion of Winter, only his right arm and leg being preserved. In his right hand he holds a small slain animal, perhaps a hare, though some call it a boar. Also on the right, on a smaller scale, are two small boys, one riding on a hare, the other on a dog, which is leaping toward the slain animal. The "season" motif on sarcophagi was a very common one at that time,[1] so that it is not unlikely that the Jew who used this one to hold the remains of some member of his family bought a modish coffin from the stock of a dealer and had a menorah carved on the medallion instead of the usual portrait of the deceased. Some, however, notably Cumont and Goodenough, see in these sculptured figures an important eschatological symbolism, significant not only to pagans but also to Hellenized Jews and early Christians.[2] In any case, it is clear that such pagan figures were not repugnant to the Jewish user (since he deliberately selected this sarcophagus), but that the figures had a positive symbolic value for him is far from established.

Another sarcophagus fragment from the Appia catacomb is more definitely Jewish in its decoration.[3] A menorah is at

---

[1] The two volumes of Hanfmann's *Season Sarcophagus* (cited in the previous note) are devoted to discussion and comparison of the numerous instances.

[2] Gressmann, in *Jewish Studies in Memory of Israel Abrahams*, 186, suggests a connection with the harvest festival of Tabernacles, but fails to realize that all four seasons are represented on the sarcophagus. Hanfmann, who has made the most exhaustive of all studies of the season sarcophagi, disputes Cumont's eschatological interpretation of this particular sarcophagus, holding that the use of a pagan sarcophagus with such a common, non-committal theme as the seasons is no proof of a belief in resurrection or of any influence of the Dionysiac mysteries (*op. cit.*, I, 195).

[3] It was last mentioned as being in the Kaiser-Friedrich Museum of Berlin. It is described and illustrated in Garrucci, *Storia della arte cristiana*, VI, 166 (illustrated in pl. 491.18, 20); *BL*, 44 f. (where it is wrongly designated as Taf. 27; the illustration is on Taf. 28); Goodenough, II, 25 f. (ill. in III, 786, 788).

the center. To the left and right are balancing series of Jewish cult objects separated by palm trees. Moving outward from the center in both directions they are, respectively, a shofar in the form of a ram's horn,[1] a palm tree, a lulab, a palm tree, an etrog, a plate. The plate at the left is empty, but that at the right is adorned with some unidentified object.[2] At each end of the sarcophagus there was a seated griffin. No longer extant, apparently, is a sarcophagus found in one of the cubicula of the catacomb and described by the excavators.[3] It showed, on one side, a man playing a lyre under the supervision of the Muse Urania; on the other side, two men, one standing, one seated, and both holding scrolls. At the center of the strigilated front was a small vessel. Goodenough thinks that these figures indicate the Jewish user's belief in some form of Dionysiac mysticism.

Goodenough was the first to call attention to several sarcophagus fragments still to be seen either in the Appia catacomb itself or in the antechamber.[4] One (G 795) shows traces of the bottom portion of a group comprising a standing man, a half-reclining and partly nude woman, a lion, and a vase from which water is flowing. The corner of a sarcophagus depicts on its two faces, respectively, a *putto*, holding a cornucopia and a curved wand (G 796), and the head of a ram (G 798). Another corner piece has a griffin and a human figure standing before a curtain (G 797). One fragment shows only the tail of a griffin (G 799). The front edge of a lid bears an attractive design of swimming dolphins (G 800). The medallion of a strigilated sarcophagus is in the form of a wreath containing a portrait, beneath which are a pair of cornucopias and a vase (G 802). The end fragment of a lid has the form of a

---

[1] So the fragmentary object is plausibly identified by Margarete Gütschow in *BL*; Goodenough (II, 26) calls it probably a "whirl rosette."

[2] These circular figures are called *matzot* in Kohl-Watzinger, *Antike Synagogen in Galilaea* (Leipzig, 1916), 187. The object in the plate at the right was identified by Garrucci (*Storia*, VI, 166) as an Aron with a volume under a curtain.

[3] Herzog in *BICA* 1861, 98 f.; Garrucci, *Cimitero*, 19-22; cf. Goodenough, II, 27 f. Garrucci did not consider this sarcophagus Jewish, but Goodenough believes that it was.

[4] Goodenough, II, 28-30; the illustrations, which appear in III, 795-804, are referred to in our text as G 795, etc.

pediment containing a wreath (G 803). Lastly, there is a piece showing Moses striking the rock (G 804). Although Goodenough feels that this fragment is probably of Jewish origin, I believe that it must certainly be from a Christian sarcophagus, since this is one of the most common motifs in early Christian art and no instance has yet been found in Rome of any Jewish treatment of a biblical theme in either painting or sculpture. As for the other fragments of this group, it is impossible to say which, if any, are Jewish. All except the last mentioned may possibly be from Jewish sarcophagi, although one may be more than dubious about the one with the portrait, since no example has yet appeared at Rome of such a use by Jews of the sarcophagus medallion. In the "Season Sarcophagus," described above, the medallion was filled with the figure of a menorah. Since it is not possible to assert that these fragments originated in the catacomb, it seems the wisest policy to adopt Ferrua's attitude that, with reference to such materials, the burden of proof rests with those who assert that they are of Jewish origin.[1]

Despite the general poverty of the community which used the Via Nomentana catacomb, as is evidenced by its simple graves, the scarcity of marble slabs, and the brevity and crudeness of the inscriptions, there were certainly some prosperous individuals among them, as is clear from the presence of a few private chambers, the decorated arcosolia, and the use of sarcophagi. All the entire sarcophagi and the fragments have been removed from the catacomb and are distributed over various parts of the grounds of the Villa Torlonia, under which the catacomb lies. While we cannot be absolutely certain which of these actually came from the catacomb, there is one about which there can be no doubt, since its inscription is the epitaph of Caelia Omnina, the wife of an archon of the Siburesians, a congregation which made use of this cemetery, as is clear from several inscriptions on the graves themselves (see above, p. 151). The front of this larger than average sarcophagus (8 ft. long, 3 ft. wide, 2 ft. 1 1/2 inches high) is covered with a simple pattern of strigilations. Each end has a splendid griffin, advancing with wings

---

[1] *RAC* 30 (1954), 238 f.

outspread, tail uplifted, and trampling a prostrate ram beneath its forelegs (Fig. 28).[1]

Another sarcophagus, its two ends adorned with seated griffins, has on its front three sculptured panels, separated by strigilations (Fig. 45).[2] The central panel shows a half-nude man, plausibly called Dionysus by Goodenough, and a youth, who is causing a snake to rise from a vessel. The narrow panel at the extreme right has a maenad, that at the left a satyr holding a wand and accompanied by a panther. It seems strange that a sarcophagus with such openly Dionysiac motifs should have been used for a Jewish burial. If so, either its user bought a fashionable type of sarcophagus without being concerned about any pagan religious ideas that these decorations might imply, or these symbols were actually, as Goodenough insists, of religious significance to him. That the Caelia Omnina sarcophagus, described in the previous paragraph, was bought ready-made and subsequently engraved with the epitaph of the deceased is obvious from the fact that the decorations are skillfully executed while the inscription itself was engraved by an unpracticed hand. The same may be true of this Dionysiac sarcophagus. It is regrettable that the epitaph, which was probably inscribed on the missing lid, is not available to offer us some clue.

Two other sarcophagi, complete except for the lids, probably came from the Nomentana catacomb. Both of these were first described and illustrated by Goodenough.[3] One, a child's sarcophagus, has no figures on the front (G 827); crossed shields and spears are on the ends (G 829). The other, a handsome case with rounded ends, stands on blocks vividly carved to represent lion heads. The strigilated front shows a small dolphin at upper center (G 832). At each end a savage lion, wearing harness, is rending an animal. Beside the lion is a man with hand upraised (G 831).

The Nomentana catacomb has yielded also a number of sarcophagus fragments, first published by Beyer and Lietz-

---

[1] See *JQR*, 42 (1952), 413-18 and pl. I, II; Goodenough, II, 42; III, 828.

[2] See *JQR*, 42, 418 and pl. III; Goodenough, II, 43; III, 833, 834.

[3] Goodenough, II, 42 f.; III, 827, 829, 831, 832; VII, 76.

mann, who regarded them as of pagan origin.[1] It is possible,
however, that, as Goodenough thinks, they are Jewish, or at
least were used by Jews, since several of the motifs occur
elsewhere in Jewish art and in some instances on the complete
sarcophagi described in the preceding paragraphs. The corner
of what must have been a very ornate sarcophagus (G 819)
has a fluted column with a richly ornamented capital, above
which are two dramatic masks. On what was the front there
is a trace of a dancing maenad, and what is left of the end
shows that it had a griffin pouncing on a ram's head, much
as on the Caelia Omnina sarcophagus. The other fragments
show, respectively, a nude male before a curtain with the hand
of another holding a scroll (G 821), a cupid picking grapes
(G 820), a lion's head (G 825), part of a hunting scene (G 823),
a satyr with a wineskin (G 822), a horse's head, and a few
other traces of human figures (G 824).

In the kitchen garden of the Villa Torlonia there lies,
neglected, a fine sarcophagus, intact with even the lid and
adorned with manifestly Jewish symbols (G 818).[2] A large,
handsome menorah at the center is flanked at left by an etrog
and shofar, at right by a lulab of the type seen on an arcosolium
inside the catacomb.[3] The simplicity of the composition
makes it particularly impressive. Paribeni, the excavator
of the Nomentana catacomb, was not sure whether the sarcophagus came from the catacomb or had been brought from
Porto, where the Torlonias had carried on excavations in the
1860s. Apparently it came from neither place, as Frey has
pointed out. He found that it was already in the Palazzo
Giraud in the Borgo, near the Vatican, by 1827, when this
palace became the property of the Torlonia family.[4] It seems
likely that the sarcophagus came originally from the Monteverde catacomb, since, as has already been noted, a number

---

[1] *BL*, 43 f. (by Margarete Gütschow) and pl. 23-25; reproduced by
Goodenough in III, 819-26 and discussed in II, 41. Cf. Gressmann
in *Jewish Studies in Honor of Israel Abrahams*, 184.

[2] On this sarcophagus see Paribeni, *N. Sc.* 1920, 155; Frey, *RAC*
8 (1931), 84; *BL*, 44 and pl. 26a; Goodenough, II, 41 and III, 818.

[3] In *BL* it is called a *Rübe*, but Goodenough rightly identified it
as a lulab.

[4] The palace, now called Palazzo Torlonia, is on Via della Concil-
iazione next to the church of S. Maria in Transpontina.

of Jewish inscriptions and other objects are known to have been carried away from that catacomb after its discovery by Bosio early in the seventeenth century.[1]

One more unquestionably Jewish sarcophagus fragment is worthy of mention at this place. It is the greater portion of a lid, the front of which is adorned with three widely separated dramatic masks (Fig. 46).[2] In the space between those at center and right is the Greek epitaph of Faustina (283), beneath which are figures of the menorah, with shofar and lulab to left and right and the Hebrew word *shalom*. Here again, the unskillful carving of the inscription contrasts with the fine workmanship of the masks, an indication that the sarcophagus was bought ready-made from a dealer's stock.[3] From the fact that this fragment was found on the Via Appia not far from the Jewish catacomb, some have assumed, as does Goodenough, that it came from that catacomb.[4] I think it more likely that, for the reason just stated, it came from the Monteverde catacomb; but this is, of course, only a conjecture. That it came from the Appia catacomb is less probable

[1] At least three fragments of sarcophagi whose inscriptions show that they must have come from the Monteverde catacomb are known to have strayed from their place of origin: No. 494, referring to the Synagogue of the Vernaclesians, is at the Ospizio Umberto I on Viale di Trastevere, about two kilometers from the catacomb; 496, with a reference to the Synagogue of the Augustesians, was found on Via Anicia in Trastevere, also some two kilometers from the catacomb; 504, referring to the Calcaresian Synagogue, was at one time in the Campus Martius near the church of S. Chiara, but what has become of it is not known. All three of the congregations mentioned on these sarcophagi buried their dead in the Monteverde catacomb, as has been shown above.

[2] Frey's illustration (*CII*, p. 199) shows only two masks, and in his note he states that two of the masks remain. He was apparently misled by a photograph of a detail, since the object itself, which I saw in a storeroom of the Terme Museum, has the three masks quite intact, as can be seen from our Fig. 46.

[3] The continually repeated inference from the masks that Faustina was an actress (cf. *VR*, 52 f.; V. Schultze, *Archäologische Studien über altchristliche Monumente* [Vienna, 1880], 271; Frey, *CII*, p. 198) has actually no basis, since such masks, as is well known, were an extremely common motif on sarcophagi.

[4] Goodenough, II, 25. The date of the discovery, given by Goodenough, following Frey, as 1722, was actually 1732; cf. *CIG* 9920. It was first published by Antonio Lupi in his *Dissertatio et animadversiones ad nuper inventum S. Severae Martyris Epitaphium* (Palermo, 1734), 177.

in that hitherto not a single inscription with a Hebrew word is known to have come from there, whereas the Monteverde catacomb has yielded a fair number of examples of Hebrew words and phrases. Besides, there is no indication that any materials from the Appia catacomb were available prior to its discovery in 1859, whereas the Faustina inscription was found in 1732.

Among the materials in a storeroom of the Terme Museum is the front of a child's sarcophagus (Fig. 47), which may be Jewish, as the inscription ἐνθάδε κοιμᾶται Ἀρτεμιδώρα ἐν εἰρήνῃ would lead one to suspect. Although, as was observed in Chapter VI, the usual beginning formula is ἐνθάδε κεῖται, the verb κοιμάομαι occurs in four inscriptions from the Jewish catacombs (150, 281, 365, 390) and the abridged form of the closing formula is found occasionally (e.g., 394, 459, 535). Although the name Artemidora does not appear in the onomasticon of the Jews of Rome, it is closely paralleled by such names as Isidora and Zenodora, which do occur. The sculptured decorations, especially appropriate for the tomb of a child, show winged putti at play, operating solid disks like hoops and rolling small round objects down an inclined board.

Sundry other sarcophagus fragments bearing inscriptions of Roman Jews have been found in Rome. In nearly all cases these were already fragments when the epitaph was carved.[1] It was obviously more economical to use such second-hand material as fragments of sarcophagi and discarded pieces of marble than to purchase a new marble slab. A few of the inscriptions, such as the Iulia Irene Arista epitaph (72), now in a cortile of the Palazzo Spada (Fig. 31), were inscribed on the sarcophagus containing the body. Since these sarcophagi and fragments have no ornamentation of either symbolic or artistic significance, no further treatment of them is called for here.

Among the objects of artistic and symbolic importance produced by the Jews of ancient Rome are the so-called "gold glasses." These were made by fastening gold leaf to the inside of the base of a glass vessel, etching the gold with the

---

[1] These are Figs. 49, 65; CII 120, 277, 494, 496, 504, 508, 511.

desired design and inscription, then fusing over it a thin layer of colorless glass, thus producing a sandwich effect.[1] Such glasses, several hundred of which have been found, were apparently used by pagans, Christians, and Jews as wine goblets.[2] Since the surviving examples were found in tombs, there was some special reason for placing such goblets with the dead, but the exact purpose can only be guessed at. Many scholars believe that some idea of salvation was involved.[3] Nikolaus Müller, on the basis of his discoveries in the Monteverde catacomb, regarded the glasses as identification marks for the graves, a view favored also by Cohn-Wiener.[4] This latter view has much to recommend it. It may well be that when one of these valuable goblets was broken, the base, with its beautifully etched figures in gold, was preserved by being used as a grave marker. Cemented into the walls of the bleak catacomb galleries, they could serve, with their sparkling gold figures, to identify tombs otherwise undistinguished. In fact, Müller found several fragments of such goblet bases still imbedded in the mortar of the grave closures.[5] The scarcity of well preserved examples is easily accounted for by the explanation that the ancient marauders, who plundered every part of the catacomb, pried these valuable objects out of the walls. That only the base of the goblet was used in the catacombs is clear from the extant specimens.

It is noteworthy that none of the oft-pictured gold glasses is recorded as having been found in a specific Jewish catacomb. There is no indication that gold glasses turned up in the Appia catacomb or in any of those discovered subsequently.

---

[1] See F. Neuburg, *Glass in Antiquity* (London, 1949), 49.

[2] Hermann Vopel, *Die altchristlichen Goldgläser* (Freiburg i. B., 1899), 84 f., thinks that they may have been favored as gifts or used at wedding feasts, anniversaries, and holidays. Lietzmann is convinced (*BL*, 23) that they were used by the Christians as drinking vessels in connection with the agape or refrigerium, and by the Jews for the meals of the Sabbath and festivals.

[3] The eschatological view is upheld, notably, by Gressmann, *op. cit.* (above, p. 216, n. 1), 181 f., and by Goodenough, II, 108-119. According to Gressmann these glasses accompanied the dead person so that "he might have his Torah shrine, his seven-branched candlestick, his sacramental cup there also."

[4] Müller, *Jüd. Kat.*, 58 (*Merk- und Erkennungszeichen*); cf. Cohn-Wiener, *Jüd. Kunst*, 128.

[5] *Jüd. Kat.*, 59-60.

One was found about 1882 in the Christian catacomb of Peter and Marcellinus,[1] but the exact provenience of the ten or eleven other extant Jewish examples is not known. Since three of these were already mentioned in Buonarroti's work on gold glasses, published in 1716, and several were included by Garrucci in his *Vetri Ornati* of 1858,[2] it is probable that most of the Jewish glasses came from the Monteverde catacomb, the only one known to that time. As has just been noted, Müller, who excavated this catacomb after its rediscovery in 1904, reported the finding of fragments of gold glasses imbedded in the walls, whereas no glasses of this type seem to have been found in the Appia and Nomentana catacombs. This circumstance, added to the fact that, as has been observed several times, a number of inscriptions and sarcophagus fragments had been removed from the Monteverde catacomb during the period of neglect after it was first discovered in 1602, would point to this cemetery as the likely provenience of most of the Jewish gold glasses whose origin is not recorded.

Now for a description of the glasses themselves. In one type of gold glass decoration the area is divided horizontally into two fields. Two glasses, one of which is in the Vatican Library (*CII* 516 = G 964, 965), the other in Poland (*CII* 517 = G 966), show in the upper half the Ark of the Law, its doors wide open so as to reveal six Torah scrolls, seen endwise and ranged on either two or three shelves. In each instance seated

---

[1] J. B. de Rossi, "Insigne vetro rappresentante il Tempio di Gerusalemme," *BAC* 20 (1882), 121-35, 137-58, Pl. VII. 1.

[2] Filippo Buonarroti, *Osservazioni sopra alcuni frammenti di vetro ornati di figure trovati ne' cimiteri di Roma*, Florence, 1716. The Jewish glasses (which are *CII* 516, 518, 520) are pictured in Pl. II.5 and III. 1, 2, and discussed on pp. 19-24; R. Garrucci, *Vetri ornati di figure in oro trovati nei cimiteri dei cristiani primitivi di Roma*, Rome, 1858 (second ed. 1864), pl. V. In Garrucci's *Storia della arte cristiana* (Prato, 1880), the Jewish glasses are described in VI, 157-58 and pictured in plate 490. The most important modern work on the gold glasses is Hermann Vopel, *Die altchristlichen Goldgläser* (Freiburg, 1899). Other substantial treatments are O. M. Dalton, "The Gilded Glasses of the Catacombs," *Archaeological Jour.*, 1901, 227-53; H. Leclercq, "Fonds de coupes," in Cabrol and Leclercq, *DACL* V, 1819-59. Leclercq has an additional discussion of "Verres juifs" in XV, 2972 f. Anton Kisa, *Das Glas im Altertume* (Leipzig, 1908) has a section on ' Die Goldgläser" (III, 834-67).

lions (presumably the lions of Judah) flank the shrine on both sides. The lower space is filled with two large menorahs, lights ablaze, accompanied by the well-known cult symbols. These are, on the one glass, a central lulab, two shofars, two flasks, an etrog, and two small unidentified objects; on the other, the central lulab is accompanied by a shofar, an etrog, and two flasks balancing each other at the extreme left and right. On another glass (*JE*, II, 107 = G 967) the open shrine in the upper half shows nine scrolls, ranged on three shelves. Instead of lions, a pair of doves (Lietzmann calls them eagles)[1] perched on globes serve as guardians of the shrine. The lower semicircle has a large lighted menorah at its center, flanked by two lions back to back, crouching as though about to spring. Here also we find the two-handled flask, etrog, shofar, lulab, and two small perforated disks which Goodenough (II, 111) thinks may represent some kind of wafer.

A fragment (*CII* 520 = G 968), now in the Vatican Library (said to be from Ostia rather than from Rome), shows the Ark, again with open doors, but with paneled compartments where one usually sees the rolled-up scrolls. A dove is perched on each door. The arched upper portion of the shrine is decorated with a menorah flanked by a shofar and etrog. To the left of the shrine is a closed scroll, shown vertically, next to which is a large rolled-up object, which Goodenough (II, 111) thinks may be a curtain rolled up from the shrine. To the left of that is a lulab. The figures to the right of the shrine are gone.

In another fragment (*CII* 518 = G 973), which is now in the Metropolitan Museum at New York, the Ark in the upper half is flanked by a pair of menorahs. Besides the scrolls seen lying within the shrine, another scroll stands upright at the left. Among the other objects only a shofar can be identified positively. In the lower half, nearly all of which is lost, there are traces of a semi-circular banquet couch and a plate containing a large fish, regarded by some as an allusion to the fish eaten at the Sabbath meal, by others as referring to the

---

[1] In *BL*, 22, n. 2.

felicity of the life beyond the grave.[1] The fish-banquet motif is seen also on a glass (*CII* 522 = G 974) which was last recorded as being at Berlin in the Kaiser-Friedrich Museum. The upper section has an open Ark with four compartments, each containing six scrolls. As in the glass of the Metropolitan Museum, there is a menorah on each side of the shrine. In this example the menorah to the left is accompanied by a shofar and a flask, that to the right by an etrog and a lulab. The lower half, fairly well preserved in this glass, shows a semi-circular couch with a small round table, on which lies a platter containing a fish.

Various fragments show repetitions, with minor variations, of the same motifs.[2] Notably different is the glass first published by De Rossi in 1882[3] as from a gallery of the Christian catacomb of Peter and Marcellinus on Via Casilina and now in the Vatican Library (*CII* 515 = G 978). A temple-like structure is shown standing in a courtyard surrounded by a colonnade. The shrine, raised on a podium with four steps, has a colonnaded front portico. A pair of doors is shown partly open. The pediment of the gabled roof is filled with a menorah. To the left and right of the shrine are two tall, free-standing columns. The front wall of the colonnade, constructed of reticulate masonry, is surmounted by a central menorah with flaming lights; at its right are two two-handled vessels and at the left a lulab, etrog, and two other vases without handles. At the right of the colonnade (and perhaps originally also at the left, which is not preserved) are two small colonnaded structures, each with a palm tree adjoining. Some scholars[4] have confidently asserted that the shrine is a repre-

---

[1] The Sabbath meal interpretation is favored by Lietzmann (*BL*, 19), Cohn-Wiener (*Jüd. Kunst*, 132), Reifenberg (*Denkmäler der jüd. Antike*, 54), and Zwarts (*Zevenarmige kandelaar*, 47). For the eschatological view see Goodenough, II, 112 and V, 45 f.

[2] Müller (*Jüd. Kat.* 59 f.) reports that the fragment of a glass fastened to a grave in the Monteverde catacomb showed some magistrate, perhaps a Roman consul, seated on a sort of throne in the attitude of one gesticulating as he spoke. Next to this figure was a flying *putto*.

[3] See above, p. 220, n. 1.

[4] Arguments for Solomon's Temple are to be found in De Rossi, *op. cit.* (above, p. 220, n. 1); Cohn-Wiener, *Jüd. Kunst*, 129; Lietzmann *BL*, 22 f. ("kein Zweifel"); Gressmann, *op. cit.* (above, p. 195 n. 1), 180 f.

sentation of Solomon's Temple and that the two unattached columns are the pillars called Jachin and Boaz in 1 Kings 7. 21. Others just as emphatically insist that the shrine cannot be the Temple. Galling, for example,[1] thinks it represents a Torah shrine accompanied by the cult objects associated with the Sukkot festival. The two pillars would be supports for the (non-existent) curtain before the shrine. With these views Reifenberg is in agreement. Goodenough, however, using the Greek inscription οἶκος ἰρήνης (House of Peace) as a clue, argues that the shrine is definitely a tomb. In that it takes the form of a shrine, it represents, he believes, the "blessed fate" of the deceased in the next world. He thinks that the two columns have nothing to do with Solomon's Jachin and Boaz, but have some undeterminable symbolic value. It would be useless to cite other interpretations. The fact is that we have no way of determining which conjecture, if any, is the correct one.

One Jewish gold glass differs from all the others in that it bears a Greek sepulchral inscription, that of Anastasia and her daughter Asther (732).[2] With its familiar Greek formulas and the addition of the Hebrew word *shalom* and the menorah and shofar, it is like many another inscription from the cata-

---

("the temple of Solomon is certainly depicted"); Frey, *CII*, p. 378 ("sans doute le Temple de Jérusalem"). Similarly, Leclercq in *DACL* XV, 2972 f. insists that it is the Temple of Jerusalem "à l'exclusion de tout autre" and thinks that it gives a clue to the actual appearance of Herod's Temple. Marucchi in *Cat. rom.* (1903 edition), 292, accepting De Rossi's identification, thinks that the glass came from the Jewish catacomb of the Via Labicana, which was located a short distance from the Christian catacomb in which it was found. The Jewish glass may, however, have come into the possession of a Christian, who used it to adorn a Christian grave, as Berliner (I, 61) points out. Incidentally, Berliner also calls the representation that of the Temple at Jerusalem. Rengstorf, *op. cit.* (above, p. 195, n. 1) 49 f., thinks that the structure is a synagogue in a court, as at Capernaum, and not the Temple of Jerusalem.

[1] For the views cited here see K. Galling, *Theol. Stud. u. Kritiken* 103 (1931), 359; Reifenberg, *Denkmäler d. jüd. Antike*, 54; Goodenough, II, 113.

[2] M. Schwabe and A. Reifenberg, "Ein jüdisches Goldglas mit Sepulcralinschrift aus Rome," *RAC* 12 (1935), 341-46; also *CII* 732 (on p. 597) and Goodenough, III, 962; cf. Leclercq in *DACL* XV, 2973. It was in the private Galleria Sangiorgi at Rome, but when I inquired there in 1951, it had already been sold.

combs, except that it is incised on a gold glass instead of being carved on marble or painted on stucco.

The inscriptions on most of the glasses refer to drinking and conviviality, an indication that their original purpose, at least, was to serve as wine goblets. One of the most frequent formulas on both the Jewish and non-Jewish glasses is the Latin transliteration of the Greek words for "drink, live," *pie, zeses* (*CII* 516, 517, 519). The adjective *hilaris* (cheerful), variously misspelled, is sometimes added (*CII* 517). One Jewish example (518) has *Bibas cum eulogia* (drink with blessing); another (520) shows the phrase *anima dulcis* (sweet spirit), found also on Christian gold glasses.[1] The one with the supposed representation of the Temple (515) bears a Greek inscription, which, if the lacunae have been supplied correctly, means "House of Peace. Take blessing with all your family." The last phrase corresponds to the Latin *cum tuis* or *cum omnibus tuis*, which is frequently found on the gold glasses. Quite different is the inscription on the glass that got from Rome to Berlin (522). It seems to indicate, in faulty grammar, that the glass was a gift from one Felix Venerius to his master Vitalis with his wife and children.[2]

Such, then, are the gold glasses from the Jewish catacombs. That they were manufactured by Jews is most probable, since it is well known that Jews were especially prominent in the glass-making industry. Neuburg, in fact, thinks that the pagan and Christian gold glasses also are products of Jewish workmanship in Rome.[3] The technique, which originated in Egypt, had been brought to Rome from Egypt and Syria. It seems clear that these glasses were used as wine goblets for festive occasions. Why they were placed in the catacombs remains an unresolved question. That they were employed for the purpose of identifying the graves, as has been intimated above, is at least a possibility.

A few words may be added on the lamps which were found

---

[1] See Vopel, *Die altchristlichen Goldgläser*, 83.

[2] The text of the inscription is as follows: *Salbo domino Vitale cum coiuge et filios ipsoru Felix Benerius.* The probable meaning is "Felix Venerius to his master italis — may he be in good health — with his wife and their children."

[3] Frederic Neuburg, *Glass in Antiquity*, 49.

in the catacombs. These are the familiar type of clay hand lamp which used olive oil as fuel. Those comparatively few that bear a decoration show the menorah in a variety of shapes.[1] Müller reported that in excavating the Monteverde catacomb he found hundreds of lamps and that there were indications that it was the custom to place a lighted lamp inside the grave by the head of the deceased. The figured decorations on the Monteverde lamps included such objects as rosettes, palmettes, a galloping horse, an ibex, a cock, and a fish. One, strangely, seems to show a figure of Venus (G 493). Three had the Christian monogram. Besides the usual seven-armed menorah, there were two with a five-armed candela-brum. In the debris from the Nomentana catacomb, not long after its discovery, I saw a number of lamps and lamp frag-ments, among which was one bearing the Christian monogram. Apparently the Jews who used these lamps were not always scrupulous about avoiding those with pagan or Christian themes.

A few small carved objects found in the Jewish catacombs are generally regarded as amulets. In the Appia catacomb Garrucci found a Medusa head carved in obsidian (G 1044).[2] It lay on the breast of a skeleton and may have been an ornament or a charm. Müller discovered in the Monteverde catacomb a coral figure of an animal, perhaps a dog, with a hole indicating that it was attached to a chain. This, in Müller's opinion, was either an ornament or an amulet.[3]

In evaluating and interpreting the figures which appear on the inscriptions and in the adornment of the tombs, tomb chambers, and sarcophagi, it would be important to know the extent to which these had a genuine symbolic and reli-gious meaning for their users. Here we find ourselves in the realm of conjecture, and the interpretations range from the views of those scholars who believe that they were primarily intended as decorative elements or, at most, to emphasize

---

[1] See the illustrations in Goodenough, III, 934, 935, 942-48. On the Monteverde lamps see Müller, *Jüd. Kat.*, 53-56 and *Diss. Pont. Acc. Rom. Arch.* Ser. II, Vol. XII (1915), 245-48.

[2] Garrucci, *Storia della arte cristiana*, VI, 165 and pl. 491.4.

[3] *Jüd. Kat.*, 50.

the Judaism of the deceased,[1] to the opinions of those at the other end of the scale, who see a mystical and eschatological significance in every such object and hold that decoration had no place in the dark subterranean galleries and tomb chambers, which were not meant to be visited and admired.

For my own part, I feel that to cite passages from the Talmud, as some scholars have done, can be of little value in helping us to a solution. The inscriptions have clearly demonstrated that there was little, if any, knowledge of Hebrew among the Jews of imperial Rome, so that the opinions of the rabbis were probably quite unknown to them. If there were any Hebrew scholars among them, we have no indication that they transmitted their knowledge of rabbinic lore to any degree among their fellow Jews. Neither will quotations from Philo help us a great deal, since Philo's allegory and mysticism were far removed from the thought and experience of the comparatively uneducated Jews of the Roman community. That the menorah and the Ark of the Law and the other cult objects had, to their original users, some symbolic and perhaps eschatological value seems entirely possible. I believe, however, that certain scholars have gone much too far in finding symbolic mysticism in every device. Marmorstein, for example,[2] holds that all the representations found in the catacombs are concerned with death and the life beyond. To Rieger all the frescoes allude to the joys of resurrection; the Sukkot symbols of etrog and lulab refer to the Messianic Era, the shofar to the trumpet with which Elijah will herald the coming of the Messiah. To Cumont the menorah symbolizes the eternal light of immortality which illumines the souls of the elect in their

---

[1] *E.g.*, Kohl and Watzinger, *Antike Synagogen in Galilaea* (Leipzig, 1916) 201, and Frey, *Biblica* 15 (1934) 288, who hold that there is no proof that the Jews used doctrinal symbolism in their funerary art. I. Zoller, *Studi e Materiali di Storia delle Religioni* 7 (1931), 150, states categorically that there is no eschatological symbolism involved, but that the figures must be taken as symbols of various aspects of Jewish religious life.

[2] These are the references for the views alluded to in this paragraph (for the works cited above on p. 195 only the pages are given): Marmorstein, 32-41; Rieger, 216-218; Cumont, *Recherches sur le symbolisme funéraire*, 495; Rengstorf, 57; Goodenough, *HUCA*, 23, 491; *Symbols*, II, 137.

heavenly abode. Rengstorf looks on the menorah as symbolic of the Torah and therefore of the light of eternal life. For Goodenough the menorah represents the hope of the Messianic Age and is the symbol of God Himself. With its seven lights, he holds, it "symbolizes the seven planets, which are the eyes of God watching (and the vehicles of God's will determining) the actions of men. It is a symbol of God as the eternal Light."

It is a familiar fact that Judaism has tended to be a this-worldly religion, placing but little stress on salvation and the future life. If, however, the Jews of Rome were so deeply concerned about the life after death and felt that the presence of the menorah or some other emblem on the tomb was actually essential in order to assure the salvation of the deceased, we may wonder why so many of the tomb inscriptions are without symbols. At least 46 % of the epitaphs from the Monteverde catacomb and 62 % from the Appia show no symbol whatsoever. Did not the Jews who inscribed these unembellished epitaphs desire the salvation of their beloved dead no less ardently than those who used such symbols? Does it not seem more plausible that, whatever their symbolic value may have been originally,[1] the menorah, shofar, lulab, etrog, and other objects associated with the ritual, had become conventionalized, merely testifying to the Judaism of the deceased, figures to be used or omitted according to the preferences of the individual? If, however, the emblems did in fact have the kind of symbolic meaning that is claimed for them, I am inclined to agree with Ferrua,[2] who points out that, in the absence of contemporary explanations, it is impossible for us to reconstruct their meaning, since we cannot hope to put our mentality in the place of that of the ancients so as to determine the specific meaning of this or that figure or to decide where decoration ends and symbolic meaning begins. The efforts of distinguished scholars, such as Marmor-stein, Cumont, and Goodenough, to achieve such a result are impressive and, for all we know, they may have attained

---

[1] As Cohn-Wiener (*Jüd. Kunst*, 90) remarks, the actual reason why the menorah came to be used as the symbol of Judaism is no better known than why the Magen David is so commonly used today.

[2] Ferrua, *RAC* 30 (1954), 242.

some measure of truth; but strong doubts must remain.

The discussions in the older writers on the extent to which the Jews of the Diaspora might permit themselves to make representations of animals and human beings in the face of the biblical prohibition of such figures are now completely pointless, in view of the discoveries in the synagogues and tombs of Palestine and the Diaspora.[1] It has become clear that even pagan mythological beings were not considered inappropriate for the decoration of Jewish tomb chambers, sarcophagi, and even synagogues. Whether such mosaics, frescoes, and sarcophagus reliefs were the work of Jewish or pagan artists is of no special significance in the face of the indisputable fact that these were deliberately selected by their Jewish users.

From the artistic point of view, many of the figures are executed with little skill, but some of the work, particularly the frescoes of the Appia and Nomentana catacombs, is, as we have seen, of a relatively high order of excellence. Students of the history of Jewish art may not ignore the artistic products in and from the Jewish catacombs of Rome.

---

[1] For example, an anonymous writer in *Rev. Bib.* 14 (1917), 318, holding that the Jews of the Hellenistic period kept strictly to the prohibition of images, rejects the "Season Sarcophagus" of the Via Appia and maintains that the interpolation of the menorah amid pagan motifs shows that it was intended for a proselyte. In reality, it seems that proselytes tended to be even more strict in their observance of religious forms than most native-born Jews. We have already seen that Frey, despite his acquaintance with the frescoes of the Dura synagogue and the mosaics of the synagogues of Palestine and North Africa, still argued that the painted rooms of the Appia catacomb were originally pagan burial places. Ludwig Blau, in *HUCA*, 2 (1926), 178-80, makes a distinction between painted figures as permissible and raised or sculptured figures as forbidden; but the reliefs on the Jewish sarcophagi make it clear that no such distinction was made, at least not by the Roman Jews.

CHAPTER TEN

THE LIFE OF THE COMMUNITY

A. Vital Data

Although most of our inscriptions offer no information on such details as the age at death, years of marriage, or size of family, and many of those which originally did bear such information are now so fragmentary that the figures are not preserved, yet sufficient data of this type can be assembled to supply statistics of some significance. In interpreting these data we must obviously apply some degree of caution, since we cannot always be certain that the results offer a typical sampling.

Age at Death	Males	Females	Sex Unknown	Totals
Under 10[1]	41	23	1	65
10-19	9	12		21
20-29	13	14	1	28
30-39	11	3		14
40-49	3	6		9
50-59	5	2		7
60-69	3	2		5
70-79	2	1[2]		3
80-89	5	5		10
90 and over	1	1		2
Totals	93	69	2	164

Out of the 534 inscriptions we can glean information on the age at death of 164 persons, of whom 93 are males, 69

---

[1] This group includes every child designated as νήπιος even when the age is not given, since this term was certainly not applied to a child as old as ten. The highest identifiable age for a νήπιος in these inscriptions is seven (161: Salvius). Sixteen boys and six girls are so designated with no statement of the actual age. Only one child is called an *infans* (273).

[2] If the conjecture ΕΤΟ in No. 307 is correct, Aurelia Zotice died at age seventy. See above, p. 97, note 4.

females, and 2 whose sex cannot be determined. The preceding table will show the distribution by age groups and sex.

It will be noted that by far the highest mortalily appears in the group under ten and that comparatively large numbers are found in the groups from 10 to 29. These figures may be deceptive in that it is entirely probable that the epitaphs tended to record the age of those who died young, or at least to indicate that they died as children,[1] and to omit the age of those living into middle life or beyond. It will be observed also that the age group 80-89 shows a higher number than any of those from 40 through 79, an indication that an advanced age was regarded as worthy of record on one's tomb. The highest ages are those of a woman, Poemenis (151), who lived to be 96 years, 10 months, 18 days, and of Pancharius (509), the Father of the Synagogue of Elaea, who died at the very ripe age of 110, devoted to his people and to his religion.

It is interesting to find that many more boys than girls seem to have died in childhood, while the mortality for girls was apparently greater in the adolescent years.[2] Although the figures are too small to be decisive, they are in accord with mortality figures that still prevail. That the infant mortality was very high is evident not alone from the figures cited above. The visitor to the Jewish catacombs (and the same is true of the Christian catacombs) will be impressed by the large number of small loculi, apparently the graves of children, unmarked by any epitaph (see Figs. 8, 9, 40).

It would be desirable to know at what age Jewish girls were married in ancient Rome. Such information is available in but six instances. Two girls married at twelve, two at fifteen, one at fifteen or sixteen, one at sixteen or seventeen. Since no later age is recorded, we may infer, even from so few examples, that fifteen was a normal age for a girl to marry

---

[1] The age of infants dying before the end of their first year is hardly ever recorded. The only extant instances are those of Judas (348), who died at seven months, and of Hermione, daughter of Pisinna (108), whose age seems to have been eight months (not eleven, as Frey thinks) and seven days.

[2] These figures must be tempered somewhat by the fact that the surviving epitaphs of males are nearly 20% more numerous than those of females.

and that some married as early as twelve.[1] There are five instances in which the girl is designated as a virgin (παρθένος)[2] and the age at death is also indicated. One was fifteen years old, two were eighteen, one nineteen, one twenty-two. We have no way of knowing whether there were many "old maids" in the community, but the likelihood, in view of the custom of arranged marriages which probably prevailed in that community as in others at the time, is that very few women reached the age of twenty without having been married. We know of one man, Aelius Primitivus (457), who married at the age of twenty-two, since his widow, Flavia Maria, recorded on his tombstone in the Monteverde catacomb that her "incomparable husband" died at thirty-eight after they had enjoyed sixteen years of married life together "without ever a complaint" (*sine ulla querela*).[3]

The number of years of marriage is recorded in thirteen instances. These range from fifteen months to thirty-four years. Every one of these marriages, needless to say, was terminated by death. There are hardly any data on size of family. We know that Veriana, entombed in the Nomentana catacomb (12), left five children; that Ursacius (129, 147, 167) and Gadias (510, 535, 543) each buried three daughters;[4] that Proculus and Euhodia were buried with their three daughters (391); that Naevia Curia was the mother of three (47); and that Cattia Ammias, "who lived a good life in Judaism," in thirty-four years of marriage "saw grandchildren from her children" (537).

Naturally, the tomb inscriptions yield no information whatsoever about divorce or multiple marriages. In two

---

[1] That Roman girls were commonly married at twelve is abundantly evident from the inscriptions and the literature. In fact, twelve was the minimum age fixed by Roman law for the marriage of girls and fourteen for boys, as is clear from Macrobius, *Saturnalia* 7.7.6; Dio 54.167; Cod. Just. 5.4.24. See H. Blümner, *Die römischen Privatalterthümer* (Munich, 1911), 343.

[2] The use of the term παρθένος involves no praise of virginity *per se*, as it often does in the Christian inscriptions. The only implication is one of pathos that the girl died before attaining marriage. On this point see Frey, *CII*, p. CXVII.

[3] On this formula see above, p. 132.

[4] On Gadias and his daughters see H. J. Leon, "The Daughters of Gadias," *TAPA*, 84 (1953), 67-72.

epitaphs the deceased woman is styled μόνανδρος (having one husband), a term which apparently recorded the fact that she did not remarry after her husband's death.[1] One was Agentia (81), who had lived with her "virgin husband" (μετὰ παρθενι-κοῦ) for nine years. The other was Rebecca (392), who died at forty-four.[2]

Interesting in this connection are the words παρθενικός, παρθενική, and *virginius*, apparently used of a spouse who had not been married before.[3] As noted just above, Agentia lived with her "virgin husband" for nine years. Then there was Sabina (242), who lived *cum virginiun sun* (for *cum virginio suo*) for three years and three days and died at the age of eighteen years and three days. Obviously, she was married on her fifteenth birthday. A woman Irene is recorded as having been the "virgin wife" (παρθενικὴ σύμβιος) of a certain Clodius (319).

That many of these marriages were very happy and that the death of the one partner brought deep sorrow to the survivor is evident from the epitaphs cited in a previous chapter (pp. 129-34). Even if we make allowance for the conventional expressions of devotion which may be expected on tomb inscriptions, many have a note which seems entirely sincere. The same is true of the expressions of sorrow which are found in the epitaphs inscribed by children to parents or by parents to children. All these point to a wholesome and devoted family life in the Jewish community of ancient Rome. It should be observed, incidentally, that there is no evidence that in the life of the family women had a position in any way inferior to that of the men. Jewish mothers, wives, and daughters were apparently regarded with no less respect and affection than fathers, husbands, and sons.

A brief paragraph may be appended here on the evidence for adoption, which is revealed in four of the inscriptions. Justus was the adopted son of Menander (3). Alexandria

---

[1] For a discussion of the meaning of this term see above, p. 129 f.

[2] There may be a third example in a fragmentary inscription (158) on which the letters NΔPOC are preserved. These point to either μόνανδρος or φίλανδρος (devoted to her husband). Frey adds 541, the epitaph of Rufina, who is also styled μόνανδρος. There is no evidence, however, that this is a Jewish inscription; cf. *HTR* 44 (1952), 171.

[3] For the meaning of these expressions see above, p. 130.

Severa inscribed an affectionate epitaph for her adopted son Notus, who died at twenty-seven after a good life with her (144). Irene, an adopted child, died at three years and seven months (21). The visitor to the Jewish Room of the Lateran Museum will see on the wall, bearing the number 116, a long epitaph by Theodotus to his adopted son Justus, who died when only four years and eight months (358). Pathetic in his sorrow, the foster-father exclaims, through the medium of the cold marble slab, "O my child Justus, would that I were able to place you in a golden coffin!" He prays to the Lord that in His justice He will allow this peerless child to sleep in peace. (Fig. 36. 116).

B. Occupations and Economic Status

The tomb inscriptions offer us, unfortunately, almost no information about the occupations of the members of the community. A certain Eudoxius, whose epitaph is still in the Appia catacomb (109), is referred to as a painter (ζωγράφος, that is, a painter of living things). It has been inferred, without further proof, that he may have painted the decorated rooms of the Appia catacomb. The same catacomb has yielded the epitaph of Alexander, "a butcher from the market (bubularus de macello), a good soul, the friend of everyone (anima bona omniorum amicus)," who died at the age of thirty (210). The inscription ends with the hope, expressed in a mixture of Latin and Greek, that this kindly man will sleep among the righteous (dormitio tua inter dicaeis). We learn that Eusebius (333) was a teacher (διδάσκαλος) and a Torah scholar (νομομαθής). A fragment in the Appia catacomb (201) seems to be part of the epitaph of a "teacher of the Law (Torah)," but since the significant word is only partly preserved, this reading, though probable, is not certain.[1] Then there was Mniaseas (= Manasseh), a "father of synagogues" (πατὴρ συναγωγίων), whatever that may mean, whose life was dedicated to scholarly pursuits (508), since he is styled "student of the sages" (μαθητὴς σοφῶν), the equivalent obviously of the Hebrew תלמיד חכם. In the catacomb of Via

---

[1] The surviving letters ΤΩΝΟΜΩΔ probably represent τῷ νομο-δ[ιδασκάλῳ] (so Frey), rather than τῷ νόμῳ δ[ικαίου] as Garrucci interpreted it (Diss. Arch., II, 152).

Appia Pignatelli, the Jewish character of which is at least doubtful, the only legible inscription reported by Nikolaus Müller was that of an ex-soldier, Rufinus (79). If Jewish, this is the only catacomb inscription which indicates military service on the part of any member of the Jewish community.[1]

Manifestly, no conclusions are justified on the basis of these scanty data. The literary sources permit a few slight additions to the list of occupations. We learn from Acts 18.3 that the Jew Aquila, who migrated from Rome to Corinth, was a tentmaker. In his autobiography (3. 16) Josephus tells of being aided on his first trip to Rome by a Jewish actor (μιμολόγος), named Alityrus, whom he met at Puteoli. This Alityrus was a favorite with Nero and introduced Josephus to the Empress Poppaea. One Menophilus, lampooned by the epigrammatist Martial (7. 82), seems to have been a Jewish comic actor. The same writer ridicules an immoral Jewish poet (11. 94).

Other references in the Roman writers indicate that the Jews of Rome were despised for their poverty and beggary rather than envied or hated for their wealth. Our sources are, to be sure, hostile witnesses, notably among them the satirist Juvenal, but their testimony, though doubtless exaggerated, must not be disregarded. Juvenal writes indignantly (3. 12-16) that the sacred spring and grove of Egeria (at the Via Appia near the Porta Capena) have been rented out for an encampment of Jews, who, with their miserable equipment of baskets and hay, have driven out the Muses and transformed that once

---

[1] The statement is frequently made that Faustina, whose sarcophagus was adorned with scenic masks, must have been an actress; e.g., V. Schultze, *Arch. Stud. über altchrist. Monumente* (Vienna, 1880), 271, and *Die Katakomben* (Leipzig, 1882), 182; Vogelstein in VR, 61 ("zweifellos") and *Jews of Rome*, 43, where he states without reservation, "The Jewish actress Faustina was living at Rome in the period of Marcus Aurelius," on the assumption, apparently from her name, that this Jewish woman was a contemporary of the Empress Faustina, wife of Marcus Aurelius. Frey also (*CII*, *ad loc.*) agrees that this is a "monument funéraire d'une actrice juive." However, the presence of the masks, a common motif on sarcophagi (see above, p. 217, n. 3), would be no indication of the profession of the deceased. Because of the name of the Synagogue of the Calcaresians, some have concluded that its members were lime burners, but, as shown above (p. 143), this view is to be rejected.

idyllic spot into a haunt of beggars.[1] He implies that synagogues also are a station for beggars (3. 296). In his Sixth Satire, the celebrated diatribe on Roman women, the satirist gives a biting description of the begging Jewess who, at a small fee, will predict the future for some superstitious Roman woman and interpret her dreams for her (6. 542-547). Martial, listing the noisy pests of the city, includes among them the Jew "taught to beg by his mother" (12. 57. 13: *a matre doctus . . . rogare Iudaeus*). Some have supposed that Martial's Transtiberine peddler, who exchanges sulphur firesticks for broken glass (1. 41. 3-5), was a Jew. This is not improbable, since Jews were the chief manufacturers of glass in the Mediterranean world at that time and the broken glass was used in the making of new glass.[2]

These indications of poverty and lowly economic pursuits among the Roman Jews are to some extent borne out by the evidence of their graves. As we have already observed, thousands of these are plain loculi, many of them marked, it seems, by no epitaph at all, others by a brief notice, crudely scrawled with paint or even just scratched on the stuccoed closures, or unskillfully carved with ill-shaped letters and in faulty grammar on pieces of discarded marble. The language of the inscriptions also, as has been seen from the preceding discussion, points to a generally low degree of literacy.

Yet, in contrast, there are signs that the various congregations had also their prosperous members and many with a good education. The attractively decorated private tomb chambers and arcosolia, the elaborate sarcophagi, the inscriptions expertly engraved by professional stonecutters on fine slabs of marble, all point to comfortable economic circumstances on the part of those who could afford to honor

---

[1] Some scholars have, on the basis of this passage in Juvenal, placed one of the principal Jewish quarters at the Porta Capena, pointing to the three Jewish catacombs in the Via Appia area as an archaeological confirmation. P. Romanelli, in *Bull. Ass. Arch. Rom.* 2 (1912), 133, asserts that this was a fine quarter for *business*, since it was on a major traffic artery. The passage in Juvenal clearly indicates a gypsy-like encampment of a motley crew of beggars, not business men; see above, p. 137.
[2] See H. J. Leon, "Sulphur for Broken Glass," *TAPA*, 72 (1941), 233-36, and F. Neuburg, *Glass in Antiquity* (London, 1949), 49.

their dead by such means. Furthermore, we can infer from the correct spelling and grammar of a good number of the inscriptions that there must have been not a few well educated persons in the Jewish community. There were even scholars, as we have just seen, and the occasional appearance of a Hebrew word or formula indicates that acquaintance with that traditionally sacred language of the Jews was not wholly absent.

As regards the occupations or professions of these wealthier members of the community, we simply have no information. Were they merchants, financiers, professional men, as are so many of the Jews in our own day? The statement is frequently made that many of them were engaged in international trade.[1] As evidence one cites the fact that the chief Jewish quarter was in the Transtiberine region near the Tiber, the busy wharves of which received merchandise brought up the river from the harbors of Ostia and Portus Traiani. This is no evidence at all, since the Transtiberine district was the squalid foreign quarter of Rome, crowded with poverty-stricken Greeks, Syrians, Jews, and other non-Romans. Prosperous merchants did not need to live close to the wharves at which their goods came in and went out. It is more likely that many of the Transtiberine Jews were humble dock workers, earning a meager livelihood by physical toil. Another piece of evidence cited for the mercantile activities of the Roman Jews is the apparent presence at the harbor city of Portus Traiani (Porto) of an important Jewish community which had close links with the Roman congregations. I have demonstrated in a separate article that there is actually no evidence for the existence of such a community, since the Jewish inscriptions which were thought to be the product of that community were in reality brought to Porto from Rome early in the nineteenth century and most probably came out of the

---

[1] So, for example, Vogelstein in VR, 61. See also S. Collon in *Mélanges d'arch. et d'hist. de l'École Française de Rome* 57 (1940), 77. Father Ferrua, in *Civ. Catt.*, 1936, IV, 310, has suggested that the use of Greek by the Jews is an indication of the commercial character of the colony; but Greek was, after all, the prevailing language of much of the Mediterranean population at this time, mercantile or otherwise. Romanelli, in the passage cited on p. 235, n. 1, states that the Jews everywhere were devoted to commerce.

Monteverde catacomb.[1] It is noteworthy also that among the numerous inscriptions hitherto found in Rome's great harbor city of Ostia there is no evidence that Jewish merchants operated there. It is a fallacy to attribute to the Jews of ancient Rome the mercantile activities that are associated with the Jews of the Middle Ages and of modern times.[2] While we need not doubt that many members of the Roman Jewish community were engaged in business activities of various kinds, there is no positive evidence of these activities in either the inscriptions or the literature. In fact, the allusions to the Jews, as has already been noted, stress their poverty, not their wealth. The scornful references to wealthy Jews which became commonplace at a later time are completely lacking in our ancient sources.

There is not a single mention in our catacomb inscriptions of either slaves or freedmen. That under the Republic many Jews had originally come to Rome as slaves is clear from Philo (*Legatio* 23. 155), who indicates that they did not long remain in servitude, since they were set free by their owners. Most probably their fellow-Jews aided many of them by providing the money needed to purchase their freedom. The conquest of Judaea by Vespasian and Titus and the bitter Jewish wars under Trajan and Hadrian must have brought to Rome many additional Jewish slaves, and we may surmise that these also came to enjoy freedom in due time. It may well be that by the time of our inscriptions there were no Jewish slaves within the Jewish community and that if any Jew died while in slavery to a non-Jew and was buried in a Jewish cemetery, the fact of his servitude was not mentioned on his epitaph. Other sources yield only two specific references to Jewish slaves at Rome. We know that the Empress Livia, wife of Augustus, had a Jewish slave woman named Acme,[3] and

---

[1] "The Jewish Community of Ancient Porto," *HTR* 45 (1952), 165-75. For the allegedly active commercial links between the Jews of Porto and Rome, see the citations in this article and Vogelstein in VR, 61 and *Jews of Rome*, 43.

[2] N. Bentwich, in *JQR*, 6 (1915), 336, agreeing with Juster (II, 313 f.), rightly points out that the Jews showed no remarkable trend toward commerce until the fifth century, when they were excluded from liberal callings.

[3] Josephus, *AJ* 17.5.7.141. In this passage Livia is referred to as

Martial seems to have owned a Jewish slave (7. 35. 2-3). The freed slaves would, after the Roman custom, have become *libertini* and have assumed the *nomen gentile* of their former master, retaining their original name as a cognomen. It is quite possible that an original freedman stock is revealed by such names of Roman Jews as Aurelius Hermias, Caelius Anastasius, Sempronius Basileus, Aurelius Ioses, Claudius Ioses, Lucius Domitius Abbas. Even a greater number of feminine names is found in this type of combination; *e.g.*, Aemilia Theodora, Aurelia Zotice, Aurelia Protogenia, Cattia Ammias, Appidia Lea, Flavia Maria. We need not conclude that all, or even any, of the bearers of such names were actually freedmen or freedwomen, but there remains the probability that a distinctive Roman *nomen gentile*, such as Aurelius, Claudius, or Domitius, derived from some ancestor who, when passing from slavery to freedom and Roman citizenship, assumed his former master's name. It was also the custom for foreigners who acquired Roman citizenship to assume the gentile name of their Roman patron (*e.g.*, Flavius Josephus),[1] and this factor also may account for some of the proud Roman names borne by Jews. Two inscriptions (256, 462) dedicated by a patron of the deceased (a proselyte in each instance) may indicate that the latter was a freed slave, since the *dominus* or *domina* of a slave would, when the slave was set free, become his *patronus* or *patrona*. Since, however, the term *patronus* was not limited to this meaning, we cannot be certain that ex-slaves are involved here.

C. National Origins

It would be illuminating to know the national origins of the members of the Roman Jewish community. That they came

---

Julia, the name which she received when she was adopted into the Julian gens (Tac. *Ann.* 1.8.1).

[1] A well-known instance is that of the Greek poet Archias, in whose behalf Cicero delivered a famous oration and who took the name Aulus Licinius Archias after Lucius Licinius Lucullus, who was his sponsor in attaining citizenship. Also noteworthy is the Jewish king, Julius Agrippa, whose Roman name was due to the patronage of the Julian family. It may be observed here that the Emperor Claudius forbade foreigners who were not Roman citizens to use Roman gentile names (Suet. *Claud.* 25.3).

to the city from various parts of the Greek-speaking Mediterranean world is clear enough. We know that many came as slaves after Pompey's capture of Jerusalem in 62 B.C.E. and later as a result of the conquest by Vespasian and Titus which culminated in the destruction of Jerusalem in 70 C.E.

The inscriptions give us a little information, since we are told the place of origin in the case of seven individuals. Two were from Caesarea, the capital of Roman-dominated Palestine. In fact, Macedonius (370) is specifically described as "the Hebrew, a Caesarean of Palestine." The other, Gelasius (25), is simply designated as "the Caesarean." A third immigrant from Palestine, Ionius (362), surnamed Acone (the Cohen?) hailed from Sepphoris in Galilee.

Another Galilean was Alypius (502), who came from the city of Tiberias and was buried at Rome with his two sons, Justus and Alypius. A Jewish woman named Ammias (296) was from Laodicea, probably the city on the coast of Syria (Laodicea ad Mare, now Latakia) rather than the great inland city of Phrygia (Laodicea ad Lycum). If an inscription which exists only in manuscript copies (501) is to be trusted, a certain Alexander came to Rome from Arca of Libanus (Lebanon), a Phoenician town near the coast.[1] The seventh person whose provenience we know is Ursacius, whose three daughters were buried in the Appia catacomb. We are told (147) that he came from Aquileia, which was an important city on the north coast of the Adriatic.

Thus, six of the seven came from Palestine or Syria, that is, from the eastern Mediterranean. The only exception is Ursacius, who was from the central Mediterranean area. It is interesting that, coming from an Italian district, he associated himself with one of the more Romanized groups which used the Appia catacomb and, although he was a Greek speaker, he gave his three daughters the Roman names of Centulia, Simplicia, and Ursacia, the last after himself.[2] He became gerusiarch

---

[1] Frey prefers the variant reading which makes Arca of Libanus the name of a synagogue in Rome. As I have pointed out above (pp. 163-65), this is very unlikely.
[2] The name Centullius is found on an inscription of Aquileia (CIL 5.1121), which was Ursacius' place of origin. Aquileia has yielded also four instances of the names Simplicius and Simplicia (CIL 5.1667, 1678, 1709, 1714), but none, so far as I am aware, of Ursacius.

of his congregation, yet was apparently not a prosperous person, since the epitaphs of his three daughters are scrawled with red paint on marble plaques instead of being carved by a stonecutter, as are the other inscriptions of the Appia catacomb.

In addition, two of the synagogues seem to have been named for the city from which most of their members, or at least their founders, came. The Synagogue of the Tripolitans clearly received its name from Tripolis, but whether this was the Phoenician or the North African city of that name cannot be determined. I have already suggested (p. 154) that the east Mediterranean city seems the more likely, since nearly all the place names mentioned on our inscriptions are of that area. Then there is the Synagogue of Elaea, which may also have been named for a city. A fairly plausible suggestion, though the matter is highly uncertain, is that the port city of Elaea in Asia Minor is meant (see p. 147). This city, on the east coast of the Aegean, is also in the east Mediterranean area.

It seems reasonable, accordingly, to assert that a considerable portion of the Jewish immigrants to Rome came from the area of the eastern Mediterranean and especially from Palestine and Syria. The evidence is too meager to permit a more definite conclusion.

D. Influence of Environment

As I have indicated from time to time in the preceding chapters, the groups which used the three largest catacombs differed from one another in the degree to which they were respectively influenced by the pagan Roman environment.[1] The chief differences appear in the language of the inscriptions, the names of the individuals, and the use of symbols and artistic motifs. It will be useful to assemble the data here for a comprehensive picture.

From the language of the inscriptions it is clear that while Greek was the dominant language of all sections of the Jewish

---

[1] See my discussion in *JQR*, 20 (1930), 309-10. Müller, (*Jüd. Kat.*, 89 f.) treats this matter briefly. Goodenough, (II, 10 and note 64) denies that such differences can be demonstrated by statistical comparisons, since the variations are, he thinks, too slight.

community, by far the largest proportion of Latin is found in the Appia catacomb and the smallest in the Nomentana. The following table will recall the percentage figures which have already been given:

	Greek	Latin
Appia	63.6%	36.4%
Monteverde	78.5	19.5
Nomentana	92.6	6.0

In fact, nearly 60 % of all the Latin inscriptions (75 out of 123) come from the Appia, although this catacomb has supplied only 35 % of the total number of inscriptions. Furthermore, practically all of the Hebrew, small though the amount is, appears on inscriptions from Monteverde. Not a single Hebrew word or Hebrew letter can be traced to the Appia catacomb,[1] while in the Nomentana I found just one poorly preserved Hebrew inscription scratched with irregular letters on the stucco closure of a loculus. From these data we are justified, I believe, in concluding that the users of the Appia catacomb formed the largest proportion of Latin speakers in the Jewish community and that those who buried in the Nomentana catacomb were almost exclusively Greek speakers. The small amount of Hebrew which was used among the Roman Jews seems to have been confined to the Transtiberine congregations, which are represented in the Monteverde catacomb.

A study of the names from the same point of view reveals similar results. To repeat the data from a foregoing chapter, the three catacombs show the following percentages:

	Entirely Latin	Entirely Greek	Entirely Semitic
Appia	50.2%	31.6%	9.1%
Monteverde	45.5	28.2	17.6
Nomentana	43.3	40.0	11.7

---

[1] This circumstance was noticed also by Müller (*Jüd. Kat.*, 90). Goodenough, however, (II, 11, n. 65), objects to this statement and cites *CII* 108, in which the name Barsheoda is spelled with the Hebrew "shin." While the provenience of this inscription is not known, it is quite certain that it did not come from the Appia catacomb (see above, p. 118, n. 1, and Append. Inscr. No. 108), and Frey was wrong in placing it among the Appia inscriptions.

These figures, based as they are on 551 names, reveal that fully half of the names among the Appia group were Latin, while the other two groups have smaller percentages of Latin names. The Nomentana group shows the largest percentage of purely Greek names, while the strongest showing of Semitic names, though the number is relatively small, is in the Monteverde catacomb. These results correspond notably with those derived from the language of the inscriptions. There is further confirmation if we consider the compound names, which involve more than one language element, such names as Aurelius Hermias, which is Latin and Greek, or Claudius Ioses, which is Latin and Hebrew. The percentage figures are as follows:

	Some Latin	Some Greek	Some Semitic
Appia	63.6%	38.1%	11.3%
Monteverde	55.0	34.3	20.1
Nomentana	48.3	45.0	11.7

Again we see that the largest proportion with one or more Latin names comes from the Appia catacomb, the smallest from the Nomentana. As regards those with at least one Greek name, the largest proportion is from the Nomentana, the smallest from the Monteverde. The Monteverde, however, shows nearly twice as large a ratio of individuals with at least some Semitic name as either of the other two groups. Thus with the name, as with the language, since several hundred instances are involved, the numbers are ample enough to give significance to the results.

The last of the three major criteria is found in the use of symbols and artistic motifs.[1] In this connection, the inscriptions from the Nomentana catacomb are much less significant, since the small area of stucco which covered the tomb closures usually left no room for a symbol after the short epitaph had been painted. In the Appia 62 % of the inscriptions bear no symbol at all,[2] whereas in the Monteverde only 46 %

---

[1] See my treatment of this matter in *JAOS* 69 (1949), 88-90, and cf. above, p. 196, notes 1 and 3.

[2] Inscriptions so fragmentary that we cannot tell whether or not they bore a symbol are not included in these figures.

are without any symbol. On the other hand, the menorah appears, with or without additional symbols, on 47 % of the Monteverde inscriptions, but on only 30 % of those from the Appia. Clearly, then, a substantial majority of the Appia group tended to mark the graves with no symbol, not even the conventional menorah; while among the more conservative element which used the Monteverde catacomb a majority displayed some significant symbol of Judaism. Such symbols as the etrog, lulab, and shofar appear twice as frequently on the Monteverde inscriptions as on those from the Appia. The Torah shrine is represented on six Monteverde inscriptions, but is not found at all in the Appia catacomb.

The paintings which adorned the cubicula and arcosolia may serve as a further indication. In the Monteverde catacomb no painted tombs or chambers were found. In the Nomentana the themes of the frescoes are recognizable as Jewish, since the most conspicuous features are, as has been seen, the menorah, the Ark, and various Jewish cult objects. In contrast, the two painted rooms of the Appia with their arcosolia are adorned with figures derived from pagan art and symbolism.

On the basis of this evidence, I believe that one can say with confidence that the several congregations for whom the Monteverde catacomb served as the cemetery represent the most conservative group of the Roman Jewish community. These gave their children a larger proportion of Hebrew names than did the others and occasionally used Hebrew expressions in their tomb inscriptions; they marked most of their graves with the menorah and other Jewish symbols and refrained from the pagan practice of painted decorations. Since the Transtiberine district in which these congregations were located was the chief foreign quarter of Rome, the environment was probably more favorable for the retention of ancestral customs. The users of the Appia catacomb were the most Romanized group, those who permitted themselves to go farthest in adopting the mores of their environment. Here we find the largest proportion of Latin inscriptions and of Roman names, no use of the Hebrew language, a relatively small proportion of inscriptions with Jewish symbols, and paintings in pagan style and theme. Finally, the group which buried in the Nomentana catacomb was the most foreign and least Romanized. Almost exclusively Greek-speaking, representing a low economic status, they show the smallest proportion of Latin inscriptions and of Roman names. Their few wealthy members, though decorating a private room and a few arcosolia in the Greek style, did, however, avoid the use of conspicuously pagan themes.

Although the differences among the three groups do not point to any such variations in religious practices as are now to be found among Orthodox, Conservative, and Reform Jews, they are of significance as showing the varying degrees to which these groups were influenced by their gentile environment.

E. Religious Ideas and Practices

We have no reason to suppose, from the available information, that the religious ideas and practices of the Roman Jews differed in any material degree from those of other communities in the Diaspora. I shall, accordingly, treat only such data as specifically concern the Roman community, since much has already been written about Judaism in the ancient Mediterranean world.[1]

The Roman writers, as we saw in the first chapter (pp. 13, 38 f.), allude to the scrupulousness of the Roman Jews in observing the Sabbath, abstaining from pork, and practicing the rite of circumcision.[2] Philo refers (*Leg.* 23. 158) to their regular Sabbath service and he informs us that the Jews of Rome would not even accept the monthly doles of money and grain if the distribution fell on the Sabbath, so that the authorities reserved their portion for distribution on the following day. A passage in the satirist Persius, already alluded to (pp. 38 f.), describes in scornful language the Jewish observance of the Sabbath with the smoking lamps displayed at the grimy window, the tunny fish sprawling in a red platter, and the

---

[1] *E.g.*, in Schürer, *Gesch. jüd. Volkes*, especially Vol. III; Juster, *Juifs dans l'Emp. Rom.*; Krauss, *Syn. Alt.*; Radin, *Jews among the Greeks and Romans*; W. Bousset, *Die Religion des Judenthums im späthellenistischen Zeitalter*, ed. 3 (Tübingen, 1926); and the various comprehensive Jewish histories.

[2] We know also from Josephus (*Apion* 2.39.282) that the Jewish Sabbath rest, fasts, kindling of lamps, and abstinence from certain foods were observed in every part of the world.

well-filled wine jar of white clay (5. 179-184). Apparently, their eating of fish, their ceremonial kindling of lamps and drinking of wine were features of the Sabbath which attracted the attention of the Roman neighbors of the Jews. The philosopher Seneca, a contemporary of Persius (both of the time of Nero), also refers with disapproval to the smoky Sabbath lamps as an undesirable method of paying homage to one's gods (*Epist.* 95. 47).

That the fast days were faithfully observed is evident from various allusions in the writers. So frequent did these Jewish fasts seem to the Romans that some thought that even the Sabbath was a fast day, a misconception shared, strangely, by the Emperor Augustus (Suet. *Aug.* 76. 2), despite his personal acquaintance with certain prominent Jews (see above, p. 13 f.). We know also, from the Philo passage just cited, that money was collected in the community to be sent to Jerusalem, a fund which the Roman rulers at various times diverted to other purposes.

Since we have no identifiable remains of any synagogue of the Roman Jews or any ancient description of such a building, we know nothing at all about the appearance of their places of worship. We cannot tell to what extent the abundant remains of synagogues found in Palestine and in various parts of the Diaspora[1] may serve as clues to those of Rome. The emblems depicted in the paintings and on the inscriptions and other articles from the catacombs do, however, afford some indications of their cult objects. From these we may be certain that every synagogue had one or more seven-branched menorahs. There was surely an Ark for the Torah scrolls, which were placed horizontally on its shelves. This Ark was, if we may trust the shape which appears consistently in the illustrations, equipped with double doors and surmounted by a pediment, and it was often, if not regularly, flanked by a pair of menorahs. We may be sure also that the shofar was sounded on the New Year and that the etrog and the

---

[1] See, most conveniently, E. L. Sukenik, *Ancient Synagogues of Palestine and Greece* (London, 1934), and Goodenough, *Jewish Symbols*, I, 178-267; II, 70-100, with the numerous illustrations in Vol. III. There is also the considerable literature on the Dura synagogue, which was found in 1932.

lulab were used at the Feast of Tabernacles. There is no good reason for believing that the use of these sacred objects differed in any important way from that which has remained a part of traditional Judaism. If the flask which is frequently depicted is actually a container for wine, as is probable, it is apparently an allusion to the ceremonial use of wine.

The religious service was conducted by the archisynagogus, perhaps aided by the hyperetes (see above, pp. 171, 190). From the scarcity of Hebrew on the tomb inscriptions we may assume that little, if any, Hebrew was used even in the synagogue and that the service was conducted in Greek, the language of the community.[1] The Torah readings also were probably in Greek, as we may infer from the fact that the very few biblical quotations found in the epitaphs appear in a Greek translation. That there were schools associated with the synagogue and a *bet hamidrash* is evident from the reference to the visit of the Palestinian rabbis in the time of Antoninus Pius and the activities of Matthias ben Heresh, as noted above (p. 38); but no specific information about these is available. It may be doubted that they exerted a great influence in the Jewish community generally, if the apparent lack of any knowledge of Hebrew can be used as a criterion.

From the epithets cited in Chapter VI, we can see that piety was held in high esteem. The most frequent of these epithets is ὅσιος (pious), which appears at least twelve times. The nearest Latin equivalent is *sanctus*, the superlative form of which appears once (233: *filiae sanctissimae*). The long verse epitaph of Regina (476) praises her piety (*pietas*) and her observance of the Law (*observantia legis*). This latter quality is alluded to in Greek by such adjectives as φιλόνομος, lover of the Law, which occurs once of a child (113) and φιλέντολος, lover of the

---

[1] See M. Simon, *Verus Israel*, 342-51, on the use of Greek for religious purposes in the Diaspora; cf. Juster, I, 365-68. For the use of the Greek language by the Jews even of Palestine see S. Lieberman, *Greek in Jewish Palestine* (New York, 1942), where evidence is cited (p. 30) that in Caesarea some Jews read the *Shema* in Greek and that rabbis quoted from Greek in the synagogues of Palestine and delivered their sermons in Greek (pp. 37-39). K. Gelling, in *Theologische Studien und Kritiken* 103 (1931), 356, agrees that Greek was the Jewish cult language, as also does I. Zoller in *Ricerche Religiose di Storia delle Religioni* 8 (1932), 462-63.

Commandments, used once of a woman (132) and once of a Father of a Synagogue (509). The epitaph of Julia Irene Arista (72), who may have been a Jewess, characterizes her as a pious observer of the Law (*iuste legem colenti*).[1] Marcia (250) is called simply "a good Jewess" (*bona Iudea*), Cattia Ammias (537) "lived a good life in Judaism," and Eparchia (228) was "a God-fearing woman."[2] Devotion to one's people and one's synagogue is heralded by the adjectives φιλόλαος, which appears twice (203, 509) and φιλοσυνάγωγος, which is used of a certain Lazar, who is described also as a pious man, lover of his children and of his brothers (321).

The Jewish virtues of charity and righteousness also come in for mention. A man entombed in the Appia catacomb is praised as having had, among other virtues, that of being φιλοπένης, a lover of the poor (203). Righteousness, as indicated by the adjective δίκαιος, is ascribed to two persons, a man and a woman (321, 363). Furthermore, righteousness on the part of the deceased is implied not only in the use of the biblical aphorism "the memory of the righteous shall be for a blessing" (Prov. 10. 7), which occurs three times, but also in the prayer that the deceased will rest "among the righteous," which is found seven times expressed in Greek and four times in Latin inscriptions (see citations above, pp. 125 f., 131).

It seems noteworthy that references to God are almost

---

[1] Frey's reconstruction (*CII*, p. 45) as *Dei virtut[em e]t fidem sationis conservatae*, which makes her also one who "cultivated the virtue of God and the faith of her preserved race," is most unlikely, since the accusatives can hardly be construed with the following *colenti*, which governs *legem*. More probably, *per* should be restored in line 2 before *Dei virtutem* (the final *R* is clearly visible on the stone) and *conservatae* taken as dative with *matri* instead of genitive with *sationis*, so that the passage would read *per Dei virtutem et fidem sationis conservatae, iuste legem colenti*, with the meaning, "preserved through the power of God and the devotion of her family, a pious observer of the Law," the reference in *conservatae* alluding probably to the woman's earlier recovery from a serious illness.

[2] Frey, inexplicably, takes *theosebes*, which is a Greek word in Latin characters, as a proper name (see above, p. 128, note 4). This adjective is used also of Agrippa of Phaena (*CII* 500), but since the provenience of the inscription is not known and the epithet is not confined to Jews, I have not counted it as Jewish.

entirely absent from the inscriptions,[1] possibly because the use of the holy name was avoided. Theodotus, in the affectionate epitaph of his foster child Justus, prays to the Lord (δέσποτα) that in His righteousness He will grant this incomparable child a peaceful sleep (358). Eparchia, as we have just seen, is called "God-fearing." Julia Irene Arista, whose epitaph has just been mentioned, is described as having been saved (from serious illness?) through the "power of God" (*per Dei virtutem*).

Belief in the Hereafter, though doubtless a part of the religious faith of the Roman Jews, as of other Jews, rarely finds expression in their sepulchral inscriptions beyond an implication of some sort of continued existence in the stereotyped formula, "In peace be his (her) sleep," which closes a large proportion of them. Twice the tomb is referred to as "the eternal home" (337: οἶκος αἰώνιος; 523: *domi heterne* [for *aeternae*] = בית עולם). The Regina epitaph (476), the longest and most elaborate of the inscriptions found in the Jewish catacombs, expresses in fairly elegant Latin hexameters a sorrowing husband's confidence that his beloved wife, who had lived with him in devoted wedlock for more than twenty years, will be rewarded for her virtues with eternal life in Paradise.[2] This inscription is of such unique interest that I am presenting it entire in a fairly close blank verse rendering:

> Here lies Regina, covered by this tomb,
> Which, to reveal his love, her husband raised.
> A score of years plus one, four months, and eight
> Days more she spent in wedlock by his side.

---

[1] Frey is wrong, however, when he asserts, in *Biblica* 12 (1931), 150, that there is no reference to God or the Lord in the Jewish inscriptions of Rome.

[2] I cannot accept Father Ferrua's contention, in *Civ. Catt.* (1936) IV, 307 f. and *Epigraphica*, 3 (1941), 38, that this is a Christian inscription reused by a Jew. His chief argument seems to be that the Jews did not use poetic epitaphs; but there is no reason to insist that some Jews with poetic propensities might not have done so. There could have been no religious scruple involved. He also regards the break in the stone after line six as deliberate, an indication to him that the stone was reused. By Ferrua's own repeatedly expressed criterion, with which I am in complete agreement, a stone found in a Jewish catacomb should be regarded as Jewish unless there are compelling reasons for rejecting it.

Again she'll live, again will see the light;
For she may hope that she will rise aloft
To that eternal life which is ordained,
As our true faith doth teach, for all the worthy
And all the pious. She has merited
To find a home in that most hallowed land.
This is assured thee by thy piety,
Thy life so chaste, thy love of all thy people,[1]
Observance of our Law, and faithfulness
Unto our marriage bond, which thou didst strive
Ever to glorify. For all these deeds
Thy future bliss is certain. In this faith
Thy sorrowing husband finds his only comfort.

Especially noteworthy as revealing a faith in immortal life
are such expressions as *rursum victura* (will live again), *reditura
ad lumina rursum* (will again return to the light), *surgat in
aevom promissum dignisque piisque* (will rise to the life promised
for the worthy and the pious), *sedem venerandi ruris* (abode
in the hallowed land, that is, Paradise). Such eternal bliss is
assured as a reward for a virtuous and pious life in this world.

In contrast, we have the cynical "My friends, I await you
here" (*Amici ego vos hic exspecto*) of Leo, surnamed Leontius
(32*), and buried in the same Monteverde catacomb as was
Regina. So shocked was Father Frey, as we have already
noted (p. 133), at the presence of this flippant sentiment
in the solemn environment of a Jewish cemetery that he
rejected the inscription and placed it among pagan inscriptions
which had found their way into the catacomb, generally
as material for sealing the loculi. There is no indication, however, that this particular stone was used in such a manner.
Leo Leontius was apparently a Jew who prided himself on
being different from the others and saw to it that his indivi-
dualistic attitude toward death was recorded on his tombstone.

If we were to follow Goodenough and other scholars in

---

[1] Ferrua (references cited in the previous note) interprets *amor
generis* as "love for your family," but *genus* is normally used in a
broader sense. The present phrase corresponds to the epithet φιλόλαος,
which, as noted above, occurs in two inscriptions (203, 509). In the
next line Ferrua translates *coniugii meritum* as "the merits of your
husband" (*il merito del tuo marito*), wrongly, I believe, since *coniugii*
properly refers to the marriage bond and *meritum* would more naturally
apply to the person addressed in an enumeration of her virtues.

interpreting the many symbols which are depicted on the tombs and inscriptions as evidences of faith in salvation, much could be added to the present discussion of the religious beliefs of the Roman Jews. Since, however, such interpretations of the symbols are highly uncertain, I feel that it is preferable not to consider them in this connection. Meager though the data have been with regard to the cult practices and religious concepts of the Jews of Rome, this is all that can be positively asserted on the basis of such information as we have.

F. PROSELYTES

It is perhaps surprising in our day to learn that the Jews of the Roman period were both active and successful in winning converts to Judaism. That the Jews in Rome itself were energetic proselytizers as early as the time of Augustus is clearly indicated by a well-known passage in the *Satires* of Horace (1.4.140-143), in which the genial poet remarks that if his critic will not permit him to indulge in the minor vice of writing about the weaknesses of his fellow men, Horace will be joined by a large band of fellow poets who, "like the Jews, will force you to come into our crowd."

It had become fashionable for the aristocratic members of Roman society to adopt certain Jewish religious practices, whether as a fad or through conviction, without, however, becoming fully converted. Observance of the Sabbath and practice of the dietary laws are most commonly mentioned in that connection. Horace's friend, Aristius Fuscus, as we have already seen (p. 12), pretended that "the thirtieth Sabbath" of the Jews prevented him from discussing business with Horace (*Sat.* 1.9.67-72). In the time of Nero, the philosopher Seneca complained bitterly, as reported by Augustine (*De Civ. Dei* 6.11), about the widespread adoption of the Jewish Sabbath, saying, "The practice of that damnable people (*sceleratissimae gentis consuetudo*) has become so prevalent that it has already been adopted in all lands. The conquered have given laws to their conquerors!" Seneca's testimony to the spread of Jewish practices is confirmed by Josephus' statement (*Apion* 2.39.282) that such Jewish religious customs as the observance of the Sabbath, fasting, kindling of lamps, and abstinence from certain foods were followed in every part of the world and even in barbarian countries.

A generation later Juvenal, who was bitterly opposed to the contamination of the traditional Roman mores by foreign superstitions, inveighs against the Roman father who, by fearing the Sabbath, so far corrupts his sons that they begin to worship the clouds and the divinity of the sky, regarding swine's flesh, from which the father abstained, as no less sacred than human, and even circumcising themselves (14.96-106). The satirist exclaims:

> Accustomed as they have become to scorning the laws of Rome, they study the Jewish Law and observe it and fear it, that Law which Moses handed down in a mysterious scroll, which instructs them not to point out the way except to one who follows the same rites nor to guide to a spring of water any but the circumcised.

Juvenal adds that the real blame is due to the father, who remained idle every seventh day, abstaining from all the duties of life. We see, accordingly, that while the father was only a "sympathizer" with Judaism to the extent of observing the Sabbath and abstaining from swine's flesh, the sons became full proselytes. Juvenal's denunciation would have little meaning were it not directed against a situation prevalent in his day.

Our historical sources, as we have seen in Chapter I, reveal only a few specific instances of prominent Romans who adopted Judaism.[1] I have already cited (p. 17) the case of the noblewoman Fulvia, wife of the influential senator Saturninus, who practiced Jewish rites and fell victim to the rapacity of a quartet of Jewish charlatans, with the result that the Emperor Tiberius banished a number of Jews from Rome. A generation later the Empress Poppaea, wife of Nero, infamous though she was in other respects, was apparently a "Judaizer," as we infer from Josephus, who calls her "God-fearing" (AJ 20. 8. 11. 195: θεοσεβής) and indicates that she was favorably inclined toward the Jews and toward Josephus himself ($Vita$ 3. 16). It has sometimes been alleged that, also

---

[1] On this topic see the recent treatment by J. S. Raisin, *Gentile Reactions to Jewish Ideals, with Special Attention to Proselytes* (New York, 1953), especially pp. 292-329.

in Nero's reign, Pomponia Graecina, wife of Aulus Plautius, a general distinguished for his conquests in Britain, was a follower of Jewish rites; but this can hardly be concluded from Tacitus' phrase, "accused of foreign religious beliefs" (*Ann.* 13. 32: *superstitionis externae rea*), although it is entirely possible that Judaism is meant. More certain is the celebrated case of Flavius Clemens, cousin of the Emperor Domitian, and his wife, Flavia Domitilla, who was the Emperor's niece. As has been demonstrated in Chapter I (pp. 33-35), there is little if any reason for doubting that they were charged with having adopted Judaism. Clemens was executed and Domitilla was banished to an island. It is of interest to recall here that Domitian's liberal-minded successor, Nerva, not only relieved the Jews of the harsh enforcement of the collection of the Jewish tax (*fiscus Iudaicus*), but also forbade accusations of "Judaizing," such as had brought about the destruction of Clemens (Dio 68. 1. 2).

The occasional repressive measures adopted by the emperors against the Jews were to some extent due to their success at winning converts and the fear, as expressed by Seneca and Juvenal, that the adoption of these un-Roman rites was undermining the traditional customs of Rome.[1] Hadrian's interdiction of circumcision was probably not so much directed toward the extermination of Judaism as animated by the purpose of checking its spread through the winning of proselytes. The same motive is clear in the action of his successor, Antoninus Pius, who, while permitting Jews to circumcise their own sons, forbade the circumcision of non-Jews (*Digest* 48. 8. 11). At the end of the second century Septimius Severus took ineffectual measures to check the spread of both Judaism and Christianity. The restrictive laws against Jewish proselytism enacted by Constantine and the Christian emperors who followed him have been treated fully by scholars and are outside the scope of the present work.[2]

---

[1] To what extent Josephus' *Jewish Antiquities*, which was written for the benefit of non-Jews in order to give them a favorable opinion of the history and traditions of the Jewish people, inspired its readers to adopt Judaism we have no way of knowing.

[2] See especially Simon, *Verus Israel*, 155-62, 316-37; Raisin, *op. cit.* (above, p. 251, n.1), 355-74. Of interest in this connection are J. E. Seaver, *Persecution of the Jews in the Roman Empire* (Lawrence,

It has long been customary to distinguish between the various degrees of proselytism to the Jewish religion, designating as partial proselytes, or "proselytes of the gate" (גרי שער) those who had adopted monotheism and some of the Jewish religious practices, and as "proselytes of righteousness" (גרי צדק) those who had become complete Jews. It was believed that the former were characterized by their contemporaries as "God-fearers" (φοβούμενοι or σεβόμενοι τὸν θεόν, or θεοσεβεῖς or *metuentes*),[1] the latter as proselytes (προσήλυ-τοι). George Foot Moore has demonstrated conclusively that the Jewish Law recognizes no demi-proselytes and that the often cited distinctions are the figment of eighteenth-century Christian writers.[2] Only such as came over completely to Judaism, accepting all its rites, including circumcision, were regarded as proselytes. That proselytes were welcomed into Judaism by the rabbis, with only a few dissenting, has been abundantly shown by scholars who have assembled the talmudic references.[3]

Our Jewish sepulchral inscriptions reveal several clear instances of proselytes. To be rejected are the four Roman inscriptions which show the term *metuens* and which Frey includes among the Jewish epitaphs. None of these is known to have come from a Jewish catacomb.[4] We do have, however,

---

Kansas, 1952) and Robert Wilde, *The Treatment of the Jews in the Christian Writers of the First Three Centuries* (Washington, 1949).

[1] For a discussion of these terms see L. H. Feldman, "Jewish 'Sympathizers' in Classical Literature and Inscriptions," *TAPA*, 81 (1950), 200-208. Feldman demonstrates correctly that such expressions are not technical terms for partial proselytes or "sympathizers," but are to be taken in each case as indicating that the individual was pious and a "God-fearer" and that they may be applied to pious Jews as well. We have already seen that a pious Jewish woman was called *theosebes* (228). On the term *sebomenoi* in Josephus, see R. Marcus, *Jewish Social Stud.* 14 (1952), 247-50.

[2] *Judaism in the First Centuries of the Christian Era*, I, 323-53, especially 340. Cf. also Schürer, III, 177 f.

[3] A useful compilation is to be found in the Brown University dissertation of W. G. Braude, *Jewish Proselyting in the First Five Centuries of the Common Era: the Age of the Tannaim and Amoraim* (Providence, 1940). See also Simon, *Verus Israel*, 318-21.

[4] That of Aemilius Valens, a Roman knight (*CII* 5), was found near the catacomb of Priscilla between the Via Salaria and the Via Nomentana; that of Larcia Quadratilla (285) was imbedded in the wall of a vineyard near St. Sebastian on the Via Appia; a portion

the epitaphs of seven indubitable proselytes, two males and five females.

Among the earliest to be copied of the Jewish inscriptions of Rome is that of the proselyte Beturia (for Veturia) Paulla, found on the fragment of a sarcophagus (523).[1] We learn from her epitaph that she was "consigned to her eternal home" (*domi heterne quostituta = domi aeternae constituta*) at the age of eighty-six years and six months, after having been a proselyte with the name of Sara for sixteen years. She was also honored as the Mother of two synagogues, those of the Campesians and the Volumnesians. It is of especial interest that when this woman, presumably a pagan, became a Jewess at the age of seventy, she assumed the Hebrew name of Sara, a name which is still the one regularly given by Jews to feminine proselytes. A similar instance is that of Felicitas (462), who died at forty-seven and had been a proselyte for six years. After she was taken into Judaism, she became known as Peregrina,[2] the feminine equivalent of the Hebrew word for proselyte (גר), which, like the Latin word, literally means "alien." It is possible that before becoming a Jewess, Felicitas had been a slave, since the inscription was set up by her *patronus*, a term commonly used of the former master of a freed slave.

The Nomentana catacomb has yielded two inscriptions of proselytes, both differing from most of the epitaphs of this cemetery in that they were carved on marble instead of being painted on the closures. One (21) is that of a foster child, Irene, who died at the age of three years, seven months, one

---

of the tomb monument of a female *metuens* (529) was found in the foundations of the Baths of Constantine on the Quirinal; the stone of Maiania Homeridida, another female *metuens* (524), was copied at the Lateran by Cittadini in the eighteenth century (*CIL* VI, 29760).

[1] This inscription has been known since the sixteenth century, when it was copied by Alonso Chacón and Philippe de Winghe (see above, p. 67 f.).It is no longer extant, so that the variants in the copies made by scholars cannot be checked with the original. Beturia's second name is variously given as Paula, Paucla (so Frey, following De Rossi), Paulina, and Paullina.

[2] I take the unintelligible NVENN, preceding *Peregrina*, as a garbling of *nomine*. Thus the language of the Monteverde inscription (*proselita ann. VI nomine Peregrina*) would exactly parallel that of Beturia Paulla, which probably came from the same catacomb (*proselita an. XVI nominae* [for *nomine*] *Sara*).

day. She is described, strangely, as an Israelite, having had a Jewish father and mother (πατρὸς καὶ μητρὸς Εἰουδέα 'Ισδραηλίτης). What is meant by these words is by no means clear. Possibly the baby girl, born of Jewish parents, had first been reared in a non-Jewish household, then adopted by a Jewish family and formally received into Judaism. Thus the epitaph emphasizes the child's Jewish origin. It seems incredible that so young a child should have been regarded as a proselyte. There is, of course, the possibility that the stone-cutter, who committed several careless errors in carving the inscription,[1] left out part of the numeral, so that Irene may actually have been an adult; but since the numeral indicating the number of years is clearly three (Γ), this suggestion must remain entirely conjectural. The other proselyte buried in the Nomentana catacomb was Cresces Sinicerius (68), designated also as a Jew (*Iudeus*). He died at thirty-five, leaving a sorrowing mother, who recorded on the stone that she had "done for her sweet son that which he ought himself to have done for me."

The Appia catacomb, like the Nomentana, reveals two proselytes who were buried there. One was Crysis (222), whose epitaph was set up by Mannacius "to his sweetest sister" (*sorori dulcissime*). The word *proselyte* seems to have been added later, since it is in smaller letters and possibly by a different hand. The other proselyte of the Appia catacomb was Nicetas (256), who, like Felicitas, may also have been a freed slave, since the woman Dionysias who set up his epitaph describes herself as his *patrona*. All that we know about this proselyte is that he was "worthy and well deserving" (*digno et benemerenti*).

The only other indication at Rome of a Jewish proselyte is on a fragment now in the epigraphic collection at the church of St. Sebastian on the Via Appia (202). It was found in the debris of the Vigna Randanini, under which lies the Jewish catacomb of the Via Appia, and it may have come from that catacomb. All that we have of the inscription is the last part of the word for Jewess ([IO]YΔEA), the first part of the

---

[1] He wrote ΤΡΕΖΙΙΤΗ for θρεπτή, ΕΙΟΥΔΕΑ for 'Ιουδαία, ICΔ-ΡΑΗΛΙΤΗC for 'Ισραηλίτης, ΗΤ for ΕΤ (abbreviation of ἔτη), ΗΜΡ for ἡμέραν.

Greek word *proselytos* (ΠΡΟCΗ[ΛΥΤΟC]), a few fragments of other words,[1] and a menorah.

Since five of the seven proselyte inscriptions are in Latin, whereas some three-fourths of all our Jewish inscriptions are in Greek, we may possibly draw the inference that proselytes were more frequent in the more Romanized element of the community. The examples are, however, so few that the preponderance of Latin inscriptions of proselytes may be due only to chance. The same may be said of the fact that five of the seven are females. It may well be that there were more feminine proselytes to Judaism, since it was easier for a woman to adopt all the Jewish rites required of women than it was for an adult male to take over all that was incumbent on a man who became a Jew. There is, besides, abundant evidence that the ancient Roman women, not unlike the women of other periods and nations, were more prone than the men to become interested in foreign cults.[2]

We may safely conclude, on the basis of both literary and epigraphic sources, that the Roman Jews welcomed proselytes and that the Jewish community had a fair number of them. These were regarded as Jews in every respect and were honored with burial in a Jewish cemetery. Those, on the other hand, who practiced a few Jewish rites, such as the worship of One God, celebration of the Sabbath, and abstinence from pork, were not regarded as Jews and did not receive a Jewish burial.

---

[1] Frey takes EOCEBI as representing θεοσεβής (God-fearing), which he regards as a surname. It is more likely that the letters EOC are the last part of a word in the nominative or genitive (cf. [γραμματ]εος in 67) and that EBI is the first part of the verb ἐβίωσεν (lived).

[2] See, for example, Franz Cumont, *Les religions orientales dans le paganisme romain* (Paris, 1929), 40.

SUMMARY

The foregoing study has revealed that a Jewish community, starting in Rome at some undetermined time, perhaps even before 100 B.C.E., had by the middle of the first century B.C.E. become important enough to attract notice and had reached a total of possibly fifty thousand souls in the era of Augustus. Largely owing to the favor of Julius Caesar and Augustus, the Jews enjoyed the full protection of the Roman Law and were permitted to practice their religion virtually undisturbed until the repressive measures of the Christian emperors after Constantine. Although some trouble-making groups were banished from the city under Tiberius and Claudius, there was never any general expulsion of the Jews from Rome, and we can be reasonably certain that the Jewish community has existed continuously in Rome from early in the first century B.C.E. until the present day. On the whole, the Jews of Rome played no great role in the annals of that imperial city, so that they are rarely mentioned by the historians, and the other writers, in their infrequent references to them, generally allude to them with ridicule and contempt.

Most of our information about the community is derived from three Jewish catacombs: those of Monteverde, the Via Appia, and the Via Nomentana, discovered, respectively, in 1602, 1859, and 1919. These subterranean cemeteries have yielded more than five hundred inscriptions, a study of which has revealed that the Jews were predominantly a Greek-speaking community, but that some used Latin, whereas Hebrew was virtually unknown. In their use of Greek and Latin no trace appears of any Jewish dialectical peculiarities in any way comparable with the Yiddish of modern times, but there are evidences of a low level of literacy on the part of a considerable portion of the community.

Although their spoken language was predominantly Greek, they preferred Latin names, especially for their daughters; still, many bore Greek names, while Hebrew and other Semitic names were not uncommon.

The large community was divided into at least eleven identifiable congregations, each completely autonomous with its own officers, both secular and religious. There is no satisfactory evidence for an all-community organization with authority over the separate congregations. Of the synagogues in which the individual congregations worshiped we know nothing at all, since no trace of any has been discovered. Data about the ritual are scanty, but enough to justify the belief that the well-known traditional forms were observed for the Sabbath and the festivals and that the service was conducted in Greek.

The symbols depicted on the tomb inscriptions and the decorations of the tombs and tomb chambers show for the most part motifs derived from the Jewish ritual, the menorah being by far the most frequently used emblem. Some groups, notably those which buried their dead in the Via Appia catacomb, reveal greater freedom in taking their subjects from pagan sources. There was manifestly no scruple, at least among the less conservative members, about the use of human and animal figures in these decorations. The extent to which these emblems bore a symbolic significance for their users remains an unresolved question.

An examination of the materials from the separate catacombs indicates clearly that different portions of the community differed in the extent to which they adopted the mores of their pagan environment. We have noticed that the users of the Via Appia catacomb represent the most Romanized group, those of the Monteverde catacomb the most conservative, and those of the Via Nomentana catacomb the most foreign and least assimilated.

From the epigraphical data, combined with the literary references, it is obvious that a distressingly large proportion of the community subsisted at a low economic level, engaged in humble pursuits, and that the lucrative mercantile activities which are associated with the Jews of later eras are not exemplified among the Jews of ancient Rome. There are indications of a wholesome family life and a respect for the marriage bond, with many evidences of devotion between husband and wife and parents and children. Proselytes were accepted as full members of the community, in contrast with

those who followed only such Jewish customs as appealed
to them.

Thanks to the data from the catacombs, we have more
information about the Jews of ancient Rome than about
any other community of the Diaspora in ancient times.
Dating as it does from the first century before the Common
Era, the Jewish community of Rome is now more than two
thousand years old and may well claim to have enjoyed a
longer continuous existence than any other Jewish community
of Europe and possibly of the world.

ILLUSTRATIONS

AND

APPENDIX OF INSCRIPTIONS

1. Via Casilina. New highway at the f the catacomb of Via Labicana.

PLATE II

Fig. 3. Vestibule of the Via Appia catacomb; northwest corner, showing triple rows of arches, reconstructed. The original arches and opus reticulatum *may be seen inside the arches at the* left. *At the extreme* left (*west wall*) *is the opening to the room which contained a well.*

Fig. 4. Vestibule of the Via Appia catacomb; east portion of north side, showing the original niches and the tufa and brick masonry.

PLATE III

Fig. 5. Vestibule of the Via Appia catacomb; east portion with reconstructed buttresses and niches containing fragments of terracotta sarcophagi. A portion of the longitudinal wall may be seen at the center. Right is the modern stairway from the ground level.

PLATE IV

Fig. 7. Site of the Monteverde catacomb, showing part of the cliff cut away for modern apartments.

PLATE V

PLATE VI

Fig. 9. Gallery of the Via Appia catacomb with loculi for adults and children and light well in the rear. The inscription is No. 179. Note axe marks in the tufa.

PLATE VII

Fig. 10. Gallery wall of the Via Appia catacomb with loculi *above and* kokim *below.*

Fig. 11. Kok (*seen from* above) *in the Via Appia catacomb (photograph by E. R. Goodenough).*

PLATE VIII

Fig. 12. Menorah painted above an arcosolium in a room of the Via Appia catacomb. In the arcosolium is a portion of a strigilated sarcophagus; loculi at left; painted decorations on the ceiling.

Fig. 13. First painted room of the Via Appia catacomb, looking into the second room; arcosolia right and left.

PLATE IX

Fig. 14. Above: *Central motif of the ceiling of the first painted room of the Via Appia catacomb; Victory crowning a youth.*

Fig. 15. Below: *Arcosolium in the first painted room of the Via Appia catacomb (at right of entrance to the second room). There are scribblings on the wall perpetrated by modern visitors.*

PLATE X

Fig. 16. Second (inner) painted room of the Via Appia catacomb with Fortuna as the central motif of the ceiling. The inscription is the epitaph of the grammateus Petronius (No. 149). At left is an arcosolium surmounted by a loculus.

PLATE XI

Fig. 17. Above: *Step at the entrance to the painted rooms of the Via Appia catacomb. The step is the inverted cover of the sarcophagus of Iocathinus, child archon (No. 120).*

Fig. 19. *Entrance to the Via Nomentana catacomb; stairway with first landing. The door and key are modern, as is the first portion of the stairway.*

PLATE XII

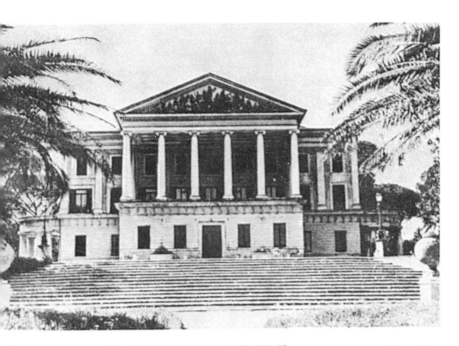

Fig. 18. Above: *Villa Torlonia, beneath which lies the Via Nomentana catacomb.*

Fig. 20. Gallery of the Via Nomentana catacomb; remnants of bones in the loculus at left; *opening of an intersecting gallery visible at* left.

PLATE XIII

Fig. 22. *Anteroom of Cubiculum I in the Via Nomentana catacomb; doorway cut out of tufa, vaulted ceiling, entrance to corridor at left.*

Fig. 21. *Crossing point of galleries in the Via Nomentana catacomb with markings on ceiling. Note partly closed loculus with closures of tufa and mortar, niche for lamp at right and lime deposits at left.*

PLATE XIV

Fig. 23. Cross vaulting of Cubiculum I in the Via Nomentana
catacomb; loculi cut into the
rear wall.

24. Graffito of menorah in
Via Nomentana catacomb.
loculus had been opened at
end by marauders.

25. Grave of Alexandria
the Via Nomentana cata-
b. The inscription (No. 8)
painted in red. Skeletal
ains are visible within the
lus. Note other loculi above
below.

PLATE XV

PLATE XVI

26. Left/Above: *Inscrip-
-s placed on the wall of an
-chamber in the Via Appia
-comb. Those visible are
t to* right), *top row: Nos. 185
-t*), *156 (part), 106 (part);
-m row: 119 (part), 106
-t*), *82.*

27. Left/Below: *Inscrip-
-s placed on the wall of an
-chamber in the Via Appia
-comb. Visible* (left *to* right)
*Nos. 271 (part), 218, 180,
-er which is 83 (part).*

Fig. 28. Sarcophagus of Caelia Omnina on the grounds of Villa Torlonia.

Fig. 29. Inscription on the sarcophagus of Caelia Omnina (No. 35a).

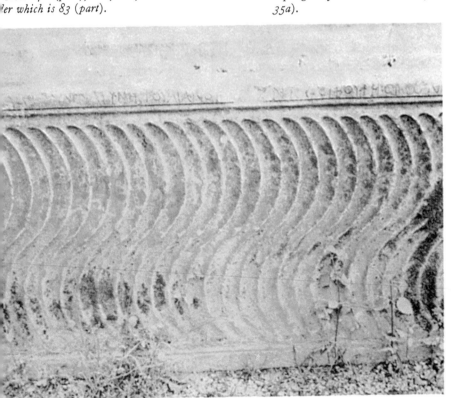

PLATE XVII

Fig. 30. Inscription of Rhodion (173).

Fig. 31. Sarcophagus of Julia Irene Arista at Palazzo Spada (No. 72).

PLATE XVIII

Fig. 32. *Inscriptions on a wall of the Sala Giudaica in the Lateran Museum.*
Top row (left to right): *CII 553 (from Capua), 538, uninscribed fragment,
296, 381, cast of CII 493a; bottom row: 540 (part), 108, 385, 506, CII 539
(from Porto).*

Fig. 33. *Inscriptions in the Sala Giudaica. First row: 470, 353; second
row: 476, 467, uninscribed fragment, 306, CII 451; third row: 322 (part),
406, 335.*

PLATE XIX

Fig. 35. Left: *Inscription with symbols (CII 200); the inscription itself, once painted within the* tabula ansata *at the top, is now invisible.*

Fig. 36. Right: *Inscription in the Sala Giudaica. First row: 370 (part), 323, 325, 311, 484; second row: 340, 361, 374; third row: 35 (part), 418, 348.*

Fig. 34. Left: *Epitaph Semoel (401).*

Fig. 37. Right: *Inscriptio in the Sala Giudaica. First row: 465, 470; second row 456, 398 (below), 474, 41 441, 476 (part); third ro 459, 354, 477, 322, 4 (part).*

PLATE XX

PLATE XXI

Fig. 38. Uninscribed slab with symbols, now the Conservatori Museum, No. 39 (= CII 49

Fig. 39. Below: *Inscriptions in the Sala Giuda First row: 330, 305; second row: 334, 377, ᷄ 408; third row: 291, 315, 317, 396 (part); fo row: 290, 369, 362, 352, 466, 363.*

PLATE XXII

Fig. 40. Corner of the cubiculum of the palm trees in the Via Appia catacomb. Note the children's loculi; at left, the entrance from the gallery. The
figure painted on the upper part of the door frame may represent a mezuzah;
it is balanced by a similar one on the other side.

PLATE XXIII

PLATE XXIV

41. Left Above: *Decorated arcosolium in the north wall of Cubiculum* *the Via Nomentana catacomb. Note the double grave, rock-cut columns* *capitals and cross vaulting, the simulated sarcophagus front below with* *figure of a lion at* right, *modern reinforcement in the rear wall, where a* *lus had been cut in, destroying the painting.*

42. Left Below: *Decorated arcosolium in the east wall of Cubiculum* *the Via Nomentana catacomb. Note the double grave, rock-cut columns,* *imulated sarcophagus front with lions. As in Fig. 41, here also a loculus* *into the rear wall destroyed the painting, leaving only the upper portion.*

Fig. 43. *Decorated arcosolium in a gallery of the* *Via Nomentana catacomb, with double grave.*

PLATE XXV

PLATE XXVI

44. The "Season Sarcophagus" from the Via Appia, now in the .. *e Museum.*

46. Sarcophagus cover with the epitaph of Faustina (283); Terme ... *eum.*

47. Sarcophagus front with the epitaph of Artemidora (733c); Terme .. *eum.*

45. Sarcophagus with griffins and "Dionysiac" scenes on the grounds .. *e Villa Torlonia.*

Fig. 49. Inscription of the painter Eudoxius (109); Via Appia.

Fig. 50. Below: Inscription of Margarita (136A); Terme Museum.

Fig. 48. Inscription of G (101); Via Ap

Fig. 51. Inscription of Margarita (136B; reverse of the preceding one); Terme Museum.

PLATE XXVIII

Fig. 52. Inscription of the grammateus Numenius (142); Via Appia.

Fig. 55. Below: Inscription of Salpingius (162); Via Appia.

53. Inscription of Alexandria
ra (144); Via Appia.

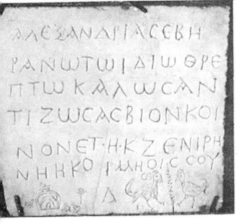

Fig. 54. Inscription of the child grammateus Honoratus (146); Via Appia.

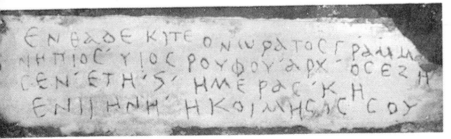

PLATE XXIX

PLATE XXX

60. *Inscription*
he priest Judas
); Sala Giudaica,
ran.

61. *Inscription of*
rammateus Judas
); monastery at
Paolo fuori le
a.

Fig. 62. Inscription of
the prostates Caelius
(365); Terme Museum.

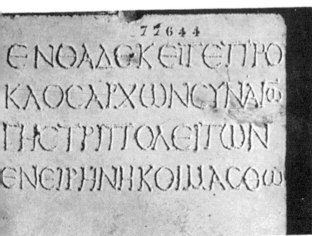

Fig. 63. Inscription of
Proclus, archon of the
Synagogue of the Tri-
politans (390); Terme
Museum.

PLATE XXXI

Fig. 65. Sarcophagus front with inscription of Caelius Quintus (505); Terme Museum.

Fig. 64. Inscription of Barzaharona and his son Paregorius (407); Terme Museum.

Fig. 66. Inscription of Salo (510); Terme Museum.

Fig. 67. Fragment with sym (545); Sala Giudaica, Lateran.

PLATE XXXII

APPENDIX OF INSCRIPTIONS

The numbers used here are those of Frey's *Corpus Inscriptionum Iudaicarum* (*CII*). Inscriptions not in *CII* have been given a subordinate numbering (*e.g.* 35a). Items found in *CII* but omitted here are those which reveal no intelligible words and those which should not, in my opinion, be counted as Jewish. A few are rejected because there is no good evidence that they came from Rome.

While the original inscriptions are written in capital letters and usually without spaces between the words, they are transcribed here in minuscules with the words separated for intelligibility. The accents and breathings, which are never indicated in the originals, are supplied for the Greek inscriptions. Non-Greek proper names, however, and Greek transliterations of Latin words are usually left without accent, except when they show Greek inflectional forms. Iota subscript, which does not appear at all in our inscriptions (whether as subscript or adscript) is not supplied. Some of the inscriptions insert points and occasionally small leaves between words or even syllables, but these are not indicated here, since they appear to have no special significance. Although the texts of the inscriptions are transcribed without punctuation, the meaning should be clear from the translations.

I have made no attempt to indicate the shapes of the letters. It may be assumed that in nearly all instances Greek sigma appears in its lunate form (like Latin C), epsilon in its rounded form (ϵ), and omega like the conventional minuscule form (ω). The Latin letters are the familiar capitals, the only variation from our modern English capital letters being the V, which (as is normal in the ancient period) is used both for the consonant and for the vowel which we represent as U.

Square brackets, [. . .], are used to indicate lacunae, that is, such parts of the inscription as were missing when it was first transcribed. The missing letters are inserted where they can be supplied with reasonable certainty. In general, however, the probable number of letters involved in the lacuna is not indicated. Parentheses (. . .), supply letters missing in the original, be it through an oversight on the part of the scribe or to mark an abbreviation or where space was lacking for the complete word or phrase. Elbow brackets, <...>, are employed to indicate letters which, though found in the original, should be deleted because they were carelessly inserted by the scribe.

The Greek numerals, usually marking the age of the deceased or the number of years of married life, are distinguished in the transcriptions by an acute accent following the numeral letters (e.g., ιβ' = 12), regardless of how they are indicated in the original. Errors in spelling and grammar are generally reproduced, since they are of value for any linguistic study of these inscriptions. Where the correct form would not be readily apparent, an explanation is offered in the notes. Mere slips on the part of the scribe, such as the frequent substitution of Λ for Α or Δ, C for E, and vice versa, are not reproduced, for they have no significance linguistically or otherwise. Those interested in such details may consult the photographs and transcriptions in CII and elsewhere. The presence of the most commonly used symbols (menorah, etrog, lulab, shofar, vase) is indicated by conventional replicas, which will be readily identified. No effort is made to characterize the shapes.

The provenience and present location of each inscription are stated, where known. The commentary has been held down to a minimum. Significant variations from CII in reading or interpretation are indicated, and, in the case of non-extant inscriptions, the more important text variants are cited. In general, I have not discussed details of language, names, symbolism, and the like, since these have been treated in the preceding chapters. For those inscriptions which appear in our illustrations the appropriate references are given.

I. Ἀμελίω τέκνω γλυκυ-
τάτω ὃς ἔζ<ζ>ησ-
εν ἔτη β' μῆν-
ας β' ἡμέρας
ε' Ἀμέλις ἄρχω(ν)
κὲ Μαρία γονεῖς τέ-
κνω ἀμμώμω ὁσείω
ἐποίησαν

Formerly in Villa Sinibaldi; not extant. To Amelius, a very sweet child, who lived 2 years, 2 months, 5 days. The Archon Amelius and Maria, his parents, set up (this inscription) to their innocent, pious child.

3. Μένανδρος   Found on the Via Salaria in 1795; now
   ἐποίησεν   in the Lateran.
   θρεπτῷ ἰδίῳ   *Menander set up (this inscription) to his*
   'Ιούστῳ ἐν ἰρή-   *own foster son, Justus. In peace his sleep.*
   νη ἡ κόρμη-
   σις αὐτοῦ
   Line 5. κορμη for κοιμη.

4. ἐνθά-   Found near the Via Salaria about 1914;
   δε κεῖτε Δ-   in the Terme Museum, No. 61633.
   ελφίνος   *Here lies the Archon Delphinus.*
   ἄρχων

Numbers 6-71 are from the Nomentana catacomb. Unless otherwise stated, they are still in the catacomb, painted or scratched on the loculi.

6. ἐνθάδε κῖτε 'Αγά-   *Here lies Agathon.*
   θων

7. ἐνθάδε κῖτε 'Αιουτωρ γραμματεὺς   *Here lies A (d)iutor, scribe of*
   Σεκηνων ἐν εἰρήνη κοίμησις αὐτοῦ   *the Secenians. In peace his*
                                    sleep.
This inscription is completely visible, although Frey indicates that several letters are missing at the end of each line.

8. [ἔν]θα 'Αλεξα(ν)δρία   *Here (lies) Alexa(n)dria.* (Fig. 25)

9. 'Ανεις Γε[ν]ειάλης   *Annius Ge[n]ialis, Gerusiarch, who lived*
   γερουσειάρχης καλῶς   *a good life to the age of 65 years, 5*
   βειώσας ὃς ἔζησεν   *months.*
   ἔτη ξε' μ(ῆνας) ε'

10 ἐνθάδε κεῖτε   *Here lies Anniano (?), a year-old baby*
   ['Αν]νιανο ἔτ(ους) α' νη- *girl.*
   πία

So Frey, after Lietzmann; or interpret line 2 as follows: ['Αν- or 'Ιου]νια Νοετα, *i.e., Annia (or Junia) Noeta,* a double name, with no age given.

11. [ἐνθάδ]ε κεῖτε Βεργ-   *Here lies Verg [ilius? or -inius?],* . . .
   [. . . . . . .] δεκανιας
The meaning of the last word is not apparent. Frey thinks it may be a name.

12. ἐνθάδε κῖτε Βηριά[νη μήτηρ Μ]αρίες κҳὶ   *Here lies Veriana,*
    'Ιούδατος καὶ Σάρες κα[ὶ' Ἰώ]σητος καὶ   *mother of Maria and*
    'Εὐφραντικοῦ κ[.........]τῶν [τέκν?]ων   *Judas and Sara and*
                                               Joses and Euphranticus
                                               [and.....], her chil-
                                               dren (?).

Frey interprets the fragmentary portion at the end as having indicated the woman's age.

13. ἐνθάδε κῖτ[ε]   *Here lies Vitalion, aged [..] years,*
    Βιταλίων ἐτῶν [..]   *son of Justus, twice archon. In peace*
    υθιὸς 'Ιούστου   *your sleep.*
    τοῦ δὶς ἄρχοντος
    ἐν ἰρήνη ἡ κύμησής
    σοῦ

Line 3. υθιος = υειος = υιός

14. ἐνεδα κῖτε   ♁ Carved on marble; formerly in the
    [....]ργο[...]ἡ κὲ ♁ stable of Villa Torlonia.
    π   *Here lies [...., a woman] also called....*

15. ἐν[θάδε κεῖ]τε Δάφνη   *Here lies Daphne.*
The EN, which is clearly visible at the beginning, is not given by Frey (or Lietzmann).

16. [ἐνθ]άδε κεῖται Δάφνο[ς] *Here lies Daphnus [....], who lived*
    [...]οιτος ζήσας ἔτη π' *80 years. In peace [his] sleep.*
    ἐν εἰρήνη κοίμη[σις..]

17. [...]ενου ... ας ἐνθάδε κῖ[τ]-   *Here lies Digitius, aged 50.*
    αι Διγίτης ἐτῶν
    ♁ ν'

The words at the beginning are not intelligible. Frey omits the menorah, though he apparently saw it, as indicated by the note in BL, p. 30, no. 13.

18. [ἐν]θάδε κῖται   *Here lies Diophatus, the scribe of the*
    Διόφατος γραμμα-   *Siburesians. In peace his sleep.*
    τεὺς Σιβουρήσων ἐν εἰ-
    ρήνη ἡ κοίμησις αὐτοῦ

Ferrua's reading Διόφαντος is incorrect (*Epigraphica*, 3, 32). The letters are clear (despite the photograph in *CII*) and there is no ligature of AN such as Ferrua suggests.

19. Δομι   *Domi*

Frey indicates a lacuna and suggests a name like Domitius, but no more than the four letters appear to have been scratched on the loculus. There is no sign of missing letters.

20. [ἐνθά]δ(ε) κῖτε Δομνος   *Here lies Domnus.* [*May he sleep?*] *in*
[....]αδω ἐν εἰρήνη   *peace.*

Possibly -αδω is due to a garbling of κοιμάσθω; compare 365, 390.

21. Εἰρήνη τρεζ-   Carved on marble; formerly in the
πτὴ προσήλυ-   stable of Villa Torlonia.
τος πατρὸς καὶ   *Irene, foster child, proselyte, her father*
μητρὸς Εἰου-   *and mother Jewish, an Israelite, lived*
δέα 'Ισδραηλίτης   *3 years, 7 months, 1 day.*
ἔζησεν ἤτ(η) γ' μ(ῆνας) ζ'
ἡμ(έ)ρ(αν) α'
Lines 1, 2: τρεζπτη for θρεπτή.

22. ἐνθάδε [κ]εῖ[ται]   [....]ου τοῦ ἄρχ[οντος]
γυνὴ Ε[ὐ]λογε[ία]   [συναγωγ]ῆ[ς τῶν] Σιβουρη[σίων]
figure of a bird

The first half of each line is read first, then the second half. *Here lies Eulogia, wife of* [....] *the Archon of the Synagogue of the Siburesians.*

More letters are actually legible than the transcription in *CII* indicates. Frey takes the fragment of a name as being that of the husband, *i.e.*, Eulogius, but the spacing shows that the husband's name is lost, except for the genitive ending.

23. [ἐνθάδε] κεῖτε γυν[ὴ . . .]λου [....]   *Here lies* [....], *the wife of*
[....]ητου καλῶς βιώσασα   [...]. *She lived a good life.*

The letters preserved of the names of the deceased and her husband are too few to permit reconstruction. The last four letters of the inscription, omitted by Frey, can be seen, though indistinctly.

24. Ε[.... υἱὸς?] Εὐόδου τοῦ γραμμάτευς   *E*[...., *son*] *of Euho-*
ἐ[ν εἰρήν]η ἡ κοίμησις αὐτοῦ   *dus, the scribe. In peace*
                                         his sleep.

Frey reads ἐ[νθάδε κεῖται] in the first line and takes EYOΔOY-

TOY as an error for the nominative of a name *Euodoutos*, a name without parallel. Since the space will hardly admit more than eight letters, it seems better to assume a short name beginning with E, followed by υἱός (son). I take γραμματευς as a misspelling for the genitive γραμματέως.

25. [E]ὐσεβὶς ὧδε [κεῖται γυ]νὴ Γελασίου   *Here lies Eusebis, wife of*
    τοῦ Κεσαρέως ἐτῶν λε′ εὐλογί-   *Gelasius of Caesarea, aged*
    αν   *35. A blessing.*

The letters AN, which Frey omits, are visible beneath the last letters of line 2.

26. [ἐνθά]δαι κῖται Εὐσέβ[ιος ἄ]ρχων ⟨symbol⟩   *Here lies Eusebius, Ar-*
    [υἱ?]ὸς Ἑρμείας ⟨symbol⟩   *chon, [son of?] Hermia.*

The interpretation of line 2 is not entirely certain. At the beginning of line 1, Frey reads MI, but the letters are actually ΛΑΙ, for ΔΑΙ. One frequently finds Λ for Δ and vice versa.

27. [ἐν]θάδε   *Here lies Euphranticus, son*
    κεῖτε Εὐφραντικὸς υἱὸς Βηριάνης   *of Veriana.*

28. ἐνθάδε κῖτε Θά-   *Here lies Thalasa, wife of Pancratius.*
    λασα γυνὴ Παν-   *She was 27 years old, having lived a*
    κρατίου ἔζησε   *good life with (her husband). Here lies*
    ἔτη κζ′ καλῶς   *Thalasa.*
    συβιώσασα
    ἔνθα κῖτε
    Θάλασα

The last two lines are scratched, while the rest is painted. It looks as though the scratched lines were inscribed first, perhaps to mark the grave, prior to the painting of the epitaph.

30. [ἐ]νθάδε κεῖται Θεοδώ[ρα ἡ κα]ὶ Γοργόνεις   *Here lies Theodora,*
    [θυ]γάτηρ Ἡλει ἀδε(λ)φὴ Ἀ[. . .]ου   *[also named] Gorgo-*
    ἐτῶν κϛ′ ⟨symbol⟩   *nis, daughter of Eli,*
    sister of A[. . .], aged
    26.

The first letter of the brother's name, A, is mistakenly taken by Frey as an error for H, but preceding it is a clear H, which Frey overlooked.

31. ⟡ ἐνθά[δε κεῖ]τε   *Here lies Theodorus, son of [Ge?]lasius,*
Θεόδωρος υἱὸς [...]   *scribe.*
λασι [.....]
γραμ[ματεύς]

Line 4, clearly showing the first four letters of γραμματεύς (scribe), was overlooked by Frey, as well as by Paribeni and Lietzmann before him. At the upper left is a crude menorah, which Lietzmann and Frey regarded as a palm branch.

32. ἐνθάδε κ[εῖται ..... γυνὴ?]   *Here lies [....., wife*
  Ἰάσωνος ἐ[ν εἰρήνη ἡ κοίμησις]   *(?)] of Jason. In peace*
  αὐτῆς   *her sleep.*

33. [....] Ἰουδας   The painted letters are so faded that the
  [....]   only intelligible word is the name Judas.

34. Ἰολείη   Carved on marble; formerly in the
  Μαρκέλ-   stable of Villa Torlonia.
  λη ἀξίη   *To Iolia (= Julia?) Marcella, a worthy woman.*

Ferrua (*Epigraphica*, 3 [1941], 32) regards this as a pagan inscription.

35. [ἐ]νθάδε   *Here lies Julia R....*
  κεῖτε Ἰουλια P[....]   *In peace her sleep.*
  ἐν εἰρήνη ἡ κο[ίμησις αὐτῆ]ς

35a. Καιλια Ὀμνινα γυνὴ Ἰουλιανου [τοῦ ἄρ]χοντος Σιβουρησίων

Carved on the upper edge of a sarcophagus on the grounds of Villa Torlonia (Fig. 29; see *JQR* 42 [1952], 413-18 and Plate II). Not in *CII*.

Here lies Caelia Omnina, wife of Julianus, the Archon of the Siburesians.

36. [....]νειναν   On two marble fragments, for-
  [Καλλ]ι νείκου γραμμ[ατέως]   merly in the stable of Villa Tor-
     lonia [...] *of Callinicus the scribe.*

37. [ἐνθάδε κεῖτ]αι Κλαυδιος   The right portion of a marble
  [ἄρχων Σιβουρ?]ησίων καὶ   slab, formerly in the stable of
  [...........] τοῦ πατὴρ   Villa Torlonia. The greater por-
  ....]ανων φινο-   tion of the stone is missing, so

[. . . . .] ἐν εἰρήνη   that only scattering words may
[ἡ κοίμησις αὐτοῦ] ἐποίησεν   be read with certainty.
[. . . . .] τινος ἔζη-   [Here lies] Claudius, [Archon of
[σεν. . . . .]ρκωλεγει   the Sibur?]esians and [. . . .] father
. . . .]ν ὧδε κειμε [. . . .] In peace [his sleep. . . .]
[. . . . .]ναμαρ   set up (this monument). [. . . . .]
                                     He lived [. . . .] Here I lie [. . . . .]

38. [ἐν]θάδε   Here [lies . . . .], aged seven.
    [κεῖται . . .]κου
    [. . . . .] ἐτῶν ζ'

39. [Κ]ρησκεντινα   Crescentina [wife of Ju? or An?]-
    [. . . .]νιανου   nianus.

41. [ἐνθάδ]ε κῖτε Μαρα 'Ιου[δαία?] Here lies Mara [the Jewess?]. In
    ἐν ἰρή(νη) ἡ κοίμ[ησις]   peace her sleep.
    αὐτῆς

In the first line, Lietzmann and Frey both read ΜΑΡΛ for
ΜΑΡΑ, but the Α at the end of the name is clear; also they
failed to read the Υ at the end of the line, though it is distinctly
visible.

42. ἐνθάδε κεῖτε Μαρινους [. . . .]   Here lies Marinus . . . . .

43. Μαρκια Τρυφερα   Carved on a marble slab; formerly in
    Μαρκειε Ζηνο-   the stable of Villa Torlonia.
    δωρε τῇ ἰδία ἀ-   Marcia Tryphera set up (this stone) to
    δελφῇ ἀγαπητῇ   Marcia Zenodora, her own beloved sister.
    ἐποίησεν

44. ⌐ἀ⌐ ἐνθάδε [κεῖται] Μαρκεια γυ-   Here lies Marcia, wife of
    νὴ Ζορτασ[ίου? . . .] ἐτῶν λγ' ἐν εἰρή- Zortas- [ius?], aged 33.
    νη ἡ κοίμησις αὐτῆς   In peace her sleep.

Frey fails to mention the menorah at upper left, but includes
it in his index.

45. Μαρκιανα π-   Carved on a marble slab; formerly in
    [αρ]θένος ἐ-   the stable of Villa Torlonia.
    τῶν ιε' ἐνθ-   Marciana, a virgin aged 15, lies here.
    άδε κεῖται

46. [ἐνθα]δε κεῖτ[αι]   *Here lies Matrona.*
Ματρωνα

47. Νεβια Κυρια ἡ καὶ Μαπ-   Indistinct letters painted on a
λικα μάτ(ηρ) τρ(ι)ῶν (τ)έκνων   tile, which Paribeni found on the
τριῶν τέκνων ἐνθάδε   ground. Neither Lietzmann nor
κεῖτε   Frey indicates whether he saw
the inscription and verified Paribeni's reading. I could not find
it. If correctly copied, the Greek
is somewhat garbled.

Naevia Cyria, also called Mapli-
ca, mother of three children, three
children, lies here.

48. Παγχάριος [.....]   *Pancharius [lies] here honorably.*
καλῶς ἐνθάδε [κεῖται]
swastika

49. Πλωτις   Carved on a piece of marble; formerly
in the stable of Villa Torlonia. It con-
tained only a single word, the name

Plotius

50. ᵺᵾ ἐνθά[δε κεῖται]   *Here lies Pr[....]. In peace his*
ᵹ Πρ[..... ἐν] εἰρή[νη]   *sleep.*
ἡ κοί[μησις αὐ]τοῦ

51. ᵺᵾ [ἐνθά]δε κεῖτε   *Here lies [Sabb?]atius, son of Zosi-*
ᵹ [....]λτεις υείὸς   *mus, who lived 4 years.*
Ζωσείμου ζήσας ἔτη δ'

52. ἐνθάδε   Painted on a *tabula ansata*. Here
κῖτε Σελευ-   *lies Seleucus.*
κους

53. ἐνθάδε κεῖτε Σουκεσσος [γραμμ]ατεός ✐   *Here lies Successus*
the scribe.

Frey fills the lacuna so as to make Successus the son of a
scribe, but the space will not admit that many letters. The
form γραμματεος for the nominative is a not uncommon
error (cf. 142).

272 THE JEWS OF ANCIENT ROME

54. Στατωρεα   Carved on marble; formerly in the
                        stable of Villa Torlonia.
    Statorea

55. ὧδε κῖτε Σωφρόνιος υἱὸς Εὐγραφίου   ♆ *Here lies Sophro-*
    ζήσα[ς ἔτη] ιβ' ἐν εἰρήνη ἡ κοίμησις αὐτοῦ   *nius, son of Eugra-*
    [μετὰ τ]ῶν ὁσίων   *phius, who lived*
                                          12 years. In peace
                                          his sleep with the
                                          righteous.

56. ἐνθάδε κῖκε [.....]   *Here lies [....], son of Faustinus,*
    υἱὸς Φοστίνου [....]   [aged?] 80 years and (?) [....]
    [......]π' κὲ [....]

Frey is probably right in reading the Π of the last line as a
numeral indicating the age of the deceased. If so, the KE is for
KAI, as commonly, and it was followed by the number of
months. Frey, like his predecessors, Paribeni and Lietzmann,
did not see the letters ΣT in the name and insisted that they
are not visible, but I saw them in 1922, and on a re-examina-
tion of the inscription in 1951 I again saw them quite distinctly, as did those who accompanied me.

58. [ἐνθά]δε κεῖτε Ν[...]   *Here lies N[....]*

62. ♆ [....]ει   [.....] *sleep] [.....]*
      [....]σε
      κοιμη
      [......]

63. ἐνθάδε   *Here lies [....]*
    κῆτε [...]μ   [......] *peace [....]*
    νη[.... εἰ]ρήνη

67. [....] θυγάτηρ   [....] *daughter of [....]*
    [... γραμματ]έος Σιβουρησίων   *scribe of the Siburesians*

The Latin inscriptions which follow (68-71) are carved on
marble plaques, which were formerly in the stable of Villa
Torlonia.

68. Cresces Sinicerius   *Cresces Sinicerius, Jew and*
    Iudeus proselitus   *proselyte, lived 35 years, laid*
    vixit ann(is) XXXV   *to rest. His mother did for her*

dormitione(m) acce-
pit mat(er) dul(ci) flu
suo fec(it) qu(o)d ips(e) mihi
deb(uit) facere VIII K(a)l(endas)
Ian(uarias)

*sweet son what he should have
done for me. December 25.*

Line 4: *dormitionem accepit*, literally means "received sleep."

Line 5: *flu* is for *filio.*

This and No. 271 are the only inscriptions from the Jewish catacombs of Rome which bear a date.

69. [. . . . . .] Ireneus
[. . . . . .] Florae coiu-
[gi cum] qua vixi an(num?)
[. . . vixi]t autem an(nis) XIII
[ἐν εἰρήνη] ἡ κοίμησίς σου

Only the right half of the slab
is preserved.
[. . . .] *Irenaeus* [. . . .] *to Flora,
my wife, with whom I lived
one(?) year. She lived 13 years.
In peace her sleep.*

Frey (as does Lietzmann) reads the numeral in line 4 as XLII, but it appears actually to be XIII, which, if correct, indicates that Flora was not over twelve when she married.

70. Xanthias
Maximine
coiugi be-
nemeren-
ti fecit

*Xanthias set up (this stone) to Maximina,
his wife, in grateful memory.*

71. [. . . . . . beneme-]
renti fecit
pater qui vi-
xit ann(os) tres
dieb(us) viginti
tres

*[To . . . . . . well-] deserving, his father
set up (this stone). He lived 3 years,
23 days.*

72. Iul(iae) Irene Aristae
m[at(ri) pe]r Dei virtu-
te[m e]t fidem sa-
tionis conserva-
tae iuste legem
colenti
Atronius Tullia-
nus Eusebius

Carved on a marble sarcophagus, now in a cortile of the
Palazzo Spada (Fig. 31). It
seems to have been found at
Sant' Agnese on the Via Nomentana about 1527. The stone is so
badly weathered that the letters
are not easily read. The reading

v(ir) o(ptimus) filius pro
debito obs-
eq[uio ann(orum)] XLI

given here is the result of a careful examination of the sarcophagus in 1951. My translation differs in material details from that of Frey; see above, p. 247, note 1.

To Julia Irene Arista, his mother, preserved through the power of God and the devotion of her family, a pious observer of the Law, Atronius Tullianus Eusebius, vir optimus, her son, in due tribute, aged 41.

Line 9: *v. o.* seems to be an abbreviation of *vir optimus*, presumably a title.

78. [. . . . . υἱὸς . . .]
ιου ἄρχοντος
ἐνθάδε κεῖται
ζήσας ἔτη κα'
ἡ κοίμησίς σου
[μετ]ὰ τῶν
[δικ]έων

Carved on a piece of marble, found in 1928 near Tor Pignatarra on the Via Labicana (now Casilina); present location unknown.

[. . . ., *son of* . . . .]*ius, the Archon, lies here, having lived 21 years. Your sleep be among the righteous.*

The formula of the last two lines was inscribed in a sort of frame to the right and left of the main inscription.

79. ὧδε κεῖτε Ρουφινος
ζήσας ἔτη ξθ' στρα-
τευσάμενος
ἀπὸ τάξεων καὶ κ-
αλῶς ἀποθανών

Painted on an arcosolium of the catacomb of Via Appia Pignatelli, in a *tabula ansata* supported by a pair of wingless, nude *putti*.Whether this is a Jewish inscription depends on whether or not the catacomb was Jewish.

Here lies Rufinus, who lived 69 years. He campaigned in the ranks and died a good death.

Numbers 81-276 (with a few exceptions, as indicated) are from the Via Appia catacomb. Unless otherwise stated, they are presumably still in the catacomb, although, when I visited it in 1951, some appeared to be missing. The epitaphs are carved on marble slabs, except as noted.

81. [ὧδε] κεῖται Ἀγεντ[ια]
[. . .]ανη μόνανδρ[ος ἡ ἔζη-]

Here lies Agentia [. . . .]*ane, married only once, who lived with her virgin*

[σ]εν μετὰ παρθε[νικοῦ αὐ-] *husband 9 years. In peace your sleep.*
[τ]ῆς ἔτη θ' ἐν εἰρή[νη ἡ]
κοίμησίς σου

82. 'Αθηνίων εἰδίω   *Athenion set up (this stone) to his*
πατρὶ ἔθηκεν   *own father, who lived a good life*
καλῶς βιώσ[ας]   *of 63 years. (Fig. 26)*
ἔτη ξγ'

Line 3: The participle should be βιώσαντι but the space admits no more than the two letters. It is strange that the name of the deceased father is not given, unless 'Αθηνίων is erroneously written for the dative. Possibly father and son had the same name.

83. Αὐρήλιος   The stone is in two pieces, each in a
Βασος Αἰ-   different part of the catacomb, the
μιλιαι   break being after the second line.
Θεοδόρ-   The lower fragment may be seen in
η ἐποίησε-   Fig. 27.
ν   *Aurelius Basus set up (this stone)*
              to Aemilia Theodora.

84. 'Αλε[ξάνδρω πατρὶ?]   Probably not extant.
γλυ[κυτάτω 'Αλέξανδ-]   *To Alexander, his very sweet father,*
ρος υἱὸς [ἐν εἰρήνη]   *(?) Alexander his son. In peace his*
[ἡ κοί]μησις [αὐτοῦ]   *sleep.*
The reconstruction is that of Frey.

85. 'Αλέξανδρος ἄρχων   *Alexander, Archon of All Dignity, to*
πάσης τειμῆς τέκνω   *his sweetest son, Alexander, Archon-*
γλυκυτάτω 'Αλεξάν-   *to-be. In peace your sleep.*
δρω μελλάνχοντι
ἐν εἰρήνη ἡ κοίμησίς σου
Line 4: μελλανχοντι for μελλάρχοντι.

86. ἐνθάδε κεῖτε 'Αμάχις   *Here lies Amachius, also called*
ὁ καὶ Πριμος μνήμη   *Primus. The memory of the just is*
δικαίου ἰς εὐλογίαν   *for a blessing and the praises accord-*
οὗ ἀληθῆ τὰ ἐνκώ-   *ed him are true. In peace your sleep.*
μια ἐν ἰρήνη<ν> ἡ
κοίμησίς σου 🕎

87. Ἀνια[.....] Scratched on a loculus.
Ania (for Annia?).
Frey prefers to regard it as part of the name Anianos.

88. ἐνθάδε κεῖτε Ἀννιανος ἄρχων (νή)πιος
υἱὸς Ἰουλιάνου πατρὸ(ς) συναγωγῆς Καμπησίων αἰτῶν η′ μηνῶν β′ ἐν εἰρήνη ἡ κοίμησις αὐτοῦ

Here lies Annianus, child Archon, son of Julianus, Father of the Synagogue of the Campesians, aged 8 years, 2 months. In peace his sleep.

89. ℣ [......]   ......in peace.......
✐ ἐν εἰρήν[η....]
απεγ′ π
The rest is not intelligible.

90. Ἀσίας τὸ   Asias, the three-year-old child. In
νήπιον   peace your sleep.
ἐτῶν γ′ ἐν
εἰρήνη ἡ κοί-
μησίς σου

91. Ἀσκληπιοδότη   Scratched on a loculus.
Asclepiodote.

92. Ἀσκληπιοδό-   To Asclepiodote, his mother, and Alexan-
τη μητρὶ καὶ Ἀ-   der, Archon, his brother, Constantius set
λεξάνδρω ἄρ-   up (this stone). In peace your sleep.
χοντι ἀδελφῶ   The letters AC were cut in the lower
Κωσταντις   right corner of the stone, at right angles
ἐποίησεν   to the main text. Possibly the cutter
[ἐ]ν εἰρήνη ἡ   started the inscription in the wrong
[κοί]μησις ὑ-   place.
μῶν.

93. [ἐν]θάδε κῖτε Ἀσστερία[ς]   Portions of the stone at the left and
πατὴρ συναγωγῆς ὅσι[ος]   the right, once seen by Garrucci,
ἄμε(μ)πτος αἰν ἱρήνη   have disappeared. See the photo-
κοίμησίς σου   graph of the extant portion in CII.
Here lies Asterias, Father of the Synagogue, pious, irreproachable. In peace
your sleep.

94. 'Αστερία   Scratched on a loculus.
                     Asteria.

95. ['Ασ]τέρις ἄρχων   The stone, badly broken, is in
    [ἐπ]όησεν τοῖς γ[ο]ν-   the Terme Museum, No. 72884.
basket ν[ε]ῦσιν αὐτοῦ 'Αστερί-   On the reverse is our No. 262.
of ω γιερουσάρχη κ[αὶ]   For a photograph see *CII*,
fruit Λουκινε τῆ μη[τρὶ αὐ]-   p. 594. The basket of fruit and
bird [το]ῦ ὃς ἔζησεν ἔτη [. . . .] the bird at the left are no
    [. . . .]ς ἐν εἰρή[νη]   longer visible.
    [ἡ κοίμησις] αὐτῶν

*Asterius, Archon, set up (this stone) to his parents, Asterius,
Gerusiarch, and Lucina, his mother. He (the father) lived [. .]
years. [. . . .] In peace their [sleep].*

96. Πολύκαρπο(ς)   *Polycarpus, the father, and Crescentina, the*
    πατὴρ καὶ Κρη- *mother, to Aurelia Maria, their worthy,*
    κεντεινα μή- *sweetest child.*
    τηρ Αὐρ(ηλια) Μαρία
    ἀξίω τέκνω γλυκ-
    (υ)τάτ(ω)

97. ἐνθάδε κῖτε   *Here lies the child Verecundus.*
    Βερεγονδος
    νέπιος

98. [ἐ]νθάδε [κεῖτα]ι Βικτο[ρ] Painted on a loculus.
    [υἱ]ὸ[ς . . . .]ωτο[υ]   *Here lies Victor, son of (?) [. . . .]*

99. ἐνθάδε κεῖτε Βιταλίω   The right half of the stone, once seen,
    γραμματεούς τὶς ἔζη[σ]- is lost. A small fragment was copied
    εν ἔτη ζ' καὶ ἡμέρας ιδ' in Velletri by Schneider-Graziosi;
    ἐν εἰρήνη οἱ κύμ[ησις] *NBAC* 21, (1915), 53 f.
    αὐτοῦ   *Here lies Vitalio, the scribe, who lived
                       7 years and 14 days. In peace his
                       sleep.*

In line 3, KAI is quite clear. Frey, following Garrucci's incorrect reading, has only K, which he wrongly combines with
the preceding Z to get a strange, inverted numeral, which
he interprets as 27.

100. ἐνθάδε κεῖτε 〽 Not extant.
Γαῖς προστάτης ⚇ *Here lies Gaius, the prostates. A pious*
ὅσιος ἔζησεν *man, he lived 72 years. In peace your*
ἔτη οβ' ἐν εἰρή(νη) *sleep.*
κοίμησίς σου

It is possible that ὅσιος is an error or misreading for ὅστις
which often precedes ἔζησεν.

101. ἐνθάδε [κεῖται . . . .]   *Here [lies] the child [. . . .]. Gaius [his*
νήπιος [. . . . .]   *father? . . . .]. In peace [your?] sleep.*
Γαῖς π[ατὴρ? . . . .]   (Fig. 48)
ἐν εἰρ[ήνη ἡ κοίμη]-
bird σι[ς . . .]

102. Γημηλλίνη νηπεία ἵτις   *Gemellina, a child who lived one year,*
ἤζησεν ἤτη μεία μήνης   *eleven months. In peace your sleep.*
ἤνδηκα ἐν ἰρήνη ἡ κοίμη-   *I, Victor the scribe, set up (this stone).*
σίς σου Βικτρω γραμματηοὺ(ς) φηκι

Nearly every word is misspelled. The last word is the Latin
feci, written in Greek letters.

103. τῶ ὁσίο [. . . .]   The reading is that of Garrucci, after
Δευτείρ(ω . . . .] -   whom nobody appears to have seen
συναγω[γῆς . . . .]   this fragment.
ἐν ε[ἰρήνη]   *To the pious [. . . .] Deuterus [. . . .] of*
ἐ κύμ[ησις]   *the synagogue [. . . . .]. In peace his*
[αὐ]το[ῦ]   *sleep.*

104. [ἐν εἰρ]ήνη Διονυ-   Scratched on a loculus. There is no
[κοίμη]σις αὐτοῦ σίας   record of its having been seen since
Garrucci.
In peace his sleep. Dionysias.

105. ἐνθάδε κ[εῖται Δ]ομιτι[α]   Apparently not extant. The reading
ἥτις ἔζησ[εν ἔ]τη ιθ'   is De Rossi's.
μετὰ τοῦ συ[μβ]ίου αὐ-   *Here lies Domitia, who lived 19 years;*
τῆς ἔτη ζ' ἐ[ν ε]ἰρήνη   *with her husband, seven years. In*
ἡ κοίμησίς σου 〽   *peace her sleep.*

106. Δουλ[κι]τιαι παρθένω   The middle of the upper portion of
μελλ[ο]νύμφῃ Πανχάρις   the stone, once read by Garrucci,
γερουσιάρχης τῇ θυγατρὶ αὐ- is now missing. For what is left, see
τοῦ ἐποίησεν ἐν εἰρήνῃ   Fig. 26, bottom row, and the
ἡ κοίμησίς σου   photograph in CII.

*To the virgin Dulcitia, bride-to-be. Pancharius, the Gerusiarch,
set up (this stone) to his daughter. In peace your sleep.*

107. [. . . .]ηναῖος   Scratched on a loculus.
[Ir? or Ath?]enaeus.

108. Ἑρμειόνη θυγατρὶ   The stone is now in
Πισιννα μήτηρ ἀνέθηκεν   the Sala Giudaica of
ἡ ἀπέδωκεν μῆν(ας) η' (κ)αὶ ἡμ(έρας) ζ' the Lateran.
ἡ(τ)ινι ἐπίκλην BARⱳEODA

There is no basis for including it among those from the Appia
catacomb, as does Frey. Since it appears to have been at
Velletri in the eighteenth century, it may, like most of that
group, have come from Monteverde; see Ferrua, *Epigraphica*,
3 (1941), 32 f.

*To Hermione, her daughter, the mother, Pisinna, set up (this
stone). She lived 8 months and 7 days. Her surname was Barsheoda.*

Frey has several erroneous readings, taken from earlier copies
although the stone itself is available (see Fig. 32. 14).

Line 3: ἀπέδωκεν is strangely used where ἔζησεν is expected.
Possibly it is for ἀπέθανεν (died). My reconstruction of the words
which follow is an attempt to interpret the letters MHNHAI-
HMZ. It appears that a K was omitted after MHNH.

Line 4: HINI seems to have lost a T and to be meant for
ἥτινι. The proper name is written in a curious combination of
letters, with Latin R and D and Hebrew *shin*.

109. ἐνθάδε   The scribe ran out of space and left
κῖτε Εὐδό-   the formula unfinished.
ξιος ζωγ-   *Here lies Eudoxius, a painter. In
ράφος ἐν   peace (his sleep). (Fig. 49).*
εἰρήνη ἡ κύ

110. [ἐνθ]άδε κεῖτε   Here lies, to Eutychianus, Archon,
    [Ε]ὐθυχιάνο ἄρχοντι   a worthy husband. Be of good spirit.
    σινβίο ἀξίω‹ν› εὐψύχι   With the just his sleep.
    μετὰ τῶν δικέων 🕎
    ἡ κύμησις αὐτοῦ 🕎

Lines 2, 3: The syntax is confused, the dative being used for the nominative.

111. 🕎 ἐνθά δε κεῖτε   The left portion of the stone is at
    Εὔκα ρπος νή-   Columbia University in New York;
    πιος ὅσιος   the right portion is still in the cata-
    φιλό νομος   comb. See H. J. Leon in *AJA* 28 (1924)
    ἐν εἰρ ήνη ἡ κοίμη-   251f.
    σίς σου   Here lies Eucarpus, a pious child, lover
                                    of the Law. In peace your sleep.

112. Τρύλλις Εὐ-   Tryllis. Eulogius set up (this stone)
    λόγις τῷ ἰδίω   to his own child.
    τέκνω ἐποί-
    ησεν

Frey takes *Tryllis* as the name of the parent and *Eulogistos* as that of the child. The ΤΩ in line 2 must, however, be the article (see above, p. 102, note 2). For the sequence of nominative of the deceased, nominative of the dedicant, dative modifiers of the deceased, and verb, compare Numbers 125, 172, 221.

113. Εὐσέβιος νε[. . . .ν]ομο-   Garruci's reading of the inscription,
    μαθῆς ἀσαλ[. . . .]ιο   which was painted in red on a slab of
    ἔζη(σεν) ἔτη [. . . .]   *cipollino verde*, is highly uncertain.
                                            Nobody else seems to have seen the
stone. The only intelligible words may be rendered as follows: *Eusebius* [. . . . .] *student of the Law* [. . . . .] *lived* [. . .] *years.* Schwabe's reconstruction (*Tarbitz* 14 [1942-43], 140 f.) of Ἀσαμωναῖος (= Hasmonean) in the second line cannot be accepted on the basis of the few unverified remains of letters.

114. Εὐσέβις   Scratched on a loculus.
                                       Eusebius.

115. Εὐτυχι[. . . .]   Scratched on a loculus.
                                       Eutychi . . .

116. Ζήνων

Scratched on a loculus.
Zenon.

117. Ζωτικὴ κα-
λῶς βιώσα-
σα ἐν εἰρήνη
ἡ κοίμησίς σου

Zotice, who lived a good life. In peace your sleep.

118. Ζωτικὸς ἄρχων [ἐν]θάδε
κεῖμε καλῶς [βιώ]σας
π[άντ]ων φ[ίλ]ος καὶ γ[ν]ωσ[τὸ]ς
[π]ᾶσ[ι ....]τρ[....]α ἀνδρὶ ἀϊ-
μνήσ[τω μετὰ] τῶν δικαίων
ἡ κοίμησίς σου ᛣ ⚹ ⚱

The stone was removed from the catacomb and is now at Pusey House, Oxford. For the text see Webster in JRS 19 (1929), 151, and Robert in Hellenica 3 (1946), 97. A photograph may be seen in Goodenough, III, 767.

I, Zoticus, Archon, lie here after a good life, the friend of all and known to all. [....] to her ever-to-be-remembered husband. Your sleep among the righteous.

In Frey's version, which is based on that of Garrucci, lines 4 and 5 are misread and misinterpreted.

119. ἐνθάδε κεῖται Θαιόφιλ[ος γερο]υσι-
άρχης καλῶς βιώσα[ς κα]ὶ κα-
λῶς ἀκούσας Θεόφι[λος κ]αὶ
Εὐσέβις πα[τρὶ γλ]υκ[υτάτ]ω
μνία σο[υ ....]

The fragment at the extreme right and the last two lines, once seen by Garrucci, are lost. See Fig. 26 and the photograph of the remaining portion in CII.

Here lies Theophilus, Gerusiarch, who lived a good life and had a good reputation. Theophilus and Eusebius to their very sweet father. Your memory [for a blessing?].

120. ὧδε κεῖτε 'Ιοκαθ-
ινος ἄρχων νήπιος

This inscription, carved on the marble lid of a sarcophagus, was lost for several decades. I rediscovered it in 1951 at the entrance to the painted cubicula, where it is used as a step (Fig. 17). See above, p. 61 and RAC 29 (1953), 101-103.
Here lies Iocathinus, child Archon.

121. ἐνθάδε κεῖ-   *Here lies Judas, scribe-to-be, who lived*
τε 'Ιουδα-   *24 years. In peace your sleep.*
ς μελ(λο)γραμ(ματεὺς)
ὃς ἔζησεν
ἔτη κδ′ ἐν
εἰρήνη ἡ κοί-
μισίς σου

122. ἐνθάδε κεῖται 🕎   *Here lies Judas, a child, son of Salutius,*
'Ιουδας νήπιος   *the scribe.*
υἱὸς Σαλουτίου
γραμματέως

123. θάρσι 'Ιουλια 'Εμιλ- *Be of good courage, Julia Emilia, aged 40*
μ′   ια   ἐτῶν   *years. You lived a good life with your hus-*
καλῶς ἔζησας μετὰ   *band. I am grateful to you for your*
τοῦ ἀνδρός σου εὐ-   *thoughtfulness and your soul.*
χαριστῶ τῇ προνοία
καὶ τῇ ψυχῇ σου

Line 2: The numeral M (= 40) is placed at the beginning of the line instead of at the end. See the photograph in *CII*.

124. τῇ ἰδία <μη>μητρὶ   *To his own mother Julia, her son Castricius*
'Ιουλιαι Καστρι-   *set up (this stone). In peace your couch.*
κις υἱὸς ἐποίη-
σεν ἐν εἰρήνη κοίτη
σου

125. 'Ιουσιος γραμματεὺς   Now at Pusey House, Oxford.
φιλοπάτωρ καὶ φι-   *Justus, the scribe, who loved his*
λάδελφος Μαρω-   *father and his brother. Maron, twice*
ν β′ ἄρχ(ων) τέκνω ἀγαπη- *Archon, to his beloved child, aged*
τῷ ὄντι ἐτῶν λζ′   *37 years.*

Line 1: IOYCIOC is for IOYCTOC.

126. ἐνθάδε κεῖται   *Here lies Joses, the sweet child,*
'Ιωσης τὸ νήπιον   *aged 2 years, 8 days. Proco-*
ἡδὺν ἐτ(ῶν) β′ ἡ(μερῶν) η′ Προ- *pius, his father, and Crispi-*
κόπις ὁ πατὴρ Κρισ-   *na, his mother. May you pray*
πινα δὲ μήτ(ηρ) προσ-   *that in peace be his sleep.*
εύχοιο ἐν εἰρήνη
τὴν κύμησιν αὐτοῦ

Lines 5-6: The shift to a verb in the second person is strange, to say the least.

127. Καλανδιω

Scratched on a loculus.
Calandio.

128. Καστος

Scratched on a loculus.
Castus.

129. ὧδε κῖτε Κεντουλια
θυγάτηρ Οὐρσακίου
ἐν εἰρήνη κύμισις αὐτῆς

Painted on a marble slab.
Here lies Centulia, daughter of Ursacius. In peace her sleep.

130. [....ό?] ἀσύκριτος
[....Κλ]αυδιος Προβινκις
[....σ]υναγωγῆς τῶν
[....]ς καὶ 'Επιφανία υἱῶ
[...έ]τη κγ' καὶ μῆνες ἕξ

Now in the Conservatori Museum. No. 40. For a photograph of the surviving portion see CII, p. 595. [... the?] incomparable [....] Claudius Provincius [....] of the Synagogue of the [....]s and Epiphanius to their son [....] aged 23 years and 6 months.

131. ἐν ἰρήνη κοίμησις
Κοσσουτίου
ὃς ἔζησεν
ἔτη κα' μ(ῆνας) ς'
ἐποίησαν
ἀδελφοί

This stone appears to be lost since the time of Garrucci. In peace the sleep of Cossutius, who lived 21 years, 6 months. His brothers set up (this stone).

132. Κρισπεινα Προκοπίου
σπουδέα φιλέντολος
ἐνθάδε κεῖται ἐν εἰρή-
νη τὴν κοίμησιν αὐ-
τῆς

The left half has disappeared since Garrucci copied it. There is a photograph of the remaining portion in CII.

Crispina, (wife) of Procopius, a fine woman, lover of the Commandments, lies here. In peace her sleep.

133. ἐν ἰρήνη κῖται Κῦρος

Scratched on a loculus.
In peace lies Cyrus.

134. [....]ο[....]
[....]κῖτε Υ[....]
Λεοντι[....]
Λεοντίου

Painted on a loculus.
[....] lies [....] Leonti[....] of Leontius.

135. ἡ δόξα
Σωφρονί-
ου Λουκιλ-
λα εὐλογη-
μένη ☙

Carved on alabaster. Last recorded
as being in Bergamo.
*The glory of Sophronius, Lucilla, a
woman highly praised.*

136. (A)
ἐνθάδε
κεῖτε Μαρια-
ριτα ἡ ἔζ[η]-
σεν ἔτη
ιθ' μ[ετὰ]
τοῦ ἀ[νδρ]-
ὸς ἔτη [δ']
ἐν εἰρήν-
η ἡ κοίμη-
σίς σου
☖

The stone, which (a fact unknown to Frey)
bears two versions on *opposite* faces, is in
the storeroom of the Terme Museum,
No. 51729 (Figs. 50, 51). See H. J. Leon,
RAC, 29 (1953), 103-105. Version A appears
to be the later, corrected version.
*Here lies Margarita, who lived 19 years,
with her husband 4 years. In peace your
sleep.*
(A) Line 2: MAPIA is for MAPΓA.
Line 7: The Δ, though lost from the stone,
may reasonably be restored from the
scrawled letter in Version B.

(B)
ΘΝΟΑΕΘ κ[εῖτε Μαργ]αιιτα
ἥτις ἔζησ[εν ἔ]τη ιθ'
μετὰ τοῦ συ[μβί]ου αὐ-
τῆς ἔτη δ' [ἐν ε]ἰρήνη
ἡ κοίμησίς σου ☖

(B) Line 1: The first word is
apparently a stupid garbling of
ἐνθάδε. At the end of the line,
ΑΙΙΤΑ is for ΑΡΙΤΑ, the name
being evidently Margarita, as
seen from Version A.

137. Μαρία βρέφος ἀγα-
πητὸν ἡ θυγάτηρ
Προκοπίου ἐνθάδε
κεῖται ἐν εἰρή(νη) ἡ κύμησις αὐτῆς

*Maria, beloved infant, the daugh-
ter of Procopius, lies here. In
peace her sleep.*

The first letter of line 3 is not a
Γ, as read by Frey, but is
intended for a π in a ligature with the following P. Exactly the
same ligature occurs in line 3 of No. 126, the epitaph of
another child of the unfortunate Procopius, who had also lost
his wife Crispina (No. 132).

138. ἐνθάδε κεῖτε
νέπιος Μαρκε-
λλος ἐν ἰρήνη
ἡ κύμισίς σου ♓

Here lies the child Marcellus. In peace your sleep.

139. Μαρκιαι
συν(βί)ω ⚙
ἰδί(α) 'Αἰλι-
ανος ἐποί-
ησεν

The portion containing the last two lines, seen by Garrucci, is now missing. See the photograph in *CII*. The menorah is inverted.
To Marcia, his own wife, Aelianus set up (this stone).

Lines 2, 3: The letters in parentheses are erased on the stone.

140. ἐνθάδε κῖτε Μαρωνις ὁ κὲ [....]ητος
ἔγγων 'Αλεξάνδρο[υ το]ῦ κὲ
Μαειου ἄρχων Σ[ιβο]υρη-
σίων ἐτῶ[ν] κδ' καὶ
μηνῶν γ' ἐν [εἰρήν]η ἡ κ[οί]-
μη[σις....]

Here lies Maronius, also named [...] etus, grandson of Alexander, also named Mathius, Archon of the Siburesians, aged 24 years and 3 months. In peace [your or his] sleep.

Line 3: MAEIOY is apparently for MAΘIOY, so that the man's surname was Mathius (= Matthew).

141. Μελιτίω μητρὶ γλυκυ-
τάτη
Δουλκιτια θυγάτηρ
ἀνέ ♓ θηκα
ἥτις ἔζη ⚱ σεν ἔτη κθ'

Now at Pusey House, Oxford. There is a photograph in Goodenough, III, No. 763.
To Melitium, my very sweet mother, I, Dulcitia, her daughter, set up (this stone). She lived 29 years.

142. ♓
Νουμένις
γραμματεός

Numenius, the scribe. (Fig. 52)

143. Νουμήνι-
ς ὁ νήπιο-
ς ἐνθάδε
κεῖται ⚘
⚱

Now at Pusey House, Oxford. There is a photograph in Goodenough, III, No. 770.
The child Numenius lies here.
Line 1: Frey's NOYMMHNI is incorrect.

144. Ἀλεξανδρία Σεβη-
ρα Νώτω ἰδίω θρε-
πτῶ καλῶς ἀν-
τιζώσας βίον κοι-
νὸν ἔτη κζ' ἐν ἱρή-
νη ἡ κοίμησίς σου
σε

Alexandria Severa to Notus, her own foster son, who lived a good life together with her for 27 years. In peace your sleep (Fig. 53). Lines 3, 4: ANTIZΩCAC is probably a scribal error for ζώσαντι, which is required by both sense and grammar; see Ferrua, *Epigraphica*, 3 (1941), 33.

round hut   tree   conical   two cocks
with four   hut   with lulab
fowls   between them

Lines 6, 7: Actually KOIMHOIC appears on the stone. The CE, written in smaller letters beneath the incorrect o, is apparently a correction, so that the form intended is KOIMHCEIC. The symbols at the bottom of the stone are crudely executed and unique among these inscriptions. See above, p. 201.

145. ἐνθάδε κεῖτε
'Ονωρατος γραμ(ματεὺς)
ὅσιος ὃς ἔζησε-
ν ἔτη ο' μ(ῆνας) η' [ἡμ(έρας)]
ιβ' Ρουφος ἄρχ(ων)
τῶ πατρὶ γλυκυ-
τάτω ἐν εἰρή-
[ν]η ἡ κοίμησίς
σου

The lower left corner, once seen, is now missing. See the photograph in *CII*. *Here lies Honoratus, the scribe, a pious man, who lived 70 years, 8 months, 12 days. Rufus, the Archon, to his most sweet father. In peace your sleep.*

146. ἐνθάδε κῖτε 'Ονωρατος γραμμα(τεὺς)
νήπιος υἱὸς Ρούφου ἄρχ(οντος) ὃς ἔζησεν ἔτη ϛ' ἡμέρας κη'
ἐν ἱρήνη ἡ κοίμησίς σου

Here lies Honoratus, the child scribe, son of Rufus, the Archon. He lived 6 years, 28 days. In peace your sleep. (Fig. 54).

147. ὧδε κῖτε Οὐρσακια θυγάτηρ
Οὐρσακίου ἀπὸ 'Ακουιλείας γερουσιάρχου ἐν εἰρήνη κύμισ(ις) αὐτῆς

Painted on a marble slab. *Here lies Ursacia, daughter of Ursacius of Aquileia, Gerusiarch. In peace her sleep.*

148. ⟨menorah⟩ ἐνθάδε κεῖτε Οὖρσος γραμμ-
ατεοὺς τὶς ἔζησεν κβ' ‹καὶ

Here lies Ursus, the scribe, who lived 22 ‹and two›

omph- δύω〉 ἔτη καὶ μῆνας τρῖς   bird *years and 3 months. The*
alos? μνεία τοῦ μελλονυμφίου   *memory of the bridegroom-*
       ἐν εἰρή(νη) οἱ κύμισ(ις) αὐτοῦ   *to-be (for a blessing?). In*
                                        peace his sleep.

Lines 2, 3: The scribe carelessly added καὶ δύω after recording the number of years by the numerals κβ. Other signs of carelessness in this inscription are the writing of Λ for A and Δ, C for E, and E for C and certain crudely formed letters, as an examination of the photograph in *CII* will reveal.

149. Ὀνορατος πατὴρ   *Honoratus, his father, the*
     γραμματεὺς Πε-   *scribe, and Petronia, his*
     τρωνια μήτηρ Πε-   *mother, to Petronius, the*
     τρωνίω γραμματέω   *scribe, their incomparable son.*
     ὑῶ ἀσυνκρίτω ἔζησεν   *He lived 24 years, 4 months,*
     ἔτη κδ' μῆν(ας) δ' ἡ(μέρας) ιε' ἐν- 15 *days. Here he lies. In*
     θάδε κεῖται ἐν εἰρή-   *peace his sleep.* (Fig. 16).
     νη κοίμησις αὐτοῦ

150. ἐνθάδε κεῖτε Μ[. . . .]   The left portion of the stone, avail-
     να Πετ(ρ)ωνια ἔζησ-   able to Garrucci, is now gone. See
     εν ἔτη νε' γυνὴ Ὀ-   the photograph of the extant por-
     ꙍ νωράτου   tion in *CII*. On the reverse of the
     καλῶς κομ-   stone is No. 246.
     οῦ μοτὰ τῶ-   *Here lies M[. . . .]na Petronia. She*
     ν δικέων   *lived 55 years, the wife of Honora-*
                                  tus. Sleep well among the righteous.

151. ἐνθάδε κῖται   Now in Pusey House, Oxford.
     Ποιμενὶς   *Here lies Poemenis, the pious wo-*
     ἡ ὁσία ἥτις   *man, who lived 96 years, 10 months.*
     ἔζησεν ἔτη   *In peace her sleep.*
     9ς' μῆνας ι'   Line 5: The numeral letters appear
     ἡμέρας ιη' ἐν ἰρήνη   to be *koppa digamma* (= 96), the
     ἡ κοίμισις αὐτῆς   former resembling our numeral 9,
                           the latter our S. See the photo-
                           graph in Goodenough, III, 766.

152. [ἐνθ]άδε κεῖτε Προβος νήπιος τὶς ἔ- *Here lies Probus, a child who*
     [ζ]ησεν ἔτη δύω καὶ μῆνα α'   *lived 2 years and one month,*
     ἡμέρας τρῖς φιλοπάτορος φ-   *3 days. He loved his father,*
     ιλομήτορος ἐν εἰρήνη οἱ κύ-   *loved his mother. In peace*
     μισίς σου ꙍ bird   *your sleep.*

153. Σαββατια   Last recorded as being in Bergamo.
Ρενάτω   *Sabbatia set up (this stone) to her brother Renatus.*
ἀδελφῶ
θῆκεν ⸲

154. ἐνθάδε κεῖτε   The letters are wretchedly scrawled
Ρμολνος (?) ἄμεμ(πτος?)   and line 2 is unintelligible. The
νήπιος ὅσιος   interpretation suggested here is
ἐν εἰρήνη ἡ κοί-   that of Frey.
μησίς σου   *Here lies Romanus (?), an irre-*
proachable (?), pious child. In
peace your sleep.

155. Λουκιος πατὴρ   *Lucius, the father, to his most sweet*
θυγατρὶ Σαβατ-   *daughter, Sabatis, aged 3 years.*
ίδι γλυκυτάτη
ἐτῶν τριῶν

156. Σαββατὶς [θυ]-   The left half, once read by Garruc-
γάτηρ Βιβί-   ci, is now missing. For a photo-
ας ἐτῶν ιγ′   graph of the remaining half see
ἐν εἰρήνη κοί-   Fig. 26, upper row, left.
μησίς σου   *Sabbatis, daughter of Vibia, aged*
13 years. In peace your sleep.

157. Σαββατὶς ἐνθά-   *Sabbatis lies here, the wife of Leus,*
δε κεῖτε γυ-   *who lived 28 years. In peace your*
νὴ Λέου ἥτις   *sleep.*
ἔζησεν ἔτη κη′
ἐν ἰρήνη ἡ κοί-
μησίς σου

158. ἐνθάδε κεῖτε Σαβειν[α]   Frey does not record any part of
ὁσία [φίλ?]ανδρος πασ[ιφίλη?]   this inscription as extant, but in
ἐν ἰρήνη κ[οίμησις . . . .]   the catacomb I saw a fragment
containing parts of the first two lines, as follows:

ΕΙΤΕ CΑΒΕΙΝ
ΑΝΔΡΟC ΠΑC

Here lies Sabina, a pious woman, [who loved her?] husband,
[beloved by?] all. In peace [her or your] sleep.

Line 2: The second word may be either φίλανδρος or μόνανδρος (*only once married*), as Frey suggests.

159. Πάρδος Σαβειν-
αι θυγατρὶ τὶς
ἔζησεν ἔτη
δέκα ἔ<σ>ξ ἐν εἰ-
ρήνη ἡ κοίμη-
σις αὐτῆς

Now at Pusey House, Oxford. *Pardus to Sabina his daughter, who lived 16 years. In peace her sleep.* Line 4: The scribe wrongly inserted a σ in the numeral. The transcription in *CII* preserves the σ but omits the ξ. Frey omits also the two menorahs. See the photograph in Goodenough, III, 764.

160. Σαβεινα Πάλμη κεῖτε

Scratched on a loculus. (*Here*) *lies Sabina Palma.*

161. Σαλβίω νη-
πίω ὃς ἔζη-
σεν ἔτη ζ'

To Salvius, a child, who lived 7 years.

162. Σαλπινγι-
ους νήπι-
ος

Salpingius, a child. (Fig. 55) The trumpets are a punning reference to the child's name.

163. Σειμο[ν?]

Scratched on a loculus. *Simon* (?)

165. Σιμον

Scratched on a loculus. *Simon*

166. ἐνθάδε κεῖτε Σιμπ[λικια μήτηρ? συ]-
ναγωγῆς φίλανδρος [. . . .]
συναγωγῆς τῇ ἰδία σ[υμβίω ἐποίησεν]

Parts at the left and right, seen by Garrucci, are now missing. For a photograph of the extant portion see *CII*. Garrucci recorded the presence of a menorah at the left, but this was overlooked by Frey.

Here lies Simplicia, Mother (?) *of the Synagogue, who loved her husband.* [Husband's name and office] *of the synagogue* [*set up* (*this stone*)] *to his own wife.*

167. ὦδε κῖτε Σινπλικι-
α θυγάτηρ Οὐρσακίου
ἐν εἰρή(νη) κύμισις αὐτῆς

Painted on a marble slab. *Here lies Simplicia, daughter of Ursacius. In peace her sleep.*

168. ἐνθάδε κεῖτε Σίριχα   The central portion, apparently
παρθένος [ἐ]τῶν ιη'   seen by Garrucci, is now lacking.
ἐν ε[ἰρήνη ἡ κοί]μησίς σου   See the photograph in *CII*.
Here lies Sirica, a virgin, aged 18 years. In peace your sleep.

169. Τρόφιμος Τροφί-   *Trophimus devotedly set up (this stone) to*
μη θυγατρὶ ἑαυτ-   *Trophime, his most sweet daughter, who lived*
οῦ γλυκυτάτη καλ-   *a year and 10 months. In peace her*
ῶς ἐποίησεν ἥτις   *sleep.*
ἔζησεν ἐνιαυ-
τὸν καὶ δέκα μῆ-
νας ἐν εἰρήνη
ἡ κοίμησις αὐ-
τῆς

170. Χρυσίο   Inscribed on a brick, according to Garrucci, the only person to record it.
To Chrysius.

171. Φαυστινος   The last three lines with the symbols at
νήπιος ἐν-   the bottom, read by Garrucci, are no
θάδε κεῖτε   longer extant.
'Αλέξες υἱός   *Faustinus, a child, lies here, son of Alexe.*
ἐν ἰρήνη ἡ κοί-   *In peace your sleep.*
μησίς σου
🕎 *calf*

172. Φλαβιος 'Ιουλι-   *Flavius Julianus, the Hyperetes. Flavia*
ανος ὑπηρέτης   *Juliana, his daughter, to her father. In*
Φλαβια 'Ιουλιάνη   *peace your sleep.*
θυγάτηρ πατρί
ἐν εἰρήνη ἡ κοί-
μησίς σου

173. [. . . . συνα]γωγῆς   The part missing at the left is by far the
[. . . .]ι 'Ροδίων   greater part of the stone. See Fig. 30.
[. . . .] εὐλογία πᾶσι   *To [name and office] of the Synagogue*
                          [. . . .] Rhodion [set up (this stone) (?)].
                          A blessing to all.

For a discussion of this inscription and a refutation of the
view that it reveals the presence at Rome of a Synagogue of
the Herodians, see above, pp. 159-62.

176. [....]ειμων   Too little remains to permit a reconstruc-
[....]ειχος Ζω-   tion of this epitaph.
[....]τος υειός   [.... S?]imon [....]icus Zo [....]tus son.

179. ἐνθάδ[ε κεῖται]   Here [lies] Amni[....] to his (or her) wife
'Αμνι [....]   (or husband) [....]
συμβίω [....]

Because of the fragmentary condition of this inscription it is
not possible to determine which spouse is the deceased.

180. ἐν[θά]δε κεῖ[ται ....]   Here lies [....], the scribe, [who
γραμματε[ὺς ὃς ἔζησ]-   lived] 7 years and [..] months.
εν ἔτη ζ' καὶ μ[ῆνας ....]   In peace his [sleep]. (Fig. 27)
ἐν εἰρήνη [ἡ κοίμησις]
αὐτο[ῦ]

185. שלום [....] ἰδία θυγα[τρὶ ....]   [....] to his own daughter, [who
♦ ἔτη ε' μῆ[νας ....]   lived] 5 years, [..] months. [In
ἡ κοίμησίς σ[ου]   peace] your sleep.

189. [....]λος γερου-   Apparently not extant.
[σιάρχη]ς καὶ Και [....]   [....] lus, Gerusiarch, and
[....]λος   Cae[....]

190. [....] μαθητὴν κα[....]   Apparently not extant.
σ[.... ε]ὐδίδακτή   [....] pupil and [....] easily
taught.

191. שלום   To [....] who lived 20 years,
♦   2 months, 3 days.
[....] μημένω
[.... δ]ς ἔζησεν
[.... ἔτ]η εἴκοσι μῆ-
[να]ς β' ἡμέρας τρεῖς

192. [....] μήτηρ   Two fragments, with seem to
[.... συ]ναγωγ[....]   be part of one inscription.
[....] ἐν εἰρήνη [....]   [....] mother [....] synagogue
[....] In peace [....]

193. [.... νο]μομαθὴς   [....] student of the Law [....]
[....] ἀμίαντος   without stain, [who lived ...
[....]ἡμέρας ιβ'   years, ... months (?)], 12 days.

[. . . .] αε μιμήσω πάτερ
[. . . .]ν τῶν
♆ scroll cow δικαίων

[. . . .]. *Always (?) will you be
remembered, father, among (?)
the righteous.*
For the interpretation, see
above, p. 125, note 2.

195. [. . . .]ΟΤΗΘ
[. . . .] μήτηρ ἱερο[. . . .]
[. . . . φί]λανδρος ἐν εἰρήνη
[. . . .]

A fragment, not extant. The
only intelligible words are
*mother, lover of her husband, in
peace.*

201. τῶ νομωδ[ιδασκάλω ? . . . .]
μνήμη δικαίο[υ σὺν]
ἐνκωμίω
ἐν ἰρήνη κοίμησίς σο[υ]

To the teacher of the Law [. . . .].
*The memory of the righteous
shall be eulogized. In peace
your sleep.*

202. [. . . . Ἰο]υδέα προσή-
[λυτος . . . .]εος ἐβί-
[ωσε βίον κοι?]νόν
[. . . .]ν ♆

This fragment is now in the
epigraphical museum of San
Sebastiano on the Via Appia.
[. . . .] *Jewess, proselyte,* [. . . .].
*She lived [her life together
with (?) . . .].*

Lines 2, 3: For the formula in my proposed reconstruction,
compare No. 144. Frey, however, interprets line 2 as containing the name *Theosebes.*

203. [. . . .]
φιλόλαος φιλ[έντο ?]-
λος φιλοπένης [ἐν εἰρήνη]
ἡ κοίμησις τοῦ α[. . . .]
τος

[. . . .] *lover of his people, lover
of the Commandments (?), lover
of the poor. [In peace] the sleep
of the* [. . . .].

204. εὐ ♆ λογεί-
α πᾶ σιν

Painted on part of a loculus.
The name of the deceased is
not preserved.
A blessing to all.

206. Cocotia qui et Iu-
da fecit fratri et
concresconio et ♆
conlaboronio meo
Abundantio qui bi-

*Cocotia, also named Juda, set
up (this stone) to his brother,
who grew up with me and worked with me. To Abundantius,
who lived 19 years, in grateful*

xit ann(is) XVIIII beneme-   *memory. In peace his sleep.*
renti iren(e) cubis(is) aut(ou)

Lines 3, 4: *Concresconio* and *conlaboronio* are unexampled nouns (*concresconiae* is found in *CIL* 6. 30467), the former meaning "one who grew up together with," the latter "coworker." Note that the person shifts from third (*fecit*) to first (*meo*). Strangely, Frey takes *Cocotia* as a feminine name, despite the *qui* (which he regards as an error for *quae*) and the surname *Iuda*.

Line 7: The common Greek formula is given in an abbreviated Latin transliteration, with *cubis* for *cymis(is)*.

207. Αγριο Ευαν-   The left portion of the stone, seen by
γελο βενεμε-   Garrucci, is no longer extant. See the
ρεντι Ρηγεινους   photograph of the remaining part in *CII*.
κολαηγα   The text is a Greek transliteration of the
Latin:
Agrio Evangelo benemerenti Reginus collega.
To Agrius Evangelus, in grateful memory. Reginus, his colleague.

208. Ael(ia) Alexandria   Taken from the catacomb and now in the
Ael(iae) Septimae   Jewish Museum, New York.
matri karis-   *Aelia Alexandria set up (this stone) to*
simae bene-   *Aelia Septima, her dearest mother, in*
mer(en)t(i) fecit   *grateful memory.* (Fig. 56).
   ram's ♂
   head

209. *ram's bovine*   *Aurelius Joses,*
head head   *Aurelia Augu-*
Aurel(ius) Ioses   *ria, in grateful*
Aurel(ia) Auguria   *memory, to their*
filio Agathopo   *son, Agathopus,*
b(e)n(e)m(e)r(enti) q(ui) v(ixit) an(nis) XV   *who lived 15*
   years. (Fig. 57)

210. Alexander   Now in Pusey House, Oxford. See the
bubularus de ma-   photograph in Goodenough, III, 765.
cello q(ui) vixit annis   *Alexander, a butcher from the Market,*
XXX anima bona om-   *who lived 30 years, a good soul, friend*

niorum amicus	*of everyone. Your sleep among the*
dormitio tua inter	*righteous.*
dicaeis 𝍦	

Lines 6, 7: *inter dicaeis* is a mixture of Latin and Greek to render the formula μετὰ τῶν δικαίων.

211. [....]thon Ann[....]   Scratched on a loculus.
[....]tasio filio   [*Aga?*]*thon, Ann*[*ia?*] *to* [*Anas?*]*tasius their son.*

The reconstruction of the names is that of Frey.

212. L(ucius) Domitius Abbas   Copied by Garrucci; not
Appidiae Leae   extant.
coniux fec(it)   *Lucius Domitius Abbas to*
et Domitia Feli-   *Appidia Lea. Her husband*
citas filia fec(it)   *set up (this stone) and Domi-*
ae Lea dormitio tua in b[onis]   *tia Felicitas, her daughter, set up (this stone). Ah, Lea, your sleep among the good.*

Line 6: AE is probably an emotional interjection, rather than a garbled abbreviation of *Appidia*, as it is usually taken. At the end of the line Frey prefers *in b*[*ono*], which he renders "dans le bonheur."

213. *basket* Sirica mater *basket*   *Sirica, the mother, to Aster,*
of fruit Asteri filie *of fruit*   *her daughter, in grateful*
venemeren-   *memory.*
ti

214. Aurelia Althea   *Aurelia Althea (nothing is missing)*

215. Σεμπρωνιους Βασει-   Greek transliteration of the
λευς Αυρηλιαι Καιλερειναι   Latin: Sempronius Basileus
κοζουγει βοναι ετ   Aureliae Caelerinae coiugi
δισκειπουλεινα βοναι   bonae et discipulinae bonae
κουν κουα βιξει αννεις XZ   cum qua vixi annis XVII
φηκιτ   fecit coiugi b(ene)m(erenti)
κοζουγει βμ

Sempronius Basileus to Aurelia Celerina, a good wife and good pupil, with whom I lived 17 *years. He set up (this stone) to his wife in grateful memory.*

Line 5: XZ is a mixture of Roman and Greek numerals and obviously represents 17. The scribe rendered Latin X by the same Greek character, but, finding no appropriate Greek transliteration for VII, used the equivalent Greek numeral. Frey, quite impossibly, interprets the numeral as 27, reading the letters as KZ, although the stone clearly shows XZ.

216. Aureliae Flaviae
Ionata archon pas-
es tessimen coiu-
[gi] be[n]em(e)re(n)t(i) fe(cit)

The stone is so imbedded in the wall that the last line, once read by Garrucci, is not visible.

To Aurelia Flavia. Jonathan, Archon of All Dignity, set up (this stone) to his wife in grateful memory.

Lines 2, 3: On *pases tessimen* see above, p. 176, note 2 and p. 177, note 2.

217. Aurelia Protoge-
nia Aur(elie) Quintille
matri karissime
que vixit annis LX
m(ensibus) V b(ene)m(erenti) posuit

ơ 🖋

Now in the Jewish Museum, New York.

Aurelia Protogenia set up (this stone) to Aurelia Quintilla, her dearest mother, who lived 60 years, 5 months; in grateful memory.

218. [. . . . A]urelio [. . . .]
[. . . .]i optim[o . . .]
[. . . . A]ur(elius) Crescen[. . . .]

[. . . .] *to Aurelius* [. . . .], *his excellent [father* or *brother], Aurelius Crescen[s* . . . .] (or *Crescentius* or *Crescentinus*) (Fig. 27).

219. Aurelius Alexan-
der Aureliae Hele-
neti coiugi be(ne)me-
renti fecit

Aurelius Alexander set up (this stone) to Aurelia Helenes, his wife, in grateful memory.

220. Iulia Afrodisia
Aur(elio) Hermiati coiugi
benemerenti fecit et

Not extant. The transcription is Garrucci's.

Julia Afrodisia set up (this stone) to

petit et rogat uti loc(us)   *her husband, Aurelius Hermias, in*
ei reservetur ut cum   *grateful memory, and she begs and*
coiuge suo ponatur   *prays that a place be reserved for her*
quam donec   *that she may be placed with her*
                               husband when the time comes.

221. Castricius   *Castricius, the scribe. Julia, his*
     grammateus   *wife, set up (this stone) to her hus-*
     Iulia coiiux   *band in grateful memory. (Fig. 58)*
     marito suo
     benemerenti
     fecit
     open scroll

222. Mannacius   *Mannacius, to his most sweet sister,*
     sorori Crysidi   *Crysis, a proselyte.*
     dulcissime
     proselyte

223. Daph(n)e   Name scratched twice on a loculus.
     Dafne   *Daphne* and *Dafne.*

224. Iustus   Transcribed by Garrucci; not ex-
     Decenbro   tant.
     fratri suo   *Justus to December, his brother. In*
     en irene ae   *peace your sleep.*
     cymesis su   Lines 4, 5: Transliteration of the
                        Greek formula.

225. Deutero gra-   *To Deuterus, a scribe most sweet, in*
     mateo bene-   *grateful memory.*
     merenti   Line 4: Frey takes *dulcis* as a pro-
     dulcis(simo)   per name, but this is a frequently
     ♂ ♈ *closed*   found abbreviation of the super-
         scroll   lative adjective.

226. Doulcitia   Name scratched on a loculus.
                        Dulcitia.

227. Dulceia   Name scratched on a loculus.
                        Dulceia.

228. hic posita Epar-
chia theose-
bes que [v]i-
xit annos LV
d(ies) VI dorm[i]-
tio tua in b[onis?]

Now in the Terme Museum, No. 72904. Frey does not mention the present location, but offers a photograph in his "Additions," p. 596. *Here lies Eparchia, a god-fearing woman, who lived 55 years, 6 days. Your sleep among the good.*

Line 6: Frey reports De Rossi as claiming to have found the fragment missing at the end with the word *bono*. He therefore reads *in bono* here, as also in No. 212; but cf. No. 250 for the same formula.

229. Esidorus
eterus
en irene qui-
mesis su

Latin transliteration of the Greek Ἰσίδωρος ἑταῖρος ἐν εἰρήνη κοίμησίς σου. *Isidorus, colleague. In peace your sleep.*

Line 2: Frey and others take *eterus* as part of the name, but see above, p. 102, note 5.

230. Eulogie matri dul-
cissime que vixit an-
nis LXXXI Castus fili-
us et Sabinus ne-
pos fecerunt

To Eulogia, most sweet mother, who lived 81 years, Castus, her son, and Sabinus, her grandson, set up (this stone).

231. Eulogi
filio
carimo
Soco nepo-
t(i)

To the son of Eulogius, the dearly beloved Socus, grandson.
Line 1: *Eulogi* is taken by Frey and his predecessors for *Eulogio* (no letter is missing in the stone) and the epitaph is interpreted as being that of two persons. It seems rather to be only that of Socus, set up by his grandfather. Presumably, Socus' father, Eulogius, had died earlier.

232. Afrodisia mater
fecit filio suo
Eutycheti qui
vixit annis XVIIII
ἐν εἰρήνη ἡ κοίμησίς σου

Afrodisia, his mother, set up (this stone) to her son Eutyches, who lived 19 years. In peace your sleep.

233. [Fa?]ustulae
Provinciae
filiae sanctis-
simae

Transcribed by Garrucci; not extant.
*To Faustula (?) Provincia, a most
pure daughter.*

234. Flavia Datiba
Flaviae Caritine<n>
baenemerenti
fecit
cabin?   ♂   ♂   ⟨menorah⟩
              with
              leaves

*Flavia Dativa set up (this stone) to
Flavia Caritina in grateful memory.*
The figure at the left, which resembles a cabin, has not been explained. It may be a *sukkah* seen from
the side, since there appears to be a
crude attempt to show slanting
roof beams.

235. Φλαβιε Βιτα-
λινι κονιου-
γι βενεμερ-
εντι Σοσσια-
νους φηκιτ

Greek transliteration of the Latin:
Flavie Vitalini coniugi benemerenti
Sossianus fecit.
*To Flavia Vitalinis, his wife, in
grateful memory, Sossianus set up
(this stone).*

236. Gaio cog-
iugi bene-
merenti fe-
cit cum fil-
io suo Ant-
onina

*To her husband Gaius in grateful
memory Antonina set up (this stone)
together with her son.*

237. Ch[. . . .] coiugi su-
e fecit Gargilie Eu-
fraxiae que vixit an-
nis XVIIII mensibus III die-
bus XII benemerenti set
sic non merenti

*Ch[. . . .] set up (this stone] to his
wife, Gargilia Eufraxia, who lived
19 years, 3 months, 12 days, well-
deserving, but not deserving this.*
Lines 5, 6: The pathetic word-
play on *benemerenti* cannot be
reproduced by rendering the
expression "in grateful memory," as elsewhere in these inscriptions.

238. Hilarus

Name scratched on a loculus.
Hilarus.

239. Ειουλια Αλε-
ξανδρα φη-

Transcription by Garrucci; not
extant. Greek transliteration of

χι κοιχι σουω   the Latin:
Ειμερω βενεβε-   Iulia Alexandra feci(t) coici suo
ρενδι μουννα   Himero benemerenti munna (?)

Julia Alexandra set up (this stone) to her husband Himerus in grateful memory. Munna (?).

Line 5: The last word has not been interpreted, despite many attempts. It is regrettable that the stone is not available for a check of the reading, since Garrucci was often careless with his transcriptions.

240. Fortunati-
anus et Ius-
ta parentes
Ireneti filiae
suae fecerunt
que vix(it) an(nis) II

Fortunatianus and Justa, the parents, set up (this stone) to Irenes, their daughter, who lived 2 years.

241. Polla fecit
Iuliae filiae
que vixit ann(is) XXXIIII

Polla set up (this stone) to Julia' her daughter, who lived 34 years.

242. [. . . .]ie Sabine coiugi
benemerenti que
vixit annis XVIII
dies III Germanus coi-
ugi benemerenti fecit
cum virginiun sun que
vixit annis III dies III

To his wife [. . . .]ia Sabina in grateful memory, who lived 18 years, 3 days, Germanus set up (this stone) in grateful memory to his wife, who lived with her virgin husband 3 years, 3 days.

243. [. . . .]-
nti incompa-
rabili Tyrisi-
a Profutura fecit

To the incomparable [. . . .] Tyrisia Profutura set up (this stone).

Line 2: Frey reads the first letters as NIE. The tops of the last two are broken off and the last one looks more like an I than a narrow E. Thus the word could be [*archo*]*nti* or the dative of a third-declension name (*e.g.,* Crescenti). Line 4: On Profutura, which may be a participle (= in a spirit of good will?) see above, p. 106, note 2.

244. Iustissima

Name scratched on a loculus.
Justissima.

245. Iusto filio
veneme(re)n-
ti par(e)ntes
fecerunt

*To Justus, their son, his parents
set up (this stone) in grateful
memory.*

246. ♆ Lucin-
us

Painted in red on the reverse of
No. 150. It is now inaccessible,
since it has been imbedded in
the wall.
Lucinus.

247. Valerius archon fecit Lu-
cretiae Faustinae coiu-
gi quae vixit annis
XXIII

Transcribed by Garrucci; not
extant.
*Valerius, the Archon, set up (this
stone) to Lucretia Faustina, his
wife, who lived 23 years.*

248. Μαρχελλους ετ Σουκ[κα?]
παρεντης Μαρκελλ[ε]
φειλιε καρισσιμε φη[κη]-
ρουν(τ) ἐν εἰρήνη ἡ κοίμη[σίς]
σου

Greek transliteration of the Latin, ending with the formula in
Greek: Marcellus et Succa (?)
parentes Marcelle filie carissime
fecerunt.

*Marcellus and Succa (?), her parents, set up (this stone) to
Marcella, their dearest daughter. In peace your sleep.*
Line 1. On the name Succa (?), see above, p. 107, note 3.

249. Μαρκ ♆ ελλαμ
θ

Greek transliteration of the Latin: Marcellam
Marcella.

Why the name is in the accusative is not clear. The meaning of
the θ in the second line is not apparent.

250. Marcia bona Iu-
dea dormi(tio) tu‹au›-
a i(n) bonis
unknown ♆ ⚱
object

*Marcia, a good Jewess. Your sleep
among the just.*
Line 2: At the end of the line is
what appears to be a ligature of
VAV. Apparently the scribe,
when confronted by TIO, follow-

ed by TVA, came out with a confused jumble.

For the unidentified symbol on the left, see the photograph in
CII or in Goodenough, III, 771.

252. Maria Maroni   *Maria set up (this stone) to Maro,*
  coniugi suo et   *her husband, and Justus to his*
  Iustus fecit pa-   *father, who lived [. .] years [. . . .].*
  tri qui vix(it) an(nis)
  [. . . .]

253. Monninus   Name scratched twice on a locu-
  Monninus   lus.
             Monninus

254. Nepia Mar-  ae bixit ann-
  osa qu-   is IIII

  The child Marosa, who lived 4 years.
  Line 1: *Nepia* is a transliteration of νηπία.

255. [. . . .] εἰρήνη   Scratched on a loculus.
  nepos Iud[. . . .]   [. . . .] *peace. Grandson Jud[as?]*
            or *of Jud[as?].*

256. Nikete proselyto   *To Nicetas, a proselyte worthy and*
  digno et benemerenti *well-deserving, his patroness Dio-*
  Dionysias patrona fecit *nysias set up (this stone).*

257. Ουλπια Μα-   Greek transliteration of the La-
  ρεινα κουαι   tin:
  βιξιτ αννεις   Ulpia Marina quae vixit annis
  κβ' βενεμερ-   XXII benemeraenti fecit.
  αιντι φηκιτ   *Ulpia Marina, who lived 22 years.*
    C   (. . . .) *set up (this stone) in*
            grateful memory.

The name or relationship of the dedicant was not placed on the
stone because of the lack of space. An irregular, second-hand
slab of marble was used (as often), and the C at the bottom
was already there when the inscription was carved. A glance
at the photograph in *CII* will reveal that the last line had to be
inscribed in smaller letters in order to get it in above the C.
Frey comments on the confused syntax, which seems to make
the dative *benemeraenti (sic)* agree with a nominative, but the
Latin should be construed with a full pause after the numeral,
starting a new sentence with *benemeraenti.*

258. Plane

Name scratched on a loculus.
Plane.

259. Pompeius Ionata
Pompeio Eutych-
eti filio qui
vixit ann(is) III
et m(ensibus) V

Transcribed by De Rossi; apparently not extant.
*Pompeius Jonathan to Pompeius
Eutyches, his son, who lived
3 years and 5 months.*

260. Aellia benemere-
nti Procle posueru-
(n)t Al- *flask* mas posuit
bixit 🕎 annis
LXXXII ⚱ mesis X

*Aellia in grateful memory set up
(this stone) to Procla. Almas set
it up. She lived 82 years, 10
months.*

Lines 2, 3: It seems that after
writing the plural verb *posueru(n)t*, the scribe, a careless
worker, as is evident from the irregular size and shape of the
letters, noticed that he had left out one of the two subjects
and so he inserted the second name with a new verb, *posuit.*
Line 3: Above the letters AL is a character like a U, which
Frey regards as part of the name, carelessly omitted by the
scribe and inserted afterward. He therefore reads the name
as *Alumas.*

261. RHBEKA
[. . .]EKA

Name scratched twice on a
loculus.
Rebeca.

Line 1: According to Frey's transcription the second letter is
Greek H. In his first publication of this graffito (*RAC* 10 [1933],
36) the first letter is given as Greek P, but in *CII* he prints it as
Latin R. Not having found this inscription, I do not know
which is correct.

262. Rufilla Pietas quae fecit
cum Celerinum a[nnos]
EV t(?)[res?] menses quattuor ODE
[e]t dies quindecem en hire-
[n]e e cymesis autoes

Painted on the reverse
of the marble slab on
which No. 95 is carved.
It is now at the Terme
Museum, but not visi-
ble because imbedded
in the wall. In 1922, however, I saw it, composed of some
twenty-five fragments, and copied it. At that time some
parts which had been copied by Garrucci were already
missing.What I copied was as follows:

RVFILLA I.....SQV
CVMCELERINVM.....
EV ....MENSESQVA....
.TDIESQVINDECE....IR
EECYMESISAVTO...

In line 3 the letters EV ODE were in the wings of the *tabula ansata* which enclosed the inscription. Only the part on the left was visible when I saw it.

Rufilla Pietas, who lived with Celerinus 3(?) *years, 4 months, 15 days in peace her sleep. Euode* (= εὐόδει, *be prosperous?*).

263. Γαιους Σαβα-   Greek transliteration of the Latin:
     τιο φιλιο φη-   Gaius Sabatio filio fecit.
     κιτ   *Gaius set up (this stone) to Sabatius, his son.*

264. Σεβηρε μα-   Greek transliteration of the Latin:
     τρι δουλκισ-   Severe matri dulcisime Severus filius. (Greek
     ειμε Σεβηρο-   formula). *To Severa, his most sweet mother,*
     υς φιλιους   *Severus, her son. In peace your sleep.*
     ἐν εἰρήνη κοί-
     μησίς σου
     bird

265. Stafylo archonti   The text is that of Garrucci, correct-
     et archisynagogo   ed by N. Müller (in MB, p. 47);
     honoribus omnibus   present location, if extant, unknown.
     fuctus Restituta coniux *To Stafylus, Archon and Archisynago-*
     benemerenti fecit   *gus, who held all honors, Restituta,*
     ἐν εἰρήνη ἡ κοίμησίς σου *his wife, set up (this stone) in grateful*
                             memory. In peace your sleep.

Line 4: If the reading is correct (MB, p. 4 has *factus*), *fuctus* is for *functus*, which should actually be in the dative, agreeing with *Stafylo*.

266. Αιλια Πατρι-   Greek transliteration of the Latin:
     κια Τουλλιο   Aelia Patricia Tullio Irenaeo coniugi
     Ειρηναιο κονιο-   benemerenti fecit diabio.
     υγι βενεμερεντ-   *Aelia Patricia set up (this stone) to*
     ι φηκιτ διαβιο   *Tullius Irenaeus, Life Archon.*

Line 5: The last word represents the title διὰ βίου, on which see above, p. 174.

267. Valerius et Si-
    monis Vale-
    riae filiae
    dulcissime
    que vix(it) ann(is) V
    mes(ibus) X die(bus) IIII

Transcription by Garrucci; not extant.
Valerius and Simonis to Valeria, their
very sweet daughter, who lived 5 years,
10 months, 4 days.

268. Βενε ρωσα
    ανρων   XVII
    εκου μαρι τους
    μησις   XV

Transcription by Garrucci; not ex-
tant. Greek transliteration of the
Latin: Venerosa anron (= annorum)
XVII e(t) cu(m) maritus mesis XV.
Venerosa, aged 17 years, and with her
husband 15 months.

269. Ζαβουττα-
    τι φιλιο αρχ-
    οντι Ζαβουτ-
    τας

Greek transcription of the Latin:
Zabuttati filio archonti Zabuttas.
Zabuttas to his son, Zabuttas, the
Archon. (Fig. 59).

270. [. . . .]
    marito bene-
    merenti feci

To [. . . .] *my husband, in grateful*
memory, I set up (this stone).

271. VII Idu(s) Ma[. . . .]
    pater et arc-
    con   Ω

        M

A fragment (Fig. 27)
Seventh day before the Ides of [March
or May], father and Archon.
Lines 3, 4: What words the Ω (of
which only the left stroke is preserved) and the Greek M introduced
cannot be guessed.

273. [. . . .]e infan-
    [ti dul]cissime
    [. . . .]us et Vi-
    [. . . .]s amato
    [parent?]es fecrut

To [. . . .]*a, a very sweet child,* [. . . .]*us*
and Vi[. . . .]*s, her loving parents (?),*
set up (this stone).
Line 4: since *amato* cannot agree with
the feminine dative, it may be part
of the word *amatores*, but the word
is not found elsewhere in these inscriptions. Line 5: *fecrut* is
for *fecerunt.*

276. [. . . .]tie [. . . .]
    bent[. . . .]
    vixit [. . . .]

A fragment, as transcribed by Garrucci; not extant.
[. . . .] *lived* [. . . .] *3 days* [. . . .] *to his*

dies tr[es. . . . coi]-   *wife in grateful memory, [who] lived*
ugi b[enemerenti . . . .]   *with her husband [. . . .] years.*
cum viro [. . . .]
vixit an[nos . . . .]

Numbers 277-81 are from the small catacomb of Vigna Cimarra. Copied by De Rossi and first published by Berliner
(*Geschichte der Juden in Rom*, I, 90-92), they have, with the
exception of 277, perished with the catacomb.

277. Ζωναθα   Carved on the front of a sarcophagus; now at
ἄρχων   the Pontificio Istituto di Archeologia Cristiana
ἐνθάδε   in Rome.
χεῖθε ἐ-   *Jonathan the Archon lies here, aged 19 years.*
θῶν XVIIII   *In peace (his) sleep.*
ἐν εἰρήνη
κοίμησην

278. [Κρ]εσκεντινα [. . . .]τ[. . . .]   The only intelligible words are the
ων κα[. . . .]οιμ[. . . .]ν   name *Crescentina* and perhaps
[ἐβ?]ιωσ[εν?] εν κε[. . . .]   *lived 25 years.*

279. ἐνθ[ά]δ[ε]   *Here lies [. . . .], scribe-to-be, who lived [. .]*
κεῖτε [. . . .]   *years.*
μελλο[γραμμ]-   Line 6: It might be surmised that the Π
ατεὺς ὁ[ς ἔζησε]-   is a numeral representing the age of the
ν ἔτησι [. . . .]   deceased, but 80 years would hardly be a
π   plausible age for a scribe-to-be. Frey
          thinks that the Σ I at the end of line 5 is
          for θι' and would = 19, but why a
          reversed numeral?

280. [. . . .]σι[. . . .]α   [. . . .] *lies here.*
ἐνθάδε κεῖτε

281. [. . . .]   A fragment of this inscription is said
συνα[γωγ]ῆς 'Ελέ-   to have been at Della Querce, a
ας ἔζησεν ἔτη   Barnabite College in Florence.
π'   [. . . .] *of the Synagogue of Elea, lived*
καλῶ ς κοιμοῦ   *80 years. Sleep well among the just.*
μετὰ τῶν δικέ-
ων

282. [. . . .]   A marble fragment now at Palazzo
[. . . .] καὶ ᾿Ισαακ [. . . .]   Corsetti in Rome (Via di Monser-
[. . . . ἀρχισυν]άγωγος [. . . .]   rato, 20), imbedded in the wall of
[. . . .] συναγωγῆ[ς . . . .]   the staircase on the second floor.
[. . . .] ἐπλήρωσ[εν ἔτη . . . .]   [. . . .] and Isaac [. . . .] Archisynagogus of the Synagogue [. . . .]. He
completed [. .] years.

Line 2: Frey thinks ὁ preceded καὶ and makes Isaac a surname
or signum.

283. ἐνθάδε κεῖ-   On a sarcophagus cover, found on the Via
ται Φαυστινα   Appia in 1732 outside the Porta San
שלום   Sebastiano and now in the Terme Museum,
No. 67613. The cover is adorned with
three masks (Frey says wrongly that only
two are left; but see Fig. 46). The inscription probably
came from the Monteverde catacomb. The masks are no
indication that the deceased was an actress, as is often
asserted; see above, p. 234, note 1.
Here lies Faustina. Peace.

284. Marcus Cvynt-   Known since early in the eighteenth cen-
us Alexus gra-   tury and copied by various scholars. It
mmateus ego t-   seems to have been found in the area of
on Augustesio-   the Praetextatus Catacomb on the Via
n mellarcon   Appia Pignatelli and was at one time in
eccion Augustesion   the portico of S. Maria in Trastevere, but
an(norum) XII   it is apparently no longer extant. The
transcriptions vary in minor details.
Marcus Cvyntus (= Quintus) Alexus,
scribe of the Augustesians, Archon-to-be of the Augustesians,
aged 12 years.

Lines 3, 4: ego ton is apparently for ἐκ τῶν, as also eccion in
line 6.

286. Προζέκτω υἱῶ Χρυσαε [καὶ . . . .]-   Found on the Via Ar-
ικη γονεῖς ἐποίησαν [ζήσαν]-   deatina near the Cata-
τι ἔτη δέκα μῆνες γ' ἡμ[έρας . . . .]   comb of Domitilla; now
ἐν εἰρήνη ἡ κο[ίμησις αὐτοῦ]   in the Sala Giudaica of
the Lateran Museum.

To Projectus, their son, Chrysas and [. . . .]ice, his parents, set *up (this stone]. He lived* 10 *years,* 3 *months,* [. .] *days. In peace [his] sleep.*

Line 1: XPYCAE is most probably for XPYCAC, the writing of E for C being a common slip.

Line 3: The stone has ΔCKA for ΔEKA. It is strange that so obvious and frequent an error should have confused Frey, who reads the boy's years as four by rejecting the C and adding I to KA, making it KAI and assuming a non-existent ligature.

289. 'Ιάσων A small marble slab found 1880 in the Tiber near the
δὶς Palazzo Farnesina. Its present location, if it is extant,
ἄρχων is not recorded.

Jason, twice Archon.

Numbers 290-489 are, except as noted, from the Monteverde catacomb. Unless otherwise stated, they are carved on marble and are now in the Sala Giudaica of the Lateran Museum. Illustrations of nearly all these inscriptions are to be found not only in *CII* but also in MB. Our illustrations show many of these on the walls of the Sala Giudaica. Many of those bearing symbols are illustrated in Goodenough, III.

290. אניה חתנה The interpretation of this Aramaic inscription
דבר כולברוה is widely disputed and uncertain. See the references and interpretations in *CII*. The first word may be a name, perhaps *Annias*. The second word is possibly חַתְנָה = son-in-law. Thus the inscription may mean:

Annias, son-in-law of Bar-Colbruah (or *Calabria?*). (Fig. 39. 21)

291. [. . . .] אסודרה ברת Aramaic and Greek.
['Ισ]ιδώρα θυγά- *Isidora, daughter of the Archon of the*
[τηρ] ἄρχ(οντος) Ἑρβέων *Hebrews.* (Fig. 39. 16)

292. שלו[ם] Painted on a fragment of tile; in a case of the Sala Giudaica.
Peace.

293. שאל שלום על Painted on a tile bearing a brick stamp (text in *CII*, p. 221, no. 111); in a case of the Sala Giudaica.
Peace on Israel.

The letters שאל (none are lost) are apparently intended for
ישראל.

296. ἔνθα χῖτε 'Αμμι-   Now in the Conservatori Museum, No. 41.
ἀς 'Ιουδέα ἀπὸ   There is a cast in the Sala Giudaica.
Λαδικίας ἥτις   (Fig. 32. 7)
ἔζησεν ἔτη   ♆   *Here lies Ammias, a Jewess from Laodicea,*
πε' ש לם   ⚓   *who lived 85 years. Peace.*

Line 5: The Hebrew characters are identified as שלם by
Chwolson, who calls them Nabatean in form (*Corp. Insc. Hebr.*,
147).

297. [νήπι?]ον 'Αμμι-   *Here[lies . . . .] the child(?) Ammi[as?].*
[. . . .ε]νθάδε

298. ♆   Now in the Terme Museum, No. 77652.
ὁσία 'Αναστασία   *Pious Anastasia lies here.*
ἐνθάδε κεῖται

299. ⊘ ἐνθάδε basket   *Here lies Aninius Sabinianus. Fla-*
κεῖτε 'Ανι- with grapes(?)   *via Flaviana set up (this stone) to her*
νιος Σαβινι-   *own husband, who lived with me*
ανος ἐποί-   *6 years, 10 months.*
ησεν Φλαβια
Φλαβιάνη τῶ
ἰδίω συμβίω
ὅστις ἔζησεν
μεθ' ἐ-
μοῦ ἔτη ϛ'
μῆν(ας)ι'

300. two lamps facing   *Here lies Annia. Her husband set up*
ἐνθάδε κ-   *(this stone).*
εῖτε 'Αννι-
α ἐποίησε-
ν σύμβιος

301. ἐνθάδε χῖτε 'Αννις   *Here lies Annius, the Gerusiarch of*
γερουσάρχης συναγω-   *the Synagogue of the Augustesians.*
γῆς 'Αγουστεσίων ἐν   *In peace his sleep.*
εἰρήνη ἡ κοίμισις
αὐτοῦ

302. [....] [.... *wife of ....]lius Anteros, aged 22 years.*
λιου 'Αντέ- *She lived with me 5 years, 9 months, 25 days.*
ρωτος ἐτ- Frey, following Bees, regards the epitaph as
ῶν κβ' ἔζη- being that of Anteros himself. It is clearly
σε μεθ' ἐμ- that of his wife, as can be seen from the geni-
οῦ ἔτη ε' μῆ- tive of the masculine name.
νας θ' ἡμέρ-
ας κε'

303. [ἐνθ]άδε κεῖται *Here lies [....]nia Anti-*
[....]νια 'Αντιπα- *pa[....], aged 2 years, 4*
[.... ἐτῶ]ν β' μῆν(ῶν) δ' *months, [..] days. Be of*
ἡμ[ερῶν]....] εὐψύχι εὐφρόνι *good spirit, be of good cheer.*
The child's name may
have been Antonia (or Junia) Antipatra.

304. ἐνθάδε κεῖτε 'Απερ ἄρχων The photograph in
Καλκαρ[ησ]ίων ἐν ἰρήνη ἡ κύ- MB (p. 97) is more
μησις [.... υἱ?]ῶ [ἐποί]ησε 'Ιουλειο- complete than
that in *CII*, which
lacks the menorah
at the left.

Here lies Aper, Archon of the Calcaresians. In peace [his] sleep.
Julius set up (this stone) to his son (?).

305. ἐνθάδε κεῖντε *Here lie the children Asterius and Nume-*
'Αστέρις καὶ Νου- *nius (Fig. 39. 6)*
μήνις νήπια

306. 'Αστήρ *bird pecking* *Aster.*
bird tree bird *at bunch* *(Fig. 33. 71)*
of grapes

307. ἐνθάδε κ[εῖ]- Not extant; the text goes back to Marangoni
τε Αὐρηλια in the eighteenth century.
Ζοτικὴ επο(?) *Here lies Aurelia Zotice, aged 70 years(?).*
Φροντων ἔγγο- *Fronto, her grandson, set up (this stone). In*
νος ἐποίησεν *peace her sleep.*
ἐν εἰρήνη ἡ κοί- Line 3: ΕΠΟ is probably either a stone-
μησις αὐτῆς cutter's slip or the copyist's error for ΕΤΟ =
ἐτ(ῶν) ο' = 70 years. Scholars have gene-
rally combined it with the following to

produce the strange name Epophronton; see above, page 97, note 4.

308. ἐνθάδε κ-
εῖτε Βαδιζ
κωπατων
σαταθοπω
σρωτωτω
ερωρωτωι
ωρ 🕎 υι

Some of the scrawled letters are dubious and the text, except for the first two words, is unintelligible.
Here lies Badiz (?).....

309. [ἐνθάδ]ε κεῖτε
[....Β?]αλσαμια
[ἐνιαύσ?]ιος καὶ μ-
[νῶν] ἐννέα

Here lies [....] *Balsamia*(?), *aged one year* (?) *and 9 months.*
Line 2: On the question of the name, see above, p. 104, note 5.

310. ἐνθάδε κῖτε θυ-
γάτηρ Κυρύλλα
Βαλεντιανω
γυνὴ 'Αννιά-
νου

Here lies the daughter of Cyrillas, Valentiano, wife of Annianus. (Fig. 39. 11)

311. Βαριη Ζωτικὴ
μητρὶ
ἥτις ἔζησεν
ἔτη κϛ' ἡμέρ(ας) ζ'
υἱοὶ αὐτῆς ἐποίησ-
αν

At the Lateran; the number (omitted by Frey) is 94. (Fig. 36. 94).
To Varia Zotice, their mother, who lived 26 years, 7 days, her sons set up (this stone).

312. Βικτ-
ωρα
🕎 🪔

Supposedly in the National Museum of Naples, but could not be located in 1951.
Victor (?)
The reading of line 2 is uncertain; a portion appears to be missing at the left.

313. Βικτω[....]

Painted on a tile; in a case of the Sala Giudaica.
Victor.

314. [ἐ]νθάδε κεῖτι Γαυδεν-
[τ]ια θυγάτηρ 'Οκλατίου
[ἐ]τῶν δέκα ἐννέα (ἐ)ποί-
ησεν αὐτῇ ἀνὶρ αὐτῆς
ἐν ἠρήνη κύμισις αὐ-

Apparently lost soon after its discovery by Paribeni in 1919.
Here lies Gaudentia, daughter of Oclatius, aged 19 years. Her

τῆς θάρσ(ει) οὐδὶς (ἀ)θάνατος

husband set up (this stone) to her. In peace her sleep. Be of good courage; nobody is immortal.

315. ἐνθάδε κῖτε 🕎 Ark of
Γαυδεντια the Law
ἱέρισα ἐτῶν κδ'
ἐν ἰρήνη ἡ
κοίμησις αὐ-
τῆς

Here lies Gaudentia, the priestess, aged 24 years. In peace her sleep.
Line 3: On ἱέρισα see above, p. 193. (Fig. 39. 17)

316. ἐνθάδε κ[ῖτε Γα]υδεν-
τις Καλκ[α]ρήσων
δὶς ἀρχ(ων) [ἐ]ν εἰ[ρή]νη

One of the four fragments visible in the photograph offered by MB (p. 98) is now missing. For what is left, see CII.

Here lies Gaudentius, twice Archon of the Calcaresians. In peace.

317. ἐνθάδε κεῖτε
Γελάσις ἐξάρχων
τῶν Ἑβρέων ἐν εἰ-
ρήνη ἡ κοίμησις
αὐ 🕎 το 🏺 ῦ

Here lies Gelasius, Exarchon of the Hebrews. In peace his sleep. (Fig. 39. 18)

318. 🕎 ᴑ 🏺 🌿 🕎
Δωνατος
γραμματεὺς
συνγωγη
Βερνακλωρω

Donatus, scribe of the Synagogue of the Vernaclians.
Line 4. Βερνακλωρω is for Vernaclorum.

319. ἐνθάδε κῖτε Εἰρήνα
παρθενικὴ σύμβιος
Κλωδίου ἀδελφὸς
Κούντου Κλαυδίου
Συνεσίου πατρὸς
συναγωγῆς Καμπη-
σίων Ρώμης שלום

Now in the Lapidary Museum of the monastery at St. Paul's on the Via Ostiense. There is no evidence that it came from the Monteverde catacomb.
Here lies Irene, virgin wife of Clodius, brother of Quintus Claudius Synesius, Father of the Synagogue of the Campesians of Rome. Peace.

Line 2: On παρθενικὴ σύμβιος see above, p. 130.

Line 3: ἀδελφός should be in the genitive, unless it is an error for ἀδελφή (= sister), but the former seems more likely in view of the names.

320. ἐνθάδε κεῖ-
τε Εἰρήνη
παρτένο-
ς

The marble slab is inscribed on both sides, the reverse being No. 362.
Here lies Irene, a virgin.

321. ἐνθάδε κε[ῖτε Λα]-
ζαρ ὅσιος δί[καιος]
φιλότεκνος φι[λαδελ]-
φῶν φιλοσυνά[γωγος]
ἐτῶν λα' ἐν [εἰρήνη]
ἡ κοίμισις αὐτ[οῦ]
〽

At the Terme Museum, No. 77650.
Here lies Lazar, pious, just, lover of his children, lover of his brothers, lover of his synagogue, aged 31 years. In peace his sleep.
Lines 1, 2: Frey prefers *Eleazar* for the name, but the space in line 1 will permit only about five letters in all.

322. ἐνθάδε κεῖτε Ἑλλῆς υἱὸς Ἀγριπ-
πείνου ἐτῶν κγ' ἐν εἰρήνη
ἡ κοίμησις αὐτοῦ

Here lies Helles, son of Agrippinus, aged 23 years. In peace his sleep. (Fig. 37. 76)

323. ἐν(θ)άδε κεῖτε <ε>
Ἐπιγενιους ἐν εἰ-
ρήνη ἡ κοίμισις
αὐτοῦ 〽

Here lies Epigenius. In peace his sleep. (Fig. 36. 92)

324. Ἑρμογένης ἄρχων
πάσης τιμῆς ἐν-
θάδε κεῖται

Hermogenes, Archon of All Dignity, lies here.

325. ἐνθάδε
κεῖτε Ἐτη-
τὸς μελλά(ρ)-
χων ἐν εἰρή-
νη ἡ κοίμη-
σις αὐτοῦ
〽

Here lies Etetus (= Aetetus), archon-to-be. In peace his sleep. (Fig. 36. 93)

326. ἐνθάδε κεῖτε
Εὐγενία νή-
πιος

Here lies Eugenia, a child.

327. 〽 εὐλογία 〽 Supposedly in the National Museum
of Naples (see on No. 312).
ark with six scrolls *Eulogia.*

Some scholars hold that εὐλογία is not a proper name here, but
= *benediction.* Eulogia is, however, found as a feminine name
in two others of these inscriptions (230, 328) and the masculine
Eulogius also occurs twice (112, 231). Still, it is not impossible
that the portion of the stone bearing the name of the deceased
is missing.

328. ἐνθάδε κῖτε   *Here lies Eulogia. In peace her sleep.*
Εὐλογία   Line 4: The letters are so poorly executed
ἐν ε(ἰ)ρή(νη) ἡ κ-   that the identity of some of them is
ύμισις α(ὐ)τῆ-   uncertain.
ς

329. ἐνθάδε κῖτε   *Here lies Eupore with your son Sabbatius,*
Εὐπόρι μετὰ   Line 2: On the name see above, p. 102,
τοῦ υἱοῦ σου   note 3.
Σαββατίου 〽

330.   ἐνθάδε κ-   *Here lies Eusebia, a tot one year old.*
bird εῖται Εὐσε- *bird*
βία μικκὴ   The birds, painted on the marble, are
ἐνιαυτοῦ   now hardly visible. (Fig. 39. 5)

331. 〽   〽   Painted on a loculus, now destroyed;
photograph in MB, p. 29, and
Goodenough, III, 78.
ἐντάδ *am-*   ε κεῖ- *Here lies Eusebius, a child of 5 (years).*
phora   τε
Εὐσέβιος
am- νήπιος
phora ε'

332. ἐνθάδε κε[ῖται]   In the Terme Museum, No. 77646.
Εὐσέβις ἄ[ρχων ?]   *Here lies Eusebius, [Archon ?],*
ἐτῶν κγ' ἐ[ν εἰρήνη τὴν]   *aged 23 years. In [peace] his sleep.*
κόμησιν αὐτοῦ
〽

333. ἐνθάδε κεῖ-
τε ὁ Εὐσέβι-
ς ὁ διδάσκα-
λος νομο-
μαθὴς συν
τῆ συμβίου αὐ-
τοῦ εἰρήνη ἡ

Here lies Eusebius, the teacher, student of the Law, with his wife. Peace .... Line 6: The dative of the article is carelessly followed by the genitive of the noun. Line 7: There was no room left on the stone for the complete formula.

334. ἐνθάδε κεῖται
Εὐτυχεὶς θυ-
γάτηρ Φιλίπ-
που ᶲ

Here lies Eutychis, daughter of Philippus. In peace her sleep. (Fig. 39. 9) Lines 5, 6: Painted on the stone with smaller letters.

ἐν εἰρήνη ἡ κοί-
μησις αὐτῖς

335. [ἐνθάδε κ]εῖτε Εὐφράσεις
ἐτῶν γ' μηνῶν ι'
θάρει Εὐφράσει   ᶲ
οὐδεὶς ἀθ[ά]νατος

Here lies Euphrasius, aged 3 years, 10 months. Be of good courage; no one is immortal. (Fig. 33. 77)

336. ἐνθάδε κεῖ-   ᶲ
τε Εὐφράσις
ἀρχισυναγώ-
γης ὁ κα[λῶς βιώσας?]

Here lies Euphrasius, Archisynagogus, who [lived a good life?].

337. οἶκος αἰώνιος ˙   *ark with*
ἐνθάδε κεῖτε Εὐ-   *four scrolls*
ψυχος δὶς ἀρχ(ων) ἀρχ(ων) π-
άσης τειμῆς καὶ φροντισ-
τής ἐν εἰρήνη κοίμησ-
ις αὐτοῦ ἐτῶν νε'

In the Terme Museum, No. 77642. *Eternal home. Here lies Eupsychus, twice Archon, Archon of All Dignity, and Phrontistes. In peace his sleep; aged 55 years.*

338. ἐν[θάδε κεῖ]τε
Ζωτ[ικὸς? ἄρ]χων
Αὐγ[ουστησίων] ἐν εἰρή-
[. . . .]

In the Terme, Museum, No. 77647. *Here lies Zoticus (?), Archon of the Augustesians. In peace [his sleep].*

339. Φηλικισ-
σιμα 'Η-
μαράν-
τω ἐ-
ποίησεν

Felicissima set up (this stone) to Emarantus (= Amarantus).

340. ἐνθάδε κῖ-
τε 'Ιακωβ
μετὰ τῶν
ὁσίων ἡ κύ-
μησις 〽
ὑτιοῦ ⚉

Here lies Jacob. With the pious his sleep. (Fig. 36. 106) Line 6: υτιου is a garbled form of αὐτοῦ.

341. [. . . .]σα 'Ιασω

Painted on a child's loculus, now destroyed.
[. . . .] *Iaso.*

342. ἐνθάδε κεῖ-
τε 'Ιλαρὰ νήπι-
ος

A portion of the stone, which is shown complete in MB, p. 104, is now lost.
Here lies Hilara, a child.

343. ἐνθάδε κῖτε 'Ιλαρὸς
ἄρχων ἀπὸ συναγωγ-
ῆς Βολυμνησίων
ζήσας ἔτη λε' ἐν ἰ-
ρήνη ἡ κοίμησις
αὐτοῦ μνί(α) αὐτοῦ

↝ ⚘ *ark with flask*
nine
two matzot (?) *scrolls*

In the Terme Museum, No. 77645.
Here lies Hilarus, Archon from the Synagogue of the Volumnesians, who lived 35 years. In peace his sleep. His memory (for a blessing?).

344. ἐνθάδε κεῖτ-
ε 'Ιου

An unfinished inscription. On the reverse is No. 30*.
Here lies Ju. . . .

345. 'Ιουδας 'Ι[. . . .]-
ου ἔγγονο[ς . . . .]
πατ[. . . .]

In the Terme Museum, No. 77656. The right half of the stone is lost.
Judas, grandson of I [. . . .], father [. . . .].

346. ἐνθάδε κῖτε
'Ιουδας ἱερε-
ούς 〽
♁ ⚉ ∅

Here lies Judas, the priest. (Fig. 60)

347. ἐνθάδε
κεῖνται
'Ιουδας καὶ

Here lie Judas and Joses, archons and priests and brothers.

Ἰωσῆς ἄρ-
χοντες
καὶ ἱερεῖς
καὶ ἀδελφοί

348. ☖ 🕎 *branch bird*   Ἰουδας   *tree   bird* 🕎
                        μηνῶν ζ'   *bird   vase* ☖
                        ἐνθάδε κεῖτε

Judas, aged 7 months, lies here. (Fig. 36. 118)

349. ἐνθάδε κῖτεν Ἰουδας   In the Lapidary Museum of the monas-
     νίπιους ἐν εἰρνε κύμυ-   tery at St. Paul's on the Via Ostiense.
     σες αὸτοῦ   *Here lies Judas, a child. In peace his*
                              sleep. Israel.
     אל 🕎 ישר

350. Ἰουδας [. . . .]   In the Terme Museum, No. 77656.
     ουσττον [. . . .]   Only the name *Judas* can be derived
     πατ[. . . .]   from this fragment.

351. 🕎 ἐνθάδε κεῖ-   🕎   In the Lapidary Museum of the
     ☖   τε Ἰουδας γρα- ☖   monastery of St. Paul's (Fig.
     🌿 μ(ματ)εὺς ἐτῶ-   61)
         ν ν' ἐν εἰρήν-   *Here lies Judas, the scribe, aged*
     ☖   η κώμισι   *50 years. In peace (his sleep).*
                              Line 5: There was no room left
                              for the rest of the formula.

352. ἐνθάδε κῖ-   *Here lies Julia Severa.* (Fig. 39. 24)
     τε Ἰουλια
     Σεβηρα

353. Ἰουλιανος   *Julianus, Gerusiarch, lies here. He*
     γερουσιάρχης   *lived on good terms with everybody.*
     ἐνθάδε κεῖται   (Fig. 33, top right)
     καλῶς βιώσας
     μετὰ πάντων

354. Ἰουλιανος   *Julianus, a Hebrew.* (Fig. 37. 74)
     Ἑβρεος

355. [ἐνθ]άδε κῖτε Ἰ[. . . .]   The stone of this fragmentary in-
     [. . . .]ος ἱερεύ[ς. . . .] scription is so badly weathered that

[. . . .]καν ἐν [. . . .]

[. . . .]ιην

some of the letters cannot be made out with certainty. Minium has been applied carelessly so that the photograph is misleading.
Here lies I [. . . .]us, priest [. . . .].

356. 'Ιουλια-
νος ἐν-
θάδε κε-
ῖται ζή-
σας ἔτη
δ'   branch

Julianus lies here. He lived 4 years.

357. ὧδε κεῖται 'Ιου-
νιος 'Ιουστος

Here lies Junius Justus.

358. Θεόδο-   εἴτε σε 'Ιουστε τέκνον ἐδυνάμην σα-   κὺς
τος τρο-   ρῶ χρυσέω θεῖναι θεψάμενος νῦν δέσ-   τῶ τ-
φεὺς τέ-   ποτα ἐν εἰρήνη κόμησιν αὐτοῦ 'Ιουστον   ροφε(ῖ)
κνω γλ-   νήπιον ἀσύκριτον ἐν δικαιώματί σου   ών
υκυτ[ά]-   [ἐ]νθάδε κεῖμε 'Ιουστος ἐτῶν δ' μηνῶν η' γλυ-
τ[ω]

The part at the extreme right is a continuation of the text, since the stone left no room for any additional lines. The part at the left should be read last, since the scribe, after using up the right margin, filled in the left margin also, leaving no spaces between this addition and the rest of the text. See Ferrua, *Epigraphica* 3 (1941), 36 f. The main text is addressed first to Justus, then to God, and is followed by words supposedly spoken by the deceased child himself. The usual dedication (at the left) ends the inscription.

Would that I, who reared you, Justus, my child, were able to place you in a golden coffin. Now, O Lord, (vouchsafe) in thy righteous judgment that Justus, a peerless child, may sleep in peace. Here I lie, Justus, aged 4 years, 8 months, sweet to my foster father. Theodotus, the foster father, to his most sweet child.

Lines 1, 2: σαρω is for σορῷ; θεψαμενος seems to be for θρεψάμενος rather than θαψάμενος, as Frey preferred.

Line 3: The syntax is confused, since the verb is omitted and κομησιν is used in place of an infinitive. If κομησιν was intended as the object of the unexpressed verb, then Ἰουστον and its modifiers should have been in the dative.

Line 4: Ferrua (*Civ. Catt.* 1936, IV, 299) interprets this as meaning "a child incomparable in Thy Law," but δικαίωμα could hardly bear the meaning of νόμος, which is regularly used of the Divine Law (Torah).

359. ἐνθάδε κεῖτε   *Here lies Justus, a child, He lived 5 years.*
    Ἰουστος νήπ-   *In peace your sleep.*
    ιος ἔζησεν ἐτ-   Line 5: The minium has been applied
    ῶν ε' ἐν ἰρήνη ἡ   incorrectly, so that the stone appears to
    κοίμισίς σου   read ΚΟΝΩΣΙΣ.

360. ἐνθάδε κ[εῖται]   *Here lies [. . . .]*
    [. . . .]ναίου
    [. . . .]

361. ἐνθάδε κεῖντε Ἰστασία γυνὴ   *Here lie Istasia, wife of*
    Ἀμαβιλίου ἐτῶν ξ' καὶ Πριμα   *Amabilius, aged 60 years,*
    θυγάτηρ Φλαβίας ἐτῶν   *and Prima, daughter of*
    ε' ἐν ἰρήνη ἡ κοίμισις   *Flavia, aged 5 years. In*
    αὐτῆς καὶ τῆς Πρίμας   *peace her sleep and Pri-*
    matzoh (?)   *ma's (Fig. 36. 107).*
    scroll

362. Ἰώνιος   This inscription is on the reverse of
    ὁ κὲ Ἀκονε   the stone bearing No. 320. (Fig.
    Σεφωρη-   39. 23)
    νός   *Ionius, also named Acone, of Sep-*
    phoris.

Line 2: On this name see above, p. 118, note 3.

363. ἐνθάδε κεῖτε Καιλια   *Here lies Caelia Euhodus, pious, just,*
    Εὐοδους ὁσία δεικέα   *lover of her children, lover of her*
    φιλόταικνος φιλαδε-   *brothers. In peace her sleep. (Fig.*
    λφῶν αἰν εἰρήνη<ς>   *39. 26)*
    ἡ κοίμησις αὐτῆς

364. ἐνθάδε κεῖται   *Here lies Caelius Anastasius, a child. In*
    Καιλιος Ἀνασ-   *peace your sleep.*
    τάσις νήπιος
    ἐν εἰρήνη ἡ κοί-
    μησίς σου

365. ἐνθάδε κεῖτε
Καιλις προστά-
της 'Αγριππη-
σίων ἐν εἰρή-
νη κοιμάσθω

In the Terme Museum, No. 77649. (Fig. 62)
Here lies Caelius, Prostates of the Agrippesians. Let him sleep in peace.

366. Κλα[υ]-
δια
Πρι-
μα

Claudia Prima.

367. ἐνθάδε κεῖ-
τη Κυιαινος
'Ιουδνος ἠ‹σ›-
τῶν μδ' ἐν
(εἰ)ρείνη εἰ κύμη-
ση(ς) αὐτοῦ

At the Lapidary Museum in the monastery at St. Paul's on the Via Ostiense. The inscription is noteworthy for its misspellings and ill-formed letters. There is no evidence that it came from the Monteverde catacomb.
Here lies Quirinus, a Jew, aged 44 years. In peace his sleep.

Line 4: Frey reads the numeral as MA = 41, but it is clearly MΔ = 44.

368. ἐνθάδε κεῖτε
Κυντιανος γερου-
σιάρχης συναγω-
γῆς Αὐγοστησίων
ὃς ἔζησεν ἔτη νδ'
ἐν ἐρήνη ἡ κοίμησις αὐτοῦ

At the National Museum in Naples (see on No. 312). For a photograph see MB, p. 154 (none in CII).
Here lies Quintianus, Gerusiarch of the Synagogue of the Augustesians, who lived 54 years. In peace his sleep.

369. ἐνθάδε κεῖτε
Λεοντία
ἐτῶν κ'

Here lies Leontia, aged 20 years. (Fig. 39. 22)

370. ἐνθάδε κῖτε
Μακεδόνις
ὁ Αἰβρῆος Κεσαρεὺς
τῆς Παλεστίνης
υἱὸς 'Αλεξάνδρου
μνία δικαίου εἰς
εὐλογίαν ἐν ἰρή-
νη ἡ κοίμισίς σου

Here lies Macedonius, the Hebrew, a Caesarean of Palestine, son of Alexander. The memory of the righteous is for a blessing. In peace your sleep.

371. ἐνθάδε κεῖτε   *Here lies Maximus, a child, son of Abas.*
    Μάξιμος νήπιο-   Line 2: It is possible that a C is lost at
    ς ᾿Αβάτος υἱός   the end of the line, since the stone is
        broken off. If so, the name of the father
        was Sabas.

372. 〽   At the Naples Museum (see on
           ἐν ἱρή-   No. 312.)
    ἐνθάδε κεῖτε νη ὐ   *Here lies Mara. She completed*
           κοίμ- OOC *80 years. In peace her sleep.*
    Μαρα ἐπλέ- ησις   The concluding formula was cut
           αὐ   at the right in smaller letters.
    οωσε ἐτῶν π′ π   The π at the bottom may be a
        repetition of the π (= 80) at the
end of the main part of the inscription. The letters OOC at the
extreme right are unintelligible.

Lines 2, 3: επλεοωσε is apparently for ἐπλήρωσε, incorrectly
followed by the genitive.

373. [ἐνθά]δε κεῖται Marcar   Painted on a loculus;
    [....]er Σαββατ[....] ἐτ[ῶν ?] destroyed with the ca-
    [ἐ]ν irene [....] η [....] αὐτ[ῆς] tacomb. If Schneider-
        Graziosi's transcription
can be trusted, the letters are a mixture of Latin and Greek.
Here lies Margarita (?), mother (?) of Sabbatius (?), aged [....].
In peace her[sleep].

Line 1: The name can have been *Marcarius*, in which case the
deceased was masculine and the ER of line 2 would be the
remnant of *pater* or even *frater*.

374. ἐντάδε κῖτε Μαρία γυ-   *Here lies Maria, wife of Salutius,*
    νὴ Σαλουτίου ὅστις   *who lived a good life with her*
    καλῶς ἔζησεν με-   *husband. In peace her sleep.*
    τὰ τοῦ ἀνδρὸς αὐτῆς   (Fig. 36. 108)
    ἐν ἰρήνη ἡ κοίμησις αὐτῆς

    ⟿ σ 〽 ✿

375. ἐνθάδε κεῖτε
    Μαρία ἡ τοῦ ἱε-   On the reverse of the stone bearing No. 379.
    ρέως   It looks as though the stonecutter failed

to complete the inscription, perhaps because he had omitted
γυνή (= *wife*) in line 2. Then the other side was used for
No. 379, possibly by the same cutter.
Here lies Maria, the (wife) of the priest.

376. ἐνθάδε κεῖτε
Μαρινα θυγάτηρ
Βενιαμειν

Here lies Marina, daughter of Benjamin.

377. ἐντάδε κῖθε Μαρ-
κια γυνὴ Μαξίμ-
ου τὶς καλῶς ἔζη-
σεν μετὰ τοῦ ἀν-
δρὸς αὐτῆς
M MAR

*Here lies Marcia, wife of Maximus, who
lived a good life with her husband. M MAR*
(Fig. 39. 10)
Line 6. The purpose of these Latin letters
does not appear. Frey interprets them
(implausibly) as M(aximus) Mar(ciae) =
Maximus to Marcia.

378. [. . . .]ητρο
[. . . .]ωρος
[πρεσβ?]ύτερος
[. . . .]ιτε

Not a single word is certain, except that
line 3 apparently refers to an *elder*, otherwise unexampled in our inscriptions. Frey
confidently reconstructs lines 1, 2 with
the name *Metrodorus.*

379. Μόνιμος ὁ καὶ Εὐ-
σαββάτις Ἑβραῖος
καὶ γλυκὺς ἔζη-
σεν ἔτη δέκα
ICA   IZ

On the reverse of the stone is No. 375.
*Monimus, also named Eusabbatius, a
Hebrew and a sweet one, lived 10 years.
ICA IZ*
Line 5: There have been sundry attempts
to explain these letters. Some have seen in
IZ the numeral for 17, but this would be
strange after the δέκα of the previous line. M. Schwabe, in
Zion 9 (1944), 47, took IC‍A as representing *Isas*, the name
of a second deceased person, who lived 17 years, but this seems
extremely unlikely.Were it not for the spacing, one might be
tempted to read ICAI as = εἰς ἀεί = *forever*, but could the Z
be an abbreviation for ζήτω = *let him live*? If so, it is without
parallel in our inscriptions.

380. ἐντάδε κεῖται
Νεικόδημος
ὁ ἄρχων
Σιβουρησίων καὶ

At the Naples Museum (see on
No. 312). There is no evidence that
this came from the Monteverde
catacomb.
Here lies Nicodemus, the Archon of the

πᾶσι φειλητὸς
αἰτῶν λ' ἡμερ(ῶν) μβ'
θάρι ἀβλαβὶ νεώτερε οὐ-
δεὶς ἀθάνατος

*Siburesians and beloved by all, aged
30 years, 42 days. Be of good courage,
innocent young man; no one is immortal.*

Line 7: ἀβλαβί is obviously a vulgar vocative of the adjective
ἀβλαβής, such epithets being common. Many, including Frey,
have mistakenly taken it as the vocative of the name *Ablabius*,
regarding this as either a second name of Nicodemus or that
of his son, later buried in the same tomb. See above, p. 128,
note 3.

381. ἐνθάδε κεῖτε
     Νωμητωρα
     παρθαίνος
     ἐτῶν ιη'
     ἐν εἰρήνη
     ἡ κοίμισις αὐτῇ[ς]

At the Conservatori Museum, No. 38.
There is a cast in the Sala Giudaica.
(Fig. 32. 8)
*Here lies Nometora (= Numitora), a
virgin, aged 18 years. In peace her
sleep.*

382. ➴ 🖋 𝜎 🕎   'Οπρω-
     μαν ἐν-
     θάδε κα-
     τάκιτε

Oproman reposes here.

383. [ἐν]θάδε κεῖτε Πολυ-
     [. .]νις ἀρχισυνγωγὸς
     [συ]ναγωγῆς Βερνα-
     [κλ]ων ἐτῶν νγ'
     [ἐν] εἰρήνη ἡ κοίμη-
     σις αὐτοῦ

*Here lies Poly[. .]nius, Archisynagogus
of the Vernaclians, aged 53 years. In
peace his sleep.*
Lines 1, 2: The name is usually restored as Πολύμνις (= *Polymnius*), but at
least two letters are required by the
space. *Polymenius* is a possibility.

For other suggestions see above, p. 103, note 3.

384. ἐνθάδε κεῖθαιν
     Πομπώνις ὁ δὶς
     ἄρχων τῆς συνα-
     γωγῆς Καλκαρησις ἔ-
     ζησεν ἐτῶν ξ' ἐν ἱρ-
     ήνη 🕎 κύμη-
     σις αὐτοῦ

At the Terme Museum, No. 77643.
*Here lies Pomponius, twice Archon
of the Synagogue of Calcaresis. He
lived 60 years. In peace his sleep.*

385.

ἐνθάδε
κεῖτε
Πριμειτι-
βα μετὰ
τοῦ ἐγγό-
νου αὐτῆς Εὐ-
φρένοντος
ἐν εἰρήνη κοί-
μησις αὐτῶν

Here lies Primitiva with her grandson Euphrenon. In peace their sleep. (Fig. 32. 15)

386. ἐνθάδε κεῖται
Προκα παρθέ-
νος ἐτῶν
δέκα κὲ ἐ-
νέα

On the other face of the irregular block is No. 424.
Here lies Proca, a virgin, aged 19 years.

387. Προκλα

Name painted on a child's loculus; destroyed with the catacomb.
Procla.

388. ἐνθάδε κεῖ-
τε Προκλα νή-
πιος
♂

Here lies Procla, a child.
What appears to be an etrog is scratched beneath the epitaph.

389. ἐνθάδε
κεῖται Προκλεινα
ἐτῶν ιη' ἡμερῶν ν'
ἐποίησεν μήτηρ
'Ακυλεινα

Here lies Proclina, aged 18 years, 50 days. Her mother Aquilina set up (this stone).

390. ἐνθάδε κεῖτε Προ-
κλος ἄρχων συναγω-
γῆς Τριπολειτῶν
ἐν εἰρήνη κοιμάσθω

In the Terme Museum, No. 77644. (Fig. 63)
Here lies Proclus, Archon of the Synagogue of the Tripolitans. Let him sleep in peace.

391. ἀνθάδε χῖτε
Πρωκουλους
ὢ δῆς ἄρχων
κὲ γυνὴ ἑαυτοῦ

Painted on a marble slab. The last two lines, crowded at the bottom of the stone, are now practically illegible.

Εὐοδία ᾽Ι‹ι›ουλια   *Here lies Proculus, twice Archon, and*
ἐτῶν ἐνέα κὲ μῆν-   *his wife Euhodia; Julia, aged 9 years*
ας ἐνέα Σαβατης ἐτῶ-   *and 9 months; Sabatis, aged 9 years;*
ν ἐνέα Εὐοδία ἐτῶν δύω   *Euhodia, aged 2 years and 9 months.*
κὲ μῆνας ἐνέα ἐν εἰρήνη   *In peace.*

Line 7: It is impossible to say whether the name is intended for Sabbatis, feminine, or Sabbatius, masculine.

Line 9: There was no room left for the full formula. The menorah at the right is so faded as to be almost invisible. It was overlooked by Frey, but may be seen in the photograph in MB, p. 111.

392. ἐνθάδε κῖται   *Here lies Rebecca, married only once, who*
Ρεβεκκα μόναν-   *lived 44 years. In peace her sleep.*
δρος ζήσας ἔτη   Minium has been applied to the letters
μδ΄ ἐν εἰρήνη   very carelessly, so that the illustration in
ἡ κοίμησις αὐτῆ-   *CII* is misleading. Frey, following the
ς   photograph instead of the stone itself, criticizes the version in MB (p. 41), which is, however, virtually correct.

393. ἐν[θάδε . . . .]   *Here [lies] Sab[. . . .].*
Σαβ[. . . .]

394. ἐνθάδε κεῖ-   *Here lies Sabatis, aged 2 years, 7 months.*
τε Σαβατις ἐ-   *In peace.*
τῶν δύο μη-   There is no way of telling whether the
νῶν ἑπτὰ ἐν   deceased child was a boy or girl, since the
εἰρήνη   name could be either masculine or feminine, depending on the accent. There was no room on the stone for the complete formula at the end.

395. Σαβ-   Painted on a loculus; destroyed with the
ατυς   catacomb; see the photograph in MB, p. 63. Sabatis (masculine or feminine).

396. ἐντάδε κεῖτε   *Here lies Sabbasa, a child. In*
Σαββασα νήπιον   *peace (her) sleep.*
ἐν εἰρήνη ἡ κοίμισις   Line 3: The final C, visible in the photograph in MB (p. 21), is now gone, as a fragment at the right has been lost. Frey

indicates also the loss of αὐτῆς at the end, but this word was never on the stone.

397. ἐνθάδε ἔκειθεν
Σαββάτις δὶς ἄρχων
ἔζησεν ἐτῶν λε'
ἐν ἰρήνη ἡ κύμησις αὐτοῦ
שלום על 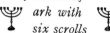 שׁי ⟶ ישראל

In the Lapidary Museum of the monastery at St. Paul's.
Here lies Sabbatius, twice Archon. He lived 35 years. In peace his sleep. Peace on Israel.
Line 5: The א in שאלום may point to the use of this letter as a vowel, or it may be only a careless slip.

398. ἐνθάδε κεῖτε
Σαβεινος διὰ
βίου Βερνακλη-
σίων

Here lies Sabinus, Life Archon of the Vernaclesians. (Fig. 37. 64)

399. ἐνθάδε
κῖται Σα-
μουηλ
νήπιος

In the Terme Museum, No. 77653.
Here lies Samuel, a child.

400. ἐνθάδε
κῖται Σα-
ρα ουρα π-
ρεσβυτνς
(menorah)

Here lies Sara ura (?), an old woman.
Line 3: OYPA is usually taken as a name, either *Ursa* or *Vera*, but a double name consisting of a Hebrew name followed by a Latin one would have no parallel in these inscriptions. The Latin name always precedes.

Line 4: ΠΡΕϹΒΥΤΝϹ seems to be for ΠΡΕϹΒΥΤΗϹ = πρεσβῦτις = *old woman.*

401. ἐνθάδε κῖτε Σεμω-
ηλ νήπιος ἐνιαυ-
τοῦ καὶ μηνῶν
πέντε ἐν εἰρήνη ὁ
κοίμησις αὐτοῦ
θάρεικ⟨ς⟩ Σαμωηλ
οὐδὶς ἀθάνατος
(menorah) ark with (menorah)
six scrolls

In the Lapidary Museum of the monastery at St. Paul's (Fig. 34)
Here lies Samuel, a child of a year and 5 months. In peace his sleep. Be of good courage, Samuel; no one is immortal.

402. ἐνθάδε κεῖτε Σικου-
λος Σαβεινος μελ-
λαρχων Βολουμνη-
σίων ἐτῶν β΄ μηνῶν ι΄

Here lies Siculus Sabinus, archon-to-be of the Volumnesians, aged 2 years, 10 months.

403. εἰτάδε χεῖθε
Σιμον ἐν ἰρή[νη] ἡ κύμ[ησις . . . .]

Painted on a loculus; destroyed with the catacomb. There is a photo-

graph in MB, p. 66.

Here lies Simon. In peace [his] sleep.

404. Στεφ[ανος?]

Painted on a tile; apparently not extant. Steph[anus?].

405. ἐντάδε ἔκιθεν
Στέφανος ἱερου-
σιάρχη[ς ἐν] εἰρή-
νη ἡ [κοίμησις αὐτοῦ]

In the Terme Museum, No. 77640. Here lies Stephanus, Gerusiarch. [In] peace [his sleep].

406. ἐνθάδε
κεῖτε
Στράτων

Here lies Straton. (Fig. 33. 76)

408. ἐνθάδε κεῖται
Σύμμαχος
εἱεροσάρχης ☰
Τριπολίτης
ἐτῶν π΄ ἐν ἐ-
ρήνη ἡ κοίμη-
σι(ς) αὐτοῦ

Here lies Symmachus, Gerusiarch of the Tripolitans, aged 80 years. In peace his sleep. (Fig. 39. 12)

409. ἐνθάδε κῖτε Σύ-
μμαχος ἐτῶ[ν . . . .]
☰

Here lies Symmachus, aged [. .] years.

410. ἐνθάδε κῖτει Σύρο[ς. . . .]
☰

*Painted on a loculus; destroyed with the catacomb.
Here lies Syrus [. . . .]*

411. ἐνθάδε κεῖτε
Τιτινια ᾿Αννα

Here lies Titinia Anna, who lived a good life with her husband for 15 years.

καλῶς βιώσα-
σα μετὰ τοῦ ἀν-
δρὸς ἔτη ιε' μῆν(ας)
δ' Πρισκιανος
ἐποίησεν

4 months. Priscianus set up (this stone).

412. ἐνθάδε
κεῖτε
Τυχικὸς
πατὴρ
Εὐτύχις
υἱῶ ἐπ[ο]-
ίησεν
shovel

Here lies Tychicus. His father, Eutychius, set up (this stone) to his son.
(Fig. 37. 66)

413. ἐνθάδε κεῖτε
Φαβια Μαυρια
Φαβίας ’Ασία[ς νή]πιος
ἐν εἰρή[νη ἡ κοίμησις αὐτῆ]ς

In the Terme Museum, No.
77654.
Here lies Fabia Mauria, a child
(daughter of) Fabia Asia. In
peace her sleep.

Line 3: Frey interprets the name as *Fabia Cassia* (!) in the
nominative, mistaking the Greek lunate sigma for Latin C,
and he regards the epitaph as that of two persons, supplying
αὐτῶν at the end, despite the clear C after the break. See
above, p. 106, note 1.

414. [. . . .]ος τῇ ἐ-
[αυτοῦ?] θυγα-
[τρὶ . . . .]ιαι Φη-
λεικιτατι [ἐποί]-
ησεν φορ[. . . .]
λα

[. . . .]us set up (this stone) to his [own?]
daughter, [. . . .]ia Felicitas. For [. . . .]-
la(?).
Lines 5, 6: The lacuna in φορ[. . . .]λα
cannot be supplied. Müller's φορ[μικου]-
λα (accepted by Frey) as the name of
the person who set up the stone will

not stand because the space will not admit as many as five
letters. Besides, it is more plausible to interpret the first word
of the inscription as the name of the father, who set up the
stone to his daughter.

415. ἐνθάδε κιετε
Φιλικεισιμα ἐν εἰ-
ρήνη ἡ κοίμισ-
ις αὐτῆς

Here lies Felicissima. In peace her sleep.

416. ἐντάδε χεῖθε Φλα-
βια ᾽Αντωνινα γυνὴ
Δατίβου τοῦ ζαβίου
ἀπὸ τῆς συναγωγ-
ῆς τῶν Αὐγουστησίων

In the National Museum of Naples (see on No. 312). There is a photograph in MB, p. 156. The inscription was executed by the same cutter as Nos. 374 and 377, as is apparent from the distinctive forms of the letters with their conspicuous serifs, the spelling ἐντάδε, and the shapes of the symbols in Nos. 374 and 416. Amusingly, Bees, in attempting to date every inscription from the Monteverde catacomb, has attributed these three inscriptions to three different periods.

Here lies Flavia Antonina, wife of Dativus, Life Archon of the Synagogue of the Augustesians.

417. ἐνθάδε κεῖτε
Φλαβιος Σαβεινο
ς
ζαβίου συναγωγῆ
ς
τῶν Βολυμνή ν
σων ἐ ν ἰρήνη
ἡ κοίμη σις αὐτῶν

In the Terme Museum, No. 77641.

Here lies Flavius Sabinus, Life Archon of the Synagogue of the Volumnesians. In peace their sleep.

Lines 2, 3: The cutter was forced by lack of space to insert one letter beneath the last letter of each line. In line 4, for some reason, he put N at the end, skipping the two intervening letters, then repeated the three letters in the next line.

Line 6: The careless scribe wrote the plural αὐτῶν instead of the singular αὐτοῦ.

418. ἐνθάδε κεῖντε Φορτουνατος καὶ Εὐτρόπις νήπιοι φιλοῦντες ἀλλήλους ὃς ἔζησεν
Φορτουνατος ἔτη τρεῖς καὶ μῆνας τέσσαρες καὶ Εὐτρόπις ὃς ἔ-
ζησεν ἔτη τρία καὶ μῆνας ἑπτὰ ἐν εἰρήνη ἡ κοίμησις
αὐτῶν
εἰς μίαν
ἀπέθαναν ἡμέραν

On the reverse of a stone bearing a pagan inscription (*CII*, 36*). (Fig. 36. 117) *Here lie Fortunatus and Eutropius, children who loved each other: Fortunatus, who lived 3 years and 4 months, and Eutropius, who lived 3 years and 7 months. In peace their sleep. They died on the same day.*

Line 4: The neuter noun is followed by the masculine of the

numeral. In line 6, however, the correct neuter form of the numeral is used.

419. ⸎ ἐνθ[ά]-
δε κε[ῖτε]
Φαυ[στι]-
να

Painted on a loculus; destroyed with the catacomb; photograph in MB, p. 78. *Here lies Faustina.*

Nos. 420-455 are fragments from the Monteverde catacomb. Only those with intelligible words are included here. Even when no more than the familiar formula is preserved, the inscription is presented, since it may be useful for linguistic data.

424. [. . . .]
γλυκυτά[τω or τη]
γονεῖς ἐποί-
ησαν

On the reverse of this fragment is No. 386. It was already broken when the later inscription was carved upon it. *To* [. . .], *their very sweet son* (or *daughter*), *the parents set up* (*this stone*).

425. [ἐνθά]δε κεῖται
[. . . .]ς γερου-
[σιάρχ]ης συ-
[ναγωγῆ]ς 'Αγρι-
[ππησίων . . . .]α (?)

Here lies [. . . .]*s, Gerusiarch of the Synagogue of the Agrippesians.*
Line 5: The only character visible in this line is the top of an A, Δ, or Λ.

427. [ἐνθά]δε [κεῖ]-
[ται . . . .]κος ν[ή?]-
[πιο?]ς ἐτῶν [.]
[καὶ μ]ῆνας ζ'

Here [*lies* . . . .]*cus, a child* (?), *aged* [. .] *years* [*and*] *7 months.*

432. [ἐνθάδ]ε κεῖτε
[. . . .]τις ἐτῶν
[. . . .] ἐν εἰρή-
[. . . .]ς

Painted on a loculus; destroyed with the catacomb.
Here lies [. . . .]*tis, aged* [. . . .]. *In peace* [. . . .].

433. ἐνθάδε κ[εῖται . . . .]-
ις γραματε[ὺς συνα]-
γωγῆς Κα[λκαρησίων ἐτῶ]-
ν με' ἐν ἰρή[νη ἡ κοίμη]-
σις αὐτ[οῦ]

Here lies [. . . .]*ius, Scribe of the Synagogue of the Calcaresians, aged* 45 *years. In peace his sleep.*

434. ἐνθάδε κεῖτε [. . . .]

Painted on a loculus; destroyed with the catacomb.
Here lies [. . . .].

435. ἐνθάδε κῖτε [. . . .]

Painted on a child's loculus; destroyed with the catacomb.
Here lies [. . . .].

436. ἐνθάδε (κεῖ)-
τε

Incomplete inscription on a slab of tufa.
Here lies

437. [. . . . ἔ]-
ζησεν ἔ-
τη κε′ μή-
τηρ καὶ ἀδ-
ελφοὶ ἐποί-
ησαν

[. . . .] *lived 25 years. (His* or *her)
mother and brothers set up (this stone).*

438. [. . . . ἔ]-
ζησεν [. . . .]
ἡ κύμησ[ις . . . .]
🕎 🕎 ?

[. . . .] *lived* [. . . .] *sleep.*

439. [ἐνθά]δε κεῖτε
[. . . .]οη (?) [. . . .]α
[. . . .]ν [. . . .]

Here lies [. . . .]

441. [ἐνθάδε κε]ῖται
[. . . .]κθωε
[. . . .]ιζωσα
[. . . .]υτης
[. . . .]υτω
[. . . . ἐποί]ησεν
amphora

[*Here*] *lies* [. . . .] *set up (this stone)*
(Fig. 37. 67)

442. [ἐνθάδε κε]ῖτε
[. . . . ἄ]ρχων

In the Terme Museum, , No. 77648.
Here lies [. . . .], *Archon.*

450. 🕎 [. . . .]νδυ
[. . . .]του
θάρσι οὐ-
δεὶς ἀθά-
νατος

[. . . .]. *Be of good courage; no one is
immortal.*

453. 🕎 🕎

[. . . . ἔ]-
τῃ ε‹ν›′ μῆνες ε′

Painted on a child's loculus; destroyed with the catacomb. There is an illustration (drawing) in MB, p. 76. [. . . . *lived*] 5 (?) *years*, 5 *months.*

If Müller's transcription is correct, the N of the numeral must be the scribe's error. Müller (followed by Frey) read the numeral in reverse as NE = 55, a strange age for a child!

454. [. . . .]
ἐν ἰρήν[η ἡ]
[κοίμη]σις α[. . . .]

[. . . .] *In peace his* (or *her*) *sleep.*

455. [. . . .] υἱὸς [. . . .]

Painted on a child's loculus; destroyed with the catacomb. [. . . .] *son* [. . . .].

456. Elius Aprilicus
grammateus qu(i)
bixit annos XXXV
coiux benemeren-
ti (f)ecit

Aelius Aprilicus, the Scribe, who lived 35 years. His wife set up (this stone) in grateful memory. (Fig. 37. 63)

457. Aelio Primitivo ma-
rito incomparabili
mellarconti qui
vixit annis XXXVIII
cum quo convixi
annis XVI sine ulla
querela coniugi d-
ulcissimo Flavia M-
aria benemereti fec(it)

In the Terme Museum, No. 77659. *To Aelius Primitivus, my incomparable husband, archon-to-be, who lived 38 years, together with whom I lived 16 years without any complaint. To her most sweet husband Flavia Maria set up (this stone) in grateful memory.*

458. locus Bellule
quiec 🕎 et in pace

Not extant. *Burial place of Bellula. She rests in peace.*

Line 2: QVIECET is probably for *quiescit.*

459. Benedicte Mariae
vere benedicte
matri et nutrici
ἐν εἰρήνη

To Benedicta Maria, truly benedicta (i.e., blessed), mother and nurse. In peace. (Fig. 37. 73)

460. λοχου
Βεσουλες
ανουρο ρε-
χεσητ χε'
ark with
8 scrolls

In the National Museum of Naples
(see on No. 312). Greek transliteration of the Latin:
Locu(s) Besules anuro (= annorum)
recessit XXV.
Burial place of Besula. She passed
away at the age of 25 years.

Line 2: On the name see above, p. 104, note 6.

461. Claudia [Bere?]-
nice Clau[die M]-
arciane fi[lie su]-
e benemere[nti]
fecit

In the Terme Museum, No. 77662.
Claudia [Bere?]nice set up (this stone)
to Claudia Marciana, her daughter, in
grateful memory.

462. Felicitas proseli-
ta ann(orum) VI nuenn
Peregrina quae
vixit ann(is) XLVII
patrona vene-
merenti

Felicitas, a proselyte of 6 years, named
Peregrina, who lived 47 years. Her
patron in grateful memory.
Line 2: NVENN is probably a garbling of nomine; cf. No. 523 and see
above, p. 254, note 2.

463. Flavius
Constanti-
us qui vixít
an[n(is)] XXIII
[diebu]s XIIII

Flavius Constantius, who lived 23
years, 14 days.

464. D
Fofoti fi[lio bene]-
merenti q[ui vixit anni]-
s II (mensibus) VII en [irene cym]-
σ   isis a[utou]

In the Terme Museum, No. 77661.
D [. .] To Fofotis, his son,
in grateful memory, who
lived 2 years, 7 months.
In peace his sleep.
Line 1: The D is usually

taken as part of the abbreviation of Dis Manibus (= to the
Divine Shades), the M having been in the lost portion of the
stone. If correct, this is the only instance of the pagan formula
in the Jewish inscriptions of Rome.

Line 4: After the S of annis the stonecutter had written M for
m(ensibus); then, on discovering that he had omitted the
number of years, he deleted the M and wrote II.

Lines 4, 5: The common Greek formula is written in Latin letters.

465. C. Furfani-
us Iulianus
exarchon
qui vixit
annis XXVIII

Gaius Furfanius Julianus, Exarchon, who lived 28 years. (Fig. 37, upper left)

466. Inpendi 🕎 anima in-
nox qui ⚱ vixsit
annos tres dies
vici inti oct(o)

The innocent soul of Impendius, who lived 3 years, 28 days. (Fig. 39. 25)

467. 🕎
Iobinu ⚱
qui vix(it) an(nos) XXX
V

Jovinus, who lived 35 years. (Fig. 33. 69)

468. Iulus Sabinu-
s fecit coiugi su-
ae Pticiae As-
teri quae vexit
annis XXXXVIII

Iulus Sabinus set up (this stone) to his wife, Pticia Aster, who lived 48 years.

469. *branch* Iust[. . . .]
🕎

Just[. . .]
The name could be Justus, Justa, Justinus, or Justina.

470. L. Maecio L. Constantio et
Maeciae L. Lucianidi et
L. Maecio Victorino et
L. Maeciae Sabbatidi filis
et Iul. Alexandriae coniugi
fecit b(ene) m(erentibus) L. Maecius I.
archon ‹s› alti ordinis

To Lucius Maecius Constantius, (son of) Lucius, and to Maecia Lucianis, (daughter of) Lucius, and to Lucius Maecius Victorinus and to Lucia Maecia Sabbatis, his children, and to Julia Alexandria, his wife, in grateful memory, Lucius Maecius, (son of) Lucius (?). Archon of High Rank, set up (this stone). (Figs. 33, upper left, and 37, upper right)

Line 5. The final I of *coniugi*, which Frey thought missing, is inserted within the G.

Line 6: The last letter of the line is not an L, as Frey asserts, but an I. It may be an error for L.

Line 7: After ARCHON there is an S, cut smaller and more shallow than the other letters. On the views with regard to its significance see above, p. 176, note 3.

471. Maeviu(s) Name painted on a tile; now in a case of the Sala Giudaica.

472. Man- Not extant; not certain that it came from the
     nus ♈ Monteverde catacomb.
            Mannus

473. Maxima Name scratched on a loculus; now in a case of the Sala Giudaica.

474. mater *His mother set up (this stone) to her son Musaeus*
     filio Muse- *in grateful memory.* (Fig. 37. 65)
     o benemern-
     ti fecit

475. ματερ Δαμνατα Ωρστωριω φιλι[ω] Painted on fragments of a terracotta sarcophagus; now in a case of the Sala Giudaica. There is a photograph in MB, p. 22. Greek transcription of the Latin: mater Damnata Orstorio filio

The mother, Damnata, to Orstorius, her son.

476. Hic Regina sita est tali contecta sepulcro
     quod coniunx statuit respondens eius amori
     haec post bis denos secum transsegerat annum
     et quartum mensem restantibus octo diebus
     rursum victura reditura ad lumina rursum
     nam sperare potest ideo quod surgat in aevom
     promissum quae vera fides dignisque piisque
     quae meruit sedem venerandi ruris habere
     hoc tibi praestiterit pietas hoc vita pudica
     hoc et amor generis hoc observantia legis
     coniugii meritum cuius tibi gloria curae
     horum factorum tibi sunt speranda futura
     de quibus et coniunx maestus solacia quaerit.

The inscription is in dactylic hexameters. For a discussion and verse translation see pp. 248-49; cf. also pp. 133-34 (Fig. 33. 68) *Here lies Regina, covered by such a tomb, which her husband set up as fitting to his love. After twice ten years she spent with him one year, four months and eight days more. She will live again, return to the light again, for she can hope that she will rise to the life promised, as is our true faith, to the worthy and the pious, in that she has deserved to possess an abode in the hallowed land. This your piety has assured you, this your chaste life, this your love for your people, this your observance of the Law, your devotion to your wedlock, the glory of which was dear to you. For all these deeds your hope of the future is assured. In this your sorrowing husband seeks his comfort.*

477. Sabbati-   *Sabbatius in peace.* (Fig. 37. 75)
     us in pace

478. 🕎 Salutia   The left half of the stone is missing.
                   Salutia.
     open scroll

479. Hoc nomen Telesini   In the National Museum of Naples
                              (see on No. 312). There is no
        evidence that it came from the
                              Monteverde catacomb, nor is it
     certain that it came from Rome.

     This is the name of Telesinius.

480. Tettius Rufinus   In the National Museum of Naples
     Melitius vicxit an-   (see on No. 312).
     nis LXXXV   *Tettius Rufinus Melitius lived* 85
     ia   bi 🕎   us   *years. Life Archon.*

Line 3: Since the base of the L of the numeral is extended beneath the following letters, it may be intended not as = 50, but as a frame for the numeral. In that case, the deceased lived only 35 years. There is a frame of that sort in No. 510, a Greek inscription. Still, in view of the high rank of Melitius, the usual interpretation of the numeral as representing 85 seems the more likely.

481. Veritas 🕎   In the Terme Museum, No. 67692.
     Amor ⚱   *Truth, Love (?) set up the inscriptions.*
     anestase   What this inscription means is an unsolv-
     titulos   ed puzzle. Some have taken *Veritas* and
                   Amor as proper names. If so, it is strange
     that the verb, a transliteration of Greek ἀνέστησε, is in the
     singular. Also, there is no explanation of the plural *titulos*.

482. The inscription of Victorina is not included here because there
     is no evidence that it came from Rome. With its cursive
     letters, its phrasing (*e.g.*, use of *plus minus, defuncta*, statement
     of date), and the shapes of the symbols, it bears no resem-
     blance to any of the inscriptions from the Jewish catacombs
     of Rome.

483. Vindicia-   In the Terme Museum, No. 77660.
     rosette   *Vindicianus, Archon-to-be.*
     nos mellarx[on]

484. [. . . .]α   Greek transliteration of the Latin:
     [. . . .]ει βενε-   [. . . .]a [. . . .]i benemere(n)ti posui.
     [μ]ερετει ποε-   *I,* [. . . .] *set up (this stone) to* [. . . .]
     υει   *in grateful memory.* (Fig. 36. 95)
     σ 🕎 ⚱   Line 3: The last letter is E for C. There
                         are also two unidentified symbols, to the
                         left and right of the menorah, respectively.

485. 🕎 [. . . .]anus Maximi   Painted on a loculus; destroyed
     ⚱ eeyr   with the catacomb.
     [. . . .]anus [son of ?] *Maximus. In peace (?)*.
     Line 2: Appears to be intended for ἐν εἰρήνη.

     Of the remaining fragments of Monteverde inscriptions given
     in *CII* (Nos. 486-493) only the following one has any intelli-
     gible words:

489. [. . . .]ter fili-   All that can be made out is that a
     [. . . . s]uo Nil (?)- parent set up (*posuit*) this inscrip-
     [. . . .]nito   tion to his or her son.
     [. . . .] fivio   Line 2: The last letter is either L
     [pos]uit   or I.
     The provenience of the inscriptions which follow is not known.
     Most of them are probably from the Monteverde catacomb.

494. ἐν[θά]δε κ-
εῖ[τε Δ]ομνο-
ς π[ατ]ὴρ συνα-
γωγ[ῆς Β]ερνάκλω-
ν τρὶς ἄ[ρχ]ων κὲ δὶς [φ]-
ρονт[ιστή]ς ἐν εἰρή-
ν[η ἡ κ]οί-
μ[ησ]ις αὐ-
[το]ῦ

Carved on the front of a marble sarcophagus; now in the cloister of the Ospizio di San Cosimato at Viale Trastevere, No. 72; most probably from the Monteverde catacomb.
Here lies Domnus, Father of the Synagogue of the Vernaclians, thrice Archon and twice Phrontistes. In peace his sleep.

Line 5: According to Vaccari, in *Biblica* 19 (1938), 342, the end of this line should read δι[ς]φ. He was deceived by a shadow in the photograph. Frey's reading is correct, since the stone clearly has C, but no φ.

495. [. . . .]
[. . . .] γυνὴ
[. . . .]υ ἐτῶν
[. . . . ἐν ε]ἰρήνη
[ἡ κοίμ]ησις αὐτῆς

On a sarcophagus fragment; now in the cloister of the Ospizio di San Cosimato.
[Here lies . . . .], wife of [. . . .], aged [. .] years. In peace her sleep.

496. [ἐνθά]δε κεῖτε
[. . . .]ια Μαρκελ-
[λα μή]τηρ συνα-
[γωγῆς] Αὐγουστη-
[σίων μ]νησθη (?)
[. . . . ἐ]ν εἰρήνη
[ἡ κοίμη]σις αὐ-
[τῆ]ς

Carved on a sarcophagus front, of which only the right half remains; now in the Conservatori Museum, No. 42.
Here lies [. . . .]ia Marcella, Mother of the Synagogue of the Augustesians. May [. . . .] be remembered (?). In peace her sleep.

Line 5: Frey's interpretation μνησθῆ (=*may she be remembered*) is possibly correct, but at least five more letters are needed in order to fill the lacuna which follows in the next line. What is lost is probably a nominative referring to the deceased.

497. ἐνθάδε κεῖται Τουβίας Βαρζααρω-
να καὶ Παρηγόριος υἱὸς Τουβία
Βαρζααρωνα
Hic est positus Tubias Barzaha-
rona et Paregorius filius
Tubiae Barzaharona

In the Terme Museum, No. 67679. (Fig. 64)
Greek with Latin translation:
Here lies Tubias Barzaharona and Pa cgorius,

[שלום] שְׁי שלום שלום שְׁי שלום שְׁי

son of Tubias Barzaha-
rona. Peace, peace, peace,
peace.

498. [. . . .]
[ε]ν ἰρήν[η]
[ἡ κοίμη]σις [. . . .]

A fragment, in the cloister of St.
Paul's on the Via Ostiense.
[. . . .] In peace [. . . .] sleep.

499. The epitaph of Sigismundus is not included, since it is medieval
and does not come within our period.

501. ἔνθα κῖτε 'Αλεξάν[δρα]
θυγάτηρ τοῦ 'Αλεξάν[δρου]
ἀπὸ τῆς πόλεως "Αρκ[ης Λιβ]-
άνου ἐν εἰρήνη ἡ κύ[μησι]-
ς αὐτῆς ἔζησε ἐτῶν [. .]
μην(ῶν) δ' ἡμερ(ῶν) θ' ψֿ

This text is found only in the
18th-century manuscripts of Migliore and Marini.
*Here lies Alexandra, daughter of
Alexander of the city of Arca of
Libanus. In peace her sleep. She
lived [. .] years, 4 months, 9 days.*

Line 3: An alternative version has ἀπὸ τῆς συναγ, which Frey
follows and makes the basis for the presence at Rome of a
Synagogue of Arca of Libanus (= Lebanon). The arguments
for rejecting this alternative are presented above, pp. 163-65.

502. 'Αλύπις Τιβερεὺς καὶ υἱ-
οἱ αὐτοῦ 'Ιουστος
καὶ 'Αλύπις 'Εβρε̄-
οι μετὰ τοῦ πατρὸς
αὐτῶν ὧδε κῖντε

In the Terme Museum, No.
67639.
*Alypius of Tiberias and his sons,
Justus and Alypius, Hebrews, lie
here with their father.*

503. ἐνθάδε κεῖτε Ζώ-
σιμος διὰ βίου συν-
αγωγῆς 'Αγριππησί-
ων ἐν εἰρήνη ἡ κοίμη-
σις αὐτοῦ ἐνθά-
δε κεῖτη Ευλλις
ἄρρων ἐτῶν
εττωιν (?) ψֿ

Known since the 16th century
and one of the earliest of our
inscriptions to be copied, but not
extant. The various transcriptions differ in details and one
cannot be sure in every instance
of the correct reading. The
inscription came most probably
from the Monteverde catacomb.

*Here lies Zosimus, Life Archon of the Synagogue of the Agrippe-
sians. In peace his sleep. Here lies Eullis (= Julius?), Archon (?), aged . . years.*

Lines 6-8: The reading of these lines is very uncertain.

Line 6: Possibly the last three letters of EYΛΛIC are intended for ΔIC so that instead of a second name, we have the information that Zosimus was twice archon.
Line 8: The word is unintelligible. It presumably indicates the age of the deceased.

504. ἐνθάδε
κεῖτε Ἰου-
λιανος ἱερευσά-
ρχων Καλ-
καρησίων υἱ-
ὸς Ἰουλιάνο-
υ ἀρχισυν-
αγώγου

Carved on the front of a sarco-phagus; apparently not extant; most probably from the Monteverde catacomb.
Here lies Julianus, Gerusiarch of the Calcaresians, son of Julianus, Archisynagogus.

505. ἐνθάδε κεῖτε
Καιλιο[ς] Κυειντ-
ος φιλοπάτωρ
β' ἄρχων ἐτῶν ιτ'
παῖς Ἑ[β]ραῖος

Carved on the front of a sarcophagus; now in the Terme Museum, No. 74102. (Fig. 65)
Here lies Caelius Quintus, lover of his father, twice Archon, aged 13 (?) years, a Hebrew boy.

Line 4: IT is probably an error for IΓ = 13. As to the phenomenon of a 13-year-old boy as twice archon, see above, pp. 178-79.

506. ἐνθάδε
κεῖτε Κου-
ιντιανη
ἐτῶν κς'
ἐν ἰρήνη ἡ
κύμισις αὐτῆς

In the Sala Giudaica of the Lateran. (Fig. 32. 16)
Here lies Quintiana, aged 26 years. In peace her sleep.

507. ἐνθάδε κῖτε
Κωνσταντ-
σα (?) νήπιου(ς)
ἐν ἰρήνη ἡ κύμη-
σις αὐτοῦ

Not extant; the exact readings are uncertain because the texts of the scholars who transcribed it do not agree.
Here lies Constantius (?), a child. In peace his sleep.

Line 3: The first two letters are given variously as TA, CA, IA. Whatever was actually on the stone may have been intended for IC, so that the child's name was perhaps Κωνστάντις = *Constantius.*

508. ἐνθάδε κεῖτε Μνι-
ασεας μαθητὴς
σοφῶν καὶ πατὴρ
συναγωγίων

Not extant.
Here lies Mniaseas (= Manasseh), *disciple of the sages and father of synagogues.*
Lines 3, 4: What is meant by the title is not clear.

509. ἐνθάδε κεῖται Παν-
χάριος πατὲρ συνα-
γωγῆς 'Ελαίας ἐτῶ-
ν ἕκατων δέκα φιλό-
λαος φιλέντολος
καλῶς βιώσας ἡν εἰρ-
ήνη ἡ κοίμησις
αὐτοῦ

In the Sala Giudaica of the Lateran.
Here lies Pancharius, Father of the Synagogue of Elaea, aged 110 years, lover of his people, lover of the Commandments. He lived a good life. In peace his sleep.

510. ὧδε κεῖ-
τε Σαλω
θυγάτηρ Γα-
δία πατρὸς
συναγωγῆς
Αἰβρέων ἐβί-
ωσεν μα'
ἐν εἰρήνη
ἡ κοίμη-
σεις αὐτῆς

Most probably from the Monteverde catacomb; now in the Terme Museum, No. 67699. (Fig. 66)
Here lies Salo, daughter of Gadias, Father of the Synagogue of the Hebrews. She lived 41 years. In peace her sleep.
Line 7: The numeral letters are enclosed in a frame resembling an L with prolonged base. Sundry scholars, including Frey, have wrongly taken it for an
L = Λ, abbreviation for λυκάβαντας,
a word for "years" which is found in poetry and in metrical epitaphs.

511. ἐνθάδε κῖ-
ται Σειλικες
γερουσιάρχης
κὲ Σωφρονία σύν-
βιος αὐτοῦ κὲ Μα-
ρία κὲ Νίκανδρος υἱοὶ
αὐτῶν

Carved on a sarcophagus; now in the Oratory of the Forty Martyrs next to the Church of Santa Maria Antiqua at the Roman Forum.
Here lies Silicius, Gerusiarch, and Sophronia, his wife, and Maria and Nicander their children.

512. [. . . .]
ἐν εἰρήνη κύ-
μησις αὐτοῦ

Known since late in the 17th century; once in the Church of Santa Sabina, but not extant.
[. . . .] In peace his sleep.

513. ἔνθα κεῖται Τι[. . . .]   Cited in 18th-century manuscripts; the
μῆνας [. . .]   slab seems to have been inserted in the
pavement of the Church of San Criso-
gono.
Here lies Ti[. . . .] months.

Numbers 515-22, inscriptions on the gold glasses, are not
included here. Although these glasses were used by the Roman
Jews and bear Jewish symbols, the inscriptions are conventional for such glasses and not distinctively Jewish.

523. Beturia Pau-
lla F domi
heterne quos-
tituta que bi-
xit an(nos) LXXXVI meses VI
proselyta an(norum) XVI
nomine Sara mater
synagogarum Campi
et Bolumni
en irenae ai cymysis
autis

Carved on a sarcophagus;
known since the late 16th
century, but not extant.
The transcriptions differ
in minor details of spel-
ling, so that a certain text
is not obtainable.
*Veturia Paulla F (?), con-
signed to her eternal home,
who lived 86 years, 6
months, a proselyte of
16 years, named Sara,
Mother of the Synagogues of Campus and Volumnius. In peace
her sleep.*

Lines 1, 2: The second name is variously given as *Paulla* or
Paulina. The oldest versions have *Paulla*.

Line 2: What was intended by the F (if correctly copied) is
not known. Frey suggests *f(ilia)* or *f(eliciter)*, neither being
plausible.

Lines 3, 4: *quostituta* is for *costituta* = *constituta*.

Lines 8, 9: The synagogues are apparently those of the Campesians and the Volumnesians.

Lines 10, 11: The transcribers differ so in their renderings of
this transliteration of the Greek formula that we cannot know
what was actually on the stone.

Numbers 524-34 are not included, since none of them demonstrably belongs to the Jews of Rome. Some are of *metuentes*
(524, 529); some are non-Jewish but refer to Jews (531-33).

Numbers 535-51e are listed as from Porto. As I have demonstrated in *HTR* 45 (1952), 165-75, most of these, if not all, belong to the Jewish community of Rome and were taken from Rome to Porto early in the 19th century. Several were taken back to Rome in 1924 and placed in the Sala Giudaica of the Lateran.

535. ἐντάδε κῖτε
τυγατέρες δύο
πατρὸς τῶν
Ἐβρέων Γα-
δίατος Κα-
ρα ἐν ἰ-
ρήνη

Carved underneath No. 543, which is the epitaph of another daughter of Gadias, who had died earlier. See H. J. Leon, "The Daughters of Gadias," *TAPA* 84 (1953), 67-72. The stone is in the Sala Giudaica.

Here lies two daughters of the Father of the Hebrews. Cara in peace.

Line 1: The verb is in the singular, either because of the stereotyped formula or because the epitaph is regarded only as that of Cara, that of her sister having been carved above.

Lines 4-6: Frey interprets the father's name as Gadia Toskara, a strange combination.

Line 6, 7: The formula is abridged because of lack of room.

536. ἐνθάδαι
κεῖται
Δωρείς
ἐν ἰρήνη ἡ κοί-
μησις αὐτῆς

Now in the Sala Giudaica. On the reverse of the stone is No. 540, probably the work of the same cutter.

Here lies Doris. In peace her sleep.

🕎

537. Καττια Ἀμμιὰς θυγάτηρ Μηνοφί-
λου πατὴρ συναγωγῆς τῶν
Καρκαρησίων καλῶς βιώσα-
σα ἐν τῷ Ἰουδαϊσμῷ ἔτη ζήσασα
τριάκοντα καὶ τέσσαρα μετὰ τοῦ
συμβίου εἶδεν ἐκ τῶν τέκνων
αὐτῆς ἔγγονα ὧδε κεῖται Καττια
Ἀμμιάς

The left half of the stone was at Porto for more than a century. In 1924 it was reunited with the right half, which was in the Sala Giudaica, where the entire stone may now be seen.

Cattia Ammias, daughter of Menophilus, Father of the Synagogue of the Carcaresians. She lived a good life in Judaism, having lived 34 years with her husband. From her children she saw grandchildren. Here lies Cattia Ammias.

Line 2: πατηρ is an error for πατρός.

Line 3: Καρκαρησιων should be Καλκαρησίων (*Calcaresians*).

538. Κλαυδιος   Now in the Sala Giudaica. (Fig. 32. 5)
Ἰωσης ἄρ-   *Claudius Joses, Archon, lived 35 years.*
χων ἔζη-
σεν ἔτη
λε'

Numbers 539 and 541 are rejected as not Jewish. See *HTR* 45 (1952), 171-72.

540. ἐνθάδε κῖτε   Now in the Sala Giudaica; on the reverse
Μαρτινα   of the stone bearing No. 536.
ἐν ἰρήνη   *Here lies Martina. In peace her sleep.*
ἡ κοίμησις
αὐτῆς
ᵗᵛᵀᵛᵀ

Numbers 542-51e, with the exception of 543, are fragments. Only those clearly Jewish and containing significant words are included here.

543. ἐνθάδει κε-   Inscribed on the same stone as No. 535,
τι Σαρρα   on which see above.
μετὰ τοῦ   *Here lies Sarra with her son. In peace.*
υἱοῦς αὐτῆς   Line 4: υιους is an error for υἱοῦ.
ἐν εἰρι   Line 5: The cutter left the last word un-
ᵗᵛᵀᵛᵀ   finished and omitted the rest of the
    formula, though there was ample space.

544. [. . . .]αμα   A fragment; in the Bishop's Palace at
[. . . .]κων οὐ[δε]-   Porto.
ἰς ἀθά[να]-   [. . . .] *No one is immortal.*
τος

545.   ἐνθ[άδε]
    κε[ῖται]   In the Sala Giudaica. (Fig. 67)
    ιε[. . .]   *Here lies* [. . . .]

---

547. ἐνθάδε κ[εῖται ....]   In the Bishop's Palace at Porto.
ἡ κύμη[σις αὐ]-   *Here lies [....]. In peace his sleep.*
το[ῦ ....]

548. [....]   In the Bishop's Palace at Porto.
[....]θουσ[....]   The last word is part of either
[....]διων και[....]   φιλοσυναγώγω (*lover of his synago-*
[....]ον παραθυρ[...]   *gue*) or ἀρχισυναγώγω (*archisyna-*
[.... σ]υναγωγω [....]   *gogus*).

Numbers 732 and 733 are in the Appendix of *CII*, pp. 597-98.

732. ἐνθάδε κεῖνται   Epitaph on a gold glass; formerly
'Αναστασία μήτηρ καὶ   in the private Galleria Sangiorgi in
'Ασθὴρ θυγάτηρ ἐν [εἰ]-   Rome, but no longer there.
ρήνη ἡ κοίμησεις   *Here lie Anastasia, the mother, and*
αὐτῶν ἀμήν   *Asther, the daughter. In peace their*
שלום   *sleep. Amen. Peace.*

733. ἐνθάδε   Now in the Museum of the Campo San-
κῖτε 'Ασθὴ-   to Teutonico in Vatican City. Although
ρ παρθένο-   some have doubted that this is a Jewish
ς ὁσία ἐτῶ-   inscription, Frey's arguments are con-
ν εἴκοσει   vincing.
δύω   *Here lies the virgin Asther, a pious*
    woman, aged 22 years.

733a. ἐνθάδε κεῖτε B-   In the Museum of the Pontificio Istitu-
ενεδικτα ἐτῶ-   to Biblico in Rome; not in *CII*; publi-
ν κβ' ἐν εἰρή-   shed by A. Vaccari in *Biblica* 19 (1938),
νη ἡ κοίμισ-   340-42.
ις αὐτῆς   *Here lies Benedicta, aged 22 years. In*
    peace her sleep.

733b. [....]ια Μαρτα ἡ [σύμ]-   In the Lapidary Museum of the
βιος 'Επαγαθοῦ τ[ο]-   monastery at St. Paul's on the Via
ῦ γερουσιάρχου ἔν-   Ostiense; not in *CII*; published by
θα κεῖτε   A. Silvagni in *Inscriptiones Chris-*
    tianae Urbis Romae, II, No. 5991.
[....]*ia Marta, the wife of Epagathus, the Gerusiarch, lies here.*

733c. ἐνθάδε   On the decorated sarcophagus of a child (Fig.
κοιμᾶται   47); in the Terme Museum, No. 67612; probably,

'Αρτεμιδώ- but not certainly, Jewish; not in *CII*. It was
ρα ἐν εἰ- transcribed by Marini in Vatican Cod. Lat.
ρήνη 9102. 218 and is cited as probably Jewish by
V. Schultze, *Die Katakomben*, 192.
Here lies Artemidora. In peace.

All the inscriptions which follow are counted as pagan by
Frey and are relegated to the Appendix of *CII*. Since, with
the exception of 11*, they were found in the Monteverde
catacomb and have no specifically non-Jewish indications,
they should be regarded as Jewish. The *CII* starred numbers
are retained. All except 11* are in the Sala Giudaica.

11*. Felicia[nus] In the Appia catacomb.
Cyriat[i] *Felicianus set up (this stone) to his wife Cyrias,*
uxori
fec[it]

24*. bull *Aurelius Olympius to his son, Bo[..]too [....]*
Aur. Oly- *in grateful memory.*
mpius fil-
io benem(e)-
renti Bo[..]
too[....]

30*. [....] The incomplete No. 344 is
[et F]elix on the reverse.
parentes *[.... and] Felix, the parents,*
Isie filiae *set up (this stone) to their*
ben(e)me(renti) fe(cerunt) *daughter, Isia, in grateful*
quae an(nis) VIIII *memory. She (lived) 9 years,*
m(ensibus) VIII *8 months.*

31*. Iulia Rufina *Julia Rufina.*

32*. Amici ego vos *Friends, I await you here;*
hic exspecto *Leo my name and Leontius*
Leo nomine et *my surname.*
signo Leontius

33*. [....]e Marcellae The stone has No. 302 on
[....]s matri sua- the reverse.

[e . . . . b]enemere-
nti

*To [. . . .]e Marcella, [. . . .]s
to his mother in grateful
memory.*

35*. Nunno Vernae
qui vixit annis
VII m(ensibus) II Vernaclus
et Archigenia filio
desiderantissimo
fecc

*To Nunnus Verna, who lived
7 years, 2 months; Vernaclus
and Archigenia set up (this
stone) to their son, whom they
greatly miss.*

Line 1: *Verna* is the word
for a slave born in the
household. It seems to be a proper name here. If not, this is
the only reference to a slave in our inscriptions.

Line 6: *fecc* is an abbreviation for *fecerunt*.

BIBLIOGRAPHY

The following list of books and articles, though extensive, is not exhaustive and omits many items to which reference is made only once or twice in the notes, where the essential bibliographical data are given. Where the applicability of a work to this study is not apparent from the title, I have usually supplied a note and, where it seemed desirable, page references to the significant passages. In citing the works of seventeenth- and eighteenth-century scholars, who provide us with the earliest copies of some of our inscriptions and on whom we must rely for reconstructing the texts of those not extant, I have specified which of the inscriptions they offer, using the numbering of *CII* and of the Appendix to the present work.

A. Important works to which frequent reference is made.

Berliner, Abraham. *Geschichte der Juden in Rom.*, 2 vols., Frankfurt-am-Main, 1893. References only to Vol. I. This work contains much valuable information, but has numerous inaccuracies, especially in dealing with the catacomb inscriptions. [Referred to here as Berliner].

Beyer, Hermann W., and Hans Lietzmann. *Die jüdische Katakombe der Villa Torlonia in Rom.* Berlin, 1930. A thorough study of the catacomb and its inscriptions. [Abbrev. BL]

Frey, Jean-Baptiste. *Corpus Inscriptionum Iudaicarum.* 2 vols., Vatican City, 1936, 1952. References are almost exclusively to Vol. I. Europe. The most nearly complete collection of the Jewish inscriptions, with commentary and numerous photographs, but marred by many errors of detail and interpretation. Frey's numbering of the inscriptions is followed in the present work. Vol. II was published posthumously in 1952, the author having died in 1939. A third volume is projected to complete the work. [Abbrev. *CII*]

Garrucci, Raffaele. *Cimitero degli antichi Ebrei scoperto recentemente in Vigna Randanini.* Rome, 1862. The first full account of the catacomb on the Via Appia and the basis for all subsequent treatments. It includes the first published texts of 63 (about half) of the inscriptions from this catacomb. [Referred to as *Cimitero*]

——, *Dissertazioni archeologiche di vario argomento.* 2 vols., Rome, 1864, 1865. Vol. II contains important material on the catacomb of the Via Appia and adds 65 inscriptions. [Referred to as *Diss. Arch.*, II]

Goodenough, Erwin R. *Jewish Symbols in the Greco-Roman Period.* Vols. I-VIII, New York, 1953-1958. More volumes are to appear. A fundamental work, although some of the views are open to question. [Referred to as Goodenough, *Jewish Symbols*, or Goodenough]

Juster, Jean. *Les juifs dans l'empire romain*. 2 vols., Paris, 1914. A work of prime importance, especially with regard to the status of the Jews of the Empire. [Referred to as Juster]

Müller, Nikolaus. *Die jüdische Katakombe am Monteverde zu Rom*. Leipzig, 1912. The description of the catacomb by the excavator. The chief source of our knowledge about this catacomb, since nothing is left of the catacomb itself. [Referred to as Müller, *Jüd. Kat.*]

———, and N. A. Bees. *Die Inschriften der jüdischen Katakombe am Monteverde zu Rom*. Leipzig, 1919. A complete collection of the inscriptions with facsimiles and commentary, brought out by Bees, since Müller had died in 1912. Bees' extensive additions to Müller's commentary are of little value and often misleading. [Abbrev. MB]

Schürer, Emil. *Die Gemeindeverfassung der Juden in Rom in der Kaiserzeit nach den Inschriften dargestellt*. Leipzig, 1879. The first extensive treatment of the organization of the Roman Jewish community; an excellent, scholarly work, but written long before the rediscovery of the Monteverde catacomb and the discovery of the Via Nomentana catacomb.

———, *Geschichte des jüdischen Volkes im Zeitalter Jesu Christi*. Ed. 4, 3 vols., Leipzig, 1901-1909, *Register* 1911. The most important work on the Jews of this period; a product of profound and extensive scholarship. [Referred to as Schürer]

Vogelstein, Hermann, and Paul Rieger. *Geschichte der Juden in Rom*. 2 vols., Berlin, 1895-1896. References are only to Vol. I. The fullest and most important treatment of the history of the Jews in Rome, but it contains many misstatements and unfounded conclusions, some of which are discussed in the foregoing text. Vol. I, pages 459-483, gives the texts (not always accurately) of all the Judeo-Roman inscriptions known to the year 1895. [Abbrev. VR]

B. Other books and articles used in the preparation of this monograph. Works dealing with the Jews more or less generally are excluded unless they contain materials of specific application to the Jews of ancient Rome. The editions of texts of ancient authors are not cited here; it may be assumed that standard modern editions have been used in all instances.

Adler, Michael. "The Emperor Julian and the Jews," *JQR* 5 (1893), 591-651.

Angelis d'Ossat, Gioacchino de. "La catacomba ebraica a Monteverde in Roma," *Roma* 13 (1935), 361-69, Plates XXXIX-XLI. Valuable discussion of the geological features.

———, *La geologia delle catacombe romane*. Vatican City, 1939. Includes important data on the Jewish catacombs. The portion on Monteverde (pp. 21-27) is largely a reproduction of the article in *Roma*.

———, *La geologia e le catacombe romane*. Vol. I, Rome, 1930. Contains some information (pp. 267, 286) on the geology of the Via Nomentana catacomb, which he seems not to have been able to visit.

Aringhius (Aringhi), Paulus. *Roma subterranea novissima.* 2 vols., Rome, 1651. Vol. II, 390-402, deals with the Jews of Rome, the data being largely taken from Bosio. Aringhi refers to the Jewish burial places in such terms as "impiorum perfidorumque hominum coemeteria," "profana Iudaeorum loca," and "ipsius Belial monumenta."

Armellini, Mariano. *Lezioni di archeologia cristiana.* Rome, 1898. Chap. III (pp. 21-31), "La Chiesa e la Synagoga nei primi tre secoli," has data on the Jewish community and the catacombs.

Ascoli, Graziadio Isaia. *Iscrizioni inedite o mal note, greche, latine, ebraiche, di antichi sepolcri giudaici del Napolitano.* Turin and Rome, 1880. Especially important for the Venosa catacomb, but has many references to the materials from Rome.

Askowith, Dora. *The Toleration and Persecution of the Jews in the Roman Empire.* New York, 1915. (Dissertation, Columbia Univ.) Treats only the period of Caesar and Augustus.

Auer, Johann. "Die Juden in Rom unmittelbar vor und nach Christi Geburt," *Zeitschrift für die gesammelte katholische Theologie* 4 (1852), 56-105. Uses the literary sources only.

Baier, Theophilus Sigifridus (Gottlieb Siegfried). *Lucubrationes de inscriptionibus Judaeorum graecis et latinis.* Regiomonti (Königsberg), 1721. Reprinted in the author's *Opuscula* (Halle, 1770), 380-410.

Baron, Salo W. *The Jewish Community.* 3 vols., Philadelphia, 1942.
——, *A Social and Religious History of the Jews.* Second edition, Vols. I and II, New York, 1952. A valuable, scholarly study, which includes data from Rome.

Bell, Harold I. *Cults and Creeds in Greco-Roman Egypt.* Liverpool, 1953. Good material on the Jews of Alexandria and their relation to the Roman authorities.
——, *Jews and Christians in Egypt.* London, 1924. Important discussion of the Claudius letter.

Benas, B. L. "Records of the Jews in Rome and their Inscriptions from Ancient Catacombs," *Proceedings of the Literary and Philosophical Society of Liverpool* 50 (1896), 45-83. Largely based on Berliner, reproducing his inaccuracies.

Bentwich, Norman. "The Rightfulness of the Jews in the Roman Empire," *JQR*, N.S. 6 (1915), 325-36. A good discussion of the privileges of the Jews, prompted by Juster's work.

Blanchinius (Bianchini), Giuseppe. Vol. I, "Le porte e mura di Roma," of Giuseppe Vasi's *Delle magnificenze di Roma antica e moderna.* Rome, 1747. On p. 57 tells of an alleged visit to the Jewish catacomb in Monteverde.

Blau, Ludwig. "Early Christian Archaeology from the Jewish Point of View," *HUCA* 2 (1926), 157-214. The attitude of the Talmud toward artistic representation.
——, "The Relation of the Bible Translations of the Jews in Romance Languages to the Ancient Versions and the Jewish Inscriptions in the Catacombs," *JQR*, N.S. 19 (1928), 157-182. Discussion of Blondheim's *Les parlers judéo-romans.*

Blondheim, David S. *Les parlers judéo-romans et la Vetus Latina.* Paris, 1925. Includes a discussion of the use of Latin by the Jews of Rome.

Bludau, August. "Die Juden Roms im ersten christlichen Jahrhundert," *Der Katholik* 83 (1903), 113-34, 193-229. A reasonably accurate and sympathetic account of the history of the community.

Blustein, Giacomo. *Storia degli Ebrei in Roma*. Rome, 1921. A work of no independent value, at least for the ancient period.

Bormann, Eugène. "Zu den neuentdeckten Grabschriften jüdischer Katakomben zu Rom," *Wiener Studien* 34 (1912), 358-69. Based on Müller's *Jüd. Kat.*

Bosio, Antonio. *Roma Sotterranea*. 2 vols., Rome, 1632. Published posthumously by Giovanni Severani in 1634, though the date on the title page is 1632. Bosio had died in 1629. The account of Bosio's famous discovery of the Monteverde catacomb is on I, 141-143.

Bousset, Wilhelm. *Die Religion des Judenthums im späthellenistichen Zeitalter*. Ed. 3 by H. Gressmann, Tübingen, 1926.

Brassloff, Stephan. "Zu den Katakombeninschriften von Monteverde," *Römische Mitteilungen* (= Mitteil. d. Deutschen Arch. Inst., Röm. Abt.) 28 (1913), 122-24.

Braude, William G. *Jewish Proselytism in the First Five Centuries of the Common Era: the Age of the Tannaim and Amoraim*. (Dissertation, Brown Univ.) Providence, 1940. Assembles the talmudic references.

Brunati, Giuseppe. *Musei Kircheriani inscriptiones ethnicae et christianae*. Milan, 1837. On pages 119-120, "Inscriptiones sepulchrales iudaicae," texts and discussion of Nos. 283 and 481, both of which were formerly in the Museo Kircheriano and are now in the Terme Museum.

Buonarroti, Filippo. *Osservazioni sopra alcuni frammenti di vasi antichi di vetro ornati di figure trovati ne' cimiteri di Roma*. Florence, 1716. For the Jewish gold glasses see pp. 19-24 and Plates II. 5, III. 1, 2.

Burgon, John William. *Letters from Rome to Friends in England*. London, 1862. On pages 162-74, "Specimens of early Jewish sepulchral inscriptions," offering texts of most of the Jewish inscriptions then known, with comments.

Cardinali, Clemente. "Iscrizioni antiche inedite," *Giornale Arcadico di Scienze, Lettere ed Arti* 11 (1821), 229-35. His Nos. XX-XXV are Roman-Jewish inscriptions with commentary. N.B. The same author's *Iscrizioni antiche inedite*, Bologna, 1819, and *Opuscoli letterarii*, Bologna, 1819, offer copies of a few more Jewish inscriptions, but Cardinali's readings in all three works are quite inaccurate.

Carmina Latina Epigraphica. Supplementum III by E. Lommatzch, Leipzig, 1926. No. 1991 = our No. 476 (the Regina inscription).

Cassuto, Milka (daughter of Umberto Cassuto). "La corrispondenza tra nomi ebraici e greci nell' onomastica giudaica," *Giornale della Società Asiatica Italiana*, N.S. 2 (1932-33), 209-30. A useful study of the Hellenized forms of Hebrew names, but some of the parallels are dubious.

Cassuto, Umberto. "Un' enigmatica iscrizione romana," *Giornale della Società Asiatica Italiana*, N.S. 2 (1932-33), 125-34. On No. 290, the Aramaic inscription.

——, "Un' iscrizione giudeo-aramaica conservata nel Museo Cristiano Lateranense," *NBAC* 22 (1916), 193-98. On No. 290.

Castiglione, Vittorio. "Intorno ad alcune lapidi giudaiche esistenti nel monastero di S. Paolo fuori le Mura in Roma," *BCACR* 36 (1908), 77-85.

Charlesworth, M. P. *Documents Illustrating the Reigns of Claudius and Nero.* Cambridge, 1939. Pages 3-5 on the letter of Claudius to the Jews of Alexandria.

Chwolson, Daniel A. *Corpus Inscriptionum Hebraicarum.* St. Petersburg, 1882. Pages 147-149, "Catacomben-Inschriften aus Rom," discuss Nos. 296 and 397.

Clermont-Ganneau, Charles. "La nécropole juive de Monteverde," *RA,* Ser. V, 11 (1920), 365-66. On the inscriptions discovered by Paribeni in 1919.

Cohn-Wiener, Ernst. *Die jüdische Kunst.* Berlin, 1929. An important work, with considerable attention to the materials from Rome (especially pp. 118-33).

Collon, Suzanne. "Remarques sur les quartiers juifs de la Rome antique," *Mélanges d'Archéologie et d'Histoire de l'École Française de Rome* 57 (1940), 72-94. Has much useful information, but is inclined to fill the gaps with unsubstantiated assumptions. Valuable for assembling of references.

Corpus Inscriptionum Graecarum [*CIG*]. 4 vols., Berlin, 1828-1859. Index vol. 1877. The Jewish inscriptions from Rome are in Vol. IV, esp. Nos. 9901-9926.

Corpus Inscriptionum Latinarum [*CIL*]. Berlin, 1863- (In progress). The Jewish inscriptions from Rome are in Vol. VI, Nos. 29756-29763.

Corsinus (Corsini), Edvardus. *Notae Graecorum, sive vocum et numerorum compendia.* Florence, 1749. Appendix II, Dissert. II, p. XXX, on No. 507.

Crook, John A. "Titus and Berenice," *AJP* 72 (1951), 162-75.

Cumont, Franz. "A propos de Sabazios et du Judaïsme," *Musée Belge* 14 (1910), 55-60. On the edict of 139 B.C.E.

———, "Catacombes juives de Rome," *Syria* 2 (1921), 145-48. On the newly discovered Via Nomentana catacomb.

———, "Un fragment de sarcophage judéo-païen," *RA,* Ser. V, 4 (1916), 1-16. On the "Seasons sarcophagus."

———, *Recherches sur le symbolisme funéraire des romains.* Paris, 1942. Pages 484-98 are a revision of his article in *RA,* above.

Dalton, O. M. "The Gilded Glasses of the Catacombs," *Archaeological Journal* 58 (1901), 227-53.

Danzetta, Fabio. Vatican MS. Lat. 8324 contains his "Schede autografe" with early copies (18th cent.) of Nos. 307 and 458 on fol. 109.

Daremberg, Ch., and E. Saglio. *Dictionnaire des antiquités grecques et romaines.* 5 vols. in 9, Paris, 1873-1919. Article "Iudaei" by Th. Reinach.

Davis, S. *Race Relations in Ancient Egypt; Greek, Egyptian, Hebrew, Roman.* London, 1951. Interesting data on the attitude of the Roman government toward the Jews.

Derenbourg, Joseph. "Eleazar le Peitan," *Mélanges Renier* (Paris, 1887), 429-441. The inscriptions at Porto on pp. 437-41.

Dictionnaire d'archéologie chrétienne et de liturgie by Henri Leclercq and Fernand Cabrol. 15 vols. in 30, Paris, 1924-1953. Especially the articles "Clemens (Titus Flavius)," "Judaïsme" (sections on La Diaspora, Organization de la communauté, L'art et les cimitières juifs, Épigraphie), "Monteverde" (includes the Jewish community and its catacombs, with very inadequate bibliography), "Verres" (especially the section on Verres juifs), all by Leclercq. [Abbrev. DACL]

Diehl, Ernestus. *Inscriptiones latinae christianae veteres.* 3 vols., Berlin, 1925-1931. "Tituli iudaici latini," Vol. II, Nos. 4851-5000.
———, *Lateinische christliche Inschriften mit einem Anhang jüdischer Inschriften.* Bonn, 1908 (*Lietzmann's Kleine Texte*). The few Roman-Jewish items are copied from *CIL* and the scanty commentary has no independent value.

Dittenberger, Wilhelm. "Römische Namen in griechischen Inschriften und Literaturwerken," *Hermes* 6 (1872), 129-55, 281-313.

Eckinger, Theodor. *Die Orthographie lateinischer Wörter in griechischen Inschriften.* (Dissertation, Zürich) Munich, 1893. Incorrect readings of the inscriptions are uncritically accepted.

Enciclopedia Cattolica. 12 vols., Vatican City, 1948-1954. Article "Cimiteri ebraici antichi" (Josi).

Enciclopedia Judaica Castellana. 10 vols., Mexico City, 1948-1951. Articles "Catacumbas" and "Roma."

Encyclopaedia Judaica (completed only through "Lyra"). 10 vols., Berlin, 1928-1934. Article "Katakomben" (Krauss).

Engers, Mauritz. "Der Brief des Kaisers Claudius an die Alexandriner," *Klio* 20 (1926), 168-178.

Engeström, A. v. *Om Judarne i Rom under äldre Tider och deras Katakomben.* Upsala, 1876. The author was acquainted with the gold glasses and only 46 of the inscriptions.

Fabretti, Raphael. *Inscriptionum antiquarum quae in aedibus paternis asservantur explicatio.* Rome, 1699. Early copies, with discussion, of Nos. 503, 504, 512, 523.

Feldman, Louis H. "Asinius Pollio and his Jewish Interests," *TAPA* 84 (1953), 73-80.
———, "Jewish 'Sympathizers' in Classical Literature and Inscriptions," *TAPA* 81 (1950), 200-208. Argues that expressions meaning "God-fearing" and the like do not necessarily apply to "sympathizers," but may be used to describe pious Jews.

Ferrua, Antonio. "Addenda et corrigenda al Corpus Inscriptionum Iudaicarum," *Epigraphica* 3 (1941), 30-46.
———, "Epigrafia ebraica," *Civ. Catt.* 1936, III, 461-73, 1936, IV, 127-37. Criticisms of *CII.*
———, "Simbolismo ebraico," *RAC* 30 (1954), 237-43. Critical review of Goodenough, I-III.
———, "Sulla tomba dei cristiani e su quella degli ebrei," *Civ. Catt.* 1936 IV, 298-311. Further criticisms of *CII.*

Ficoronius (Ficoroni), Franciscus. *Dissertatio de larvis scenicis et figuris comicis antiquorum Romanorum.* Ed. 2, Rome, 1754. Page 106 and Plate 81 deal with our No. 283.

Fiorelli, Giuseppe. *Catalogo del Museo Nazionale di Napoli. Raccolta epigraphica.* Naples, 1868. The Jewish inscriptions from Rome are his Nos. 1954, 1956, 1958-1960, 1962-1965.

Foerster, W. *Das Judenthum Palästinas zur Zeit Jesu und der Apostel.* Ed. 2, Hamburg, 1955.

Frey, Jean-Baptiste. "L'ancienneté des catacombes juives à Rome," *Rendiconti della Pontificia Accademia Romana di Archeologia,* Ser.

III, 7 (1936), 185-198. On the dating of the catacombs (first to third centuries).

——, "La catacombe juive de la voie Nomentane," *RAC* 8 (1931), 359-63. Review of BL.

——, "Una comunità giudaica di Arca del Libano a Roma nel 3° secolo secondo una iscrizione inedita," *Bulletino del Museo dell' Impero Romano* I (1930), 97-106 (= Appendix to *BCACR*, Vol. 58). Argument for the synagogue supposedly revealed in No. 501.

——, "Les communautés juives à Rome aux premiers temps de l'Église," *Recherches de Science Religieuse* 20 (1930), 267-97, 21 (1931), 129-68. On the congregations and their organization.

——, "Il delfino col tridente nella catacomba giudaica di Via Nomentana," *RAC* 8 (1931), 301-314. Color plate on page 308.

——, "Inscriptions inédites des catacombes juives de Rome," *RAC* 5 (1928), 279-305, 7 (1930), 234-60. These were later included in *CII*.

——, *Inscriptions juives de Rome et d'Italie*. Paris, 1932. Includes items previously published in *RAC*.

——, "Inscriptions juives inédites," *RAC* 8 (1931), 83-125. Chiefly on the Porto materials with an account of the supposed Jewish community at that place.

——, "Le judaïsme à Rome aux premiers temps de l'Église," *Biblica* 12 (1931), 129-56. Much of this material was subsequently incorporated in the Introduction to *CII*.

——, "Nouvelles inscriptions inédites de la catacombe juive de la Via Appia," *RAC* 10 (1933), 27-50. The previously unnoticed *graffiti*, later introduced into *CII*. There is a new plan of the Appia catacomb opposite page 184.

——, "La question des images chez les juifs à la lumière des récentes découvertes," *Biblica* 15 (1934), 265-300. Argues, with numerous examples, for a much freer use of images by Jews than previously realized; maintains that these are primarily for decoration and not doctrinal symbolism.

——, "La signification des termes MONANΔPOC et UNIVIRA. Coup d'oeil sur la famille romaine aux premiers siècles de notre ère.)" *Recherches de Science Religieuse* 20 (1930), 48-60. Argues for the meaning "not divorced" in the Jewish inscriptions.

——, "La vie de l'au-de-là dans les conceptions juives au temps de Jésus-Christ," *Biblica* 13 (1932), 129-68. Contrasts Jewish ideas of the hereafter with pagan and Christian.

Friedmann, K. "Ancora sulla persecuzione di Domiziano," *Atene e Roma*, N.S. 11 (1931), 69-83. Maintains that there was a persecution of the Jews by Domitian.

Gabrieli, G. *Itala judaica*. Rome, 1924. Bibliographical material.

Galling, K. "Die jüdischen Katakomben in Rom als ein Beitrag zur jüdischen Konfessionskunde," *Theologische Studien und Kritiken* 103 (1931), 352-60. Offers eschatological interpretations of the symbols.

Garrucci, Raffaele. "Descrizione del cimitero di Vigna Randanini sulla Via Appia." *Civ. Catt.*, Ser. V, 3 (1862), 87-97.

——, "Nuove epigrafi giudaiche di Vigna Randanini." *Civ. Catt.*, Ser. V, 6 (1863), 102-117. This article and the preceding one were later incorporated in his *Diss. Arch.*, II.

——, *Storia della arte cristiana*. 6 vols., Prato, 1873-1880. For the

Jewish materials see I, 9-13; VI, Plates 489-92, with discussion on pages 156-67.

——, *Vetri ornati di figure in oro trovati nei cimiteri dei cristiani primitivi di Roma.* Rome, 1858; also ed. 2, Rome, 1864, in which Plate V has Jewish gold glasses.

Gatti, G. *BCACR,* Ser. V, 28 (1900), 223-24 (on No. 496 and the Augustesians); N.Sc. 1892.345 (on No. 505); N.Sc. 1900.88 (on No. 496); N.Sc. 1904.297 (on *CII* 288, which is not demonstrably Jewish).

Ginsburg, Michael S. "Fiscus Iudaicus," *JQR,* N.S. 21 (1931), 281-91.

Goodenough, Erwin R. "The Crown of Victory in Judaism," *Art Bulletin* 28 (1946), 139-59. Application of this symbolism to the paintings of the Jewish catacombs.

——, "Early Christian and Jewish Art," *JQR,* N.S. 33 (1943), 403-417. Chiefly concerned with Dura-Europus.

——, "The Evaluation of Symbols Recurrent in Time, as Illustrated in Judaism," *Eranos-Jahrbuch* 20 (1952), 285-319.

——, "The Menorah among the Jews in the Roman World," *HUCA* 23, pt. 2 (1950-51), 449-92. Largely incorporated in *Jewish Symbols,* IV, ch. 4.

Graetz, Heinrich. *Geschichte der Juden von den ältesten Zeiten bis auf die Gegenwart.* 11 vols. in 13, Leipzig [1897-1911]. Various other editions in German and in translation. The American edition is in 6 vols., Philadelphia, 1891-1898.

——, "Die jüdischen Proselyten im Römerreiche unter den Kaisern Domitian, Nerva, Trajan, und Hadrian," *Jahresbericht d. jüd.-theolog. Seminars,* Breslau, 1884.

Greppo, J. G. H. *Notices sur des inscriptions antiques tirées de quelques tombeaux juifs à Rome.* Lyon, 1835. Has texts, with commentary, of nine inscriptions from the Jewish catacombs, none at firsthand; unacquainted with those found in 1748 at Monteverde.

Gressmann, Hugo. "Die Inschriften der jüdischen Katakombe am Monteverde zu Rom," *Deutsche Literaturzeitung* 41 (1920), 305-310. Discussion of MB.

——, "Jewish Life in Ancient Rome," *Jewish Studies in Memory of Israel Abrahams* (New York, 1927), 170-191. Extensive discussion of the catacomb materials, especially of the painted rooms of the catacombs of the Via Appia and Nomentana.

Gsell, Stéphane. *Essai sur le règne de l'empereur Domitien.* Paris, 1894. Pages 290-310 treat the Jews under Domitian and the problem of Clemens, Domitilla, and Glabrio.

Guignebert, Ch. *Le monde juif vers le temps de Jésus.* Paris, 1935. The 1950 edition is a reprint of the earlier one.

Guterman, Simeon L. *Religious Toleration and Persecution in Ancient Rome.* London, 1951.

Hamburger, J. *Real-Encyclopädie für Bibel und Talmud.* Strelitz, 1883. Article "Rom."

Hanfmann, George M. A. *The Season Sarcophagus in Dumbarton Oaks.* 2 vols., Cambridge, Mass., 1951. The "Season Sarcophagus" from the Via Appia is discussed, especially I, 195; II, 88, note 339.

Hardy, G. F. *Studies in Roman History.* London, 1906. Contains materials on the Jews at Rome in the first century C.E.

Heidel, W. A. "Why were the Jews Banished from Italy in 19 A.D.?" *AJP* 41 (1920), 38-47. An unconvincing attempt to explain the action of Tiberius.

Herzog, E. "Le catacombe degli Ebrei in Vigna Rondanini," *BICA* 1861, 91-104. The earliest account of the Via Appia catacomb, published while it was being excavated.

Hospers-Jarsen, Anna M. A. *Tacitus over de Joden, Hist. 5. 2-13.* Groningen, 1949. Discussion of the sources of Tacitus' account of the Jews.

Hudson, (Miss) E. H. *History of the Jews in Rome, B.C.* 160- *A.D.* 604. London, 1882. An uncritical study from the point of view of a pious Christian "unacquainted with the dead languages."

Huidekoper, Frederic. *Judaism at Rome.* New York, 1876. Has nothing on the catacomb materials, although much was available at that date.

Inscriptiones Graecae. Vol. XIV, *Inscriptiones Italiae et Siciliae,* ed. by G. Kaibel, Berlin, 1890. Only Nos. 945, 946, 949 (= our 535, 536, 538) are Jewish inscriptions, all of the Porto group.

Janne, Henri. "Impulsore Chresto," *Mélanges Bidez* (= *Annuaire de l'Institut de Philologie et d'Histoire Orientales,* II, 1934), 531-553. On the expulsion by Claudius as due to disturbances over Christ.

——, "Lettre de Claude aux Alexandrins et le Christianisme." *Mélanges Franz Cumont* (= *Annuaire de l'Institut de Philologie et d'Histoire Orientales,* IV, 1936), 273-95.

Jewish Encyclopedia [*JE*]. 10 vols., New York and London, 1907. Especially the following articles: "Alphabet, the Hebrew" (Lidzbarski), "Ark of the Law" (Casanowicz), "Art, Attitude of Judaism toward" (Kohler), "Ass-Worship" (Krauss), "Burial" (Kohler), "Candlestick" (Nowack), "Catacombs" (Krauss), "Etrog" (Casanowicz), "Lulab" (Casanowicz), "Paleography—Greek and Latin Inscriptions" (De Ricci), "Rome" (Ochser), and the individual articles on the various writers, emperors, and other historical characters alluded to in this study.

Jones, H. Stuart. "Claudius and the Jewish Question at Alexandria," *JRS* 16 (1926), 17-35.

Jordan, H. "Das Templum Deae Syriae in Rom," *Hermes* 6 (1872), 314-22. On pages 319-20 he deals with the Jewish settlements in Rome.

Jüdisches Lexikon. 4 vols. in 5, Berlin, 1927-1930. Especially the following articles: "Kaiser, Römische, Stellung zu den Juden" (Rieger), "Katakomben" (Rieger), "Römische Schriftsteller über Juden" (Posner), "Rom" (Rieger).

Juster, Jean. *Les droits politiques des juifs dans l'empire romain.* Paris, 1912.

——, *Examens critiques des sources relatives à la condition juridique des juifs dans l'empire romain* (Doctoral Dissert.) Paris, 1911. This work and the preceding one were incorporated into the author's *Les juifs dans l'empire romain.*

Kanzler, R. "Scoperta di una nuova regione del cimitero giudaico della Via Portuense," *NBAC* 21 (1915), 152-57.

Kaufmann, Carl M. *Handbuch der altchristlichen Epigraphie.* Freiburg-im-Breisgau, 1917. Includes references to Jewish inscriptions.

——, *Handbuch der christlichen Archäologie.* Ed. 3, Paderborn, 1922. Has references to the Jewish catacombs.

Kohl, Heinrich, and Carl Watzinger. *Antike Synagogen in Galilaea*. Leipzig, 1916. Makes some use of the materials from Rome for illustrative purposes.

Kraus, F. X. *Roma Sotterranea. Die römischen Katakomben*. Ed. 2, Freiburg, 1879. Includes the Jewish catacombs known at that time.

Krauss, Samuel. *Synagogale Altertümer*. Berlin and Vienna, 1922. Pages 247-59 on the Roman synagogues and their officials.

——, *Talmudische Archäologie*. 3 vols., Leipzig, 1910-1912.

Kretschmer, Paul. "Die Inschriften der jüdischen Katakombe am Monteverde zu Rom," *Glotta* 12 (1923), 192-93. Review of MB.

Lanciani, Rodolfo. *New Tales of Old Rome*. Boston, 1891. "Jewish Memorials in Rome," pages 215-59.

——, "Ricerche topografiche sulla città di Porto," *Annali dell' Instituto di Corrispondenza Archeologica* 40 (1868), 144-95. Texts of two Jewish inscriptions then in Porto (Nos. 535, 536) on page 191.

——, *BCACR* 9 (1881), 8. On No. 289.

La Piana, George. "The Church and the Jews," *Historia Judaica* 11 (1949), 117-44.

——, "Foreign Groups in Rome during the First Centuries of the Empire," *HTR* 20 (1927), 183-403. Pages 341-93 are an important contribution on the Jews of Rome, their districts, synagogues, cemeteries, privileges, cults, proselytism. An Italian version appeared as "L'immigrazione a Roma nei primi secoli dell' impero" in *Ricerche Religiose* 4 (1928), 193-248.

Laqueur, Richard. "Der Brief des Kaisers Claudius an die Alexandriner," *Klio* 20 (1926), 89-106.

Le Blant, Edmond. *Comptes-Rendus de l'Académie des Inscriptions et Belles-Lettres* 12 (1884), 52-53 (on the Via Labicana catacomb), 208-209 (on the Jewish catacombs), 14 (1886), 194-96 (on the Porto inscriptions).

Leclercq, Henri. *Manuel d'archéologie chrétienne*. 2 vols., Paris, 1907. "L'art et les cimetières juifs," I, 495-528; "Chandelier à sept brauches," II, 215 f.

Lehmann, Karl. "The Dome of Heaven," *Art Bulletin* 27 (1945), 1-27. Used by Goodenough to demonstrate this motif in the frescoes of the Appia and Nomentana catacombs.

Lenormant, François. *Essai sur la propagation de l'alphabet phénicien dans l'ancien monde*. Ed. 2, 2 vols., Paris, 1872. I, 264-67 on the inscriptions of the Monteverde catacomb; II, 109 on the Semitic letters of No. 296.

Leon, Harry J. "The Daughters of Gadias," *TAPA* 84 (1953), 67-72, Plates I-II. On Nos. 535, 543, 510.

——, "De Iudaeorum antiquorum sepulcretis Romae repertis quaestiones selectae," *Summaries of Theses*, Harvard University, Cambridge, 1931, pp. 8-9. The thesis itself (unpublished) is available in the Harvard University Library.

——, "The Jewish Catacombs and Inscriptions of Rome: an Account of their Discovery and Subsequent History," *HUCA* 5 (1928), 299-314.

——, "The Jewish Catacombs of Rome," *AJA* 31 (1927), 83-84. Summary of paper.

——, "The Jewish Community of Ancient Porto," *HTR* 45 (1952), 165-75.

——, "A Jewish Inscription at Columbia University," *AJA* 28 (1924), 251-52. On No. 111.
——, "The Jews of Venusia," *JQR*, N.S. 44 (1954), 267-84.
——, "The Language of the Greek Inscriptions from the Jewish Catacombs of Rome," *TAPA* 58 (1927), 210-33.
——, "The Names of the Jews of Ancient Rome," *TAPA* 59 (1928), 205-224.
——, "New Material about the Jews of Ancient Rome," *JQR*, N.S. 20 (1929), 301-312.
——, "One Hundred Per Cent Romanism," *South Atlantic Quarterly* 26 (1927), 146-60. On the attitude of the Romans toward foreign elements, including the Jews.
——, "Symbolic Representations in the Jewish Catacombs of Rome," *JAOS* 69 (1949), 87-90.
——, "The Synagogue of the Herodians," *JAOS* 49 (1929), 318-21. On No. 173.
——, "Two Jewish Inscriptions of Rome Rediscovered," *RAC* 29 (1953), 101-105. On Nos. 120, 136.
——, "An Unpublished Jewish Inscription at Villa Torlonia in Rome," *JQR*, N.S. 42 (1952), 413-18, Plates I-II. On No. 35a.
——, Reviews: of MB, in *AJA* 31 (1927), 392-94; of Loevinson, *Roma Israelitica*, in *JQR*, N.S. 24 (1933), 159-60; of *CII*, in *JQR*, N.S. 28 (1938), 357-61; of Goodenough, I-III, in *Archaeology* 7 (1954), 261-62; IV, *ibid.* 9 (1956), 154; V-VI, *ibid.* 11 (1958), 135-36; VII-VIII, *ibid.* 13 (1960) 155.
Leoni, Umberto, and Giovanni Staderini. *On the Appian Way.* Rome, 1907. Pages 48-49 on the Jewish catacombs.
Lévi, Israel. "Le prosélytisme juif," *REJ* 50 (1905), 1-9, 51 (1906), 1-31.
Lévy, Isidore. "Tacite et l'origine du peuple juif." *Latomus* 5 (1946) 331-340. Considers the sources of each of Tacitus' conjectures about the Jews.
Levy, M. A. "Epigraphische Beiträge zur Geschichte der Juden," *Jahrbuch für die Geschichte der Juden* 2 (1861), 259-324. Numerous inaccuracies and misinterpretations in both the texts of the inscriptions and the commentary.
Liebermann, Saul. *Greek in Jewish Palestine.* New York, 1942.
Loeb, Isidore. "Chandeliers à sept branches," *REJ* 19 (1889), 100-105. On various forms of the menorah.
Loevinson, Ermanno. "Il cimitero degli antichi Ebrei sulla Via Portuensis," *BCACR* 47 (1921), 206-210. Discussion of MB.
——, *Roma Israelitica.* Frankfurt, 1927. Has some good material on the catacombs and inscriptions.
Lowrie, Walter. *Art in the Early Church.* New York, 1947.
Lupi, Antonio Maria. *Dissertatio et animadversiones ad nuper inventum S. Severae Martyris epitaphium.* Panormi (Palermo), 1734. Includes texts of several Jewish inscriptions with comments.
Maffei, Scipione. *Museum Veronense.* Verona, 1749. Page 321 has our No. 481.
Magnus, Laurie. *The Jews in the Christian Era.* London, 1929. Discussion of anti-Jewish bias among the Romans.
Manfrin, Pietro. *Gli Ebrei sotto la dominazione romana.* 4 vols., Rome, 1888-1897. Diffuse and fantastic.
Manna, Belisario. "L'epigrafia del cimitero giudaico di Via Nomentana," *BCACR* 48 (1922), 205-223.

Marangoni, Giovanni. *Acta S. Victorini Episcopi Amiterni et Martyris.* Rome, 1740. Page 151 has our No. 284.

Marchi, Giuseppe. *I monumenti delle arti cristiane primitive nella metropoli del cristianesimo.* Rome, 1844. Pages 20-22 on the Monteverde catacomb.

Marcus, Ralph. "The *Sebomenoi* in Josephus," *Jewish Social Studies* 14 (1952), 247-50. On the use of the word *sebomenoi* for gentile "godfearers."

——, "A Selected Bibliography of the Jews of the Hellenistic Roman Period," *Proceedings of the American Academy of Jewish Research* 16 (1946-47), 97-181.

Marini, Gaetano. *Gli atti e monumenti de' Fratelli Arvali.* Rome, 1795. Pages 341, 342, 347 on our Nos. 349, 401.

——, "Epitaphia Hebraeorum." In Vatican MS. Lat. 9074, pp. 938-41. Copies of the Jewish catacomb inscriptions known in the late eighteenth century.

——, "Iscrizioni cristiane greche." In Vatican MS. Lat. 9102. Copies of Jewish inscriptions on ff. 60, 114, 197, 212, 217, 218.

——, In Vatican MS. Lat. 9115, f. 176, our No. 380.

Marmorstein, A. "Jüdische Archäologie und Theologie," *Zeitschrift für die neutestamentliche Wissenschaft* 32 (1933), 32-41. Eschatological interpretations of the symbols in frescoes and inscriptions.

Marucchi, Orazio. *Breve guida del cimitero giudaico in Vigna Randanini.* Rome, 1884. Later reprinted in the 1905 edition of *Le catacombe romane*, pp. 227-247, and (in a French version) in *Éléments d'arch. chrét.*, II, 208-226.

——, *Le catacombe romane.* Rome, 1905. The revised edition of 1933 (by E. Josi) greatly reduces the material on the Jews and their catacombs. Most of my references are, accordingly, to the earlier edition.

——, "La chiesa di S. Maria Antiqua nel Foro Romano," *NBAC* 6 (1900), 285-320. Page 311 on our 511.

——, "Di un nuovo cimitero giudaico sulla Via Labicana," *Dissertazioni della Pontificia Accademia Romana di Archeologia*, Ser. II, 2 (1884), 499-532. Reproduced in the 1905 edition of his *Catacombe romane*, pp. 279-97, and (in French version) in his *Éléments*, II, 259-274.

——, *Éléments d' archéologie chrétienne.* Ed. 2, 2 vols., Paris, 1906, 1903. Vol. II, 208-226 on the Via Appia catacomb, 259-74 on the Via Labicana catacomb.

——, "Scavi nella Vigna Randanini," *Cronichetta Mensuale*, Ser. III, tom. II, ann. II (1883), 188-90.

——, "Scoperta di un nuovo cimitero giudaico sulla Via Nomentana," *NBAC* 26 (1920), 55-57.

——, *BAC*, Ser. IV, 2 (1883), 79 f.; 3 (1884), 42 f. Reports on the investigation of the Via Labicana catacomb.

——, *Dissert. Pontif. Accad.*, Ser. II, 2 (1884), 24-26. On the discovery of our No. 72.

Menestrier, Claude (died 1639). Vatican MS. Lat. 10545. Early copies of our inscriptions: f. 150 has No. 523, f. 239 has No. 503.

Merrill, Elmer T. *Essays in Early Christian History.* London, 1924. Pages 102-108 on Claudius and the Jews; 148-73 on the Flavius Clemens problem and the persecution under Domitian.

——, "The Expulsion of the Jews from Rome under Tiberius," *CP* 14 (1919), 365-72.

Migliore, Gaetano (died 1789). "Ad inscriptionem Flaviae Antoninae commentarius sive de antiquis Iudaeis exercitatio epigraphica." In Vatican MS. Lat. 9143, ff. 113-170. Includes the author's transcriptions of the then known Jewish inscriptions.

Modena, Aldo Neppi. "A proposito del P. Lond. 1912. 73-104," *Aegyptus* 7 (1926), 41-48. On the letter of Claudius to the Jews of Alexandria.

Momigliano, Arnaldo. *Claudius: the Emperor and his Achievements.* Oxford, 1934. A translation (by W. D. Hogarth) with revisions and editions of the Italian work of 1932, listed below.

——, "I nomi delle prime 'sinagoghe' romane e la condizione giuridica della communità in Roma sotto Augusto," *Rassegna Mensile di Israël* 6 (1931), 283-92.

——, *L'opera dell' Imperatore Claudio.* Florence, 1932.

——, "Severo Alessandro Archisynagogus." *Athenaeum*, N.S. 12 (1934), 151-53.

Mommsen, Th. *Inscriptiones regni neapolitani latinae.* Leipzig, 1882. Includes texts of two Roman Jewish inscriptions of the Naples Museum. His No. 6727 = our 479; 7190 = 480.

Moore, George Foot. *Judaism in the First Centuries of the Christian Era: The Age of the Tannaim.* 2 vols., Cambridge, Mass., 1927.

Müller, Nikolaus. "Le catacombe degli Ebrei presso la Via Appia Pignatelli," *Römische Mitteilungen* (= *Mitteilungen des Deutschen Archäologischen Instituts. Römische Abteilung*) 1 (1886), 49-56.

——, "Cimitero degli antichi Ebrei posto nella Via Portuense," *Dissertazioni della Pontificia Accademia Romana d' Archeologia*, Ser. II, 12 (1915), 205-318, Plates IX-XII. A posthumous account, Müller having died in 1912. The material is largely the same as that in the author's German monograph of 1912 (listed in Section A, above).

——, *BAC*, ser. IV, 3 (1884-85), 139-41. Report on the discovery of the Appia Pignatelli catacomb.

Münz, J. B. "Neuaufgefundene römische Inschriften aus einer jüdischen Katakombe," *Monatsschrift für Geschichte und Wissenschaft des Judentums* 59 (1915), 77-81. On the Monteverde catacomb.

Muratori, Ludovicus Antonius. *Novus thesaurus veterum inscriptionum.* 4 vols., Milan, 1739-1742. Has the following Roman Jewish inscriptions: I 152.4 = 504, II 708.3 = 504 with altered readings, II 1129.6 = 1, III 1674.3 = 283, IV 2045.7 = 284. Muratori's readings and explanations are undependable.

Neubauer, A. "On Non-Hebrew Languages Used by Jews," *JQR* 4 (1891), 9-19.

Neuburg, Frederic. *Glass in Antiquity* (trans. by R. J. Charleston). London, 1949. Includes the gold glasses from Rome and data on Jews in glassmaking.

Nicolai, Johannes. *De sepulchris Hebraeorum.* Lugduni Batavorum (Leyden), 1706. Still useful.

Nicolai, Niccola Maria. *Della Basilica di S. Paolo.* Rome, 1815. On pages 161-63 there are texts and translations (both very inaccurate) of the Jewish inscriptions in the monastery at St. Paul's on the Via Ostiense (San Paolo fuori le Mura).

Nohl, Hermann. *Wochenschrift für klassische Philologie* 30 (1913), 66 f. On No. 476.

Northcote, J. S., and W. R. Brownlow. *Roma Sotterranea or Some Account of the Roman Catacombs.* Ed. 2, London, 1879. Includes brief data on the Jewish catacombs.

Nuovo Bullettino di Archeologia Cristiana [NBAC]. Reports at Conferenze di Archeologia Sacra: 20 (1914), 97, on new discoveries at Monteverde; 27 (1921), 54-55, on the excavation of the Via Nomentana catacomb; 28 (1922), 110, discussion of the Synagogue of the Calcaresians.

Odericus, G. A. *Dissertationes et adnotationes in aliquot ineditas veterum inscriptiones et numismata.* Rome, 1765. On pages 253 f. there are copies of Nos. 307 and 458, based on Marangoni.

Oehler, Johann. "Epigraphische Beiträge zur Geschichte des Judentums," *Monatschrift für Geschichte und Wissenschaft des Judentums* 63 (1909), 292-302, 443-52, 525-38. Does not include the inscriptions from the Via Appia catacomb, although they had been published long before.

Orelli, J. C., and W. Henzen. *Inscriptionum latinarum selectarum amplissima collectio.* 3 vols., Turici (Zürich), 1828-1856. The Roman Jewish inscriptions are No. 2522 (= our 523), 2524 (= 481), 3222 (= 284).

Osann, Friedrich Gottheil. *Sylloge inscriptionum antiquarum graecarum et latinarum.* Leipzig, 1834. For the Jewish inscriptions of Rome see pages 430, 432, 441, 472, 474, 485.

Paribeni, Roberto. "Catacomba giudaica sulla Via Nomentana," *N. Sc.* 1920, 143-55. First official report of the excavation of the catacomb.

——, "La collezione cristiana del Museo Nazionale Romano," *NBAC* 21 (1915), 95-118. The Jewish materials are on pages 95-97 and Plate IV. 1.

——, "Culti e religioni in Roma imperiale secondo recenti scoperte archeologiche," *Atene e Roma,* N.S. 1 (1920), 169-83. Pages 181-183 on the Via Nomentana catacomb.

——, "Iscrizioni del cimitero giudaico di Monteverde," *N. Sc.* 1919, 60-70.

Parker, John Henry. *The Archaeology of Rome.* Part XII. *The Catacombs.* Oxford and London, 1877. Pages 119-122 and Plate III on the Jewish catacombs.

Paulys Real-Encyclopädie der classischen Altertumswissenschaft [RE], by Georg Wissowa (later vols. by W. Kroll and K. Mittelhaus). Stuttgart, 1894- (in progress). Especially the articles "Berenike" (Wilcken), "Fiscus Iudaicus" (Rostowzew), "Flavius Clemens" (Stein), "Flavia Domitilla" (Stein).

Perret, Louis. *Catacombes de Rome.* 6 vols, Paris, 1851-1855. Plates XXIV, XXVIII show Jewish gold glasses; material on the Jews in VI 43, 122, 125.

Radin, Max. "A Jewish Sepulchral Inscription from Rome," *JQR,* N.S. 7 (1917), 281-83. On No. 111.

——, *The Jews among the Greeks and Romans.* Philadelphia, 1915. Makes no great use of the archeological materials from Rome.

——, *CP* 20 (1925), 368-75. Review of Bell's *Jews and Christians in Egypt* with discussion of the Jews of Alexandria.

Raisin, Jacob S. *Gentile Reactions to Jewish Ideals with Special Reference to Proselytes*. New York, 1953. Pages 292-329 deal with the Jews of Rome.

Raponi, Ignazio Maria. "Inscriptiones ad Iudaeos Italicos spectantes Velitris in Museo Borgiano MDCCLXXXVIIII." In Vatican MS Mus. Borg. 278, pp. 154-60. Accurate texts of the Jewish inscriptions which were then at Velletri and most of which were later transferred to the Naples Museum.

Reifenberg, Arthur. *Ancient Hebrew Arts*. New York, 1950. Especially pp. 129-138 art of the catacombs, 144-147 on lamps, 148-152 on glass.

——, *Denkmäler der jüdischen Antike*. Berlin, 1937.

——, "Jüdische Lampen," *Journal of the Palestine Oriental Society* 16 (1936), 166-79.

Reinach, Salomon. "Synagogue juive à Phocée," *Bulletin de Correspondance Hellénique* 10 (1886), 327-35. Pages 329-30 deal with the Roman Synagogue of Elaea.

Reinach, Théodore. "Le cimetière juif de Monteverde," *REJ* 71 (1920), 113-26.

——, "Une nouvelle nécropole judéo-romaine," *REJ* 72 (1921), 24-28. On the Via Nomentana catacomb.

——, "La pierre de Myndos," *REJ* 42 (1901), 1-6. Page 4 on No. 496.

——, "Quid Iudaeo cum Verre?" *REJ* 26 (1893), 36-46. On Cicero's alleged jest about Caecilius.

——, *Textes d'auteurs grecs et romains relatifs au Judaïsme*. Paris, 1895.

Rengstorf, Karl Heinrich. "Zu den Fresken in der jüdischen Katakombe der Villa Torlonia in Rom," *Zeitschrift für neutestamentliche Wissenschaft* 31 (1932), 33-60.

Riba, Maximilian. "Neuaufgefundene römische Inschriften aus einer jüdischen Katakombe an der Via Portuense bei Rom," *Programm des K.K. Staats-Obergymnasium zu Wiener-Neustadt*, 1914, 3-20.

Ricci, Seymour de. "Catacombe juive de la Via Portuensis," *Comptes-Rendus de l' Académie des Inscriptions et Belles-Lettres*, 1905, 245-47. On the rediscovery of the Monteverde catacomb.

Rieger, Paul. "Zu den Fresken in der jüdischen Katakombe der Villa Torlonia in Rom," *Zeitschrift für die neutestamentliche Wissenschaft* 33 (1934), 216-18.

Ripostelli J., and O. Marucchi. *La Via Appia*. Rome, 1908. Page 103 on the Jewish catacomb.

Robert, Louis. "Un corpus des inscriptions juives," *REJ* 101 (1937), 73-86. Criticism of *CII*.

——, "Un corpus des inscriptions juives," *Hellenica* 3 (1946), 90-108. Amplification of the preceding article.

——, "Inscriptions juives grecques et latines à Oxford," *REJ* 102 (1937), 121. Identification of the Pusey House inscriptions as from the Via Appia catacomb.

Roller, Théophile. *Les catacombes de Rome*. 2 vols, Paris, 1881. On the Jewish catacombs see I 11-16 and Plates IV, V.

Roma e dintorni (Guida d' Italia). Milan 1950. On the Via Appia catacomb see pages 300-301.

Romanelli, Pietro. "I quartieri giudaici dell' antica Roma," *Bullettino dell' Associazione Archeologica di Roma* 2 (1912), 132-39.

Romanoff, Paul. "Jewish Symbols on Ancient Coins," *JQR*, N.S. 33 (1942-43), 1-15, 435-44; 34 (1943-44), 161-77, 299-312, 425-40.

Rossi, Giovanni Battista de. "Insigne vetro rappresentante il Tempio di Gerusalemme," *BAC* 20 (1882), 121-35, 137-58 and Plate VII; 21 (1883), 92. Also a French version: "Verre représentant le Temple de Jérusalem," *Archives de l'Orient Latin* 2 (1884), 439-55.

——, *La Roma sotterranea cristiana.* 3 vols., Rome, 1864-1877. The Jewish catacombs on I, 90.

——, "Scoperta d'un cemetero giudaico presso l'Appia," *BAC* 5 (1867), 16. On the Vigna Cimarra catacomb.

——, *BAC* 3 (1865), 90-95, on the early relations between Christianity and Judaism; 4 (1866), 40, on the Porto inscriptions.

Roth, Cecil. "Messianic Symbols in Palestinian Archaeology," *Palestine Exploration Quarterly*, 1955, 151-64.

Scaglia, Sixte. *La promenade archéologique.* Rome, 1911. Pages 100-105 on the Via Appia catacomb.

Schneider-Graziosi, Giorgio. "La nuova Sala Giudaica nel Museo Cristiano Lateranense," *NBAC* 21 (1915), 13-56. Has texts of all the inscriptions.

Schultze, Victor. *Archäologische Studien über altchristliche Monumente.* Vienna, 1880. Jewish materials on pages 263 f., 271, 277, 281.

——, *Die Katakomben.* Leipzig, 1882. Jewish materials on pages 19-22, 87, 182, 193.

Schulze, Wilhelm. *Zur Geschichte lateinischer Eigennamen.* Berlin, 1904.

Schwabe, Moshe. "Die neue jüdische Inschrift von der Via Labicana in Rom," *Journal of the Palestine Oriental Society* 12 (1932), 248-250. On No. 78.

——, *Tarbitz* 14 (1942-43), 140 f. On No. 113 [Hebrew].

——, *Zion* 9 (1943-44), 46 f. On Nos. 535, 543. *Ibid.*, 47. On No. 379 [Hebrew].

——, and A. Reifenberg. "Ein jüdisches Goldglas mit Sepulcralinschrift aus Rom," *RAC* 12 (1935), 341-46. On No. 732.

——, "Ein unbekanntes jüdisches Goldglas," *RAC* 15 (1938), 319-29. On a gold glass in Cologne, possibly from Rome.

Scramuzza, Vincent M. *The Emperor Claudius.* Cambridge, Mass., 1940.

Seaver, James E. *Persecution of the Jews in the Roman Empire.* Lawrence, Kansas, 1952.

Silvagni, Angelo. *Inscriptiones christianae urbis Romae septimo saeculo antiquiores.* Nuova serie, 2 vols., Rome, 1922, 1935. No. II 5991 = our No. 733b.

Simon, Marcel. "Le chandelier à sept branches, symbole chrétien?" *RA* 31-32 (1948-49), 971-80.

——, "Θάρσει οὐδεὶς ἀθάνατος. Étude de vocabulaire religieux," *Revue de l'Histoire des Religions* 113 (1936), 188-206.

——, *Verus Israel. Étude sur les relations entre chrétiens et juifs dans l'empire romain* (135-425). Paris, 1948. An important study.

Smallwood, E. Mary. "The Chronology of Gaius' Attempt to Desecrate the Temple," *Latomus* 16 (1957) 3-17.

——, "Jews Under Tiberius," *Latomus* 15 (1956) 314-329.

——, "The Legislation of Hadrian and Antoninus Pius Against Circumcision," *Latomus* 18 (1959) 334-347.

Solomon, S. J. "Art and Judaism," *JQR* 12 (1901), 533-66.

Spon, Jacob. *Miscellanea eruditae antiquitatis.* Lugduni (Lyon), 1685. Early copies of Nos. 503, 504, 523 on pages 371 f.

Sturtevant, E. H. *The Pronunciation of Greek and Latin.* Ed. 2, Philadelphia, 1940.

Styger, Paul. *Juden und Christen im alten Rom.* Berlin, 1934. Has many inaccuracies and shows a marked anti-Jewish bias.

Sukenik, E. L. *Ancient Synagogues in Palestine and Greece.* London, 1934.

Supplementum Epigraphicum Graecum. Vol. IV (Leyden, 1929), Nos. 143, 144 = our 537, 111.

Thumb, Albert. *Die griechische Sprache im Zeitalter des Hellenismus.* Strassburg, 1901.

Thylander, Hilding. *Étude sur l' épigraphie latine.* Lund, 1952. "Le gentilice des Juifs," on 139-40; "Les surnoms des Juifs," on 167-69; also page 178.

Universal Jewish Encyclopedia. 10 vols. New York, 1939-1943. Especially the articles "Catacombs, Jewish" (Rieger), "Roman Writers on Jews," "Rome" (with cross references).

Vaccari, Alberto. "Ancora le iscrizioni giudaiche del Museo Cristiano Lateranense," *NBAC* 28 (1922), 43-52, Plate IV.

——, "Osservazioni sopra alcuni iscrizioni giudaiche del Museo Cristiano Lateranense," *NBAC* 23 (1917), 31-45.

——, "Pontius Maximus," *Rassegna Italiana di Lingue e Lettere Classiche* 2 (1919-20), 326-28. On the date of the election of archons by the Jews.

——, *Biblica* 19 (1938), 340-42. Discussion of *CII.*

Vaglieri, Dante. "Nuove scoperte e nuovi studi al Foro Romano," *BCACR,* Ser. V, 28 (1900), 266-98. Page 295 on No. 511.

Venuti, Ridolfino. "Dissertazione sopra due antiche greche iscrizioni," *Giornale dei Letterati,* 1748, 145-58. Includes discussion of several of the Jewish inscriptions of Rome.

Vessillo Israelitico, 1884, 261 f. Report of the discovery of the Via Labicana catacomb.

Vieillard, R. "Codices et volumina dans les bibliothèques juives et chrétiennes: Notes d' iconographie," *RAC* 17 (1940), 143-48. Includes data on representations of the Ark of the Law.

Visconti, C. L. "Scavi di Vigna Randanini," *BICA* 1861, 16-22. Discovery of materials outside the Via Appia catacomb.

Vogelstein, Hermann. *History of the Jews in Rome* (trans. by Moses Hadas). Philadelphia, 1940.

Vopel, Hermann. *Die altchristlichen Goldgläser.* Freiburg im Breisgau, 1899. Includes Jewish gold glasses.

Waal, Anton de. "Die jüdische Katakombe an der Via Portuensis," *Römische Quartalschrift für christliche Altertumskunde und für Kirchengeschichte* 19 (1905), 140-42.

Webster, T. B. L. "The Wilshire Collection at Pusey House in Oxford," *JRS* 19 (1929), 150-54. Includes Jewish inscriptions removed from the Via Appia catacomb.

Wesseling, Petrus. *Diatribe de Iudaeorum archontibus ad inscriptionem Berenicensem.* Traiecti ad Rhenum (Utrecht), 1738. Discusses Nos. 1, 504, 508.

Wilde, Robert. *The Treatment of the Jews in the Greek Christian Writers of the First Three Centuries.* Washington, 1949.

Willrich, Hugo. "Zum Brief des Kaisers Claudius an die Alexandriner," *Hermes* 60 (1925), 482-89.
——, *Berliner Philologischer Wochenschrift*, 1895, 987-89. Additions to Reinach's *Textes relatifs au Judaïsme*.
Winghius (de Winghe), Philippus (died 1592). MS in Royal Library of Brussels, Cod. 17872-17873. Contains the earliest known copies of any Jewish inscriptions of Rome, our Nos. 503 and 523.
Wischnitzer, Rachel. "La catacombe de la Villa Torlonia," *REJ* 91 (1931), 102-107.
Withrow, William H. *The Catacombs of Rome and their Testimony Relative to Primitive Christianity*. Rome, 1877. On the Jewish catacombs, pages 50-54, 188.
Zabeo, Ugo. "Osservazioni di meteorologia nelle catacombe," *RAC* 22 (1946), 63-88. Useful data on temperature and humidity inside the catacombs.
Zeitlin, Solomon. Review of Goodenough, I. *JQR*, N.S. 45 (1954), 66-73.
Zoller, I. "Iscrizioni sepolcrali nelle catacombe giudaiche," *Ricerche Religiose di Storia delle Religioni* 8 (1932), 461-65.
Zolli, Israel. "Zu Frey: Corpus Inscriptionum Iudaicarum," *Monatschrift für Geschichte und Wissenschaft des Judentums* 82 (1938), 56-57. Zolli's review of *CII* is in 81, 303-305.
Zunz, Leopold. *Namen der Juden*. Leipzig, 1837. Also in his *Gesammelte Schriften*, II (Berlin, 1876), 1-82.
Zwarts, Jacob. "De zevenarmige Kandelaar in de romeinse diaspora." (Amsterdam dissertation) Utrecht, 1935. A survey of occurrences and types of the menorah.

INDEX

Though extensive, this Index is not intended to be exhaustive, in that it does not include every passing reference, but is, in general, limited to matters of some significance. Only the more important references to ancient authorities, such as Josephus and Philo, are cited here. Similarly, it seemed of little value to include every reference to the work of modern scholars, some of whom, notably Frey, Goodenough, Schürer, and Vogelstein, are cited very frequently in the text. Accordingly, this Index refers only to pages where their views are described or discussed.

References to the Appendix of Inscriptions are not included in the Index, since the inscription numbers can, in most instances, readily be located from the catalogue of names (pp. 95-107).

Greek and Hebrew words are presented in transliteration. The use of the letter *n* after a page number (e.g. 85n.) indicates that the reference will be found in the notes on the page specified, but the separate notes are not indicated.

APPENDIX TO THE REVISED EDITION: NEW INSCRIPTIONS

Nos. 1#–32# are new inscriptions from the Villa Torlonia catacomb, published by Fasola, "Le due catacombe ebraiche di Villa Torlonia," *Rivista Archeologia Cristiana* 52 (1976) 7–62.

1#. ☩

Ἐνθάδε κεῖται	*Here lies*
Φίλιππος ὁ φιλάδελφος	*Philip, of brotherly love,*
ζήσας ἔτη τριάκοντα	*who lived thirty-*
τρία.	*three years*

Fasola, p. 12 with photo. *Année épigraphique* (1976) 78. Found on the ground near entrance A. A small marble slab, 18 x 23 cm., 0.8 cm. thick, letters 2 cm. high. According to Fasola, it must have been affixed next to the loculus, rather than on the closure, a method not unusual in the Jewish cemeteries.

2#. ☷

Ἐνθάδε κ[εῖται]	*Here l[ies]*
Ζώσιμο[ς]	*Zosimo[s]*
εὐδ . . .	*[happy?]*
σ . . . ν . . .	*s . . . n . . .*

Fasola, p. 14. Found *in situ* at the bottom of stairway A, entrance to upper catacomb. Letters painted in red, very poorly preserved. The menorah is 16 cm. high.

3#.

['P]ουφί[νος]	*[R]ufi[nus]*
[ἐ]ν εἰρήν[ῃ]	*[i]n peac[e]*
[ἐτ]ῶν . . .	*[ye]ars . . .*

Fasola, p. 18. Area A2, painted on a piece of plaster, letters 5–7 cm.

4#.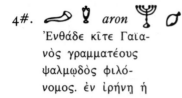

'Ενθάδε κîτε Γαϊα-
νὸς γραμματέους
ψαλμῳδὸς φιλό-
νομος. ἐν ἰρήνῃ ἡ
κοίμισις αὐτοῦ

Here lies Gaia-
nos, scribe,
cantor, lover of the
law. In peace be
his sleep.

Fasola, pp. 19–20, with photo. *Année épigraphique* (1976) 79. Fasola's transcription (p. 19) corrects the spelling, but the photo (p. 20) shows it as given here. In gallery AI, slab *in situ*, at the center of the closure, the rest in plastered tiles. This is the eighth inscription of a scribe at Villa Torlonia, the only known of a cantor in the Roman inscriptions.

5#. 'Ενθάδε κîτε Ι[. . . ἀπὸ τῆς]   Here lies I[. . . from]
    'Αχαίας ἐν ἰρη[νῃ . . .]   Achaia in pea[ce . . .]

Fasola, p. 20. Red paint on plastered tile, broken but *in situ*.

6#. 'Ενθάδε κîτε Εὐμένις   Here lies Eumenis

Fasola, p. 21. Painted at the top edge of the lowest loculus on the wall of gallery AI, across from A3. Fasola emends the name to Εὐμένι(ο)ς, but it could also be Εὐμένης.

7#. Βλερίνος   Verinus

Fasola, p. 21. In gallery AI, next to the entrance to A6. Written in fresh plaster above the loculus of a child. The candelabra is five-branched.

8#. Σιν·πλί·χ[ι]-   Simplic[i]-
    ως·αἐ·τῶν   us, years
    δέ·κα·αε·ν εἰ-   ten, in pe-
    ρένῃ   ace

Fasola, p. 21; photo, p. 22. *Année épigraphique* (1976) 80. Found on the ground in gallery AI. The divisions between letters are made with ivy leaves or simple points. The letters are filled in in red and inscribed on previously drawn lines. The last word was originally spelled HPENH, then the first mistake was partially corrected by the inscriber.

9#. Μάξιμος Θαβρακενός   *Maximus of Thabraca*

Fasola, pp. 21–22; photo, p. 23. *Année épigraphique* (1976) 81. A small slab, 13 x 20 x 1.5 cm., found at the junction of galleries A1 and A3. Because of its small size, the slab must have been affixed next to the loculus rather than on it, as with #1 above. But because it was not discovered *in situ*, it is not known whether this is the inscription of a child, as is no. 1#. The place of origin of the deceased is Thabraca in Numidia.

10#. Ἐνθάδε κῖ[ται] ἐν ἰρήν[ῃ ἡ]   *Here li[es] in peac[e be]*
     Σπουδέος   κοίμησις αὐτο   *Spoudeos   his sleep*

Fasola, p. 23. Inscription spread across four tiles sealing a burial. Letters to the left are on the first tile to the left; the second, small tile was removed by robbers. The letters on the right side are spread across the third and fourth tiles. Fasola emends the name to Σπουδαῖος.

11#. [Πομ]πώνια Θε . . . .   *[Pom]ponia The . . .*
     [ἐνθάδ]ε κ[εῖται]   *[lie]s h[ere]*

Fasola, pp. 23–24. Painted fragments found among others on the ground, probably belonging to the same inscription which still has a menorah *in situ* above.

12#. Ὗκος εἰρήνης   ἐν ἰρή-   *House of peace   in pea-*
     Κερδῶν μετὰ εὐλογίας νη   *Kerdo with blessing   ce*

Fasola, p. 24. Intact loculus in gallery A5, inscription in carbon on tile closure. Ὗκος for οἶκος, indicative of the pronunciation of the Greek diphthong. To the right of the burial a glass vial for spices is affixed.

13#. Ⴠ ⬟ aron ⚬ ⛎

'Ενθάδε κῖτε 'Ιουσ-
τος υἱὸς 'Αμαχίου
τοῦ Κατανέου
ἐτῶν κβ' ἐν ἰρήνῃ
ἡ κοίμισις αὐτοῦ

Here lies Jus-
tos son of Amachios
of Catania
22 years. In peace
be his sleep.

Fasola, pp. 25–26, with photo. *Année épigraphique* (1976) 82. Fasola's transcription corrects the spelling, but the photo shows it as given here. Found out of place in gallery A6–A7. The symbols are similar to those on no. 4# above, though not identically placed. The ark in the center contains nine scrolls, as opposed to twelve in the inscription of Gaius.

14#. *Locus Maran*
     ⛎ *aron* ⛎

Burial of Maran

Fasola, p. 26, with photo. Found in same place as no. 13#. Only the fifth Latin inscription from Villa Torlonia (cf. nos. 68#–71#). Though the first word is clearly Latin, the name, probably Semitic, appears to be written in Greek: MAPAN. The ark is peculiar in having eight scrolls inside on four shelves, but three more on each open door. The design above the ark is probably a five-branched candelabra as in no. 7# above.

15#. ⛎ 'Ενθάδε κῖτε ⛎
      'Αναστάσιους
      ἀρχιγερουσιάρ-
      χης υἱὸς 'Αν[ασ]
      τασίου οι[. . . .]

Here lies
Anastasius
archigerousiarch
son of An[as]-
tasios, aged (?)

Fasola, pp. 36–37, with photo. *Année épigraphique* (1976) 83. Found out of place in area B. Though the title of gerousiarch of local synagogues occurs elsewhere in the inscriptions, this is the first known archigerousiarch, possibly another title for the same position, or possibly an official at a higher level. The son who is commemorated has taken his father's name but latinized it, a common phenomenon. Fasola emends the final letters to the beginning of the word ἐτῶν, since that is the most likely conclusion, and the corruption αἐτῶν is not unusual. Though the bottom right of the inscription is broken off, there is room for three more letters at most, and no further lines, since the whole inscription is enclosed in a *tabula ansata*, the menorahs placed in the *ansae*. Above the left menorah is an anomalous circle that could be an etrog.

16#. *Dis*   *To the*
     mani[bus]   *divine spi[rits]*
     Cuspia[e filia-]   *for Cuspi[a his daughte-]*
     e Cusp[ius]   *r Cusp[ius]*
     pat[er posuit or fecit]   *her fat[her set this up]*

Fasola, p. 38. *Année épigraphique* (1976) 85 as a pagan inscription. One of two inscriptions found together in area B that Fasola doubts are Jewish, perhaps reused stones in the catacomb. But the use of *dis manibus* is not unknown on Jewish or Christian inscriptions: cf. Horsley, *NewDocs* 1.76 for argument to accept this one as Jewish. If so, it would add to the small number of Latin Jewish inscriptions.

17#. Σεβέρο[ς]   *Severu[s]*
     . . . σεα . . .   *. . . sea . . .*

Fasola, p. 45. In gallery E5 in the lower catacomb. One of three inscriptions found in place, letters painted on cement spread on the closure. Fasola reports that the full inscription is four lines long, but of the third and fourth line, only an M and a P are legible. The second inscription is not sufficiently preserved to yield any information.

18#. . . . μετος   *. . . metos*
     δὶς ἄρ[χων]   *twice ar[chon]*

Fasola, p. 45. The third of three inscriptions begun at no. 17# above. Four letters of this inscription, MET of the first line and P beneath it, appear in *CII* 66, read by Lietzmann. Fasola reads the other six.

19#. Ῥουφεῖνος φι-
    λογονέους
    Ἔζησεν ἔτη
    δέκα δύω

                    Rufinus lo-
                     ver of parents
                     lived twelve years

Fasola, p. 46, with photo. *Année épigraphique* (1976) 86. Found in area E out of place. The spelling out of the numerals is unusual.

20#. Ἀβῖβο[ς] . . .
    ἀπὸ Λίν[δ]-
    ου ἐνθάδε
    κεῖται ἔζη-
    σεν ἔτη λ'

                     Avivo[s]
                     from Lin[d-]
                     os here
                     lies, who lived
                     thirty years

Fasola, pp. 46–47, with photo. *Année épigraphique* (1976) 87. Area E. The upper right part of the tablet is broken off, so that there is room for several more letters after the name, but also after the first three letters of Lindos. Thus the name could have been longer, or a symbol could have been placed there, or a title, such as ἄρχων, Fasola's speculation. *Année épigraphique* omits the last three words, plainly visible on fig. 21, p. 47 of Fasola, and misreads the name as Ἀκρῖβος; the first five letters are clearly legible as ABIBO. Fasola provides the rough breathing on the opening letter of the name.

21#. *Julius* . . .
    Juliae F . . . [coniu-]
    gi cum [qua annis]
    XVIII vixi[t]
    ἐν ἰρήνῃ ἡ [κοίμησις αὐτῆς]

                     Julius . . .
                     to Julia F . . . [his wife]
                     with [whom he lived
                     18 years
                     in peace [be her sleep]

Fasola, pp. 46–47, with photo. Area E. The sixth Latin inscription found at Villa Torlonia, but with Greek conclusion. The slab is broken off the entire right side.

22#. *Ioulius*
    Archon

                     Joulius
                     archon

Fasola, p. 47. Area E. Letters painted on a tile. A Latin name spelled partially in Greek, and the Greek term ἄρχων written in Latin.

23#. Ἰουδ[ας]   *Joud[as]*
     μεν γ´   *three months (?)*

Fasola, p. 47. Area E. Letters painted on a tile. The fourth letter could also be λ, hence the name could be Ἰουλ(ιος) or Ἰουλ(ία).

24#. [Εὐ]πρέπιος 🕎   *[Eu]prepios*

Fasola, p. 48. In gallery E6. There are two more lines to the inscription, but they are indecipherable.

25#. Ὀκ[λά]τια Πία γυνή   *Oc[la]tia Pia, wife (?)*
     ἐ[νθάδε κεῖται ?]   *[lies here?]*

Fasola, p. 49. In gallery E6, on a double burial, one on top of the other within a loculus with arcosolium, a method seemingly unique to the Villa Torlonia cemetery. Description in Fasola, pp. 50–52. The rest of the inscription on plaster has fallen off. As Fasola recognizes, the initial E of the second line may really be the beginning of the name of the husband.

26#. [Ἐνθά]δε [κεῖται]   *[He]re [lies]*
     [Φιλόδ]οξο[ς] (?)   *[Philod]oxo[s] (?)*

Fasola, p. 49. In gallery E7. The first line is surely correct, but there are other possibilities for the name.

27#. [Ἐ]νθάδε κ[εῖται]   *[H]ere l[ies]*
     παιδὶν Ἰουλία   *the child Julia*

Fasola, p. 49. In gallery E1, east of the crossing of E9. Παιδίν for παιδίον. See another variant spelling in no. 28# below.

28#. Ἐνθάδε [κεῖται]   *Here [lies]*
     πεδὶν Ἀπ[ελλῆς ?]   *the child Ap[elles ?]*

Fasola, p. 49. Same location as no. 27#. Πεδίν for παιδίον. The completion of the name is a guess based on the space available.

29#. Ἐνθάδε κῖτε　　　　Here lies
　　Γερόντις　　　　　　Gerontis
　　ζήσας ἔτη δύο　　　who lived two years
　　παρὰ ἡμέρας ί　　　less ten days

Fasola, p. 49; photo, p. 50. In gallery E1. A complete marble inscription found out of place, damaged by later secondary use.

30#. Ἐνθ[άδε κεῖται]　　　　Her[e lies]
　　Γερο[. . . .] [ἐν εἰρήνῃ]　　Gero[. . . .] [in peace]
　　[ἡ κοίμησ]ις αὐ[τοῦ or αὐτῆς]　[be his/her sleep]

Fasola, p. 50. In gallery E1. Painted in red on cement smeared on a tile. The name could be of a man or a woman.

Nos. 31#–39# are from area D, where other inscriptions have already been published by Paribeni, Lietzmann, Frey, Leon, and others. These were apparently not noticed by previous investigators.

31#. Ἀθη[ναῖος ? . . . ἐν εἰρή-]　　Athe[naios ? . . . in pea-]
　　νη ἐτῶ[ν] . . .　　　　　　　ce, ? year[s]

Fasola, p. 56. In gallery D2 on the south wall near the stairs. The name could be masculine or feminine.

32#. [Λ]εόντις　　　　　　[L]eontis

Fasola, p. 56. In gallery D2, north wall near crossing with D5.

33#. Αὐια νέπια　　　　　Avia, infant

Fasola, p. 56. In gallery D2. Painted on fresh plaster. Avia is a Latin name that can also mean grandmother, but obviously does not here. Νέπια for νήπια, also found in the masculine form in CII 97, 138.

34#. [Ἐνθάδε κ]εῖτε   *[Here l]ies*
    . . . υτα Σάρα   *. . . uta Sarah*

Fasola, p. 56. In gallery D3, north wall, soon after branching from D1.

35#. ἐτῶν . . . ἐν εἰρήνη   *. . . years . . . in peace*
    [ἡ κοίμησις] αὐτοῦ   *[be] his [sleep]*

Fasola, p. 56. In gallery D3. An inscription of four lines, of which only the third and fourth are legible.

36#. . . . ος δὶς [ἄρχων ?]   *. . . os twice [archon?]*
    ἐν εἰρήν[ῃ ἡ κοίμησις]   *in peac[e be] h[is sleep]*
    [α]ὐτοῦ

Fasola, p. 57. In gallery D3. The deceased held an office twice, perhaps that of archon: see no. 18# above.

37#. Ἐνθά[δε] . . . καὶ Επα[. . . .]   *Her[e] . . . and . . . Epa[. . . .]*
    τ[. . . .] θεια [εὔ]τεκνος   *t[. . . .] theia, [good] child-*
    ἐν ἐρή[νῃ ἡ κοίμη-]   *bearer, in pea[ce be his sl]e[ep]*
    σ[ις] αὐτοῦ μετὰ τῶν ὁσίων   *with the holy ones*

Fasola, p. 57. Gallery D7, west wall. A very long inscription, only partly decipherable. If the reading of the second line is correct, the name ending is feminine, but Fasola reads the masculine adjective in the last line. Much is obviously lost from the inscription.

38#. ⸸ Ει . . .   *Ei . . .*
    ἐν ε[ἰρήνη ἡ κοίμησις α]ὐτο[ῦ] *in p[eace be h]is [sleep]*

Fasola, p. 57. Gallery D9, east wall.

39#. [Ro]mana   *[Ro]mana*

Fasola, p. 57. In gallery D10, south wall, painted in large lettering, a woman's name in Greek or Latin.

No. 40# was copied by Antonio Ferrua in 1982 among a number of Christian inscriptions in the private collection of Federico Zeri: "Iscrizioni paleocristiane in una raccolta privata," *Rivista Archeologia Cristiana* 59 (1983) 321–33.

40#.[ός ἔζη]σεν ἐτῶν πε[ν-   *[who li]ved fi[fty] years*
 τήκον] τα ἐν ἰρήνη ἡ κο[ί- *in peace be his sl[eep]*
 μησις] αὐτοῦ ♆

Ferrua, "Iscrizioni paleocristiane," pp. 328–29; sketch, p̣. 327. Fragment of marble slab, broken on all sides. The formula ἔζησεν ἐτῶν is grammatically irregular, but not unknown elsewhere in the Jewish inscriptions: see 359, 384, 397. Because all three are from Monteverde, Ferrua speculates that this inscription also comes from there.

41#. [. . . Κ]ατιλία Εὐτυχι- *[. . . C]atilia Eutychi-*
 [. . . ἐ]πύησα ἔνπρο- *[. . . m]ade in the pres-*
 [σθεν ? . . .]μυς· Ἑρμιόνην *[ence of . . .]mus. Hermione,*
 [τρο]φ[ίμην ἐτ]ῶν δ´ Ἑρμιᾶ- *dear four-ye[ar-old fo]s[ter]*
 δος φιλίην ἥδε σορὸς κα- *child, of Hermias this tomb*
 τέχι· Πούπλις Κατίλις Ἑρμι- *contains. I, Publius Catil-*
 ᾶς ἔνπορος ἐνθάδε κῖμαι *is Hermias, merchant, age*
 ἐτῶν λε´· ἐ δέ τις ταύτην τὴν *35, lie here. Anyone who*
 σορὸν ἀν(ύξ)η καὶ ἔτερόν τινα *opens this tomb and places*
 θάψη. θήσι τῷ ταμίῳ * ´ ε´ · εἰ δέ *another will pay 5000 denarii.*
 τις ἢ τύνβον πρίατα ἢ γράμ- *Of anyone who buys the tomb*
 μα μιώση ἐξόλεσι ουκιν *or ruins the inscription,*
 σύνπαν γένος ἡ θεοῦ *may the wrath of God destroy*
 ὀργή *all descendants.*

Museo Nazionale Romano, inv. 72932, probably from Vigna Randanini. Moretti, "Iscrizioni greco-giudaiche di Roma" (215–18), argues that this is a Jewish inscription, dated orthographically to the late second or early third century, on the basis of its association by provenance with other Jewish inscriptions, the absence of usual Greco-Roman funerary expressions, and the final allusion to the wrath of God. Ουκιν in third to last line for ἐκείνου.

ADDENDA ET CORRIGENDA
TO THE FIRST EDITION

The following are some corrections later made to Leon's readings. Only rereadings or substantial observations that shed new light are included here, not differences of opinion. For further suggestions, see Lifshitz, pp. 25–42.

No. 11. The final word is δεκανίας, Greek translation of *decuria*, translated "of the section." "The epitaph belonged to a member of a *decuria*, whatever the meaning of it may be" (Lifshitz, p. 25).

No. 12. In the last line, Fasola (p. 57) reads with Ferrua the last word as ὁσίων, (with the) saints, not τέκνων, children.

No. 16. The final σοῦ, conjectured by Frey but not restored by Leon, does exist, and can be read off the cement, on the tufa below (Fasola, p. 57).

No. 25. The final AN of εὐλογίαν read by Leon and criticized by Lifshitz, p. 26, Fasola (pp. 57–58) emends to Π and reads four more letters after, so that the final line reads (εὐλογί)α πᾶσιν, blessing to all.

No. 35a. Instead of Καιλία for the first name, L. Moretti ("Iscrizioni Greco-Giudaiche di Roma," p. 219) reads on the sarcophagus ['Io]υλία. J. and L. Robert (*Bulletin épigraphique* 68 [1955] no. 293) emends Ὀμνῖνα το Δομνῖνα. Further, Moretti claims there is no room for the article του as third to last word. Thus the whole inscription should read: ['Io]υλία Δομνῖνα γυνὴ 'Ιουλιανοῦ [ἄρ]χοντος Σιβουρησίων, *Julia Domnina, wife of Julianus, archon of the Siburesians.*

No. 44. Fasola, p. 58, sees several things not reported by others. The stamp of Sapricius is applied about 25 times to the wet plaster. To the left of the menorah is the word εὐλογία, blessing, with loulab to the left and shofar to the right. To the right of the inscription, the name *Sapricius* with etrog to its left.

No. 239. As interpretation of the final word MOYNNA,
M. Schwabe (review of *CII* in *Qiryat-Sepher: Bibliographical
Quarterly of the Jewish National and University Library* 14
[1938] 498–513, in Hebrew) had proposed the first letters of
the Hebrew formula אמן נפש נוח שכבו ("his tomb a place of
rest for the soul. Amen"), with reference to no. 611, where
the same formula appears with שלום as the final word instead
of אמן (Lifshitz, p. 32).

No. 249, l. 2. Single Θ unrecognized by Leon is read by
J. M. Reynolds (*Classical Review* n.s. 13 [1963] 332–33) as
equivalent of *obiit*.

No. 733 b. Published by Ferrua, "Iscrizioni paleocristiane,"
p. 329, seemingly unaware that Frey and Leon had already
published it, as well as Silvagni in *Inscriptiones Christianae
Urbis Romae Septimo Saeculo Antiquores* (New Series; ed. Giovanni Battista de Rossi, Angelo Silvagni, Antonio Ferrua;
Rome: Pontifical Institute of Christian Archeology, 1922—),
2.5991. But Ferrua comments that the first letter is unsure;
only the bottom remains, so that it could as well be Γ, Π, or
T, and the two letters could be a fragment or abbreviation of
a *gentilicium* of Martha, or a second name, like Πία or Λία.

UPDATED BIBLIOGRAPHY

The following bibliography contains major works on Jews in the Roman world and more detailed studies on the Jews of Rome since 1960. Like the bibliography of the first edition, it is not meant to be exhaustive. Abbreviations follow the Society of Biblical Literature format, except that where there is a discrepancy with those given at the beginning of this volume, Leon's system is followed.

Blumenkranz, B. "Quelques notations démographiques sur les Juifs de Rome des premiers siècles." In *Studia Patristica* 4.2. Edited by F. L. Cross. Pages 341–47. Berlin: Akademie Verlag, 1961.

Brooten, Bernadette J. *Women Leaders in the Ancient Synagogues*. BJS 36. Chico, Calif.: Scholars, 1982.

Chilton, Bruce. "The Epitaph of Himerus from the Jewish Catacomb of the Via Appia." *JQR* 79 (1988/89) 93–100.

Clauss, M. "Probleme der Lebensalterstatistiken aufgrund römischer Grabinschriften." *Chiron* 3 (1973) 395–417.

_____. "Ausgewählte Bibliographie zur lateinischen Epigraphik der römischen Kaiserzeit (1.–3 Jh.)." *ANRW* 2.1 (1974) 796–855.

Cohen, Shaye J. D. "Epigraphical Rabbis [Catalog of Jewish Inscriptions Referring to Rabbis]." *JQR* 72 (1981) 1–17.

_____, ed. *The Jewish Family in Antiquity*. BJS 289. Atlanta: Scholars, 1993.

Dinkler, E. "Shalom–Eirene–Pax: Jüdische Sepulkralinschriften und ihr Verhältnis zum frühen Christentum." *Rivista Archeologia Cristiana* 50 (1974) 121–44.

Fasola, Umberto M. "Le due catacombe ebraiche di Villa Torlonia." *Rivista Archeologia Cristiana* 52 (1976) 7–62.

Ferrua, Antonio. "Iscrizioni paleocristiane in una raccolta privata." *Rivista Archeologia Cristiana* 59 (1983) 321–33.

Figueras, Pau. "Epigraphic Evidence for Polytheism in Ancient Judaism." *Immanuel* 24–25 (1990) 194–206.

Frey, Jean-Baptiste. *Corpus inscriptionum iudaicarum*. 2 vols. Rome: Pontifical Institute of Christian Archeology, 1936–1952; reprint of vol. 1 with a Prolegomenon by Baruch Lifshitz. New York: Ktav, 1975.

Fuks, Gideon. "Where have all the freedmen gone? On an Anomaly in the Jewish Grave-Inscriptions." *JJS* 36 (1985) 25–32.

Horsley, G. H. R. and Stephen Llewelyn, eds. *New Documents Illustrating Early Christianity,* 6 vols. (to date). North Ryde, N.S.W.: Macquarie Ancient History Documentary Research Centre, 1981– .

Horst, Pieter W. van der. *Ancient Jewish Epitaphs: An Introductory Survey of a Millennium of Jewish Funerary Epigraphy (300 BCE – 700 CE).* Contributions to Biblical Exegesis and Theology 2. Kampen, Netherlands: Kok Pharos, 1991.

_____. "Das Neue Testament und die jüdischen Grabinschriften aus hellenistische-römischer Zeit." *BibZeit* 36 (1992) 161–78.

_____. "The Jews of Ancient Crete." *JJS* 39 (1988) 183–200.

Kajanto, Iro. *Onomastic Studies in the Early Christian Inscriptions of Rome and Carthage.* Acta Instituti Romani Finlandiae 2.2. Helsinki: Tilgmann, 1963.

_____. *A Study of the Greek Epitaphs of Rome.* Acta Instituti Romani Finlandiae 2.3. Helsinki: Academia Scientiarum Fennica, 1963.

Kant, Laurence H. "Jewish Inscriptions in Greek and Latin." *ANRW* 2.20.2 (1987) 671–713.

Konikoff, A. *Sarcophagi from the Jewish Catacombs of Ancient Rome: A Catalogue Raisonné.* Stuttgart: Franz Steiner, 1990.

Kraabel, A. Thomas. "Jews in Imperial Rome." *JJS* 30 (1979) 41–58.

Kraemer, Ross S. "Jewish Tuna and Christian Fish: Identifying Religious Affiliation in Epigraphic Sources." *HTR* 84 (1991) 141–62.

_____. "A New Inscription from Malta and the Question of Women Elders in the Diaspora Jewish Communities." *HTR* 78 (1986) 431–38.

_____. "Non-Literary Evidence for Jewish Women in Rome and Egypt." *Helios* 13 (1986) 85–101.

_____. "On the Meaning of the Term 'Jew' in Greco-Roman Inscriptions." *HTR* 81 (1989) 35–53.

Lampe, Peter. *Die stadtrömischen Christen in den ersten beiden Jahrhunderten.* WUNT 18, 2d ser. 2d expanded ed. Tübingen: J. C. B. Mohr (Paul Siebeck), 1989. [ET forthcoming by Fortress]

Lapp, E. C. "Jewish Archaeological Evidence from the Roman Rhineland." *JJS* 44 (1993) 70–82.

Le Bohec, Y. "Inscriptions juives et judaïsantes de l'Afrique romaine." *Antiquités africaines* 17 (1981) 165–207.

Marcos, N. F. "Singagoa e iglesia primitiva: Arquitectura e institución." *Sefarad* 53 (1993) 41–58.

Mayer, G. *Die jüdische Frau in der hellenistische-römischen Antike.* Stuttgart: Kohlhammer, 1987.

Miranda, E. "Due iscrizioni greco-giudaiche della Campania." *Rivista Archeologia Cristiana* 55 (1979) 337–41.

Moretti, Luigi. "Iscrizioni greco-giudaiche di Roma." *Rivista Archeologia Cristiana* 50 (1974) 213–19.

Murphy-O'Connor, Jerome. "Lots of God-fearers? Theosebeis in the Aphrodisias Inscription." *RB* 99 (1992) 418–24.

Noy, David. *Jewish Inscriptions of Graeco-Roman Egypt.* New York: Cambridge University Press, 1992.

———. *Jewish Inscriptions of Western Europe.* Vol. 1. New York: Cambridge University Press, 1993.

Patterson, J. R. "The City of Rome: From Republic to Empire." *JRS* 82 (1992) 186–215.

Penna, Romano. "Les Juifs à Rome au temps de l'apôtre Paul." *NTS* 28 (1982) 321–47.

Rajak, Tessa. "Inscription and Context: Reading the Jewish Catacombs of Rome." In *Studies in Early Jewish Epigraphy.* Edited by Jan Willem van Henten and Pieter W. van der Horst. Pages 226–41. Leiden: Brill, 1994.

——— and David Noy. "Archisynagogi: Office, Title, and Social Status in the Greco-Roman Synagogue." *JRS* 83 (1993) 75–93.

Rutgers, L. V. "Archaeological Evidence for the Interaction of Jews and Non-Jews in Late Antiquity." *AJA* 96 (1992) 101–18.

———. "Überlegungen zu den jüdischen Katakomben Roms." *JAC* 33 (1990) 140–57.

Safrai, S. and M. Stern, eds. *The Jewish People in the First Century: Historical Geography, Political History, Social, Cultural and Religious Life and Institutions.* 2 vols. CRINT 1.1–2. Vol. 1: Philadelphia: Fortress Press, 1974 / vol. 2: Amsterdam: Van Gorcum, 1976.

Schürer, Emil. *The History of the Jewish People in the Age of Jesus Christ (175 B.C.–A.D. 135).* New ed. Rev. Geza Vermes, Fergus Millar, and Martin Goodman. 3 vols. (vol. 3 in 2 pts.). Edinburgh: T. & T. Clark, 1973, 1979, 1986, 1987.

Smallwood, E. Mary. *The Jews under Roman Rule: From Pompey to Diocletian.* Leiden: Brill, 1976.

Solin, Heikki. "Juden und Syrer im westlichen Teil der römischen Welt: Eine ethnisch-demographische Studie mit besonderer Berücksichtigung der sprachlichen Zustände." *ANRW* 2.29.2 (1984) 590–789.

———. "Die Namen der orientalischen Sklaven in Rom." In *L'onomastique latine.* Edited by Noël Nuval. Pages 205–20. Colloques internationaux de Centre National de la Recherche Scientifique 564. Paris: Centre National de la Recherche Scientifique, 1977.

———. "Onomastica ed epigrafia: Riflessioni sull'esegesi onomastica delle iscrizioni romane." *Quaderni Urbinati di Cultura Classica* 18 (1974) 105–32.

Spyridakis, Stylianos V. "Inscriptiones Creticae II, xiii, 8: A Jewish In-
    scription?" *HTR* 82 (1989) 231–32.
Stern, M. *Greek and Latin Authors on Jews and Judaism.* 3 vols. Jerusa-
    lem: Israel Academy of Sciences and Humanities, 1974–1984.
Tcherikover, Victor A., et al., eds. *Corpus Papyrorum Judaicarum.* 3 vols.
    Jerusalem: Magnes Press (Hebrew University), 1957–64.
Walters, James C. *Ethnic Issues in Paul's Letter to the Romans: Changing
    Self-Definitions in Earliest Christianity.* Valley Forge, Pa.: Trinity,
    1993.
White, L. Michael. "The Delos Synagogue Revisited: Recent Fieldwork
    in the Graeco-Roman Diaspora [figs.]." *HTR* 80 (1987) 133–61.